# Lecture Notes in Artificial Intelligence   984

Subseries of Lecture Notes in Computer Science
Edited by J. G. Carbonell and J. Siekmann

# Lecture Notes in Computer Science

Edited by G. Goos, J. Hartmanis and J. van Leeuwen

**Springer**
*Berlin*
*Heidelberg*
*New York*
*Barcelona*
*Budapest*
*Hong Kong*
*London*
*Milan*
*Paris*
*Santa Clara*
*Singapore*
*Tokyo*

Jean-Paul Haton  Mark Keane
Michel Manago (Eds.)

# Advances in
# Case-Based Reasoning

Second European Workshop, EWCBR-94
Chantilly, France, November 7-10, 1994
Selected Papers

Springer

Series Editors

Jaime G. Carbonell, Carnegie Mellon University, USA

Jörg Siekmann, University of Saarland, DFKI, Germany


Volume Editors

Jean-Paul Haton
Université Henri-Poincaré, Nancy I
CRIN/INRIA-Lorraine, BP 239, F-54506 Vandoeuvre, France

Mark Keane
University of Dublin, Department of Computer Science
Trinity College, Dublin 2, Ireland

Michel Manago
AcknoSoft
58 a rue du Dessous des Berges, F-75013 Paris, France


Cataloging-in-Publication Data applied for


Die Deutsche Bibliothek - CIP-Einheitsaufnahme

**Advances in case based reasoning** : second European workshop
; selected papers / EWCBR-94, Chantilly, France, November 7
- 10, 1994. Jean-Paul Haton ... (ed.). - Berlin ; Heidelberg ;
New York ; Barcelona ; Budapest ; Hong Kong ; London ;
Milan ; Paris ; Tokyo : Springer, 1995
  (Lecture notes in computer science ; Vol. 984 : Lecture notes in
  artificial intelligence)
  ISBN 3-540-60364-6
NE: Haton, Jean-Paul [Hrsg.]; EWCBR <2, 1994, Chantilly>; GT


CR Subject Classification (1991): I.2

ISBN 3-540-60364-6 Springer-Verlag Berlin Heidelberg New York

© Springer-Verlag Berlin Heidelberg 1995
Printed in Germany

Typesetting: Camera ready by author
SPIN 10485692      06/3142 – 5 4 3 2 1 0      Printed on acid-free paper

# *Preface*

Artificial intelligence has experienced an important evolution over the past few years; an evolution that has been centrally influenced by Case-based reasoning (CBR), especially in the area of knowledge-based decision support. CBR has close relationships to many other AI paradigms like machine learning, induction, classification, analogy, information retrieval, and knowledge acquisition. This book considers some of the current advances that have been made in CBR and some of the papers explore these relationships to other areas of AI.

The Second European Workshop on Case-Based Reasoning took place at the Abbaye de Royaumont nearby Paris, France in November 1994. This workshop followed the first EWCBR that was hosted by the University of Kaiserslautern, Germany in November 1993. EWCBR-94 was largely successful, attracting more than 150 participants from all over the world. The scientific program included invited talks, oral presentations, posters, panel discussions, system demonstrations and an industry day, thus covering the main research and application issues of CBR. Out of 60 submissions, the program committee selected 19 papers for oral presentation and 18 for the poster sessions.

This book contains revised and extended versions of a subset of 22 papers that were selected by the program committee after the Workshop among the initial contributions. It shows that methods and tools related to CBR are in constant evolution. Simultaneously, substantial progress has been made in the applications domain, especially in the fields of architecture and computer-aided design, task planning, chemical synthesis, maintenance and diagnosis, and law.

We would like to thank all the people who contributed to the success of EWCBR-94: the participants for the good atmosphere during and between the sessions, the staff at AcknoSoft (in particular Eric Auriol, Jerome Guiot, Sylvie Garry and Christophe Deniard), Martine Kuhlmann, Amedeo Napoli and Jean Lieber from CRIN/INRIA, and also Jacqueline Reynal and Eunika Mercier-Laurent. We also thank the French association for Artificial Intelligence (AFIA), AI Watch and IEEE that publicized the announcements for the workshop.

We also gratefully acknowledge the support of the following sponsors:
- AcknoSoft (Paris, France)
- Conseil Régional d'Ile de France
- French Délégation Générale à l'Armement (Direction des Recherches, Etudes et Techniques, direction scientifique, section soutien à la recherche, contrat n° 94-1205/A000)
- European Commission (COMETT program)
- INGENIA corporation (Paris, France)
- tecInno GmbH (Kaiserslautern, Germany).

*Nancy, May 1995    Jean-Paul Haton, Mark Keane, Michel Manago*

# Table of Contents

# Part I

# Methods and Tools

# Integrating Induction in a Case-based Reasoner

Eva Armengol          Enric Plaza

Artificial Intelligence Research Institute, IIIA
Spanish Scientific Research Council, CSIC
Campus de la Universitat Autónoma de Barcelona
08193- Bellaterra, Catalonia, Spain
{eva | enric}@iiia.csic.es

**Abstract.** This paper focuses on two key issues in building case-based reasoners (CBRs). The first issue is the knowledge engineering phase needed for CBRs as well as knowledge-based systems (KBS); the second issue is the integration of different methods of learning into CBRs. We show that we can use a knowledge modelling framework for the description and implementation of CBR systems; in particular we show how we used it in developing a CBR in the domain of protein purification. In order to encompass CBR (and learning in general) our knowledge modelling framework extends the usual frameworks with the notion of memory. Including memory we provide the capability for storing and retrieving episodes of problem solving, the basis of case-based reasoning and learning. We show here that this framework, and the supporting language NOOS, allows furthermore to integrate other learning methods as needed. Specifically, we show how a method for the induction of class prototypes can be implemented and integrated with case-based methods in an uniform framework.

## 1 Introduction

This paper focuses on two key issues in building case-based reasoners (CBRs). The first issue is the knowledge engineering phase needed for CBRs as well as knowledge-based systems (KBS); the second issue is the integration of different methods of learning into CBRs. Regarding knowledge engineering, the last years have shown that knowledge modelling frameworks are adequate methodologies for building KBS (Steels, 1990; Wielinga, 1992).We show that we can use a knowledge modelling framework for the description and implementation of CBR systems; in particular we show how we used it in developing a CBR in the domain of protein purification. In order to encompass CBR (and learning in general) our knowledge modelling framework extends the usual frameworks with the notion of memory. Including memory we provide the capability for storing and retrieving episodes of problem solving, the basis of case-based reasoning and learning (Arcos and Plaza, 1993). We show here that this framework, and the supporting language NOOS, allows furthermore to integrate other learning methods as needed. Specifically, we show how a method for the induction of class prototypes can be implemented and integrated with case-based methods in a uniform framework. The structure of the paper is the following. First, we describe our knowledge modelling framework and its supporting object-oriented frame-based language named NOOS. Section 3 shows how a case-based reasoner on the domain of chromatography applied to protein purification can be developed in the framework and implemented using the NOOS language. Finally, related work and conclusions are outlined.

# 2 The Knowledge Modelling Framework

Our knowledge modelling framework augments the ideas of the components of expertise (Steels, 1990) with the notion of episodic memory: the memorization of problem-solving episodes allows learning methods to be integrated since they require to access the past experience to improve the system performance. The elements of our knowledge modelling framework are tasks, methods, theories and models. Tasks are goals to be achieved by the system in a problem setting. Problem solving methods are specifications of ways to achieve tasks. Usually, tasks are decomposed into subtasks by means of a problem-solving method, e.g. the generate-and-test method applied to a task decomposes it into the generate and test subtasks. Other methods are elementary methods (like union and intersection of sets). Case models and theories embody the domain knowledge modelled for our problem. A case model contains all the factual knowledge of a topic and consists on the set of tasks that make sense for it; for instance, the case model of John are those tasks we have solved about John (like his fever being 39) and those tasks to be solved (like finding his diagnosis). Thus solving a problem consists on completing the case model of the problem (e. g. finding the diagnosis of John) by means of a method (e.g. generate-and-test). As the case model is characterized by its tasks, a theory is defined by the methods declared usable to solve the tasks of a case model.

How can we integrate case-based reasoning and learning into this framework? The first step involves the memorization of successful methods and the fact that all solved case models are also memorized as cases to be used by a case-based method. The second step involves a metalevel (called *inference level*) consisting of inference methods and inference theories. An inference method (e.g. the CBR-method) is invoked when a domain method is missing. The result is retrieving and selecting a method from a past case able to solve the task at hand. This method is then instantiated into the current task and executed there (like in derivational replay). In fact, several methods can be retrieved from different cases in memory and tried out to see whether one can solve the current task. Different CBR methods can be described uniformly in a retrieve/select/reflect decomposition by using different methods in the retrieve and select subtasks; these different methods embody the domain-dependent knowledge that may be used in case-based reasoning (Arcos and Plaza, 1993). Inference theories hold several inference methods plus some preferences to choose among them. Examples of this are shown in section 3. Other kinds of inference methods are inheritance that retrieves domain methods from super type theories (e.g. John may inherit domain knowledge from theory person and theory mammal), see (Plaza, 1992).

## 2.1 The Framework Implementation: The NOOS Language

The knowledge modelling framework described above is supported by the implementation of the object-oriented frame-based language NOOS in which every concept is represented as an object. The dynamic of NOOS is impasse-driven: every time a lack of knowledge to do something is detected, an impasse is generated and an opportunity for learning arises. As in SOAR (Newell, 1990), there are two kinds of impasses: either the next step is unknown (e.g. there is no known method to solve a task) or there are several ways to proceed (e.g. there are several possible methods that may be applicable to a task). Every time an impasse is generated the NOOS language generates a task whose goal is to solve that impasse.

The results of solving an impasse in a task are stored into that task for future usage and future decisions may be based on this precedent (they are cases that record method utility). This is called the self-model of NOOS and can be used by NOOS learning methods to reason about its own performance and about method usage. In a uniform way, inference methods (that succeed or fail) are also recorded at the inference level task so the system may learn from their usage. Finally we mention two aspects of NOOS implementation: automatic backtracking and consistency maintenance. It is possible to declare in a metafunction several methods applicable to a specific task. NOOS assures that a method will be tried out to see if it solves the task (selected according to the declared preferences), backtracking to other declared methods if it fails. When all methods for a task fail, and this task is a subtask generated by a method of a super ordinate task, that method fails and a higher-level backtracking to new possible methods is performed. Thus, backtracking in NOOS assures that all methods declared in all tasks will be explored until a solution to the overall task is achieved, and that methods will be selected according to the preferences expressed in metafunctions. Moreover, NOOS has a consistency maintenance mechanism that supports incremental knowledge modelling. Every time some NOOS object (theory, method, task, etc.) is changed the consistency maintenance mechanism invalidates all objects that depend on that change.

## 3 The Chromatography Domain Application

In this section we will explain an application of the knowledge modelling framework and the support provided by the NOOS language to the integration of several case-based and inductive methods. First we describe the application domain of protein purification using chromatographic techniques. After that, CHROMA, an application program written in NOOS, is explained in detail. In particular, the different tasks and methods of CHROMA, and their integration, are described.

### 3.1 Introduction to the Chromatography Domain

Our domain of application is the purification of proteins from biological sources (animal tissues, bacteriological cultures, etc.) for industrial and research purposes. Purification is an essential process in the analysis of the properties of molecules from biological origin and widely used in industries and in research. Proteins are a type of biological macromolecules that are purified by a sequence of laboratory operations. These operations can use different techniques but the more used for molecule purification are chromatographic techniques. They exploit the different distribution of molecules between both a stationary and a moving phase. There are different chromatographic techniques according to the physic-chemical principle in which are based: Ion Exchange is based in the Coulomb's law; Hydrophobic Interaction is based in the Van der Vaals law; Gel Filtration separates the molecules according its size; Affinity exploits the existence of specific unions between certain types of molecules; etc. A plan to purify a molecule can be composed by several steps involving one or more chromatographic techniques. There is no unique way to purify a molecule but there are multiple useful purification plans according the expected use of the purified molecule. To find the adequate purification plan the experience of an expert is required. Usually, a human expert makes a focused search in the literature in order to obtain adequate precedent cases of purification and then he analyzes them to choose the most appropriate. From a blind search he should obtain many experiments and probably an apprentice cannot choose between them. The literature search has to be focused according the molecule to purify, the sample origin (species, tissue, etc.), the future study with the purified molecule, etc. It is necessary much domain knowledge in order to decide how to do the search and how to choose between the obtained precedents. This domain knowledge is complex and difficult to formalize. Let's suppose that we have proteins classified according to the substance to which they have affinity and the protein to purify belongs to one of these classes. In that situation, the protein may be purified using an affinity chromatography technique with the substance of the specified class. Nevertheless, this classification is not useful if the protein has no affinity with any substance or to decide if other steps can be applied.

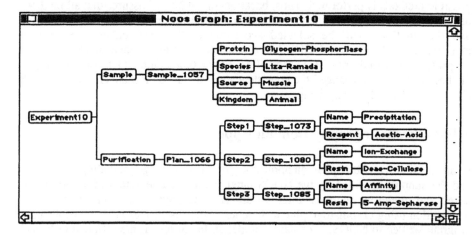

**Fig. 1.** Description of an experiment from case-base in CHROMA application. An experiment is composed of the sample from which the protein has to be extracted and the purification plan.

### 3.2 Solving the Purification task

From a knowledge engineering phase we detected that searching a case-base of purification experiments is an essential part in the human expert solving the purification task. Our goal is to build a system that, based on purification cases, will be capable to find precedent cases useful for solving new experiments. This system has to capture enough domain knowledge to allow it to focus the case-base search in an efficient and expert-comparable level. We limit the action field to the biological macro-molecules called proteins and exclude macro-molecules as the nucleic acids or the polysaccharides. A requirement that emerged in the knowledge engineering phase was that the user of the system has to have the final decision about which plan is finally chosen. This requirement arises from the fact that the user is knowledgeable of the chemical domain and wants to maintain control on the purification process. The CHROMA application supports the user in inspecting the candidate cases proposed for taking his final decision.

The main task of the CHROMA application is the purification task. Given a new experiment, CHROMA has to determine a purification plan using either a memory of cases or domain knowledge. The memory of cases is composed by objects named *experiments* having two slots: a sample (an animal tissue, bacteriological culture, etc.) and a purification (a plan to purify a specific protein from the sample). Figure 1 shows an experiment in the case-base. A sample is described in turn by four features: the protein to purify, the species where the sample comes from, the source of the sample (an animal or vegetal tissue, a culture, etc.) and finally, the kingdom to which the species belongs (animal, bacteria, protozoa, etc.). The purification is a plan composed by a variable number of chromatography steps. Each step has the name of the technique (affinity, gel filtration, etc.) and the name of the substance (reagent or resin) used to purify the protein. A new experiment to purify has only the sample and the task is to find an appropriate purification plan for it.

In order to obtain a purification plan, purification task can use four methods: equal-sample, classify-by-prototype, analogy-by-determination and default-plan (see figure 2). The equal-sample method detects if there is an experiment in the base of cases having the same sample as our current experiment. The classify-by-prototype method uses domain knowledge in the form of generalized experiments (prototypes) that are generated from the case-base of experiments by an inductive method. The analogy-by-determination method retrieves experiments purifying the same protein as our current experiment but from different species or source. Finally, default-plan is a domain method based on statistical analysis of purification experiments. This method is used when there is no experiment in the case-base purifying the protein we are interested in and the other methods have failed. In the next sections we will explain the four methods in detail and their interaction.

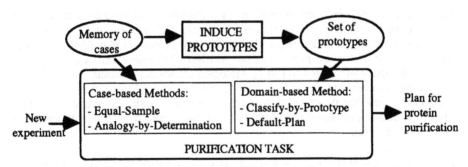

**Fig. 2.** Methods used in the purification task of CHROMA.

### 3.2.1 Equal-Sample Method

The equal-sample method is a case-based method constructed as a NOOS inference method for purification task. It is composed by two tasks (figure 3): retrieve and reflect. Method for retrieve task is retrieve-by-pattern that is a NOOS built-in method that considers the pattern as a graph and retrieves from the memory those cases (considered as graphs) that are subsumed by the pattern; subsumption is defined in NOOS as the usual subsumption between directed acyclic graphs (see section 3.2.3). In this situation, this method takes the *sample* of the current case as a pattern and searches the base of cases for experiments having at least that sample. In practice it will retrieve experiments with an identical sample since both pattern and experiments are graphs with the same links: protein, species, source and kingdom. Reflect task instantiates as solution to purification task the purification plan of the retrieved experiment. This method fails if there is no experiment having the same sample that the new one. This method is useful to solve routine purifications with commonly occurring samples and proteins and assures a correct solution.

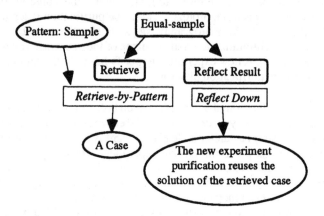

**Fig. 3.** Task-method decomposition of Equal-Sample method.

### 3.2.2 Analogy-by-Determination Method

The analogy-by-determination method is a case-based method constructed as a NOOS inference method for purification task. This method uses the domain knowledge embodied in a *determination* stating that the correct plan for purification task is determined by the protein to be purified. Determinations are functional dependencies that can be used to justify analogical reasoning (Russell, 1990)[1]. In the analogy-by-determination method the determination used states that the solution for purification task depends on the value of protein task. The method can then justify a solution purification plan from the fact that a precedent case with the same protein used that plan.

The analogy-by-determination method is composed by three tasks (figure 4): retrieve, select and reflect. The retrieve task uses a method named retrieve-by-determination that searches into the base of cases for those experiments purifying the same protein than the current problem. When it retrieves more than one experiment, the task select uses the method select-&-prefer in order to select only

---

1 The classical example of an analogy justified by a determination is the following: the usual language spoken by a person is determined by the person's nationality. We know a case, Janos, that is Hungarian and speaks Magyar. The task language of another person can be solved by an analogy-by-determination method. If this method finds that a person is Hungarian then it concludes that he speaks Magyar because of the determination *and* the Janos precedent.

one experiment. The `select-&-prefer` method has two subtasks: `select-relevant` and `preferences`. From the set of retrieved experiments, `select-relevant` goal is to select those experiments with a sample that has either the same species or the same source as the new experiment. The task `preferences` starts when there is more than one experiment purifying the same protein (with the same species and/or source or not). If there are some experiments purifying the protein in the same species or source, `preferences` task has no effect because it is sure that the retrieved experiments belong to the same kingdom. Otherwise, experiments purifying proteins in species of the same kingdom are preferred. If more than one experiment is obtained all they are presented to the user who must choose one of them. Finally, the `reflect` task instantiates as solution to the current experiment the purification plan of the selected case. The `analogy-by-determination` method fails if there is no experiment in the case base purifying the protein we want in our current experiment (i.e., it fails when there is no case fulfilling the protein determination).

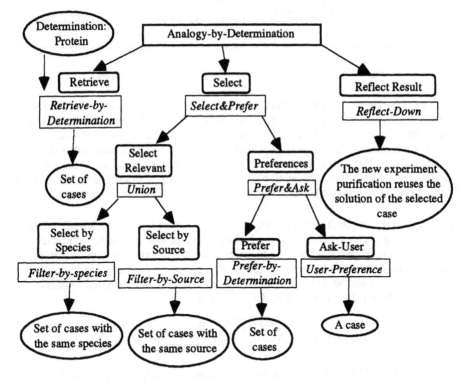

**Fig. 4.** Task-method decomposition of Analogy-by-determination method.

### 3.2.3 Classify-by-Prototype Method

The `classify-by-prototype` method is a domain method that uses domain knowledge to classify a sample in terms of a solution purification plan. In the Chromatography domain there is knowledge (molecular structure, source of the sample, etc.) that is implicitly used for the experts in order to search a good purification plan. Classes of experiments having the same purification plan are represented by prototypes. As can be seen in Figure 5, a prototype is like an experiment with several values allowed for each slot in the sample. Prototypes are generated by induction using classify-by-prototype method.

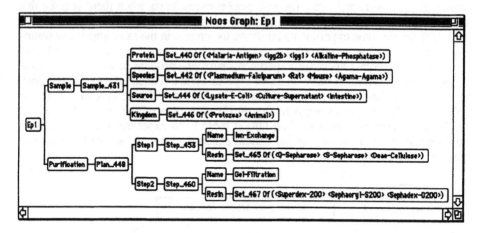

**Fig. 5.** A purification prototype induced from the base of cases.

The classify-by-prototype method is composed by four tasks (figure 6): generate-prototypes, plausible-prototypes, select and reflect. The generate-prototypes task accesses the domain knowledge (prototypes) required for the classify-by-prototype method in the form of purification prototypes. If this knowledge does not exist then the NOOS language generates an impasse that is solved using the induce-prototypes method (see next section). Other activations of classify-by-prototype do no produce any impasse because the prototypes are already generated.

Once retrieved the purification prototypes the plausible-prototypes task selects, using subsumption-matching method, only those prototypes subsuming the new experiment sample. We saw in 3.2.1 the retrieve-by-pattern method that uses the same subsumption method to retrieve cases from memory. Subsumption in an object-oriented language like NOOS is similar to pattern-matching in rule-based systems[2]. An object A is subsumed by an object B, $A \subseteq B$, when:

$$\{F\}_A \subseteq \{F\}_B,$$
$$\forall\, F_i \in \{F\}_A,\, F_i\,(A) = V_j\,,\, F_i\,(B) = V_k \;\Rightarrow\; V_j \subseteq V_k$$

I.e., for all slots $\{F\}_A$ in A, B has all those slots ($\{F\}_A \subseteq \{F\}_B$) and the set of values of each slot in A ($F_i\,(A) = V_j$) is subsumed by the corresponding set of values of the same slot in B ($F_i\,(B) = V_k$ and $V_j \subseteq V_k$). For instance the following experiment-3 is subsumed by the prototype Ep1 shown in Figure 5.

---

2 Subsumption among objects is a very useful method for classification tasks in object-oriented languages, see [Napoli, 1992] for a complex classification method using subsumption.

```
(define experiment-3
    (sample (define (sample)
    (protein alkaline-phosphatase)
        (species rat)
        (source intestine)
        (kingdom animal)))))
```

When more than one purification prototype is retrieved, the select task has the user-preference method that asks the user for the best purification plan: as in the previous method the final decision has to be the one of the user and NOOS supports the inspection of the alternatives. As in all inference methods, finally the reflect task instantiates in the current experiment the purification plan of the prototype. The classify-by-prototype method fails when there is no prototype subsuming the current experiment sample. In this situation the CHROMA application tries the analogy-by-determination method to search a case for solving the purification task.

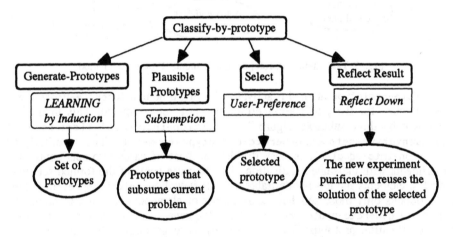

**Fig. 6.** Task-method decomposition of Classify-by-prototype method.

### 3.2.4 Induce-Prototype Method

As we have seen, the domain knowledge contains purification prototypes obtained by induction from the base of cases. These prototypes represent classes of experiments that have the same purification plan. Thus a prototype is like a rule of the type

$$situation \Rightarrow plan$$

where *situation* describes the general features that the *sample* of an experiment has to fulfil to be classified in the solution class that is the *plan*. The subsumption method we have seen acts as a pattern-matcher that compares a specific experiment to the generalized experiment (prototype); if they match, the classification recommends the prototype's purification plan as the plan for the current experiment. A purification prototype has the same slots that an experiment. The difference is that each sample slot of a purification prototype can have more than one value (see Fig. 5). The advantage provided by these purification prototypes is that sometimes a case retrieval method may propose to the user different experiments to choose but all they have the same purification. Using the purification prototypes, that summarize this information into one single (generalized) case, CHROMA can produce results without the user's intervention.

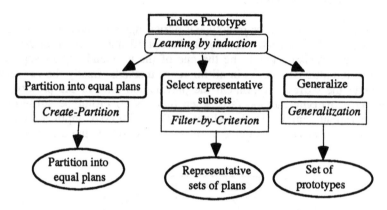

**Fig. 7** Task-method decomposition of Induce-Prototypes method.

The induce-prototype method is activated the first time that Generate-Prototypes task searches for the purification prototypes not yet computed. This method is composed by three subtasks (figure 7): partition-into-equal-plans, select-representative-sets and generate-prototype-from-set. The method of partition-into-equal-plans task divides the base of cases into sets containing experiments with the same purification plan. Because some of the formed sets may have few elements and it is not desirable to make induction, select-representative-sets obtains only those sets having a number of elements above a threshold. The method of generate-prototype-from-set task generates from each representative set a purification prototype. Its main concern is to generalize the samples of the experiments belonging to a representative set. The sample of a prototype is created with its slots having the union of the values of each slot of the experiment samples belonging to a representative set. The prototype purification plan is the common purification plan of all the experiments into that representative set.

### 3.2.5 Default-Plan Method

The default-plan method is a domain-based method that starts if all the other methods have failed. This occurs only when the protein of the current experiment has never been purified before and thus no case with that protein purification exists in memory. This default purification plan has been obtained from a statistical study where many purification plans were analyzed. The conclusion of this study was that the most frequently used chromatographic techniques in each step of a purification plan are the following: 1) Clarification, 2) Ion-Exchange, and 3) Gel-Filtration. As we said in section 3.1 there are several plans that can be used to purify a protein; although some plans are more adequate (more efficient or with a better degree of purity in the obtained protein), when there is no literature on a particular protein subject, the expert uses general or default plans, less adequate but nonetheless appropriate for purification. The default-plan method captures this general domain knowledge useful for the CHROMA application.

### 3.3 Integration

In previous sections several methods solving the purification task have been presented. Is it efficient to use all them? The answer is that it depends on the way in which they are combined. NOOS allows us to define a metalevel method that selects which method to apply in a case-by-case basis. This is the Selection method of the combinations analyzed below. We decide the possible combinations and their efficiency.

**Combination 1.** Purification task can be solved using two methods: analogy-by-determination and Default-plan. Default-plan is a valuable tool to give an approximate solution but the proposed solutions are not as good as those of a specific method. In fact solutions proposed by analogy-by-determination are better that those proposed by default-plan. Nevertheless, the base of cases is not complete and there are some proteins with no available information (i.e. there are no experiments in the base of cases purifying them) that commonly be solved by default-plan. The Selection method in Combination 1 checks if there are some experiments using the same protein that we want to purify. If the protein already exists in the base of cases, selection method proposes to apply analogy-by-determination. Otherwise default-plan is applied. Using selection method the time used in solving $Q_t$ new cases is the following:

$$T_1 = Q_d * T_d + Q_a * T_a + \Delta * Q_t \qquad \text{where } Q_t = Q_a + Q_d$$

where $T_d$ and $T_a$ are the mean times used by default-plan and analogy-by-determination respectively in solving a problem; $Q_d$ is the number of cases that are solved using default-plan; $Q_a$ is the number of cases that are solved using analogy-by-determination; $\Delta$ is the time used by the selection method to assess the applicability of the methods. The selection method is executed for all the cases to be solved ($Q_t$).

**Combination 2.** Now we will introduce a combination that includes a third method, say classify-by-prototype that has a mean execution time of $T_p$ seconds. The selection method used in this combination of CHROMA can be viewed in Figure 8. If the selection method is capable know when each method is applicable without error, the total time to execute the $Q_t$ new cases is the following:

$$T_2 = Q_d * T_d + Q_a' * T_a + Q_p * T_p + \Delta * Q_t \qquad \text{where } Q_a = Q_a' + Q_p$$

$Q_t$ is the same that in Combination 1. This means that for the $Q_a$ cases that in Combination 1 have been executed using analogy-by-determination, now $Q_p$ cases have been solved using classify-by-prototype and others ($Q_a'$) have been solved using analogy-by-determination.

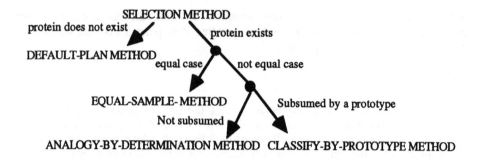

**Fig. 8.** Description of the selection method in combinations 2 and 3.

**Combination 3.** This combination is the same as Combination 2 but assuming that Selection method may have errors, i.e. may choose a method that eventually will not be able to solve the current problem. In particular, the Selection method can propose as applicable classify-by-prototype but there may be no prototype subsuming the sample of the new experiment. In this situation the selected method fails and Selection method has to choose another one, such as analogy-by-determination. Thus, from the $Q_t$ new cases to solve, for $Q_p$ of them selection method may propose classify-by-prototype For $Q_{p'}$ cases this method succeeds but for $Q_f$ of them this method fails and analogy-by-determination is used in a second choice. Time spent to solve these $Q_f$ cases is $T_p + T_a$, i.e. time used by classify-by-prototype that fails, and time used by analogy-by-determination that succeeds. Total time spent in this Combination 3 is the following:

$$T_3 = Q_d * T_d + Q_{a'} * T_a + Q_f * (T_p + T_a) + Q_{p'} * T_p + \Delta * Q_t \quad \text{where} \quad Q_p = Q_f + Q_{p'}$$

### 3.3.1. Analysis of the efficiency of the proposed combinations

The efficiency of a combination is evaluated with the spent time in solving $Q_t$ new cases. A combination should also be evaluated regarding its solution quality but the quality of a purification plan depends on the quantity of protein produced (some chromatographic techniques produce more and some less from a given source) and on the degree of purity of the protein produced (it also depends on the chromatographic techniques). We will not discuss here the quality of solution issues since this depends on the later use of the purified protein.

Combination 1 is the easiest combination producing good purification plans. Thus, other combinations are justified if they are more efficient that Combination 1. Combination 2 is more efficient than Combination 1 if $T_2 \leq T_1$ It is easy to see that this relation holds only if $T_p \leq T_a$ (i.e. classify-by-prototype is more efficient than analogy-by-determination). This relation is true in our domain since $T_p = 20.937$ seconds and $T_a = 27.175$ seconds.

Combination 3 represents a real situation because it may be difficult to obtain a selection method discriminating all the situations in which each method is applicable without any error (as combination 2 assumes). For example, in our domain all the new experiments that are solved using classify-by-prototype can also be solved using analogy-by-determination. Therefore, Combination 3 is more efficient that Combination 1 if the relation $T_3 \leq T_1$ holds. It is easy to see that for that inequality to hold it is required the following:

$$\frac{Q_f}{Q_{p'}} \leq \frac{T_a - T_p}{T_p}$$

From this inequality we can see that the efficiency of Combination 3 does not depend on the selection method time but only on the number $Q_p$ of cases that can be solved using classify-by-prototype and the number of cases over which the selection method fails ($Q_f$). In our domain $T_p = 20.937$ seconds and $T_c = 27.175$ seconds. Therefore, if $0.298 Q_p \geq Q_f$ it is better to use Combination 3 because is more efficient that Combination 1. In particular, if we have 100 new cases that can be solved using classify-by-prototype, if error in the selection method is less than a 23%, Combination 3 is more efficient.

Finally, we want to remark that equal-case is not considered for simplicity in the obtained expressions since it execution time is a constant that has to be added in all the expressions.

We have shown how CHROMA can use a selection method that is easy to represent in the NOOS language because it is just a method solving the task of choosing among possible methods. This form of method combination is more efficient than the simple sequential combination as used in other systems. On the long run it would be interesting to learn to select the best methods based on features of the current problem and of the task environment. The important issue is that an integrated framework as NOOS allows us to freely implement, combine and experimentally evaluate the quality and efficiency of methods and method-combinations and tailor the final system to the task requirements in an application domain.

## 4 Related Work

We have presented a knowledge modelling framework and its supporting language, NOOS, that incorporate the notion of memory and impasse-driven learning for integrating case-based and inductive methods for learning. Other knowledge modelling frameworks, like components of expertise (Steels, 1990), KADS (Wielinga, 1992), PROTEGE-II (Puerta et al., 1991), etc, do not integrate learning methods. Our approach is closer to components of expertise. However, components of expertise lacks the two layers of NOOS: domain theories and methods and inference theories and methods, having only the domain layer. The basic building blocks in PROTEGE-II, are implemented in Lisp and thus new mechanisms require new programs in Lisp. The philosophy of NOOS is different: methods can be decomposed in a finer grain into elementary subtasks that use a set of elementary methods (e.g. conditionals, set intersection, etc.) provided by NOOS. There is a difference between our goals and the goals of COMMET, KADS, PROTEGE-II, etc., but they are complementary. The knowledge modelling community is interested in acquiring a wide library of components, while we are interested in integrating learning methods with those libraries of components.

There is some work dealing specifically with the combination of case-based methods and knowledge produced by inductive methods. The KATE system (Manago, 1989) induces a decision tree and combines decision-tree classification with case-based classification. The combination of methods is fixed: decision-tree classification is tried first and if it "fails" (because of a missing attribute) then a case-based method is used. The INRECA project (Manago, 93) follows a similar approach integrating the induction of decision trees (using KATE) and case-based reasoning using PATDEX. Currently KATE and PATDEX are able to interchange results through the format of the CASUEL language, and their combination is again fixed. The integration of the multiple inference methods is easily realized by the support given by NOOS language to the knowledge modelling of the CHROMA application. As we have seen all methods (case-based, inductive, knowledge-based) can be described in our knowledge modelling framework and then implemented using the NOOS language. This is a tighter integration than other proposals for integrating inductive and case-based methods; for instance the INRECA project is based on the establishment of the syntax of an interchange format called CASUEL. Different modules (CBR, induction) read from and write to this format but each module uses a different representation language.

## 5 Conclusions and future work

In this paper, we have presented a knowledge modelling framework for KBS modelling and its implementation into the NOOS language. A more detailed explanation of NOOS and its case-based capabilities can be found in (Arcos and Plaza, 1993). We have focused on the integration of case-based and inductive methods in our knowledge modelling framework. The basis for this integration is the capability of NOOS for ascribing several alternative methods to any task, selecting among them based on a language of preferences, and automatically backtracking to other alternative methods. Learning methods, case-based or inductive, are integrated in an impasse-driven manner. This general setting allows us to ascribe appropriate learning methods to specific tasks, as shown in the CHROMA application. The multiplicity of methods raises the issue of how to combine them in an efficient way. We have shown that meta-knowledge about their applicability range can be incorporated in the form of an oracle that selects the most adequate method for every case to be solved. Other learning methods, like induction of decision trees, could be integrated in our framework if it is useful to solve specific tasks.

Our current work involves several systems where CBR methods are integrated with other methods. For instance, a classification-based system for sponge identification is being developed in NOOS using a method of top-down classification called recognize-prototype-and-refine. This work is a test for comparing our approach to a classical rule-based expert system on the same domain developed at our Institute and may help us understand the differences and the utility of our knowledge modelling framework for KBS design and the utility of learning methods for different subtasks. Moreover, research on planning as a general form of problem solving is currently under way. We focus on case-based planning, non-linear search-based planning, and interleaving case-based/search-based planning. Comparing it to other systems, like derivational analogy (Veloso, 1992) NOOS supports its two main capabilities: non-linear planning and interleaving planning and learning. Comparison of planning domains in KBS knowledge modelling frameworks will be pursued, specifically using the workbench project Sisyphus on floor planning, used as a standard for comparison by the KBS knowledge acquisition community.

### Acknowledgements

The research reported on this paper has been developed at the IIA inside the ANALOG Project funded by CICYT grant 122/93 and a MEC fellowship. We would like to thank Dr. Lluis Bonamusa for kindly providing his expertise on the Chromatography domain.

# References

Arcos, J. L., and Plaza, E. (1993). A Reflective Architecture for Integrated Memory-based Learning and Reasoning. In *First European Workshop on Case-based reasoning*. Kaiserslautern: Germany.

Napoli, A. (1992). Subsumption and Classification-based Reasoning in Object-based Representations. *Proceedings of the European Conference on Artificial Intelligence (ECAI'92), Vienna, Austria*, p.425-429.

Manago, M. (1989). Knowledge Intensive Induction, *Proceedings 6th International Machine Learning Workshop*. Morgan Kaufman.

Manago, M., Alhoff, K. D., Auriol, E., Traphöner, R., Wess, S., Conruyt, N., Maurer, F. (1993). Induction and reasoning from cases. *First European Workshop on Case-based reasoning*. Kaiserslautern: Germany..

Newell, A. (1990). *Unified Theories of Cognition.* Cambridge MA: Harvard University Press

Plaza, E. (1992). Reflection for analogy: Inference-level reflection in an architecture for analogical reasoning. *Proceedings of IMSA'92 Workshop on Reflection and Metalevel Architectures*, Tokyo, November 1992, p. 166-171.

Puerta, A., Egar, J., Tu, S., Musen, M. A. (1991). A multiple-method knowledge acquisition shell for the automatic generation of knowledge acquisition tools. In *Proceedings of AAAI-KAW*.

Russell, S. (1990). *The Use of Knowledge in Analogy and Induction*. Morgan Kaufmann.

Steels, L. (1990). The Components of Expertise, *AI Magazine*, 11(2):30-49.

Veloso, M., (1992). *Learning by analogical reasoning in general problem solving*. Ph.D. thesis, Carnegie Mellon University, Pittsburgh, PA.

Wielinga, B., Schreiber, A., Breuker, J. (1992). KADS: A modelling approach to knowledge engineering. Knowledge Acquisition 4(1).

# Integrating Induction and Case-Based Reasoning: Methodological Approach and First Evaluations

Eric Auriol[1], Michel Manago[1], Klaus-Dieter Althoff[2], Stefan Wess[2], Stefan Dittrich[3]

**Abstract.** We propose in this paper a general framework for integrating inductive and case-based reasoning (CBR) techniques for diagnosis tasks. We present a set of practical integrated approaches realised between the KATE-Induction decision tree builder and the PATDEX case-based reasoning system. The integration is based on the deep understanding about the weak and strong points of each technology. This theoretical knowledge permits to specify the structural possibilities of a sound integration between the relevant components of each approach. We define different levels of integration called "cooperative", "workbench" and "seamless". They realise respectively a tight, medium and strong link between both techniques. Experimental results show the appropriateness of these integrated approaches for the treatment of noisy or unknown data.

## 1    Introduction

Integration of case-based reasoning and other learning paradigms is a growing research area today. The representation and use of additional domain knowledge, e.g., rules or deep causal models, is an important issue for dealing with real world applications (e.g., [1] and [2]). Numerous case-based systems have experimented on integrated use of problem solving methods. Some suggestions for the integration between case-based reasoning and model-based knowledge acquisition are given in [17]. The MOBAL system [26] integrates manual and automatic knowledge acquisition methods. The CASEY system [19] integrates a model-based causal reasoning program to diagnose heart diseases. An example of integrating rules and cases is the BOLERO system [21]. The MOLTKE approach [8] integrates different kinds of knowledge—technical and heuristic—to deal with a complex technical application (Computerised Numeric Control Machining Centre).

We focus in this paper on the integration between the PATDEX case-based reasoning tool [5] and the KATE-Induction inductive learning tool [23] for diagnosis tasks in complex structured domains. This idea has an origin in Schank's approach [33] who wrote: "In essence, case-based reasoning means no more than reasoning from experience. The issue of whether something is best called a case, or a rule, or a story, is one of understanding how experience get encode in memory". In a very simplified approach, we can say that human reasoning is based on rules (that are abstract and general knowledge about a domain) and cases (that represent particular experiences). The problem of integrating both reasoning schemes is the main topic of the INRECA project (ESPRIT project n° 6322). However, before speaking about implementation or test, it seems important to understand why, where and how we need integration. The

---

1    AcknoSoft, 58a, rue du Dessous-des-Berges, 75013 Paris, France

2    University of Kaiserslautern, Dept. of Computer Science, PO Box 3049, 67653, Kaiserslautern, Germany

3    tecInno GmbH, Sauerwiesen 2, 67661 Kaiserslautern, Germany

"why" has been already addressed in a previous paper [23], where we discuss the advantages and drawbacks of each technique. Briefly speaking, the integration is motivated by keeping together the "goodies" of each system. In particular, we are likely to keep the information gain measure [28] used in KATE for building a decision tree from a set of data, the similarity measure and the retrieval mechanism defined in PATDEX. In this paper, we try to answer the "where" and the "how" problems. Note that though the starting points of this work have been the KATE and the PATDEX systems, the results described here are system-independent and apply to a set of problems that can be generally handled using induction and/or case-based reasoning. We propose in Sect. 2 an architectural framework that enables a global system description. Inside this framework, we define a four-level integration architecture, where each level corresponds to a specific degree of interaction between the tools. In Sect. 3, we present three specific applications of this framework for truly integrating KATE and PATDEX. We evaluate these integration possibilities in Sect. 4 through a set of statistical criteria measured on various databases.

## 2 Methodological Approach

We present in this section an architectural framework. It helps in separating the different components of a case-based system and in explaining the logical flow of information when using such a system on a diagnosis problem. We propose a four-level integration approach, whose application is proved to be sound on the various parts of the framework.

### 2.1 Architectural Framework

In technical diagnosis domains, different users have various needs. The engineer who develops the application requires other forms of integration than the end-user who just wants to consult the system. We use the following architectural framework to structure our collection of integration possibilities that clarifies the applied terminology (Fig. 1).

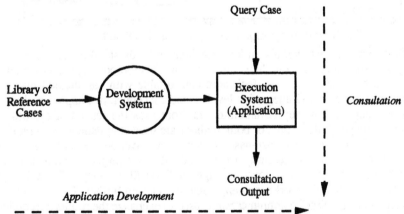

**Fig. 1.** Architectural framework (due to [35])

From this framework we conclude the following basic terminology:

- *Development System*      Functional component for the construction and maintenance of the application system. It is devoted to the development engineer.

- *Application Development*    Process of using the development system.
- *Execution System*        Resulting application system. The end-user that uses the execution system may be a skilled expert, or a maintenance technician, etc.
- *Consultation*            Process of using the execution system.

Note that even if there is no separation between the execution system and the development system in a particular implementation, we use the distinction on a logical level to ease the definition and application of the integration possibilities. We think that both development and execution systems address different categories of users.

## 2.2 Four Integration Levels

We define four possible levels of integration between the induction and the case-based reasoning technologies (Fig. 2). Each level aims at developing specific integration possibilities on the different parts of a system.

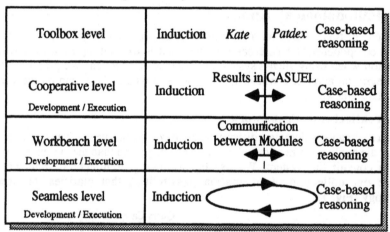

**Fig. 2.** Four integration levels between KATE and PATDEX

The first level consists simply in keeping both tools as stand-alone systems and letting the user choose the one he is interested in. This toolbox approach should not be rejected because a user may feel more comfortable with one method than with another one. In the second integration level, called the cooperative approach, the tools are kept separated but they collaborate. One tool uses the results of the other to improve or speed up its results, or both methods are used simultaneously to reinforce the results. For instance, the case-based reasoning tool can be used at the end of the decision tree when some uncertainty occurs. In the INRECA project, communication of results between the tools is achieved through the CASUEL language[1]. The third level of integration, called the workbench approach, goes a step further. The tools are still separated but a "pipeline" communication is used to exchange the results of individual modules of each technique. For instance, PATDEX produces a similarity measure between a set of cases that may be used by KATE to supplant the information gain

---

[1] CASUEL is the European standard language for cases and knowledge representation used in INRECA.

measure. The final level of INRECA aims at reusing the best components of each method. It builds a powerful integrated tool that avoids the weaknesses of each separate technology and preserves their advantages. By doing this, we keep in mind the application fields of INRECA, that are decision support and diagnosis (e.g., [27]). The evaluation of the different integration possibilities takes care of this specific final goal (e.g., [3]).

# 3. Integrating KATE and PATDEX

A very exciting challenge in using together a decision tree and a case-based system seems to be their mutual integration in the execution system. Therefore, the first two levels of integration focus on the consultation system. In the cooperative level, the consultation starts with a decision tree and switches to the case-based reasoning mode when an unknown value is met during consultation. In the workbench level, the consultation switches in presence of an unknown value between the KATE decision tree and PATDEX. This enables the system to determine the most similar cases to a given situation. The most probable value for the unknown attribute in this subset of cases is chosen and switched back to the decision tree.

On the other hand, integration can be applied into the development system. It results in a simpler and more generic development interface. In the seamless level, specific parts of each inductive and case-based technique are interlaced in a common tool in two ways: One for building a decision tree that should be more resistant to noise; one for building a more efficient indexing structure in the case-based reasoning tool. The seamless level implies the creation of a single system, that can deal with diagnosis problems resolved by CBR as well as by induction.

## 3.1 Cooperative Level: Switching Between Decision Tree and CBR

The architecture tested for the cooperative level consists in switching between the decision tree and the case-based reasoning system when the value of a test is unknown at a given consultation node. The query is a full case description and the decision tree is used as an indexing mechanism. When an unknown value is met during tree consultation, the decision tree calls the CBR system instead of following all possible branches of the current node. The case-based system finds the most similar cases among the current subset of cases and delivers the most probable diagnosis among them (Fig. 3).

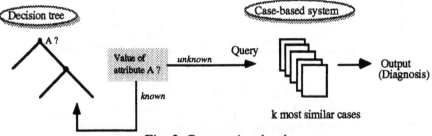

**Fig. 3.** Cooperative level

This cooperation brings two advantages. From a practical point of view, it speeds up the case-based reasoning process, because the retrieval is generally made on a small subset of the whole database. The speed gain can be important on big databases, or when the cases are stored on a hard disk and have to be reached through a net. From a more semantic point of view, it helps the user in selecting a subset of "interesting" cases on which he can concentrate himself. In this case, the decision tree can be viewed as an intelligent request maker on the database. The user is free to use the retrieved cases as he needs.

Instead of using a decision tree before the retrieval step, we could do the contrary. The idea is to retrieve first a subset of cases (for example; a number defined by default), and then to generate "on the fly" a set of possible tests that guides the research on the remaining cases. Instead of being driven by the system as in the former integration scheme, the user conducts the research towards what seems important to him. Nevertheless, this approach shows a few inconveniences: It requires a quick case-based matching for dealing with the whole database, and a very powerful decision tree builder. This integration scheme has not been tested yet for technical reasons. It will probably be of interest of developing it in a vertical system.

## 3.2 Workbench Level: Balancing Between Decision Tree and CBR

In the workbench level, we define a double switch between the decision tree and the case-based reasoning system. Given a query Q (defined as previously by the current situation in the decision tree until an unknown value A is met), the case-based reasoning system retrieves the most similar cases. It looks among these cases for the most probable value for A. The decision tree can continue its diagnosis further by using this answer. Several jumps can be used consecutively during the same consultation, what gives its name to this "workbench". The retrieval mechanism is the same as the one presented earlier. Figure 4 sketches the relations between the techniques in this integration level.

As in the cooperative level, the workbench level can be used in batch. This is of interest for running the tests automatically.

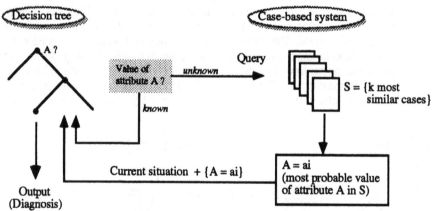

**Fig. 4.** Workbench level

Another possibility of a workbench integration is to choose automatically another test from the database subset for realising a dynamic decision tree generation (as it is done in KATE 4.1 throughout the "Dynamic Consultation" module). In any case, the user is strictly guided by the system.

### 3.3 Seamless Level: Using a Decision Tree During the Retrieval Step

Some important components of KATE and PATDEX are especially valuable according to the state of the art of the techniques.

- The most interesting part of the Kate technology to be used in CBR seems to be the information gain measure (based on Shannon's entropy, cf. [34]). Information gain is a heuristic that enables the most discriminating attributes for a given target attribute to be selected, such that the resulting tree is minimal in some sense. In average, a few questions are asked in order to reach a conclusion [22].

- The similarity measure is the basis of the process in a case-based reasoning system. Much attention has been paid in PATDEX to the definition of the similarity measure. Various aspects that are usually neglected in the classical distance measures (Euclidean, $\chi^2$, etc.) are taken into account in PATDEX (cf. [5], [31]). To summarise these advantages, one can say that the similarity measure allows the system to be flexible and incremental in a "clever" way.

In the seamless level we define a combination of entropy and similarity to create a better and more flexible retrieval index in the case-based reasoning system. Another advantage of this approach is that both systems and criteria's decisions are merged such that there exists only one system. The same tree can be used as a decision tree as well as an index tree in all parts of the system.

The main idea of tree building is to structure the search space based on its observed density (respectively on its classification goal) and to use this pre computed structure for efficient case retrieval (respectively for efficient diagnosis). In PATDEX, a multidimensional tree called $k$-d tree [16] is used to pre-process the entered attribute values in a way that the number of interesting cases can be reduced [38]. Thus, it works like a fixed indexing structure for the case retrieval. Within the $k$-d tree an incremental best-match search is used to find the m most similar cases (nearest neighbours) within a set of n cases with k specified indexing attributes. Application-dependent similarity measures based on user-defined value ranges enable the system to guide the search. The similarity measures used in PATDEX are constructed according to Tversky´s contrast model [36].

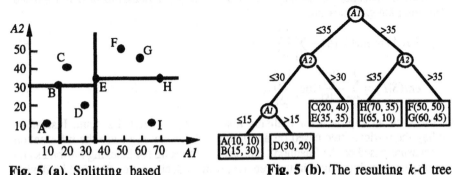

**Fig. 5 (a).** Splitting based on the interquartile distance

**Fig. 5 (b).** The resulting $k$-d tree

Every node within the $k$-d tree represents a subset of the cases of the case base and the root node represents the whole case base. Every inner node partitions the represented case set into disjoint subsets. A selection criterion permits to choose the next partitioning attribute within the tree. For instance, figure 5 shows a $k$-d tree built with the maximal interquartile distance criterion (cf. [18]). Splitting in the median of the discriminating attribute makes the k-d tree an optimal one (the tree is optimal if all leaf nodes are at adjoining levels).

Tree building needs to select at each node the best partitioning attribute. A good partition has to reflect the structure and the density of the underlying case base. Several *a priori* similarity measures can be used (there is an equivalence relation between similarities and distances, cf. [30]).

- The interquartile distance (1) computes the distance between the first and the third quartile. The bigger the distance between these quartiles, the bigger the dispersion of the selected attribute values. The attribute having the maximal dispersion is selected as the partitioning attribute.

$$dint = 1 - sim(q1, q3) . \tag{1}$$

- The maximum distance takes the greatest distance between to consecutive values $v_i$ of an attribute $A$ (2).

$$d_{max} = \max \{1 - sim(v_i, v_{i+1}), \text{ for } i = 1, ..., range(A) - 1 . \tag{2}$$

These distances are only available for numerical or totally ordered attributes.

In an another paper [39], the same authors propose some alternative strategies for creating a k-d tree based on an *a posteriori* estimation: The category utility of COBWEB [15], the entropy measure and an average similarity measure.

- The average similarity measure (3) estimates the dispersion of cases according to a given partition of the database $M = \{M_1, ..., M_l\}$. The partitioning attribute is the one with the greatest average similarity for a chosen partition.

$$sim_{ave} = \frac{2}{|M_i|^2} \sum_{a,b \in M_i} sim(a,b) . \tag{3}$$

- The information gain measure computes the difference of entropy between a case base M and its partition $\{M_1, ..., M_l\}$ built from an attribute $A$ (4). The entropy evaluates the impurity of a set of cases S with respect to a special attribute $T$ called the target, that has $K$ values $T_1, ..., T_K$ (5). The discriminating attribute selection procedure computes the attribute that provides the best normalised information gain measure.

$$IG(A) = ent(M|A) - \sum_{i=1}^{l} \frac{M_i}{M} ent(M_i|A) . \tag{4}$$

$$ent(S|T) = \sum_{k=1}^{K} -\frac{|S_k|}{|S|} \log_2 \frac{|S_k|}{|S|} . \tag{5}$$

We use such an approach for realising a seamlessly integrated system. Instead of building the retrieval tree based on an interquartile distance, we use the information gain measure based on the Shannon's entropy for choosing the indexing attributes and their respective value ranges in the tree, i.e., using a decision tree-like fixed indexing structure for case retrieval. Note that as decision trees are generally not binary trees—a symbolic attribute can generate many children nodes—the k-d tree mechanism required extensions in order to cope with multiple search paths and with unknown values during retrieval. The resulting system is a completely integrated one. The same tree can be used simultaneously as a k-d tree in the CBR process for cases indexing and retrieval, or as a decision tree in the induction process for cases' generalisation. The interactions between both approaches are greatly enhanced. We do not expect especially a higher retrieval speed or an increased accuracy rate, but rather a more flexible and convivial tool, that should be easier to use and to maintain. However, these advantages are difficult to measure.

Some authors have also looked at specific combinations between distances and entropy for selecting a partition of attributes for numeric or ordered values. For instance, [37] proposes to combine the entropy with an intra class similarity measure for detecting the "natural" classes of a partition on numerical attributes. In a similar way, [13] uses geometric features for defining a new attribute selection measure that takes the distance between pairs of examples near the frontiers into account. [14] integrates the information gain measure with the Minimum Description Length Principle for choosing the splitting point for numerical attributes. Furthermore, they propose a multi-interval discretization based on this criterion.

All these works show clearly that there is not a unique solution to the attribute selection problem for tree building. Some authors even advanced that a random attribute selection could achieve better (or at least, as good as) results than any other selection technique [24] and that the important thing was tree pruning [25]! Fortunately, further work has been realised on the same data sets, that shows that Minger's results have been misinterpreted [12]. Without exhausting the subject, the importance of attribute selection has been definitely rehabilitated [20].

Although each approach claims to be better than the classical one and demonstrates its advantages on well-known data sets (and it is probably the right way to do), we think that a specific choice cannot be made for real-life applications. To turn the things otherwise, we argue that a generic technology is not directly applicable and it has to be declined in vertical platforms for various domains such as maintenance, help-desk, etc. According to the type of applications and to the kind of data to work with, several degrees of integration become necessary.

## 4 Experimental Results

Many criteria are of interest for evaluating a case-based reasoning system: Technical, ergonomic, economic, etc. In this paper, we focus on some well-defined technical criteria as they can be easily measured and understood. As we said previously, we have to keep in mind that other advantages of integration (such as flexibility, completeness, adaptability, etc.) can be forgotten in such a prosaic evaluation. The interested reader can refer to our report on commercial CBR tools [7] for a deeper look on these criteria. We briefly present the test protocol and the databases on which these criteria are applied. We evaluate the benefits of integration on several databases (see Sect. 4.2). The obtained results show a clear advantage towards the case-based reasoning approach in terms of accuracy percentage, especially when the rate of noisy data increase. Unfortunately, the time spent for it remains high compared to a decision tree consultation. An intermediary approach seems to be the adequate way for most of databases' types.

### 4.1 Protocol Description

We aim at testing the merits of each integrated tool on several application domains. Each database is cut in two parts. The learning data set enables to build the system and the test set enables to consult it. The test set is chosen randomly, and the experiments are repeated five times. Both learning set and test set are exclusive (75%—25%). We use the following default values: The *reduced information* increases from 0 to 60%, by steps of 15%; at each step the average results on the five runs are computed onto the following indicators:

- The classification accuracy;
- The error rate;
- The no-answer rate;
- The time used to perform the consultation.

Two kinds of information reduction mode are defined: The *deletion* of existing values of an attribute simulates *unknown* values; the *modification* of existing values simulates *noise* in the data. The information reduction applies only onto the test set.

The tests have been systematically performed onto eight consultation systems:

- The pure decision tree system with unknown data;
- The pure decision tree system with noisy data;
- The pure case-based reasoning system with unknown data;
- The pure case-based reasoning system with noisy data;
- The cooperative system with unknown data;
- The workbench system with unknown data[1];
- The seamless level, where a decision tree is used as a retrieval structure, with unknown data;
- The seamless level, where a decision tree is used as a retrieval structure, with noisy data.

All the experiments have been automatically processed through a handy test editor. A test session involves several application domains and several consultation types.

## 4.2 Databases

The databases used for test cover a wide range of application domains. The number of cases varies from 205 to 1470. The attributes' types are numeric as well as symbolic. Table 1 summarises these databases.

In the "DEVELOPER" domain, one has to decide which kind of chemical is necessary when knowing the type of development film, the current temperature, etc. These data have been provided by tecInno. The "TRAVEL AGENCY" domain is a classical problem that arises in many travel agencies: Given traveller's wishes (price, destination, type of holidays, etc.), the agency has to find an adequate hotel. The data on the "TRAVEL AGENCY" domain were provided by Mario Lenz to who we are indebt. The "AIRCRAFT" domain deals with the maintenance of planes' engines. The database, that is a subset of a real application data set, has been provided by AcknoSoft. In the "CAR" domain, one has to determine a risk estimation factor for car insurance companies, based on several attributes such as manufacturing, price, technical data, etc. The "CAR" domain comes from the UCI Repository of Machine Learning Databases and Domain Theories, USA.

---

[1] Since the decision tree switches to CBR in presence of unknown data only, the cooperative and the workbench systems tested with noisy data provide the same results as the pure decision tree with noisy data.

**Table 1.** Overview of the test domains

| Domain Name | DEVELOPER | TRAVEL AGENCY | AIRCRAFT | CAR |
|---|---|---|---|---|
| # of cases | 280 | 1470 | 621 | 205 |
| # of attributes | 10 | 9 | 7 | 26 |
| # of numeric attributes | 3 | 3 | 0 | 14 |
| # of values per attribute (average) | 18 | 26 | 33 | 6 |
| % unknown values (average) | 26 | 0 | 17 | 1 |
| # of classes | 65 | 11 | 55 | 7 |
| Database characteristics | well-balanced domain | big size, average number of values per attribute is high | high unknown values rate, only symbolic attributes | well-balanced domain, no unknown values |

## 4.3 Results

Due to the lack of place, we present only partial results on accuracy rate and time, that concern the tests made with *deleted* values. For more complete results, please contact the first author of this article.

The four first graphs (Fig. 6) demonstrate again a well-known advantage of CBR compared to induction. The CBR approach supports much more easily unknown values in the query [23]. Therefore, all the integrated approaches that involve a decision tree in the first part of the problem solving process (decision tree, cooperative and workbench levels) lead to a lower accuracy rate. However, it does not mean that these approaches have to be rejected. Even if they fail in filling some accuracy criteria, we argue that they encompass very important "non measurable" criteria like flexibility of the resulting executive system, acceptance by the user etc. More precisely, three points are of major interest when dealing with real-world applications:

- They may better correspond to the user's wishes;
- They are more effective in some situations;
- They lead much quicker to the results.

One can notice that the workbench approach provides better results than the two other decision-tree-based approaches, especially on the Developer and Travel Agency databases. This comes from the fact that the data are more regular—from a statistical point of view—in these databases. The overall conclusions about accuracy are:

- The case-based system performs much better as the decision tree when the information reduction percentage is growing. It gives always an answer because we did not define a minimal threshold for the similarity measure.
- The cooperative and the workbench approach give slightly better results than the decision tree according to the accuracy and no-answer indicators.
- The accuracy rates of the pure CBR and of the seamless level are roughly the same. The seamless approach only intends to speed up the case retrieval; it leads normally to the same results.

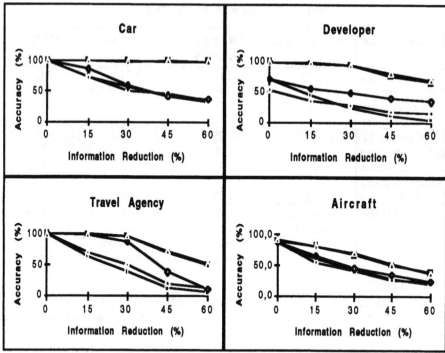

**Fig. 6.** Accuracy percentage comparison

Therefore, the seamless approach may be preferable if the results are obtained quicker.

The four next graphs (Fig. 7) show the average time spent for case retrieval with the decision tree, the pure CBR and the seamless approach.

- As expected, the decision tree consultation is almost instantaneously (some hundredths of second).
- The time used to consult the case-based reasoning system decreases with the information reduction rate. This is quite understandable because the least the number of features a query has, the least the number of local similarities the system has to calculate.
- The time used by the seamless approach is longer than the pure CBR for all databases but CAR. This point may seem surprising and requires further explanations.

In the seamless approach, a decision tree is used as a k-d tree to index the cases of the database. It results in a lower number of examined cases. Thus, unlike a "normal" k-d tree, the decision tree is not binary: Each node may have many branches when it describes a symbol attribute. When backtracking in such a node, the number of tests to be made is very high. In fact, we discovered that one of the tests (the "Ball-Within-Bounds" test, cf. [4], [6]) was responsible for 80% of the time spent during case retrieval. This makes the decision tree quite inefficient for boosting the retrieval step.

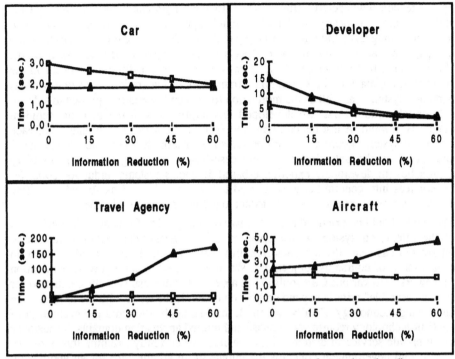

**Fig. 7.** Time comparison (decision tree, CBR and seamless level)

Despite its apparent lack of efficiency, we intend to further work on this approach for two reasons:

- Once a decision tree has been generated, it can be used as a $k$-d tree as well as a pure induction tree during the consultation phase. For the applications where there exist symbolic attributes, it can be used only as a pure decision tree.

- The tests have been made with all the data stored in high memory. In reality, the database is often stored on a central site that is accessed by the application through a network. Therefore, the number of accesses to the database is a crucial point that has not to be underestimated. We made a few tests with databases stored on hard disk. In this case, the $k$-d tree leaded to a big gain of time, compared to the flat CBR retrieval, even on databases that have only symbolic attributes. As the $k$-d tree tries to minimise the number of examined cases, the time spent for the bound tests during retrieval is compensated by the low number of visited cases.

## 5    Discussion

More than successful algorithms or results, this paper proposes a methodology for integrating CBR with other learning paradigms like induction. The four-levels approach acts as a framework that enables CBR to migrate from academia to industry. It opens the door to allow real-world problems to be solved by CBR-like methods, by offering flexible use and integration of the techniques in the user's environment. With respect to this approach, we already realised some applications where CBR and Induction are more or less coupled (diagnosis of airplane engines [9], diagnosis of robots [10].

From a technical perspective, this research discusses at *practical* level combining CBR and induction. It is nearly similar to Quinlan's approach who discusses at *technical* level integrating CBR and other learning paradigms [29]. The approaches described in this paper are also similar in some aspects to the integration of CcC+ with BUBE [11], or to the IKBALS project [40]. However, some major differences occur in the conceptual approach to the integration—framework of integration levels onto various parts of a system—as well as the motivation for a deep integration opposed to side-to-side collaboration. First, we developed this approach with the goal of technical diagnosis in mind. A test bench permits to verify systematically the validity of each integrated system according to various statistical criteria that take into account noise and errors on the data. Induction and case-based reasoning are complementary approaches for developing experience-based diagnosis systems. Induction *compiles* experiences into general knowledge used to solve problems. Case-based reasoning directly *interprets* experiences. Both technologies complement each other.

This work should be extended at least in two directions. The first one is the evaluation of the integrated system with respect to other criteria. For instance, the users' interaction easiness, the system's flexibility, etc. The problem caused by such an evaluation is of course its subjectivity. We already tried to apply a wider evaluation framework onto various CBR tools [7]. It appears that the results of the evaluation for "non measurable" criteria depend on how confident is the tester with the tools and the underlying technology. Finally, we think that the application and the evaluation of the CBR technology require very precise and limited application domains, for instance the after-sale service in technical maintenance (we currently examine this domain). The second development concerns the choice of an architecture for an application domain. The integration level required depends mainly on the application type and on who is supposed to use the final applicative system. The development methodology is not the same for a help-desk application than, for example, for a troubleshooting manual based on experience or for an electronic maintenance manual. This problem is currently under investigation.

# 6 Acknowledgement

Funding for INRECA has been provided by the Commission of the European Communities (ESPRIT contract P6322) to which the authors are greatly indebted. The partners of INRECA are AcknoSoft (prime contractor, France), tecInno (Germany), Irish Medical Systems (Ireland), the University of Kaiserslautern (Germany). KATE is a trademark of Michel Manago. S3-CASE is a product of tecInno GmbH. The data on the "Travel Agency" domain were provided by Mario Lenz to which we are indebt. The "CAR" domain comes from the UCI Repository of Machine Learning Databases and Domain Theories, U.S.A. We wish to thank Ralph Traphöner and Guido Derwand for their contribution to this work, and the reviewers for their helpful comments.

# 7 References

[1]    Aamodt, A.: Explanation-driven Retrieval, Reuse, and Learning of Cases. Richter, Wess et al. (1993) 279-284

[2]    Aamodt, A., Plaza, E.: Case-Based Reasoning: Foundational Issues, Methodological Variations, and System Approaches. AI COM **Vol. 7 No. 1** (1994) 39-59

[3]    Althoff, K.-D: Machine Learning and Knowledge Acquisition in a Computational Architecture for Fault Diagnosis in Engineering Systems. M. Weintraub (ed.), Proc.

International Machine Learning Conference, Workshop on "Computational Architectures for Supporting Machine Learning and Knowledge Acquisition", Aberdeen (1992)

[4]   Althoff, K.-D., Bergmann, R., Maurer, F., Wess, S., Manago, M., Auriol, E., Conruyt, N., Traphöner, R., Bräuer, M., Dittrich, S.: Integrating Inductive and Case-Based Technologies for Classification and Diagnostic Reasoning. E. Plaza (ed.), Proc. ECML-93 Workshop on "Integrated Learning Architectures" (1993)

[5]   Althoff, K.-D., Wess, S.: Case-Based Knowledge Acquisition, Learning, and Problem Solving in Diagnostic Real World Tasks. Proc. EKAW-91, Glasgow & Crieff (1991)

[6]   Althoff, K.-D., Wess, S., Bergmann, R., Maurer, F., Manago, M., Auriol, E., Conruyt, N., Traphöner, R., Bräuer, M., Dittrich, S.: Induction and Case-Based Reasoning for Classification Tasks. H. H. Bock, W. Lenski & M. M. Richter (eds.), Information Systems and Data Analysis, Prospects-Foundations-Applications, Proc. 17th Annual Conference of the GfKl, University of Kaiserslautern, 1993, Springer Verlag, Berlin-Heidelberg (1994) 3-16

[7]   Althoff, K.-D., Auriol, E., Barletta, R., Manago, M: A Review of Industrial Case-Based Reasoning Tools. A. Goodall (ed.), AI Intelligence, 1995

[8]   Althoff, K.-D., Faupel, B., Kockskämper, S., Traphöner, R., Wernicke, W.: Knowledge Acquisition in the Domain of CNC Machining Centers: the MOLTKE Approach. J. Boose, B. Gaines & J.-G. Ganascia (eds.), EKAW-89 (1989) 180-195

[9]   Auriol, E., Manago, M.: Integrating Induction and Case-Based Reasoning for Troubleshooting CFM-56 Aircraft Engines. XPS'95, Workshop Fallbasiertes Schließen - Grundlagen & Anwendungen, University of Kaiserslautern (1995)

[10]  Auriol, E., Manago, M.: Roboterdiagnose bei Sepro Robotique. XPS'95, Workshop Service-Support-Systeme - Innovative Techniken für Kundendienst, Wartung und Serviceaufgaben, University of Kaiserslautern (1995)

[11]  Bamberger, S. K., Goos, K.: Integration of Case-Based Reasoning and Inductive Learning Methods. Richter, Wess et al. (1993) 296-300

[12]  Buntime, W., Niblett, T.: A Further Comparison of Splitting Rules for Decision-Tree Induction. Kluwer Academic Publishers, Machine Learning 8 (1992) 75-85

[13]  Elomaa, T., Ukkonen, E. (1994). A Geometric Approach to Feature Selection. Springer-Verlag, Proc. of ECML-94 (1994) 351-354

[14]  Fayyad, U. M., Irani, K. B.: Multi-Interval Discretization of Continuous-Valued Attributes for Classification Learning. Bajcsy, R. (ed.), Proc. of the 13th IJCAI (1993) 1022-1027

[15]  Fisher, D.: COBWEB: Knowledge Acquisition via Conceptual Clustering. Machine Learning II (1987) 139-172

[16]  Friedman, J. H., Bentley, J. L., Finkel, R. A.: An Algorithm for Finding Best Matches in Logarithmic Expected Time. ACM Trans. Math. Soft. 3 (1977), 209-226

[17]  Janetzko, D., Strube, G.: Case-Based Reasoning and Model-Based Knowledge Acquisition. Springer Verlag, F. Schmalhofer, G. Strube & T. Wetter (eds.), Contemporary Knowledge Engineering and Cognition (1992) 99-114

[18]  Koopmans, L. H.: Introduction to Contemporary Statistical Methods. Second Edition, Duxbury Press, Boston (1987)

[19]  Koton, P.: Using Experience in Learning and Problem Solving. Massachussets Institute of Technology, Laboratory of Computer Science (PhD Diss). MIT/LCS/TR-441 (1989)

[20]  Liu, W. Z., White, A. P.: The Importance of Attribute Selection Measures in Decision-Tree Induction. Kluwer Academic, Machine Learning 15 (1994) 25-41

[21]  Lopez, B., Plaza, E.: Case-Based Planning for Medical Diagnosis. Proc. of ISMIS'93, Trondheim (1993) 96-105

[22] Manago M.: Knowledge Intensive Induction. Morgan Kaufmann, Proc. of the sixth International Machine Learning Workshop (1989)

[23] Manago, M., Althoff, K.-D., Auriol, E., Traphöner, R., Wess, S., Conruyt, N., Maurer, F.: Induction and Reasoning from Cases. Richter, Wess et al. (1993), 313-318

[24] Mingers, J.: An Empirical Comparison of Selection Measures for Decision-Tree Induction. Kluwer Academic Publishers, Machine Learning 3 (1989) 319-342

[25] Mingers, J.: An Empirical Comparison of Pruning Tree Methods for Decision-Tree Induction. Kluwer Academic Publishers, Machine Learning 4 (1989) 227-242

[26] Morik, K., Wrobel, S., Kietz, J. U., Emde, W.: Knowledge Acquisition and Machine Learning: Theory, Methods, and Applications. Academic Press (1993)

[27] Pfeifer, T., Faupel, B.: The Application of MOLTKE: Fault Diagnosis of CNC Machining Centres (in German: Die Anwendung von MOLTKE: Diagnose von CNC-Bearbeitungszentren). Pfeifer and Richter (1993) 42-67

[28] Quinlan, R.: Learning Efficient Classification Procedures and their Application to Chess End Games. Morgan Kaufmann, R. S. Michalski, J. G. Carbonell and T. M. Mitchell (eds.), Machine Learning: An Artificial Intelligence Approach Vol. 1 (1983)

[29] Quinlan, R., Cameron-Jones, R.: FOIL: a Midterm Report. Proc. of ECML-93, P. Bradzil (ed.), Springer-Verlag (1993) 3-20.

[30] Richter, M. M.: Classification and Learning of Similarity Measures. Springer Verlag, Proc. 16th Annual Conference of the German Society for Classification (1992)

[31] Richter, M. M., Wess, S.: Similarity, Uncertainty and Case-Based Reasoning in PATDEX. Kluwer Academic Publishers, Automated Reasoning - Essays in Honor of Woody Bledsoe (1991)

[32] Richter, M. M., Wess, S., Althoff, K.-D., Maurer, F. (eds.): Proc. 1st European Workshop on Case-Based Reasoning (EWCBR-93). SEKI-REPORT SR-93-12, University of Kaiserslautern (1993)

[33] Shank, R.: Dynamic Memory. A Theory of Reminding and Learning in Computers and People. Cambridge University Press (1982)

[34] Shannon & Weaver: The Mathematical Theory of Computation. University of Illinois Press, Urbana (1947)

[35] Traphöner, R., Manago, M., Conruyt, N., Dittrich, S: Industrial Criteria for Comparing Technologies in INRECA. INRECA D4, Esprit Project P6322 (1992)

[36] Tversky, A.: Features of Similarity. Psychological Review 84 (1977) 327-352

[37] Van de Merckt, T.: Decision Trees in Numerical Attribute Spaces. Bajcsy, R. (ed.), Proc. of the 13th IJCAI (1993) 1016-1021

[38] Wess, S., Althoff, K.-D., Derwand, G.: Improving the Retrieval Step in Case-Based Reasoning. Richter, Wess et al. (1993) 83-88

[39] Wess, S., Althoff, K.-D., Derwand, G.: Using $k$-d Trees to Improve the Retrieval Step in Case-Based Reasoning. Springer-Verlag, S. Wess, K. -D. Althoff & M. M. Richter (eds.). Topics in Case-Based Reasoning (1994)

[40] Zeleznikov, J., Hunter, D., Vossos, G.: Integrating Rule-Based and Case-Based Reasoning with Information Retrieval: the IKBALS System. Richter, Wess et al. (1993) 341-346

# Experimental Study of an Evaluation Function for Cases Imperfectly Explained

Carlos Bento

José Exposto   Victor Francisco   Ernesto Costa

Departamento de Engenharia Informática
Universidade de Coimbra
Vila Franca - Pinhal de Marrocos
3030 Coimbra - PORTUGAL
E-mail: bento@alma.uc.pt   ernesto@moebius.uc.pt

**Abstract.** This paper describes an evaluation function which deals with similarities and dissimilarities in cases imperfectly explained. Our explanation-based evaluation function represents an alternative to other approaches that use case explanations for selection and retrieval of past cases. This function is used by a diagnosis system called $RECIDE_{clinic}$. We present the experimental results obtained in the domain of neurologic diseases. These results illustrate the role of similarity and dissimilarity terms as they are defined within our framework.

## 1   Introduction

The power of a Case-Based Reasoning (CBR) System [7, 5, 13] is greatly determined by its capability to retrieve the relevant cases for prediction of the solution to a new problem.

A nearest neighbour algorithm for case retrieval, described by Duda and Hart (1973), searches through every case in memory, applies a similarity metric and returns the case (or k cases) with the past problem most similar to the new one. This similarity metric counts the number of facts that the past and the new problem have in common.

Two systems CYRUS [6] and UNIMEM [10] index cases by facts in the past problem description that are predictive of other facts in the solution description. Predictiveness of the facts is determined by some correlation calculations. This has some drawbacks, specially when calculations are performed on a small data set [11].

The combination of nearest neighbour and knowledge-guided techniques led to the development of knowledge-based retrieval systems [1, 9, 11, 12, 3]. These systems use domain knowledge for the construction of explanations of why a problem had a specific solution in the past.

The CBR approach is appropriate for domains where a strong theory is not available and past experience is accessible. The absence of a strong theory implies that in general case explanations are imperfect. We report three kinds of imperfections in explanations: (1) incomplete set of explanations; (2) partial explanations; (3) broken explanations. Partial and broken explanations are not considered in current explanation-based similarity systems. We propose a function that computes degree of match for cases imperfectly explained. We will refer to this function as an evaluation function [8].

We introduce the results obtained with RECIDE$_{clinic}$ (REasoning with Cases Imperfectly Described and Explained in a Clinical Domain) an expert system based on RECIDE - an implementation of our CBR approach. RECIDE$_{clinic}$ has a case library of past successful diagnoses in the domain of neurology. We present the results obtained with our evaluation function and make some remarks on them.

## 2   An Explanation-Based Evaluation Function

In this section we introduce how a case is represented within our framework. We describe a new explanation-based evaluation function that is an extension of one previously proposed by Bento and Costa (1994).

### 2.1   Case Representation

Within our approach a case is represented by a triple $< P, S, R >$ (Figure 1) with $P$ and $S$, respectively, a set of facts representing a past problem and a solution, and $R$ a set of rules representing a causal justification. The causal justification is in the form of a set of explanations. An explanation is a proof tree that links facts in the problem with a fact in the solution. We consider three kinds of imperfections in explanations: (1) incomplete set of explanations; (2) partial explanations; (3) broken explanations.

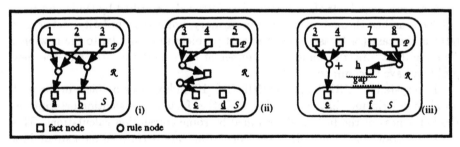

**Fig. 1.** A case with (i) a complete set of explanations; (ii) an incomplete set of explanations; (iii) a partial and broken explanation

In a case with an incomplete set of explanations some solution facts are not explained and hence are not the conclusion for any proof tree (e.g., Cases ii and iii , in Figure 1. Facts d̲ and f̲ in these case solutions are not leaves of a proof tree). A partial explanation is one whose proof tree omits some branches.

This means that one or more steps in the proof tree apply a rule for which the conditions are necessary but not sufficient. Rule nodes representing these rules are labelled by '+' (e.g., In Figure 1, case iii, the proof tree at the left). A broken explanation is one in which there is a gap between the proof tree and the case solution (e.g., In Figure 1, case iii, the proof tree at the right).

## 2.2 Case Matching

As outlined before we use an explanation-based retrieval approach in which explanations are assumed possibly imperfect. Explanations determine subsets in the set of facts describing the case problem (Figure 2). Those subgroups are called footprints, a concept introduced by Veloso (1992). A footprint is a set of facts that are the origin (premises) of an explanation for a fact in the case solution[1]. We extend the concept of footprint by considering four types of footprints: strong (Sfp) , weak (Wfp), undetermined (Ufp), and strongly undetermined (SUfp). Those four types of footprints are used for case indexing, evaluation, and retrieval.

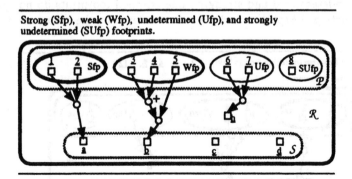

**Fig. 2.** Strong, weak, undetermined, and strongly undetermined footprints

The footprint type is determined by the kind of proof tree (explanation) for which the footprint facts are premises. Depending on the proof tree being complete[2], partial or broken the footprint is strong (e.g., In Figure 2, the set of facts $\{1, 2\}$ in the problem description concerning fact $\underline{a}$ in the solution), weak (e.g., In Figure 2, the set $\{3, 4, 5\}$ concerning fact $\underline{b}$ in the solution), or undetermined (e.g., In Figure 2, the set $\{6, 7\}$ concerning fact $\underline{h}$ before the gap).

---

[1] In M. Veloso (1992) approach these explanations link the initial state and the goals in a planning system.

[2] It is important to distinguish between a complete set of proof trees (explanations) and a complete proof tree (explanation). As outlined before, when any fact in the solution is leave of a proof tree we say that the case has a complete set of proof trees. A proof tree is complete when it is not broken or partial.

A fact that is not origin of any proof tree establishes a strongly undetermined footprint (e.g., In Figure 2, the set {8} in the problem description).

The reason to consider four types of footprints is the assumption that facts origin of complete, partial, or broken explanations, or no explanation at all, play distinct roles in case evaluation and must be assigned different relevance for case retrieval. It is assumed a footprint origin of a complete explanation is strongly relevant for the solution. A footprint origin of a partial explanation is relevant in an unknown extension for the solution (a partial explanation uses rules that are generalisations not guaranteed to be valid). A footprint origin of a broken explanation is undetermined in the sense that it is not known if it is relevant for the solution, although the creation, by the expert, of a broken explanation presupposes some importance is given to the premises for this broken explanation. A footprint (single fact) not origin of any explanation is strongly undetermined in the sense that it is unknown whether it has any relevance for the solution or not.

When a case has a complete set of complete explanations, undetermined and strongly undetermined footprints become irrelevant. In those cases footprints in the problem description that are premises for the complete set of complete explanations establish the necessary and sufficient conditions for the solution. Therefore undetermined and strongly undetermined footprints do not play any role in predicting the solution and are not considered by the evaluation function.

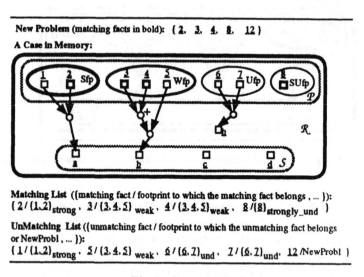

**Fig. 3.** Case matching

Matching between a past case and a new problem is represented by two lists of matching and unmatching facts (Figure 3). Each list is composed of pairs fact/footprint. The fact in a pair of a matching list represents a matching in the case problem. The footprint is the one to which the fact belongs. The left part in a pair of an unmatching list represents a fact in the case problem or in the new problem that does not match. If the right part has the symbol 'NewProbl' this means that the unmatching fact occurs in the new problem. Figure 3 shows an example of a matching between a case in memory and a new problem. In this example the matching facts are 2, 3, 4, and 8 (in bold). Matching fact 2 belongs to the strong footprint composed of facts 1, and 2. Facts 3 and 4 belong to the weak footprint composed of facts 3, 4, and 5. Fact 8 belongs to the strongly undetermined footprint composed of fact 8. The unmatching facts are 1, 5, 6, 7, and 12. Unmatching fact 1 belongs to the strong footprint composed of facts 1, and 2. Fact 5 belongs to the weak footprint composed of facts 3, 4, and 5. Facts 6 and 7 belong to the undetermined footprint composed of facts 6 and 7. Fact 12, belongs to the new problem.

## 2.3   Evaluation Function

The matching and unmatching lists described above (abbreviated, *ML* and *UML*) are the arguments for the function 'evalt' which evaluates the degree of similarity and dissimilarity between a new problem and a partially-matching case:

$$evalt(ML, UML) = sim(ML) - dissim(UML) \qquad (1)$$

Functions 'sim' and 'dissim' calculate similarity and dissimilarity values between a case and a new problem and are described below:

$$sim(ML) = \kappa \sum_{i=1}^{l} relev(f_i, Sfp) + \lambda \sum_{j=1}^{m} relev(f_j, Wfp) + \mu \sum_{k=1}^{n} relev(f_k, Ufp) +$$

$$\nu \sum_{l=1}^{o} relev(f_l, SUfp) \qquad (2)$$

with $f_i$ , $f_j$ , $f_k$ , and $f_l$ , respectively, matching facts in the case problem that belongs to strong, weak, undetermined, and strongly undetermined footprints;

$$dissim(UML) = \rho \sum_{i=1}^{l} relev(g_i, Sfp) + \sigma \sum_{j=1}^{m} relev(g_j, Wfp) + \tau \sum_{k=1}^{n} relev(g_k, Ufp) +$$

$$\upsilon \sum_{l=1}^{o} relev(g_l, SUfp) + \omega \sum_{m=1}^{o} g_m \qquad (3)$$

with $g_i$ , $g_j$ , $g_k$ , and $g_l$ , respectively, unmatching facts in the case problem that belong to strong, weak, undetermined, and strongly undetermined footprints; $g_m$ unmatching facts in the new problem; and

$$relev(FACT, FOOTPRINT) =$$

$$\frac{1}{cardinality of the FOOTPRINT to wich FACT belongs} \qquad (4)$$

Constants *l*, *m*, *n*, and *o* are, respectively, the number of matching facts in the matching list belonging to strong, weak, undetermined, and strongly undetermined footprints. Constants *p*, *q*, *r*, and *s* are the number of unmatching facts in the unmatching list belonging to strong, weak, undetermined, and strongly undetermined footprints, and *t* is the number of unmatching facts in the new problem.

The four terms in the 'sim' function relate (from left to right) to matching facts belonging, respectively, to strong, weak, undetermined and strongly undetermined footprints. Constants $\kappa$, $\lambda$, $\tau$, and $\nu$ assign a different weight to terms for facts belonging to different footprints.

The first four terms (from left to right) in the 'dissim' function correspond to the ones in the 'sim' function but relative to unmatching facts. Constants $\rho$, $\sigma$, $\tau$, and $\upsilon$ assign a different weight to terms for facts belonging to strong, weak, undetermined, and strongly undetermined footprints. The fifth term from the left relates to unmatching facts in the new problem. Constant $\omega$ assigns a weight to this term.

Function 'relev' assigns a relevance to each (un)matching fact inversely proportional to its footprint cardinality. It is assumed the (un)matching of a fact from a small set of facts premises for an explanation is more relevant than the (un)matching of one from a bigger set of facts.

As an example, consider the value returned by the evaluation function with $\kappa=22$, $\lambda=15$, $\tau=10$, $\nu=1$, $\rho=22$, $\sigma=15$, $\tau=10$, $\upsilon=1$, and $\omega=7$, for the case and new problem in Figure 3:

$$[22 * (1/2) + 15 * (1/3 + 1/3) + 10 * 0 + 1 * (1/1)] - [22 * (1/2) + 15 * (1/3) + 10 * (1/2 + 1/2) + 1 * 0 + 7 * 1]$$

The first term within the first square brackets relates to the matching fact $\underline{2}$ belonging to the strong footprint $\{\underline{1}, \underline{2}\}$ with length two implying a fact relevance of $1/2$ which is multiplied by constant $\kappa$. The second term is due to matching facts $\underline{3}$ and $\underline{4}$ belonging to the weak footprint $\{\underline{3}, \underline{4}, \underline{5}\}$ with length three and hence each fact has relevance $1/3$ which is added and multiplied by $\lambda$. The third term relates to the undetermined footprint without any fact matching the new situation. The fourth term deals with matching fact $\underline{8}$ belonging to the strongly undetermined footprint $\underline{8}$ with length one implying a fact relevance $1/1$ which is multiplied by $\nu$.

Terms within the second pair of square brackets relate to unmatching facts in the case problem and new problem. The first of the five summing terms relates to the unmatching fact $\underline{1}$ belonging to the strong footprint $\{\underline{1}, \underline{2}\}$ with length two implying a fact relevance $1/2$ which is multiplied by constant $\rho$. The second term relates to unmatching fact $\underline{5}$ belonging to the weak footprint $\{\underline{3}, \underline{4}, \underline{5}\}$ with length three and hence the fact has relevance $1/3$ which is multiplied by $\sigma$. The third term relates to unmatching facts $\underline{6}$ and $\underline{7}$ belonging to the undetermined footprint $\{\underline{6}, \underline{7}\}$ with length two and accordingly with relevance $1/2$ which is multiplied by constant $\tau$. The fourth term deals with the strongly undetermined footprint {8} which does not have any unmatching fact. The fifth term relates to unmatching fact 12 in the new problem. Each fact in the new problem is considered individually, so its relevance is assumed to be 1/1 which is multiplied by constant $\omega$.

As reported before, this metric is an extension of another one defined by Bento & Costa (1994). In the next section we describe $RECIDE_{clinic}$ an expert system in the domain of neurology which applies this metric.

## 3 Test Domain

The tests we present in this paper come from an application in the domain of neurology. The task is the diagnosis of neurologic diseases. $RECIDE_{clinic}$ determines a patient pathology supported on previous successful diagnoses.

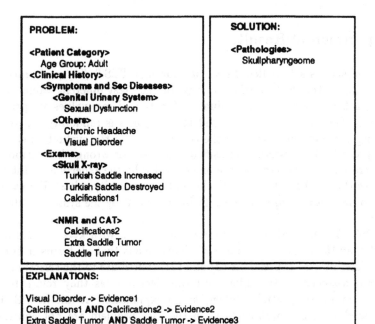

**Fig. 4.** A case in the domain

A past case (Figure 4) comprises a problem description composed of a patient categorisation together with her/his clinical history and a solution description in the form of a set of pathologies. The patient categorisation comprises information about her/his age and sex. The clinical history is described by two groups of facts - symptoms/secondary diseases, and exams, both being root of an hierarchy of subgroups[3]. Domain vocabulary comprises 61 attributes for patient categori-

---

[3] The taxonomy introduced for problem and solution description is only relevant at the user's level. For matching between a new problem and cases in memory $RECIDE_{clinic}$ considers only ground facts organized in a flat structure.

sation and clinical history description. The cases currently available cover eight diseases.

In the case represented in Figure 4, all explanations are broken. It describes an adult patient with a sexual dysfunction, chronic headache, and visual disorder. The X-ray exams showed an increased and destroyed turkish saddle and calcifications. The Nuclear Magnetic Resonance (NMR) and Computerised Axial Tomography (CAT) exams suggest calcifications, an extra saddle tumour and a saddle tumour. The pathology that has been diagnosed for this case is a skullpharyngeome. The explanations provided by the experts for this diagnosis are: (1) visual disorder is an evidence for the pathology, (2) calcifications detected by the X-ray and NMR/CAT are another evidence, (3) extra saddle and saddle tumours detected by the NMR/CAT are a third evidence.

In the current library almost all cases have broken explanations. In fact the experts seldom created partial or complete explanations during the elicitation sessions.

## 4 Experimental Results

We describe six tests (labelled TEST #1 through TEST #6) performed with RECIDE$_{clinic}$ in the domain of neurology. In each test different values are assigned to each parameter in the evaluation function. Those values are presented in Figure 5. The set of past cases used in these tests is randomly ordered and this sorting is maintained along all the experiments. In the evaluation step each solution given by the system is classified as correct or wrong. A solution is assumed correct if it is the same as the one provided by the experts and if it comes from a case that is the only one with the highest similarity value[4]. For each new problem, a new case is input if the solution provided by the system is classified as wrong.

In TEST #1 the evaluation function was applied with k=22, l=15, m=10, n=1, r=22, s=15, t=10, u=1, and w=7. This means that all terms in function 'sim' and 'dissim' (see expressions (2) and (3)) contribute to the selection value. The weight assigned to the different terms decreases as they relate to facts premise of complete, partial, broken, or no explanation at all. In TEST #2 terms related with unmatching facts in the case problem are not considered. The other terms are assigned the same weight as in TEST #1. In TEST #3 only the terms related to matching facts in the case problem contribute to the value returned by the evaluation function and the relevance attributed to them is the same as in TEST #1. In TEST #4 only the terms related to unmatching facts are considered. The weight associated to these terms is the same as in

---

[4] When the system presents more than one case with the highest similarity value this means the evaluation function does not have enough discriminating power as it assigns the same selection value to several disctinct cases. When this happens the solution is classified as wrong.

|            | κ  | λ  | μ  | ν | ρ  | σ  | τ  | υ | ω |
|------------|----|----|----|---|----|----|----|---|---|
| TEST #1    | 22 | 15 | 10 | 1 | 22 | 15 | 10 | 1 | 7 |
| TEST #2    | 22 | 15 | 10 | 1 | 0  | 0  | 0  | 0 | 7 |
| TEST #3    | 22 | 15 | 10 | 1 | 0  | 0  | 0  | 0 | 0 |
| TEST #4    | 0  | 0  | 0  | 0 | 22 | 15 | 10 | 1 | 7 |
| TEST #5    | 1  | 1  | 1  | 1 | 1  | 1  | 1  | 1 | 1 |
| TEST #6 (relev = 1) | 1 | 1 | 1 | 1 | 0 | 0 | 0 | 0 | 0 |

**Fig. 5.** Test parameters

TEST #1. In this test the value returned by the evaluation function is always less than or equal to zero (see expression (1)). The closer this value is to zero the higher it is the chance for the case to be selected. In TEST #5 all terms are assigned the same weight. In TEST #6 only the terms related to matching facts in the case problem are considered. All terms on matching facts are assigned the same weight and function 'relev' (see expression (4)) is modified to return the unitary value independently of the footprint a fact belongs to. This means the evaluation function becomes (compare with expressions (1) through (4)):

With constants l, m, n, and o, respectively, the number of matching facts in the matching list belonging to strong, weak, undetermined, and strongly undetermined footprints, function 'evalt' returns the number of facts in the case problem matching the new problem, that is, the function proposed by Duda & Hart (1973).

Figures 6 and 7 summarise the results obtained with the six tests. Figure 6 represents the cumulative number of correct solutions for new problems. Figure 7 shows the number of cases that were given the system.

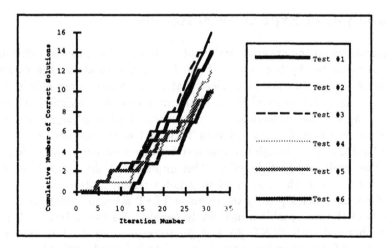

**Fig. 6.** Cumulative number of correct solutions

The best results are obtained with TESTS #2 and #3. In those tests the progression in the number of correct solutions (Figure 6) is similar until the 22nd iteration. At the end the performance achieved with TEST #2 is slightly better than with TEST #3. The worst results are obtained with TESTS #5 and #6.

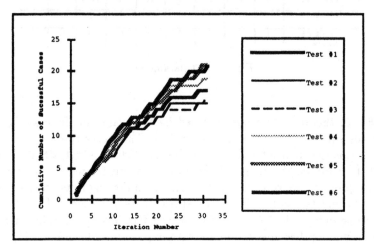

**Fig. 7.** Progression in the number of successful cases in memory

Figure 7 represents the number of cases input in the sequence of wrong solutions. The best results are obtained with TESTS #2 and #3 in which at the end, respectively, 15 and 16 cases had to be input. The results obtained with TEST #1 are between the ones obtained with TESTS #2 and #3, and the ones produced by TESTS #4, #5, and #6. With TESTS #5 and #6 after the 31st iteration 21 cases are in memory.

## 5    Analysis of Experimental Results

Considerations on the experimental results relate, at first, to the solutions (diagnoses) suggested by the system. From Figure 6 wich shows the cumulative number of correct solutions, it is clear that the best results are obtained when different weights are assigned to the similarity terms and dissimilarities in facts representing the case problem are not considered (TESTS #2 and #3). The reason for the worse result obtained with TEST #1 when compared with TESTS #2 and #3 is that, although not assumed during elicitation, some facts describing a case problem are disjunctive. This implies that the occurrence of some unmatching facts in the case problem is not a reason to decrease the selection value for a case. Consequently the terms in TEST #1 which relate to unmatching facts in the case problem incorrectly penalise the case selection. The poor results obtained with TEST #5 and #6 correspond to what is expected. In TEST #5 all facts are assigned the same weight independently of being premise or not of an explanation. TEST #6 shows the results obtained with a classical nearest neighbour function. The worst results are obtained with this test. This makes clear that assigning decreasing relevance to facts premises of complete, partial, broken, or no explanations at all improves the selection quality as has been shown with TESTS #1, #2, and #3. The relative low number of cases correctly selected in TEST #4 considering only dissimilarities is coherent with the considerations made about disjunctive facts in case problems.

Another aspect to be considered is the number of cases in memory. Figure 7 shows that in TESTS #2 and #3 15 cases had to be input which is the lowest number of cases given to RECIDE$_{clinic}$. This emphasises the assertion that the best results are obtained when different weights are assigned to facts in the case problem premises of different types of explanations and the dissimilarities due to unmatching facts in the case problem are not considered. In TESTS #1 and #4, respectively, 17 and 19 cases were input. In TESTS #5 and #6 the performance in terms of number of cases in memory is quite bad. In these tests, after the 33rd iteration 21 cases were provided by the experts.

## 6 Conclusions

Case-Based Reasoning is a well suited approach when a perfect theory on the domain is not available and past cases are accessible. As it was pointed up in this paper, when explanation-based retrieval is performed it is important to consider imperfections in explanations. In our approach the concepts of strong, weak, undetermined, and strongly undetermined footprint are central to the matching process. The proposed evaluation function is also supported on these concepts.

In our metric we consider two groups of terms. One relates to similarities and another to dissimilarities between cases and new problems. In each group the different terms are associated to different types of footprints to which the (un)matching facts belong. The relevance function assigns higher relevance to facts that belong to smaller footprints.

The results reported in this paper show that the way in which dissimilarities contribute to case selection has to be considered with care. In cases where facts describing the problem are mainly disjunctive, considering for evaluation unmatching facts in the case problem may lead to discouraging results.

RECIDE$_{clinic}$ always performed correctly after the 24th iteration provided the parameter values in the evaluation function were those assigned in TEST #2. With those parameter values 15 cases were necessary for a good coverage of the domain and the system produced a number of correct solutions 50% higher than with Duda & Hart (1973) approach.

Although we believe the lessons provided by these results are valuable for different tasks in different domains it must be kept in mind that they relate to a specific task in a specific domain.

# 7  Acknowledgements

We would like to thank the physicians working at the Neuroradiology and Endocrinology Department at the Hospitais da Universidade de Coimbra (HUC) for their valuable contribution, and the anonymous reviewers of this paper for their helpful comments. Fundação Luso-Americana para o Desenvolvimento (FLAD) financially supported our contacts with other groups working on CBR in the USA.

# References

1. Barletta, R., and Mark, W., Explanation-Based Indexing of Cases, in Proceedings of a Case-Based Reasoning Workshop, Morgan-Kaufmann, 1989.
2. Bento, C., and Costa, E., A Similarity Metric for Retrieval of Cases Imperfectly Explained, in Wess, S.; Althoff, K.-D.; and Richter, M. M., eds., Topics in Case-Based Reasoning - Selected Papers from the First European Workshop on Case-Based Reasoning, Springer Verlag. Berlin: Germany, 1994a.
3. Cain, T., Pazzani, M. J. and Silverstein, G., Using Domain Knowledge to Influence Similarity Judgments, in Proceedings of a Case-Based Reasoning Workshop, Morgan-Kaufmann, 1991.
4. Duda, R., and Hart, P., Pattern Classification and Scene Analysis, New York: Wiley, 1973.
5. Hammond, K., Case-Based Planning: An Integrated Theory of Planning, Learning and Memory, Ph D Dissertation, Yale University, 1986.
6. Kolodner, J., Retrieval and Organizational Strategies, in Conceptual Memory: A Computer Model. Hillsdale, NJ.: Lawrence Erlbaum Associates, 1984.
7. Kolodner, J., and Riesbeck, C., Experience, Memory, and Reasoning, Lawrence Erlbaum Associates, Hillsdale, NJ, 1986.
8. Kolodner, J., (1993). Case-Based Reasoning (pp. 328-329), Morgan-Kaufmann Publisher, 1993.
9. Koton, P., Using Experience in Learning and Problem Solving, Massachusets Institute of Technology, Laboratory of Computer Science (Ph D diss., October 1988), MIT/LCS/TR-441, 1989.
10. Lebowitz, M., Concept Learning in an Rich Input Domain: Generalization-Based Memory, in Michalski, R., Carbonell, J., and Mitchell T. (Ed.), Machine Learning, Vol. 2, Los Altos, Ca.: Morgan Kaufmann Publishers, 1986.
11. Pazzani, M., Creating a Memory of Causal Relationships: An Integration of Empirical and Explanation-Based Learning Methods, Hillsdale, NJ.: Lawrence Erlbaum Associates, 1990.
12. Porter, B., Bareiss, R., and Holte, R., Concept Learning and Heuristic Classification in Weak Theory Domains. Artificial Intelligence, vol. 45, no. 1-2, 229-263, 1990.
13. Riesbeck, C., and Schank, R., Inside Case-Based Reasoning, Lawrence Erlbaum Associates, Hillsdale, NJ, 1989.
14. Veloso, M., Learning by Analogical Reasoning in General Problem Solving. Ph D Thesis. School of Computer Science, Carnegie Mellon University, Pittsburgh, PA, 1992.

# Reasoning with Cases Imperfectly Described and Explained

Carlos Bento  Luís Macedo  Ernesto Costa

Departamento de Engenharia Informática
Universidade de Coimbra
Vila Franca - Pinhal de Marrocos
3030 Coimbra - PORTUGAL
E-mail: bento@alma.uc.pt  ernesto@moebius.uc.pt

**Abstract.** This paper introduces RECIDE, an implementation of our approach to case-based reasoning. A qualitative and a quantitative metric are used for case retrieval. RECIDE has a library of successful and failure cases. Generation of new solutions is driven by splitting and merging operations on successful cases. Failure cases are in the form of indivisible and incompatible cases and represent constraints on the application of splitting and merging operators. Both types of cases are acquired interactively during problem-solving. We present the algorithms for generation of new cases with a solution that potentially applies to the new problem. RECIDE$_{PSY}$, an application of RECIDE in the domain of psychology, is introduced in this paper.

## 1  Introduction

A Case-Based Reasoning (CBR) System depends strongly on its methods for retrieval and reuse of previous experiences. This distinguishes these systems from those relying on the generalisation of solutions from first principles (abstract knowledge).

The combination of CBR and abstract knowledge-guided techniques led to the development of knowledge-based retrieval systems [9]. These systems use domain knowledge for construction of explanations of why a problem had a specific solution in the past. Explanations are necessary to judge the relevance of the facts describing a past problem [1, 5, 11, 2].

In our work on CBR we are mainly concerned with two aspects. One has to do with the fact that the CBR approach is mostly used when a strong theory is not available and past experience is accessible. Lack of a strong theory means that, in general, case explanations are imperfect. We consider three kinds of imperfections and use them for retrieval [2]. A second aspect relates to the role of failure cases in CBR. Some current CBR systems make use of failure cases to represent and explain past unsuccessful experiences [6, 7] in our approach, failure cases represent *intra* and/or *inter*-case dependencies that were violated during case reuse.

This paper introduces how our qualitative [3] and quantitative [2] metrics are used for case retrieval. We present failure cases, as they are defined in our approach and describe their role in the construction of new solutions from successful cases in memory. Failure cases are indivisible or incompatible. Indivisible cases represent constraints on the application of splitting operators on cases in memory that potentially contribute to the solution of a new problem. Incompatible cases represent constraints on the application of merging operators. Our CBR approach is implemented in a system called RECIDE (REasoning with Cases Imperfectly Described and Explained). RECIDE$_{PSY}$ is an application of RECIDE in the domain of psychology. In this domain the task is to suggest a set of intervention strategies for students with underachievement problems. We present the structure of successful cases and the types of failure cases encountered in this task. We show the experimental results obtained in the domain.

## 2   Overview of RECIDE

RECIDE functional structure comprises: a case retriever, and a case reuser (Figure 1). The case retriever accesses successful cases in the case library. For case selection we use a qualitative and a quantitative metric.

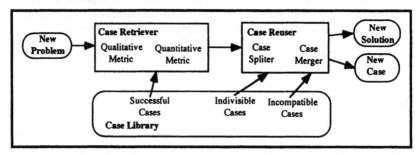

**Fig. 1.** Functional Structure of RECIDE

The qualitative metric clusters past cases by the way in which they are potentially useful for creation of a new solution. The quantitative metric ranks cases in each cluster by its similarity with the new problem. The case reuser takes case clusters ordered by decreasing similarity and generates new cases that potentially have the same solution as the new problem. New cases are generated by applying splitting and merging operators, constrained by indivisible and incompatible cases. The need for splitting and merging operations on past cases follows from the fact that in general it does not exist a case in memory that comprises a complete solution for the new problem. In those situations catching the case pieces that have part of the solution for the new problem and merging them hopefully leads to a case comprising the new solution. This method of generating a solution shows to be particularly suitable for design tasks. The drawback of it is that when a case is split, some *intra*-case constraints may be violated making this operation illegal. Also, in the merging step may be *inter*-case dependencies forbidden the synthesis of a new case from case pieces.

Within our approach *inter* and *intra*-case dependencies are represented in the form of indivisible and incompatible cases which are two kinds of failure cases. Their syntax is similar to the one for successful cases. Indivisible cases represent case pieces that when occurring in a case cannot be split. Incompatible cases represent case pieces that cannot occur in a new case by means of merging case parts from different cases. The semantic for failure cases is formally introduced in this section.

## 2.1 Case Library

The case library comprises: successful, indivisible, and incompatible cases. A successful case is represented by a triple $<P, S, R>$ (Figure 2) with $P$ and $S$, respectively, a set of facts representing past problem and solution, and $R$ a set of rules given by the expert, representing a set of causal explanations. An explanation is a proof tree that links facts in the problem with a fact in the solution. We consider three kinds of imperfections in explanations: (1) incomplete set of explanations; (2) partial explanations; (3) broken explanations.

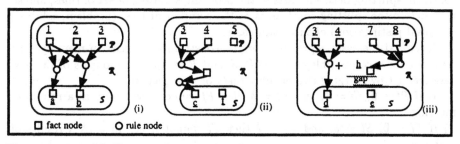

**Fig. 2.** A case with (i) a complete set of explanations; (ii) an incomplete set of explanations; (iii) a partial and broken explanation

In a successful case with an incomplete set of explanations some solution facts are not explained and hence are not conclusion for any proof tree (e.g., Cases ii and iii in Figure 2. Facts $f$ and $e$ in these cases solution are not leaves of a proof tree). A partial explanation is one whose proof tree omits some branches. This means that one or more steps in the proof tree apply a rule for which the conditions are necessary but not sufficient. Rule nodes representing these rules are labelled by '+' (e.g., In Figure 2, case iii, the proof tree at the left). A broken explanation is one in which there is a gap between the proof tree and the case solution (e.g., In Figure 2, case iii, the proof tree at the right).

Failure cases (indivisible and incompatible), are represented by a triple $<Pf, Sf, Rf>$ with $Pf$ and $Sf$ the sets of facts representing, respectively, the problem and solution components, and $Rf$ a set of rules. The semantic for these cases is different from the one defined for successful cases and is related to the splitting and merging operations performed during case reuse. The semantic for indivisible cases is ($P$, $S$, and $R$ represent, respectively, the components of the case candidate for splitting):

i) If $Pf \neq \emptyset$, $Sf = \emptyset$, $Rf = \emptyset$ and $Pf \subseteq P$ then the subset $Pf$ in $P$ cannot be split.

ii) If $Pf = \emptyset$, $Sf \neq \emptyset$, $Rf = \emptyset$, and $Sf \subseteq S$ then the subset $Sf$ in $S$ cannot be split.

iii) If $Pf = \emptyset$, $Sf = \emptyset$, $Rf \neq \emptyset$, and $Rf \subseteq R$ then the subset $Rf$ in $R$ cannot be split.

iv) If $Pf \neq \emptyset$, $Sf \neq \emptyset$, $Rf \neq \emptyset$, and $Pf \subseteq P \wedge Sf \subseteq S \wedge Rf \subseteq R$ then subsets $Pf$, $Sf$, and $Rf$ in $P$, $S$, and $R$ have to remain in the same past case piece after the splitting process.

v) If $Pf \neq \emptyset$, $Sf \neq \emptyset$, $Rf = \emptyset$, and $Pf \subseteq P \wedge Sf \subseteq S$ then the subsets $Pf$ and $Sf$ in $P$ and $S$ have to remain in the same past case piece after the splitting process.

vi) If $Pf = \emptyset$, $Sf \neq \emptyset$, $Rf \neq \emptyset$, and $Sf \subseteq S \wedge Rf \subseteq R$ then the subsets $Sf$ and $Rf$ in $S$ and $R$ have to remain in the same past case piece after the splitting process.

vii) If $Pf \neq \emptyset$, $Sf = \emptyset$, $Rf \neq \emptyset$, and $Pf \subseteq P \wedge Rf \subseteq R$ then the subsets $Pf$ and $Rf$ in $P$ and $R$ have to remain in the same past case piece after the splitting process.

Indivisible cases of types i, ii, and iii constrain the splitting of facts in a problem or solution, or in a set of rules. So, they determine splitting constraints at the fact level in a successful case. Indivisible cases of type iv through vii constrain splitting between parts of the problem, solution, or set of rules, and so they determine splitting constraints at the component level (problem, solution, or causal justification) of successful cases.

Incompatible cases represent merging constraints on cases in memory. The semantic for incompatible cases is ($P$, $S$, and $R$ are the components of the new case created by merging two or more cases or case pieces):

i) If $Pf \neq \emptyset$, $Sf = \emptyset$, and $Rf = \emptyset$ then $Pf$ cannot occur in $P$ as a results of merging.

ii) If $Pf = \emptyset$, $Sf \neq \emptyset$, and $Rf = \emptyset$ then $Sf$ cannot occur in $S$ as a results of merging.

iii) If $Pf = \emptyset$, $Sf = \emptyset$, and $Rf \neq \emptyset$ then $Rf$ cannot occur in $R$ as a results of merging.

iv) If $Pf \neq \emptyset$, $Sf \neq \emptyset$, $Rf \neq \emptyset$ and $Pf \subseteq P \wedge Sf \subseteq S \wedge Rf \subseteq R$ then $Pf$, $Sf$, and $Rf$ cannot occur all together in the new case as a result of merging.

v) If $Pf \neq \emptyset$, $Sf \neq \emptyset$, $Rf = \emptyset$ and $Pf \subseteq P \wedge Sf \subseteq S$ then $Pf$ and $Sf$ cannot occur all together in the new case as a result of merging.

vi) If $Pf = \emptyset$, $Sf \neq \emptyset$, $Rf \neq \emptyset$ and $Sf \subseteq S \wedge Rf \subseteq R$ then $Sf$ and $Rf$ cannot occur all together in the new case as a result of merging.

vii) If $Pf \neq \emptyset$, $Sf = \emptyset$, $Rf \neq \emptyset$ and $Pf \subseteq P \wedge Rf \subseteq R$ then $Pf$ and $Rf$ cannot occur all together in the new case as a result of merging.

As with indivisible cases, incompatible ones of type i, ii, and iii relate to merging constraints at the fact level. Remaining case types report to constraints at the case component level.

## 2.2 Case Retrieval

Case retrieval is performed on a flat memory of successful cases. The retrieval process involves two steps:

i) Clustering of potentially useful past cases.
ii) Ranking of case clusters.

In the first step five clusters of past cases are created. Let $S$ be the set of facts representing the solution for a case in memory and $S'$ the set of facts representing the solution for a new problem. Each cluster comprises the following cases (in the examples that follow it is assumed the case library is composed by cases in Figure 2, and represented again in Figure 3):

**CLUSTER_1** - Cases with $S = S'$.
e.g. If the new problem is described by the set of facts $\{\underline{1}, \underline{2}, \underline{3}\}$, CLUSTER_1 will be composed of case i (see Figure 2). Case i is completely explained, that is, facts $\{\underline{1}, \underline{2}, \underline{3}\}$ describing case problem and the new problem are necessary and sufficient for the solution $S = \{\underline{a}, \underline{b}\}$, therefore the new problem solution is $S' = S = \{\underline{a}, \underline{b}\}$.
**CLUSTER_2** - Cases possibly with $S = S'$.
e.g. For a new problem described by the set $\{\underline{3}, \underline{4}, \underline{5}\}$, CLUSTER_2 will be composed of case ii. As the new problem is the same as the one described in case ii it is possible that case solution and new problem solution are also similar. The reason why we are not certain about this is that case ii is not completely explained. Therefore we do not know if fact $\underline{5}$ is causally linked with fact $\underline{f}$ in the solution. This means the problem that has the solution $S = \{\underline{c}, \underline{f}\}$ may be different from the one represented in case ii provided it contains facts $\underline{3}$ and $\underline{4}$.
**CLUSTER_3** - Cases possibly with $S \supset S'$.
e.g. Considering a new problem $\{\underline{1}, \underline{2}\}$, case i is the one in CLUSTER_3. As $\underline{1}$ and $\underline{2}$ are the causal premises for fact $\underline{a}$ in this case's solution, it is possible that the new problem solution is $\{\underline{a}\} = S' \subset S$. The uncertainty about this is due to unknown *intra*-case dependencies which may be violated by splitting case i.
**CLUSTER_4** - Cases possibly with $S \subset S'$.
e.g. With a new problem $\{\underline{1}, \underline{2}, \underline{3}, \underline{4}, \underline{5}\}$, cases i and ii are the ones in CLUSTER_4. As case i has the solution $S = \{\underline{a}, \underline{b}\}$ for problem $\{\underline{1}, \underline{2}, \underline{3}\}$ and case ii solution $\{\underline{c}, \underline{f}\}$ is supposed to be the one for problem $\{\underline{3}, \underline{4}, \underline{5}\}$ then it is possible that $\{\underline{a}, \underline{b}\} = S_i \subset S'$ and $\{\underline{c}, \underline{f}\} = S_{ii} \subset S'$, with $S_i$ and $S_{ii}$, respectively, the solutions for cases i and ii. We are not certain about this as we do not know the *inter* and *intra*-case dependencies between and within cases i and ii.
**CLUSTER_5** - Cases possibly with $S \cap S' \neq \emptyset$.
e.g. Assuming the new problem is $\{\underline{1}, \underline{3}, \underline{6}, \underline{9}\}$, CLUSTER_5 is composed by case i. As $\underline{1}$ and $\underline{3}$ are necessary and sufficient for $\underline{b}$ in the context of case i then $S_i \cap S' = \{\underline{b}\}$. The uncertainty on this is related to possibly unknown *intra* and *inter*-case dependencies.

Clusters above are not mutually exclusive. Considering, for instance, a new problem $\{\underline{3}, \underline{4}, \underline{5}\}$ case ii will belong to CLUSTER_2, as explained above, but it will also belong to CLUSTER_5 as it is possible that fact $\underline{5}$ in case ii is not the one responsible for fact $\underline{f}$ in the solution. If this happens then as $\underline{3}$ and $\underline{4}$ are necessary and sufficient for $\underline{c}$ in the context of case ii then $S_i \cap S' = \{\underline{c}\}$, with the constraint that no *intra* and *inter*-case dependencies are violated.

Cases within each cluster are ranked by an explanation-based similarity metric [2]. It assigns a distinct relevance to each fact in a case problem that matches a fact in the new problem, depending on the fact being premise of a complete, partial, broken, or no explanation at all. Clusters are sorted by decreasing similarity values.

Clustering of cases for retrieval embodies two main properties: (1) case clustering organises memory cases accordingly to their kind of potential usefulness for the new problem solution; and (2) it provides information on the most suitable method for creation of a new case. In the next subsection we describe how the reuse unit deals with these clusters.

## 2.3 Case Reuse

RECIDE reuse unit works with successful cases in terms of case pieces. Four types of pieces are considered (Figure 3): strong, weak, undetermined, and unexplained.

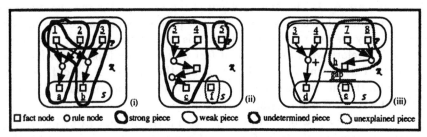

**Fig. 3.** Types of case pieces

A complete explanation, the facts that are premises of it, and the fact that is its conclusion determine a strong piece (e.g. In Figure 3, the pieces in case i). A partial explanation, its premises and its conclusion embody a weak piece (e.g. In Figure 3, case iii, the case piece at its left). A broken explanation and its premises or any single fact that is not premise of an explanation form an undetermined piece (e.g. In Figure 3, case ii, the piece composed by the single fact $\underline{5}$ and the piece in case iii at top right). Any fact in a case solution that is not conclusion of an explanation determines an unexplained piece (e.g. In Figure 3, single facts $\underline{f}$ and $\underline{e}$ in cases ii and iii are unexplained pieces). Case splitting is performed at the case piece level.

As described in section 2.2, after giving the system a new problem, successful cases in memory are clustered accordingly to their usefulness for the generation of a new solution. The reuse unit gets those clusters and performs the following steps:

1) generation of new cases;
2) selection of the new case most promising for the solution of the new problem;
3) validation of the solution provided by the selected case.

Figure 4 shows the algorithm for generation of new cases. Each new case is created by splitting and merging operations on cases from a cluster. In the figure assignment operations are represented by the '<-' symbol.

```
01. GIVEN: CLUSTER_1, ..., CLUSTERS_5
02. OUTPUT: a set of NEWCASES that, presumably, have the same solution as the new problem
    MAIN PROGRAM:
03. NEWCASES <- Ø;
04. IF length(CLUSTER_1) = 1 THEN
05.   NEWCASES <- "The case in CLUSTER_1"
06. ELSE
07.   IF length(CLUSTER_2) ≥ 1 THEN
08.     NEWCASES <- "The case in CLUSTER_2 with the highest similarity value"  FI;
09.   IF length(CLUSTER_3) ≥ 1 THEN
10.     CASE_PIECES <- "The pieces created by splitting the case in CLUSTER_3 with the highest similarity value";
11.     NEWCASE <- "The case composed of the pieces in CASE_PIECES which are potentially useful for the new
                   problem";
12.     NEWCASES <- NEWCASES ∪ NEWCASE        FI;
13.   IF length(CLUSTER_4) ≥ 2 THEN
14.     CASE_PIECES <- "The pieces created by splitting the cases in CLUSTER_4";
15.     NEWCASES1 <- "The cases assumed to have the same solution as the new problem and created by
                     merging pieces from CASE_PIECES that are potentially useful for the solution of the
                     new problem";
16.     NEWCASES <- NEWCASES ∪ NEWCASES1       FI;
17.   IF length(CLUSTER_5) ≥ 2 THEN
18.     CASE_PIECES <- "The pieces created by splitting the cases in CLUSTER_5";
19      NEWCASES1 <- "The cases assumed to have the same solution as the new problem and created by merging
                     pieces from CASE_PIECES that are potentially useful for the solution of the new problem";
20.     NEWCASES <- NEWCASES ∪ NEWCASES1       FI
21. FI
```

**Fig. 4.** Algorithm for generation of new cases

If CLUSTER_1 is not empty a new case is generated from it[1]. The case it contains is assigned to NEWCASES without any modification and the solution for it is definitely the solution for the new problem. Therefore it is not necessary to create alternative new cases. If CLUSTER_1 is empty, new cases are created from each cluster with a sufficient number of cases for case generation. The first one of these clusters to be considered is CLUSTER_2. Cases in CLUSTER_2 probably have the same solution as the new problem. From this cluster it is chosen the case with the highest similarity value and assigned to NEWCASES. Cases in CLUSTER_3 are expected to have a solution represented by a set of facts that contains the facts representing the new solution. To create a new case from this cluster, the system selects its case with the highest similarity value. The case pieces from this case with a solution fact supposed to be part of the new solution are the ones included in the new case. NEWCASES set becomes composed by the new case plus its previous set. Cases in CLUSTER_4 have a solution supposed to be part of the solution for the new problem. Cases in

---

[1] If CLUSTER_1 is not empty then it is expected to contain only one case. If it has more than one case this means the same problem has multiple solutions.

CLUSTER_5 have a solution supposed to have facts in common with the facts representing the new solution. Generation of NEWCASES1 from CLUSTER_4 and 5, comprises splitting the cases in the cluster into pieces and merging those pieces that have a conclusion fact (a leaf of an explanation) that potentially contributes to the new problem solution. This means catching the case pieces for which it is presumed that $S_{p1} \cup ... \cup S_{pn} = S'$, with $S_{pi}$ the solution fact in a case piece and $S'$ the set of facts representing the new solution. The new cases generated from those clusters are assigned to NEWCASES1. NEWCASES set becomes composed by the cases in NEWCASES1 plus its previous cases. The code related to CLUSTER_4 and 5 (lines 13 through 20 in Figure 4) differs in which relates to the treatment of unexplained pieces. The unexplained pieces within cases that contribute to the new case in CLUSTER_4 are included in the new case. The reason for this is that it is assumed cases in CLUSTER_4 comply with $S \subset S'$. Therefore unexplained pieces are assumed to be part of the new solution. Unexplained pieces within cases in CLUSTER_5, which is presumed to observe $S \cap S' \neq \emptyset$ , are not included in the new cases as it is reasonable to assume those unexplained pieces do not belong to set $S'$.

Two heuristics are applied for selection of the new case most likely to have the same solution as the new problem:

H1: Prefer new cases with higher similarity values.

H2: Prefer new cases from clusters with lower index (e.g. CLUSTER_1 over CLUSTER_2).

Heuristic 1 assumes cases with a problem description closer to the new problem description (matching more facts in the new problem, weighted the fact of being premise of a complete, partial, or interrupted explanation) have a higher chance of comprising the same solution as the new problem.

Heuristic 2, favours cases from those clusters with lower indexes. The reason to choose CLUSTER_1 is obvious. It is the only cluster that, if not empty, has a case known to have the correct solution. For the other clusters preferring those with lower index means to choose new cases that required fewer splitting and merging operations for its generation. The more splitting and merging operations are performed, the more likely it is that unknown *intra* and/or *inter*-case dependencies are disregarded.

The next step comprises the validation of the solution provided by the selected new case. The validation algorithm is described in Figure 5.

In the validation step, RECIDE searches for a new case for which the splitting and merging operations involved in its construction do not violate the constraints imposed by the failure cases in memory (lines 6 through 8 in Figure 5). Then it outputs the new case solution and the cases in the origin of it. If the user accepts the solution then the validation process ends.

If the new solution is not accepted, the user is encouraged to give the *intra* and *inter*-case dependencies in the origin of the wrong solution. Those descriptions are recorded as indivisible and/or incompatible cases (lines 14 through 16). With the memory of indivisible and incompatible cases updated in this way the system starts another validation cycle selecting a new case that does not conflict with the updated library of failure cases.

01. **GIVEN:** the selected new case that, presumably, has the same solution as the new problem;
02.         ORIGCASES, the set of cases in the origin of the new case
03. **OUTPUT:** a new solution;
04.             occasionally a new case is recorded
  **MAIN PROGRAM:**
05. SOLUTION_VALIDATED <- 'NO';
06. **WHILE** SOLUTION_VALIDATED = 'NO' **DO**
07.   **WHILE** "New case violates constraints imposed by indivisible and incompatible cases in memory" **DO**
08.       "Select an alternative new case"       **OD**;
09.   "Output the solution for the new case";
10.   "Output ORIGCASES";
11.   **IF** "The solution is accepted by the user" **THEN**
12.       SOLUTION_VALIDATED <- 'YES'
13.   **ELSE**
14.       **IF** "The user inputs failure cases in support of her/his rejection" **THEN**
15.           "Record failure cases";
16.           "Select an alternative new case"
17.       **ELSE**
18.           "Ask for the new problem solution and a causal justification for it ";
19.           "Record new problem, solution, and justification as a new successful case" ;
20.           SOLUTION_VALIDATED <- 'YES'     **FI**     **FI**
21. **OD**

**Fig. 5.** Validation of a new case's solution

If the user cannot explain why the new solution is wrong in terms of indivisible and incompatible cases then she/he is asked to give the solution for the new problem together with a causal justification. This input is recorded as a new successful case and the process is completed (lines 18 though 20).

## 2.4 An Example

In this subsection we illustrate the solving/learning cycle described before. It is assumed the library of successful cases comprises the cases in Figure 3 reproduced in Figure 6 for convenience.

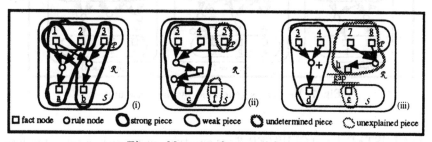

**Fig. 6.** Memory of successful cases

Suppose a new problem is represented by facts $\{\underline{1}, \underline{2}, \underline{3}, \underline{4}, \underline{6}\}$. The retrieval unit creates the empty sets CLUSTER_1 and 3, the sets CLUSTER_2 and 4 with case i, and CLUSTER_5 with cases i, ii, and iii.

Case i is not in CLUSTER_1 as facts 1, 2, and 3 are the ones necessary and sufficient for its solution and the new problem involves two additional facts 4 and 6. This prevents the system of stating that the solution for case i is the one for the new problem. The problem component of cases ii and iii does not include facts 1 and 2. Cases ii and iii are also not completely explained. These considerations cumulatively determine that their solution is not the one for the new problem and so they are not in CLUSTER_1.

CLUSTER_3 does not contain cases i, ii, and iii as this cluster comprises cases presumed to have a solution represented by a set of facts being a subset of the facts representing the new solution. As the facts representing the new problem are not a subset of the facts representing the problem in cases i, ii, and iii, inclusion above is not possible. Therefore none of these cases has a chance of belonging to CLUSTER_3.

Case i is the one in CLUSTER_2. As facts 1, 2, and 3 are necessary and sufficient for this case solution, and the new problem includes those facts, it is possible that it has the same solution as case i provided facts 4 and 6 in the new problem are irrelevant. Cases ii and iii are not supposed possible to have the same solution as the new problem as both have facts in their problem that do not match facts in the new solution[2].

Case i is the one in CLUSTER_4. Problem facts in case i are necessary and sufficient for its solution and match the new problem. Therefore it is assumed its solution facts are possibly contained in the set of new solution facts. A similar supposition cannot be made about cases ii and iii as they have problem facts that do not match the new problem.

Cases i, ii, and iii are in CLUSTER_5. Some groups of facts in their problem match with the new one. Those matching facts are necessary or necessary and sufficient for the solution facts in those cases. Therefore it is possible that some solution facts in cases i, ii, and iii are common with the new solution. The reuse unit creates a NEWCASES set comprising cases represented in Figure 7 (see algorithm in Figure 4).

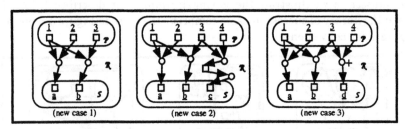

(new case 1)    (new case 2)    (new case 3)

**Fig. 7.** New cases generated by the reuse unit

As CLUSTER_1 and CLUSTER_3 are empty no new case is constructed from

---

[2] Within a more liberal approach, fact 5 in case ii and facts 7 and 8 in case iii would be assumed possibly irrelevant and therefore those cases solution could be considered to be the one for the new problem.

them. The single case in CLUSTER_2 is in the origin of new case 1 in Figure 7. Generation of new cases from CLUSTER_4 implies merging two or more cases. As in this example CLUSTER_4 has only one case it is impossible to create a new one from it. New case 2 and 3 are generated from CLUSTER_5. New case 2 (Figure 7) is a consequence of merging the two strong pieces in case i and the strong piece in case ii whose problem facts match the new problem. New case 3 (Figure 7) is constructed by merging the two strong pieces in case i and the weak piece in case iii.

Selection of the case potentially most useful for the solution of the new problem comprises the application of heuristic H1. In this example new case 2 is the one selected by this heuristic as this case is the one with the highest similarity value [4]. Heuristic H2 is not applied as a tie does not occur within heuristic H1.

The next step is the validation of the solution provided by new case 2. As the case library does not have failure cases yet, new case 2 is not tested against constraint violations and the solution for it is suggested by the system. In this example, the user classifies the solution composed of the set $\{\underline{a}, \underline{b}, \underline{c}\}$ as wrong with the justification that facts $\underline{a}$ and $\underline{c}$ are incompatible. This is represented by an incompatible case with $P = \emptyset$ , $S = \{\underline{a}, \underline{c}\}$, and $R = \emptyset$.

In sequence of the failure case given by the user, the alternative new case 3 is selected (it has a higher similarity value than new case 1). In the validation step new case 3 passes the test on merging conflicts represented by the incompatible case previously input. The new case solution $\{\underline{a}, \underline{b}, \underline{d}\}$ is suggested to the user. Supposing she/he does not accept it, the alternative new case 1 is suggested as a solution. If the user also classifies this solution as wrong then she/he is asked to give the correct one and a justification for it. This new case given by the user is recorded by RECIDE as a new successful case.

At the end, RECIDE has learned an incompatible case and a successful one composed by the solution for a new problem together with a justification for it.

# 3  An Application in the Domain of Psychology

In this section we present an application of RECIDE in the domain of psychology. Results obtained with this application are also described in this section.

## 3.1  The Domain

RECIDE$_{PSY}$ is an advising system for scholar underachievers. It suggests a new program for improvement of scholar performance supported on previous successful experiences.

A past experience comprises a context (past problem) in which a set of intervention strategies (past solution) was applied successfully. Figure 8 represents a case in the domain as it is output by RECIDE$_{PSY}$[3]. A '->' symbol in the explanations represents a complete explanation and a '->+' a partial explanation.

---

[3] The taxonomy introduced for context and recuperation strategies is only relevant at the user's level. For matching of a case with a new problem, RECIDE$_{PSY}$ only considers ground facts organized into a flat structure.

```
PROBLEM:

<Subject Data and Familiar Background>
   Sex: Male
   Age: 12 - 14
   Num. of Siblings: 2
   Siblings are: Younger
   Familiar Relationship: Conflicting

<Educational Background>
   Degree achieved: 6
   Educational Branch: Primary School
   Siblings' Educational Achievements:
                      Induces NegativeComparision

<Phycological Struct and Development Tasks>
   Interpersonal Relationship:  Low

<Learning Characteristics>
   Num of Areas with Underachiev.:  more than 3
   Influencial Dispersion Sources:  Internal
   Underachiev. Started: Years Ago
```

```
SOLUTION:

<Main Strategies>
   Assertiveness Training
   Selman's Interpersonal
                 Negotiation Strategies
   Enhancement of Learning Skills

<Complementary Strategies>
   Self-knowledge Enhancement
   Familiar Support Mobilization

<Behavioral and Cognitive Strats>
   Role Playing
   Thinking Cut-off
   Recording of Thoughts,
            Behaviors and Emotions
   Disfunctional Behaviors Evaluation
```

```
EXPLANATIONS:

Sex : Male AND Age: 12 - 14 -> Adolescence Crisis
 Familiar Relationship: Conflicting  AND Siblings' Educational Achievements: Induces Negative
            Comparision AND Adolescence Crisis -> Confict Situations
Confict Situations AND Interpersonal Relationship: Low -> Lack of Interpersonal Skills
Num of Areas with Underachiev.: more than 3 AND Underachiev. Started: Years Ago ->
            Enhancement of Learning Skills
Confict Situations ->+ Self-knowledge Enhancement
Confict Situations -> Familiar Support Mobilization
Lack of Interpersonal Skills -> Assertiveness Training  AND Selman's Interpersonal Negotiation
            Strategies AND Recording of Thoughts, Behaviors and Emotions AND Disfunctional
            Behaviors Evaluation
Influencial Dispersion Sources:  Internal -> Thinking Cut-off
```

**Fig. 8.** A successful case

This case describes a male client between 12 and 14 years old, with two siblings, both younger and with a conflicting relation with relatives. The level of education achieved is six years of basic education and he is unfavourably compared with his siblings due to their scholar achievements. Interpersonal relationship is low. His grades comprise more than three unsuccessful disciplines, shows internal sources of dispersion and has a long history of underachievement.

The main intervention strategies being applied are assertiveness training, Selman's interpersonal negotiation strategies, and enhancement of learning skills. The complementary strategies are self-knowledge enhancement and familiar support mobilisation. The behavioural and cognitive intervention strategies are role playing, thinking cut-off, recording of thoughts, behaviours and emotions, and disfunctional behaviours evaluation.

The explanations provided by the experts for this intervention program are: (1) being a male client aged between twelve and fourteen are causing an adolescence crisis, (2) a conflicting familiar relationship marked by negative comparison, associated with the adolescence crisis characterise a conflict situation, (3) the conflicting situation under development and his low level of interpersonal relationship describe his lack of interpersonal skills, (4) the number of underachievement areas being higher than three and the duration of this problem (starting years ago) cause the need for enhancement of learning skills, (5) the conflicting situation is a partial cause (the only partial explanation step in this case) for using self-knowledge enhancement, (6) the conflict situation is the cause for mobilisation of familiar support, (7) the lack of interpersonal skills is the motive for applying assertiveness training, Selmans interpersonal negotiation strategies, recording of thoughts, behaviours and emotions, and evaluation of disfunctional behaviours, and (8) presence of internal sources of dispersion is the cause for using thinking cut-off.

In this task indivisible cases are of types i and ii (see subsection 2.1.). Incompatible cases are of types ii, iii, and v. The set of cases given by the experts comprises 38 successful cases and 78 failure cases (45 indivisible and 33 incompatible).

## 3.2  Empirical Results

Three types of tests were performed. In the first test only successful cases were given to the system. In the second, successful and indivisible cases were input. The last test involved the input of successful and incompatible cases. Each test comprised a set of 38 iterations[4]. Each iteration involves the input of the problem component of a randomly selected case. The system creates and presents a new case with a solution presupposed to be the one for the new problem together with the cases that were in the origin of the new case. If the system gives a wrong solution the user inputs indivisible cases (in test two), and incompatible cases (in test three). If the system still solves the problem wrongly the user gives it the correct solution and its justification.

In the first test only two correct solutions were suggested along the 38 iterations, six wrong solutions were produced and the remaining 30 solutions were ambiguous[5]. In the second test, after the 30th iteration all answers created by the system were correct except in the 34th iteration in which a wrong solution was built. In the third test two correct answers were given, like in the first test, but the number of wrong solutions along the 38 iterations decreased by three.

## 4  Final Remarks

Our last comments concern to the way RECIDE solves and learns, and to future work we think worth doing.

---

[4] A more detailed analysis of these results is available in a paper by Bento, Machado & Costa (1994).

[5] The criterion for considering a solution correct, ambiguous, or wrong was the following one. If a solution contains more than 70% of the intervention strategies suggested by the expert and the number of unsuitable strategies in this solution are less than 30% of the total number of strategies suggested by the experts then it is classified as correct; a solution with a percentage of unsuitable strategies higher or equal to 30% is classified as wrong. Solutions with a percentage of suitable and unsuitable strategies out of these intervals are classified as ambiguous.

With respect to problem solving, the retrieval method used by RECIDE takes into consideration two important aspects - usefulness, and similarity - assigning a higher importance to usefulness. As pointed out by other authors [8, 10] we believe that search driven by usefulness plays a main role in case retrieval. Case clustering, as performed within our approach, relates to the role cases can play in the construction of a new one. Similarity is only considered for case ranking within clusters.

Failure cases as they are defined within our framework constrain the generation of new cases by *intra* and *inter*-case dependencies. Many times, the reason why cases created by splitting operations do not have the correct solution is due to *intra*-case dependencies that were not perceived *a priori*. A similar problem appears when case pieces are merged due to *inter*-case dependencies. Indivisible and incompatible cases are a powerful way to represent those dependencies.

An aspect that needs to be taken into consideration is that if the combination strategies used for case generation are not maintained under control the process leads to combinatory explosion. This is prevented by limiting combination of case pieces to the most promising cases within each cluster.

In the task we describe in section 3, indivisible cases lower the number of successful experiences needed for domain coverage. Incompatible cases lower the number of wrong solutions given by the system.

In RECIDE, the learning process comprises interactive acquisition of failure and successful cases. In general the acquisition *a priori* of *intra* and *inter*-case dependencies is not feasible. The problem-solving process provides a context of failure in which the analysis of the cases in the origin of a wrong solution is a way to detect violated dependencies that were the cause for the wrong solution. Incompatible cases (as in the example of section 3) also make possible to represent that a solution proposed by the system is incompatible with the new problem given to the system.

Among the tasks to be accomplished in the future we consider that it would be interesting to know the performance of the system on a bigger set of new situations and, hopefully, to confirm that the domain is well covered with 31 cases.

A second task relates to coexistence of indivisible and incompatible cases. In section 3 it has been shown that indivisible cases decrease the number of successful experiences necessary for domain coverage. Incompatible cases decrease the number of wrong solutions output by the system. It would be interesting to study the system behaviour when the two types of failure cases coexist.

A third aspect worth studying would be the effect of changing the input ordering of the new problems and cases. Intuitively this ordering influences the performance of the system. In our tests the order randomly created is the same for all the tests which allows to make comparisons between them. It would be interesting to know if a change in the order of new problems, entails a significant change in the results.

# 5 Acknowledgements

We would like to thank the anonymous reviewers of this paper for their helpful suggestions. Fundação Luso-Americana para o Desenvolvimento (FLAD) financially supported our contacts with other groups working on CBR in the USA.

# References

1. Barletta, R., and Mark, W., Explanation-Based Indexing of Cases, in Proceedings of a Case-Based Reasoning Workshop, Morgan-Kaufmann, 1989.
2. Bento, C., and Costa, E., A Similarity Metric for Retrieval of Cases Imperfectly Explained, in Wess, S.; Althoff, K.-D.; and Richter, M. M., eds., Topics in Case-Based Reasoning - Selected Papers from the First European Workshop on Case-Based Reasoning, Springer Verlag, Berlin: Germany, 1994a.
3. Bento, C., and Costa, E., A Qualitative Approach for Retrieval of Cases Imperfectly Described and Explained. Technical Report, DEE-UC-001-94, Univ. de Coimbra: Portugal, 1994b.
4. Bento, C., Machado, P., and Costa, E., Evaluation of RECIDE$_{PSY}$ - An Adviser in the Domain of Psychology, in AAAI-94 Workshop on Case-based Reasoning, Seattle, USA, 1994.
5. Cain, T., Pazzani, M. J. and Silverstein, G., Using Domain Knowledge to Influence Similarity Judgments, in Proceedings of a Case-Based Reasoning Workshop, Morgan-Kaufmann, 1991.
6. Hammond, K., CHEF: A Model of Case-Based Planning, in Proceedings of AAAI-86, Cambridge, MA: AAAI Press / MIT Press, 1986.
7. Hinrichs, T., and Kolodner, J., The Roles of Adaptation in Case-Based Design, in Proceedings of AAAI-91, Cambridge, MA: AAAI Press / MIT Press, 1991.
8. Kolodner, J., Judging Which is the Best Case for a Case-Based Reasoner, in Proceedings of a Case-Based Reasoning Workshop, Morgan-Kaufmann, 1989.
9. Koton, P., Using Experience in Learning and Problem Solving, Massachusets Institute of Technology, Laboratory of Computer Science (Ph D diss., October 1988), MIT/LCS/TR-441, 1989.
10. Smyth, B., and Keane, M., Retrieving Adaptable Cases: The Role of Adaptation Knowledge in Case Retrieval, in Wess, S.; Althoff, K.-D.; and Richter, M. M., eds., Topics in Case-Based Reasoning - Selected Papers from the First European Workshop on Case-Based Reasoning. Springer Verlag, Berlin: Germany, 1994.
11. Veloso, M., Learning by Analogical Reasoning in General Problem Solving. Ph D Thesis. School of Computer Science, Carnegie Mellon University, Pittsburgh, PA, 1992.

# Interacting Learning-Goals: Treating Learning as a Planning Task

Michael T. Cox and Ashwin Ram

Georgia Institute of Technology. Atlanta, GA 30332-0280

{cox,ashwin}@cc.gatech.edu

**Abstract.** This research examines the metaphor of goal-driven planning as a tool for performing the integration of multiple learning algorithms. In case-based reasoning systems, several learning techniques may apply to a given situation. In a failure-driven learning environment, the problems of *strategy construction* are to choose and order the best set of learning algorithms or strategies that recover from a processing failure and to use those strategies to modify the system's background knowledge so that the failure will not be repeated in similar future situations. A solution to this problem is to treat learning-strategy construction as a planning problem with its own set of goals. Learning goals, as opposed to ordinary goals, specify desired states in the background knowledge of the learner, rather than desired states in the external environment of the planner. But as with traditional goal-based planners, management and pursuit of these learning goals becomes a central issue in learning. Example interactions of learning-goals are presented from a multistrategy learning system called Meta-AQUA that combines a case-based approach to learning with non-linear planning to achieve goals in a knowledge space.

## 1 Introduction

As case-based reasoning research addresses more sophisticated task domains, the associated learning issues involved become increasingly complex. Multistrategy learning systems attempt to address the complexity of such task domains by bringing to bear many of the learning algorithms developed in the last twenty years. Yet the goal of integrating various learning strategies is a daunting one, since it is an open question as how best to combine often conflicting learning-mechanisms. This paper examines the metaphor of goal-driven planning as a tool for performing this integration. Learning is viewed as a planning problem to solve. The planning problem is formulated by posting learning goals (such as goals to answer a question or to reconcile two divergent assertions) that, if achieved, accomplish some change in the system's background knowledge. A plan is assembled by choosing various learning algorithms from the system's repertoire and ordering them in such a way as to achieve the system's learning goals.

In formulations with conjunctive goals, however, numerous difficulties arise such as goal interactions, protection intervals, and many-to-many relationships between goals and algorithms. For instance, a familiar goal conflict in planning systems is the "brother-clobbers-brother" goal interaction [35] whereby the result of one plan that achieves a particular goal undoes the result or precondition of another plan serving a different goal. If a learning goal specifies a state change to the background knowledge of the system, rather than a state change in the world, then learning plans can have similar effects. Changes to specific knowledge may affect previous changes to the background knowledge performed by other learning algorithms.

This paper presents an approach to learning with multiple interacting learning goals in which learning is treated as a planning task. The theory is implemented in a multistrategy learning system called Meta-AQUA. The performance task in Meta-AQUA is story understanding. That is, given a stream of concepts as the representation for a story sequence, the task is to create a causally connected conceptual interpretation of the story. The story-understanding strategies available to the system are case-based reasoning, analogy, and explanation. If the system fails at its performance task, its subsequent learning-subtasks are (1) use case-based methodologies to analyze and explain the cause of its misunderstanding by retrieving past cases of meta-reasoning; (2) use these cases to deliberately form a set of learning goals to change its knowledge so that such a misunderstanding is not repeated with similar stories; and then (3) use nonlinear planning techniques to construct some learning method by which it achieves these goals.

In more general terms, Ram and Cox [26] have argued that the above three fundamental learning-subtasks must be solved by all learners to learn effectively in an open world where many sources of failure exist. The subtasks are referred to as the *blame-assignment* problem [18], *deciding what to learn* [12, 24, 27], and the *strategy-construction* problem [5]. In operational terms, the following three stages characterize our learning approach that addresses these problems. Note that each corresponds to the steps 2a through 2c of Meta-AQUA's learning algorithm outlined in Figure 1.

**Blame assignment.** (step 2a, Figure 1) *Take as input a trace of the mental and physical events that preceded a reasoning failure; produce as output an explanation of how and why the failure occurred, in terms of the causal factors responsible for the failure.*

The input trace describes how results or conclusions were produced by specifying the prior causal chain of mental and physical states and events. The learner retrieves an abstract explanation-pattern (XP) called a Meta-XP[1] from memory and applies it to the trace in order to produce a specific description of why these conclusions were wrong or inappropriate. This instantiation specifies the causal links that would have been responsible for a correct conclusion, and enumerates the difference between the two chains and two conclusions (what was produced and what should have been produced). Finally, the learner outputs the instantiated explanations.

**Deciding what to learn.** (step 2b, Figure 1) *Take as input a causal explanation of how and why failure occurred; generate as output a set of learning goals which, if achieved, can reduce the likelihood of the failure repeating.*

The previously instantiated explanation-pattern assists in this process by specifying points in the reasoning trace most likely to be responsible for the failure. The learner includes with the output both tentative goal-dependencies and priority orderings on the goals. Section 2 will discuss this phase of the learning task in the context of a working example.

---

1. Explanation-Pattern Theory has roots in the work of Schank [32] and Ram [24, 25]. See Ram and Cox [26] and Cox [4] for specific details on the algorithm used to retrieve and utilize Meta-XPs. The algorithm is adapted from standard XP algorithms. See also [13] and [33] for additional uses of XP theory.

## 0. Perform and Record Reasoning in Trace

## 1. Failure Detection on Reasoning Trace

## 2. If Failure Then
   Learn from Mistake:

- 2a. *Blame Assignment*

   Compute index as characterization of failure
   Retrieve Meta-XP
   Apply Meta-XP to trace of reasoning
   If XP application is successful then
      Check XP antecedents
      If one or more nodes not believed then
         Introspective questioning
         GOTO step 0
   Else GOTO step 0

- 2 b. *Create Learning Goals*

   Compute tentative goal priorities

- 2 c. *Strategy Construction*

   Translate Meta-XP and goals to predicates
   Pass goals and Meta-XP to Nonlin
   Translate resultant plan into frames

- 2 d. *Apply Learning Algorithm(s)*

   Interpret plan as partially ordered network of actions
      such that primitive actions are algorithm calls

## 3. Evaluate Learning (not implemented)

---

Fig. 1. Meta-AQUA's learning algorithm

**Strategy construction.** (step 2c, Figure 1) *Take as input a trace of how and why a failure occurred and a set of learning goals along with their dependencies; produce as output an ordered set of learning algorithms to apply that will accomplish the goals along with updated dependencies on the set of goals.*

The final learning-strategies are organized as plans to accomplish the learning goals. The plans are sequences of steps representing calls to specific learning algorithms. The plans are created by translating the learning goals and context from a frame representation into predicate logic format, then passing them to a Common LISP version of Tate's [36] Nonlin planner [9]. The learner instantiates, then executes the learning plans (in step 2d, Figure 1). Section 3 will provide details for this learning phase.

Previous publications [4, 6, 26] have dealt with the blame assignment stage. This paper explores how learning goals are spawned when deciding what to learn (Section 2) and how these goals are satisfied in the strategy-construction phase (Section 3). A simpler system might forego explicit learning-goals altogether, and directly map a failure to a learning algorithm. The discussion of Section 3 explains, not only how learning goals are managed, but what leverage is gained over and above a direct mapping itself. Finally, Section 4 concludes by specifying the relation between the Meta-AQUA system and traditional case-based reasoning approaches. It also briefly discusses related systems, limitations with Meta-AQUA, and areas for future research.

## 2 Deciding What to Learn

Given some failure of a reasoner, the task of the learning system is to adjust its knowledge so that such reasoning failures will not recur in similar situations.[2] The learner is therefore modeled as a planning system that spawns goals to achieve this overall task [12, 27]. The learner subsequently attempts to create plans resulting in desired new states of its background knowledge[3] that satisfy these knowledge goals. The overall aim is to turn reasoning failures into opportunities to learn and to improve the system's performance.

Learning goals represent what a system needs to know [24, 25, 27, 28] and are spawned when deciding what to learn. Learning goals help guide the learning process by suggesting strategies that would allow the system to learn the required knowledge. Learning goals specify the desired structure and content of knowledge, as well as the ways in which knowledge is organized in memory. Learning goals also facilitate opportunistic learning [11, 24, 25, 27]; that is, if all information necessary for learning is not available at the time it is determined what is needed to be learned (e.g., when a question is posed), then a learning goal can be suspended, indexed in memory, and resumed at a later time when the information becomes available.

Some learning goals seek to add, delete, generalize or specialize a given concept or procedure. Others deal with the ontology of the knowledge, i.e., with the kinds of categories that constitute particular concepts. Many learning goals are unary in that they take a single target as argument. For example, a *knowledge acquisition goal* seeks to determine a single piece of missing knowledge, such as the answer to a particular question. A *knowledge refinement goal* seeks a more specialized interpretation for a given concept in memory, whereas a *knowledge expansion goal* seeks a broader interpretation that explores connections with related concepts. Other learning goals are binary in nature since they take two arguments. A *knowledge differentiation goal* is a goal to determine a change in a body of knowledge such that two items are separated conceptually. In contrast, a *knowledge reconciliation goal* is one that seeks to merge two items that were mistakenly considered separate entities. Both expansion goals and reconciliation goals may include/spawn a *knowledge organization goal* that seeks to reorganize the existing knowledge so that it is made available to the reasoner at the appropriate time, as well as modify the structure or

---

2. The learner could also adjust its circumstances in the physical world, such as placing items in a cupboard in the same place to aid memory. This paper, however, will not entertain such possibilities. See [10] for an approach to such task interactions and associated learning.

3. The background knowledge includes more than simple domain knowledge. It also contains meta-knowledge, heuristic knowledge, associative knowledge, and knowledge of process.

content of a concept itself. Such reorganization of knowledge affects the conditions under which a particular piece of knowledge is retrieved or the kinds of indexes associated with an item in memory.

A program called Meta-AQUA [26] was written to test our theory of understanding, explanation and learning. Given the drug-bust story of Figure 2, the system attempts to understand each sentence by incorporating it into its current story representation, explain any anomalous or interesting features of the story, and learn from any reasoning failures. Numerous inferences can be made from this story, many of which may be incorrect or incomplete, depending on the knowledge of the reader. Meta-AQUA's background knowledge includes general facts about dogs and sniffing, including the fact that dogs bark when threatened, but it has no knowledge of police dogs. It also knows cases of gun smuggling, but has never seen drug interdiction. The learning task in Meta-AQUA is to learn from failures, incrementally improving its ability to interpret new stories.

S1: A police dog sniffed at a passenger's luggage in the airport terminal.
S2: The dog suddenly began to bark at the luggage.
S3: The authorities arrested the passenger, charging him with smuggling drugs.
S4: The dog barked because it detected two kilograms of marijuana in the luggage.

---

Fig. 2. The drug-bust story

In the drug-bust story, sentence S1 produces no inferences other than that sniffing is a normal event in the life of a dog. However, S2 produces an anomaly because the system's definition of "bark" specifies that the object of a bark is animate. Moreover, the program (incorrectly) believes that dogs bark only when threatened by animate objects (see Figure 3 for the representation[4] produced by Meta-AQUA during blame assignment). Since luggage is inanimate, there is a contradiction, leading to an incorporation failure. This anomaly causes the understander to ask why the dog barked at an inanimate object. It is able to produce but one explanation: the luggage somehow threatened the dog.

S3 asserts an arrest scene which reminds Meta-AQUA of a past case of weapons smuggling by terrorists; however, the sentence generates no new inferences concerning the previous anomaly. Finally, S4 causes the question generated by S2, "Why did the dog bark at the luggage?" to be retrieved. Instead of revealing the anticipated threatening situation, S4 offers another hypothesis: "The dog detected drugs in the luggage."

The system characterizes the reasoning error as an expectation failure caused by the incorrect retrieval of a known explanation ("dogs bark when threatened by objects," erro-

---

4. Attributes and relations are represented explicitly in Meta-AQUA and in this figure. For instance, the ACTOR attribute of an event Dog-bark.12 with the value Dog.4 is equivalent to the explicitly represented relation ACTOR.21 having a domain value of Dog-bark.12 and a co-domain value of Dog.4. In addition, all references to TRUTH attributes equal to out refer to the domain being out of the current set of beliefs. See [4] and [26] for further representational details. The "Internal Structures Window" of Figure 4 shows the top-level frame representation corresponding to Figure 3.

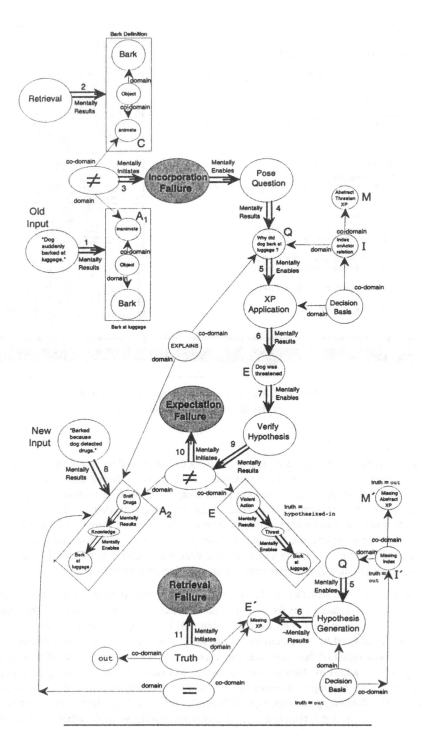

Fig. 3. Instantiated composite meta-explanation

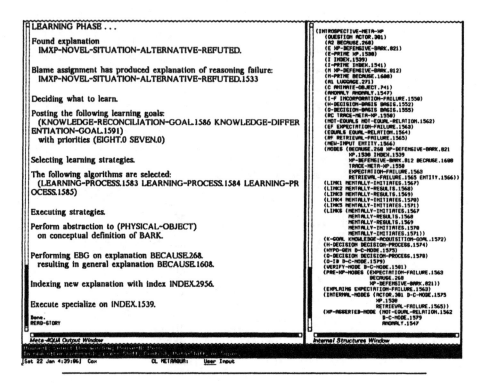

Fig. 4. Meta-AQUA output and frame representation of the meta-explanation used in example story

neously assumed to be applicable), and a missing explanation ("the dog barked because it detected marijuana," the correct explanation in this case). During blame assignment, Meta-AQUA uses this characterization as an index to retrieve an abstract case called a Meta-XP [5, 26] that is applied to a trace of the reasoning that produced the failure. The instantiation results in an explanation of its reasoning error, as shown in Figure 3. This composite meta-explanation consists of three parts: a Novel-Situation centered around "Retrieval Failure," an Erroneous-Association centered around "Expectation Failure" and an Incorrect-Domain-Knowledge centered around "Incorporation Failure."

Faced with the structure of the reasoning error produced by the blame-assignment phase, the learner determines the learning goals for the system. First, since the seemingly anomalous input (marked "Old Input" in Figure 3) has been incorporated into the story and later reinforced by the coherence of the story structure, and since no contradictions occurred as a result of this inference, the learner posts a knowledge reconciliation goal. The goal is to adjust the background knowledge so that neither dogs barking at animate objects nor dogs barking at inanimate objects will be considered anomalous by the understander. This learning goal is appropriate because even though one item is an instantiated token (a particular dog barked at a specific inanimate object), while the other is a type definition (concept specifying that dogs generally bark at animate objects), they are similar enough to each other to be reconcilable.

Secondly, given that an expectation failure triggered the learning, and (from the blame assignment phase) given that the failure resulted from the interaction of misindexed knowledge and a novel situation, Meta-AQUA posts a goal to differentiate between the two explanations for why the dog barked (nodes M and M' in Figure 3). Since the conflicting explanations are significantly different (for example, they do not share the same predicate, i.e., detect versus threaten), a knowledge-differentiation goal is licensed, rather than a goal to reconcile the two types of explanations. The differentiation goal is achieved if the system can retrieve proper explanations given various situations. The original misunderstanding of the story occurred, not because the explanation that dogs bark when threatened is incorrect in general, but rather because the system did not know the proper conditions under which this explanation applies.

In addition to posting these two learning goals, Meta-AQUA places a tentative ordering on their execution (see Figure 4 for program output when deciding what to learn). With no other specific knowledge concerning their respective relations, a good default heuristic is to order them by the temporal sequence of the failures involved in the original reasoning trace. The reason this may be useful is that if it is determined that the first failure was indeed not an error but a misunderstanding or was caused by faulty input, then the reasoning that followed from the first failure (or other assumptions depending on the nature of the first failure that led to the second) may have contributed to the cause of the second. Thus, learning acquired about the first failure may show that the subsequent reasoning was irrelevant, or it may yield more information to be used on the second goal. Therefore, the decide-what-to-learn stage outputs the knowledge-reconciliation goal with priority over the knowledge-differentiation goal.

## 3 Strategy Selection and Combination

In the strategy-construction stage, Meta-AQUA builds a learning plan to realize the learning goals posted by the previous stage (see Figure 4 for program output during the strategy-construction phase). This entails not only choosing the algorithms and operators to achieve the learning goals, but perhaps also spawning new subgoals. To help the system create a plan for a learning goal with two arguments, the following types of questions can be posed about the reasoning chain. For example, with the knowledge-differentiation goal, the focus starts at the error that triggered the introspective-explanation episode, that is, at the expectation failure. Given that the reasoner expected explanation E to be correct, but later decides that $A_2$ is the actual explanation, the system needs to determine:

- Was the actual occurrence, $A_2$, foreseeable?
- If so, was $A_2$ considered?
- Is there still a possibility that $A_2$ is incorrect?
- Is there still a possibility that E is correct?
- How confident is the system in $A_2$ or input associated with establishing $A_2$?
- How much experience exists with $A_2$ and E's abstract progenitors?

The answers to these questions enable the system to choose learning algorithms, strategies, or operators. For example, since the story provides an explanation ($A_2$) that provides more coherence to the representation of the story, the system assumes that there is no error in the input. However, because the system has no prior experience with the instance (and thus the system neither foresaw nor considered the explanation), the learner posts another goal to expand the concept, thus producing $M'$. Explanation-based generalization (EBG) [7, 19] can then be selected as an appropriate learning algorithm.

A more difficult problem is to differentiate the applicability conditions for the two generalized explanations ($M'$, the one produced by generalizing the detection explanation, $A_2$, and M, the original abstract pattern that produced the initial threaten explanation, E) by modifying the indexes ($I'$ and I) with which the system retrieves those explanations. If the two problems of erroneous association and novel situation were to be treated independently, rather than as a problem of interaction, then an indexing algorithm would not be able to ensure that the two explanations would remain distinct in the future. That is, if the learner simply detects a novel situation and automatically generalizes it, then indexes it by the salient or causal features in the explanation, and if the learner independently detects an erroneous retrieval, and re-indexes it so that the same context will not retrieve it in the future, then there is no guarantee that the resultant indexes will be mutually exclusive. Instead, the system must re-index E with respect to $A_2$, not simply with respect to the condition with which E was retrieved. Therefore, a direct mapping from blame assignment to strategy selection without the mediation of learning goals is problematic.

The problems to be solved, then, are determining the difference between $A_2$ and E, and, in the light of such differences, computing the minimal specialization of the index of E and the maximally general index of $A_2$ so they will be retrieved separately in the future. In the case of the story above, the problem is somewhat simplified. The difference is that retrieval based on the actor relation of barking actions (dogs) is too general. The threaten explanation applies when dogs bark at animate objects, while the detection explanation is appropriate when dogs bark at containers.

The learning goal to reconcile the fact that the conceptual definition of dog-barking is limited to animate objects and the fact that a particular dog barked at a piece of luggage can be thought of as a simple request for similarity-based learning (SBL) or inductive learning (for example, UNIMEM's SBL algorithm in [16] or abstraction transmutation as in [17]). The system is simply adding an additional positive example to the instances seen. An incremental algorithm is required because this instance has been discovered after an initial concept has been established some time in the past.

An interesting interaction can occur, however, if the system waits for the result of the EBG algorithm required by the knowledge-expansion subgoal spawned by the knowledge-differentiation goal discussed above. The algorithm will generalize the explanation (that this particular dog barked at a particular piece of luggage because it detected marijuana) to a broader explanation (that dogs in general may bark at any container when they detect contraband). Thus, the example provided to the inductive algorithm can be more widely interpreted, perhaps allowing its inductive bias to generalize the constraint, C, on the object of dog-barking to physical-object (the exhaustive case of animate-object and inanimate-object), whereas a single instance of a particular breed of dog barking at a specific brand of luggage, $A_1$, may limit the inductive inference if no additional domain knowledge is available.

Unfortunately, however, because the EBG algorithm uses the representation of the dog-bark definition, and the inductive algorithm changes this definition, the induction must occur first. Thus, the learner cannot take advantage of the opportunity cited in the previous paragraph. One important implication of this point is that in systems which plan to learn, if the reasoner does not anticipate this second interaction (thus placing EBG before the induction), the system must be able to perform dynamic backtracking on its decisions.

To notice these types of interactions, however, requires a least-commitment approach such as that used in a non-linear hierarchical planner like Nonlin [9, 36]. Likewise, the system must detect any dependency relationships so that goal violations can be avoided. For example, when the definition of dog-barking is modified by generalizing its constraint of what dogs bark at to physical-object from animate-object, any indexing based on the modified attribute must occur after this modification, rather than before it, to avoid indexing with obsolete conceptual knowledge.[5]

Figure 5 shows a learning-operator definition for the indexing algorithm that manages mutual indexing between two concepts. The operator schema determines that both items must be independently indexed before they are indexed with respect to each other. The action schema has filter conditions that apply when both are indexed and both are XPs. An unsupervised condition specifies that if there exists a change in the explained action, then it must occur before the execution of this schema. That is, a linearization must be performed on external goals to reorder any other schema that may establish the change. It says in effect that we want all attributes of the target concept to be stable before it operates on the concept; no other operator can change an attribute in order for the changes performed by indexing to be unaffected. Note that the action schema of abstraction in Figure 6 has an effect that includes such a change to its addlist. Therefore, if both schemas are being instantiated, Nonlin will automatically order the abstraction before the indexing. A similar unsupervised condition prevents generalization from occurring before the concept is stable.

Therefore, the final learning plan Meta-AQUA constructs is (1) perform an abstraction transmutation on the new example of dog barking (realizing that dogs bark at containers); (2) perform EBG on the new explanation (producing a generalized version); (3) index the generalized XP in isolation; and finally, (4) use the new concept definition to mutually differentiate and index the two generalized explanations of why dogs bark.

Subsequently, Meta-AQUA can accept a similar story as input. In this story a police officer and a canine enter a suspect's house, the dog barks at a garbage pail, and the suspect is arrested for possession of some marijuana found in the pail. The new story causes no anomaly when the dog barks at the inanimate container. Indeed, Meta-AQUA expects some type of contraband to be found in the container after it reads that the dog barked, but before it is told of the contraband's existence in the story. Thus, the previous learning improves both understanding and prediction.

---

5. This result supersedes the conjecture by Ram and Hunter [27] that, unlike standard planning techniques, interactions and dependencies do not occur with learning goals.

```
(opschema mutual-index-op
      :todo   (index-wrt-item ?x ?y)
      :expansion (
              (step1 :goal (indexed ?x))
              (step2 :goal (indexed ?y))
              (step3 :action
                      (index-dual-items ?x ?y)))
      :orderings(
              (step1 -> step3)
              (step2 -> step3))
      :conditions (
              (:precond (indexed ?x)
               :at step3 :from step1)
              (:precond (indexed ?y)
               :at step3 :from step2)
              (:use-when (not (equal ?x ?y))
                      :at step1))
      :effects   ()
      :variables (?x ?y))


(actschema do-mutual-xp-indexing
      :todo   (index-dual-items ?x ?y)
      :expansion ( (step1 :primitive
                      (perform-mutual-indexing ?x ?y)))
      :conditions (
              (:use-when (indexed ?x) :at step1)
              (:use-when (indexed ?y) :at step1)
              (:use-when (isa xp ?x) :at step1)
              (:use-only-for-query
                      (explains ?explains-node ?x)
               :at step1)
              (:use-only-for-query
                      (domain ?explains-node
                       ?explained-action)
               :at step1)
              (:unsuperv (changed true ?explained-action)
               :at step1)
                      )
      :effects   (
              (step1 :assert (indexed-wrt ?x ?y))
              (step1 :assert (indexed-wrt ?y ?x)))
      :variables (?x ?y ?explains-node ?explained-action))
```

Fig. 5. Mutual-indexing schemas

```
(actschema do-abstraction-change
      :todo   (abstracted ?r1 ?r2)
      :expansion ( (step1 :primitive (perform-abstraction ?r1 ?r2)))
      :conditions (
              (:use-when (isa relation ?r1) :at step1)
              (:use-when (isa relation ?r2) :at step1)
              (:use-when (relation ?r1 ?r1-type) :at step1)
              (:use-when (relation ?r2 ?r2-type) :at step1)
              (:use-only-for-query (domain ?r1 ?r1-domain) :at step1)
              (:use-only-for-query (co-domain ?r1 ?c) :at step1)
              (:use-only-for-query (co-domain ?r2 ?a) :at step1)
              (:use-only-for-query (parent-of ?c ?c-parent) :at step1)
              (:use-only-for-query (parent-of ?a ?a-parent) :at step1)
              (:use-when (equal ?r1-type ?r2-type) :at step1)
              (:use-when (equal ?c-parent ?a-parent) :at step1))
      :effects   (
              (step1 :assert (co-domain ?r1 ?c-parent))
              (step1 :assert (changed true ?r1-domain))
              (step1 :delete (co-domain ?r1 ?c))
              (step1 :delete (changed false ?r1-domain)))
      :variables (?r1 ?r2 ?r1-type ?r2-type ?r1-domain
                  ?c ?a ?c-parent ?a-parent))
```

Fig. 6. Abstraction schema

# 4 Conclusions

Although Meta-AQUA is firmly in the case-based reasoning tradition, our approach diverges from it somewhat. Three elements traditionally characterize case-based reasoning. First, case-based reasoning usually processes instances or concrete episodic cases. However, some systems emphasize the integration of generalized knowledge and cases (e.g., [1, 25]), and moreover, like Meta-AQUA, some case-based reasoning systems actually process abstract cases, including XPs (see [13, 25, 33]). Secondly, case-based reasoning emphasizes the role of memory retrieval of past examples, rather than reasoning from first principles. This focus has led to research on indexing vocabulary and case adaptation. However, Meta-AQUA is a hybrid system that combines the case-based reasoning of the first two learning phases with the nonlinear planning of the third. Finally, traditional case-based reasoning systems stress goal-directed activity to focus both processing and learning [14, 27, 31]. Our approach to learning is also goal-directed, but in a very different style. Meta-AQUA is the first case-based reasoning system to specifically plan in the knowledge space using goals that specify changes in that space. Unlike INVESTIGATOR [12], which creates plans in the external world to achieve learning goals (e.g., access a database to answer a question), Meta-AQUA's plans operate on the internal world of the system's background knowledge. Although many computational systems use a reflective reasoning approach [3, 8, 20, 21, 34], and a few have used the planning metaphor in learning [12, 23, 27, 28, 29], none of these systems have applied the planning metaphor as strictly as Meta-AQUA has; none execute a planner like Nonlin upon its own knowledge.

The planning and problem-solving literature suggest that use of explicit goals have many benefits over *ad hoc* processing. Many of these benefits apply to leaning-goal processing as well as standard-goal processing. First, learning goals decouple the many-to-many relationship between failures and algorithm. Secondly, an opportunistic approach to solving learning problems can be achieved by suspending the goals and resuming their pursuit at a time when satisfaction is more likely. Thirdly, learning goals allow chaining, composition, and optimization of the means by which learning goals are achieved. Fourthly, because nonlinear plans allows parallelism, learning algorithms may be executed concurrently. Finally, the use of learning goals allows detection of dependency relationships so that goal violations can be avoided.

Future research is directed toward incorporating more learning strategies. One of the weak points of the current system is that it reasons during learning at a macro-level. Meta-AQUA recognizes the functional difference between generalization and specialization and therefore can choose an appropriate algorithm based on which algorithm is most appropriate. For example, it cannot currently select between competing algorithms that both perform generalization. Meta-AQUA does not reason at the micro-level, as do systems that address the *selective-superiority problem*[6] in inductive learning (see, for instance, [2, 22, 30]), although the scope of learning problems solved by Meta-AQUA is greater than these other systems.

---

6. Empirical results suggest that various inductive algorithms are better at classifying specific classes or particular distributions of data than others. Each algorithm is good at some but not all learning tasks. The selective superiority problem is to choose the most appropriate inductive algorithm, given a particular set of data [2].

Another limitation of the Meta-AQUA implementation is that learning self-evaluation (step 3 of Figure 1) is not yet implemented. Thus, Meta-AQUA cannot cross-validate or compare various successful algorithms, nor can it currently judge when learning fails and another algorithm must be chosen. Just as it detects, explains, repairs and learns from reasoning failures, an interesting line of future research would be to allow Meta-AQUA to reason about its own learning. See Leake [15] for approaches to this problem.

To perform multistrategy learning, a case-based reasoning system must consider a number of factors that are not significant in isolated learning systems. In particular, a system must be able to handle insufficient resources and knowledge and manage dependency relations between learning algorithms at run-time. Many alternative solutions and interactions may occur, even when reasoning about simple situations. Treating the learner as a planner is a principled way of confronting these difficulties. Many of the techniques and results from the planning literature can be appropriated in case-based systems to provide a better level of robustness and coverage in situations where many types of failure may occur. The aim is to transform these failures into opportunities to learn and improve the system's overall performance.

## Acknowledgments

This research is supported by AFOSR under contract #F49620-94-1-0092 and by the Georgia Institute of Technology. We also thank Jennifer Snow Wolff and the anonymous reviewers for the helpful comments on earlier drafts of this document.

## References

1. Aamodt, A.: Explanation-driven case-based reasoning. In S. Wess, K.-D. Althoff, and M. M. Richter (Eds.), Topics in case-based reasoning (EWCBR-93). Berlin: Springer-Verlag (1994) 274-288

2. Brodley, C. E.: Addressing the selective superiority problem: Automatic algorithm / model class selection. Machine Learning: Proceedings of the Tenth International Conference. San Mateo, CA: Morgan Kaufmann (1993) 17-24

3. Collins, G., Birnbaum, L. Krulwich, B., Freed, M.: The role of self-models in learning to plan. In A. L. Meyrowitz and S. Chipman (Eds.), Foundations of knowledge acquisition: Machine learning. Boston: Kluwer Academic Publishers (1993) 117-143

4. Cox, M. T.: Introspective multistrategy learning (Cognitive Science Tech. Rep. No. 2). Atlanta: Georgia Institute of Technology, College of Computing (1993)

5. Cox, M. T., Ram, A.: Using introspective reasoning to select learning strategies. In R. S. Michalski and G. Tecuci (Eds.), Proceedings of the First International Workshop on Multistrategy Learning. Washington, DC: George Mason University, Center for Artificial Intelligence (1991) 217-230

6. Cox, M. T., Ram, A.: Multistrategy learning with introspective meta-explanations. D. Sleeman and P. Edwards (Eds.), Machine Learning: Proceedings of the Ninth International Conference. San Mateo, CA: Morgan Kaufmann (1992) 123-128

7. DeJong, G., Mooney, R.: Explanation-based learning: An alternative view, *Machine Learning* 1(2) (1986) 145-176

8. Fox, S., Leake, D.: Modeling case-based planning for repairing reasoning failures. In M. Cox and M. Freed (Eds.), Proceedings of the 1995 AAAI Spring Symposium on Representing Mental States and Mechanisms. Menlo Park, CA: AAAI Press (1995) 31-38

9. Ghosh, S., Hendler, J., Kambhampati, S., Kettler, B.: UM Nonlin [a Common Lisp implementation of A. Tate's Nonlin planner]. Maintained at the Dept. of Computer Science, University of Maryland, College Park, MD. Available by anonymous ftp from cs.umd.edu in directory /pub/nonlin (1992)

10. Hammond, K. J.: Learning and enforcement: Stabilizing environments to facilitate activity. B. W. Porter and R. Mooney (Eds.), Machine Learning: Proceedings of the Seventh International Conference. San Mateo, CA: Morgan Kaufmann (1990) 204-210

11. Hammond, K., Converse, T., Marks, M., Seifert, C.: Opportunism and learning. In J. L. Kolodner (Ed.), *Case-based learning*. Boston: Kluwer Academic (1993) 85-115

12. Hunter, L. E.: Planning to learn. Proceedings of the Twelfth Annual Conference of the Cognitive Science Society. Hillsdale, NJ: LEA (1990) 261-276

13. Kerner, Y.: Case-based evaluation in computer chess. In M. Keane, J.-P. Haton, and M. Manago (Eds.), *Topics in case-based reasoning (EWCBR-94)*. Berlin: Springer-Verlag (this volume)

14. Kolodner, J. L.: Case-based reasoning. San Mateo, CA: Morgan Kaufmann (1993)

15. Leake, D.: Evaluating explanations: A content theory. Hillsdale, NJ: LEA (1992)

16. Lebowitz, M.: Experiments with incremental concept formation: UMIMEM. Machine Learning 2 (1987) 103-138.

17. Michalski, R. S.: Inferential theory of learning: Developing foundations for multistrategy learning. In R. S. Michalski and G. Tecuci (Eds.), Machine learning: A multistrategy approach IV. San Francisco: Morgan Kaufmann (1994) 3-61

18. Minsky, M. L.: Steps Towards Artificial Intelligence. In E. A. Feigenbaum and J. Feldman (Eds.), Computers and thought. New York: McGraw Hill (1963) 406-450

19. Mitchell, T., Keller, R., Kedar-Cabelli, S.: Explanation-based generalization: A unifying view, Machine Learning 1(1) (1986) 47-80

20. Oehlmann, R., Edwards, P., Sleeman, D.: Changing the viewpoint: Re-indexing by introspective questioning. In Proceedings of the Sixteenth Annual Conference of the Cognitive Science Society. Hillsdale, NJ: LEA (1994) 675-680

21. Plaza, E., Arcos, J. L.: Reflection and analogy in memory-based learning. In R. S. Michalski and G. Tecuci (Eds.), Proceedings of the Second International Workshop on

Multistrategy Learning. Fairfax, VA: George Mason University, Center for Artificial Intelligence (1993) 42-49

22. Provost, F. J., Buchanan, B. G.: Inductive policy. Proceedings of the Tenth National Conference on Artificial Intelligence. Menlo Park, CA: AAAI Press (1992) 255-261

23. Quilici, A.: Toward automatic acquisition of an advisory system's knowledge base. Applied Intelligence (to appear)

24. Ram, A.: A theory of questions and question asking. Journal of the Learning Sciences 1(3&4) (1991) 273-318.

25. Ram, A.: Indexing, elaboration and refinement: Incremental learning of explanatory cases. Machine Learning 10(3) (1993) 201-248.

26. Ram, A., Cox, M. T.: Introspective reasoning using meta-explanations for multistrategy learning. In R. S. Michalski and G. Tecuci (Eds.), Machine learning: A multistrategy approach IV. San Francisco: Morgan Kaufmann (1994) 349-377

27. Ram, A., Hunter, L.: The use of explicit goals for knowledge to guide inference and learning. Applied Intelligence, 2(1) (1992) 47-73

28. Ram, A., Leake, D.: Learning, goals, and learning goals. In A. Ram and D. Leake (Eds.), Goal-driven learning. Cambridge, MA: MIT Press/Bradford Books (to appear)

29. Redmond, M. A.: Learning by observing and understanding expert problem solving (Tech. Rep. No. GIT-CC-92/43). Doctoral dissertation, Atlanta: Georgia Tech (1992)

30. Schaffer, C.: Selecting a classification method by cross-validation. Machine Learning, 13(1) (1993) 135-143

31. Schank, R. C.: Dynamic memory: A theory of reminding and learning in computers and people. Cambridge, UK: Cambridge University Press (1982)

32. Schank, R. C.: Explanation patterns: Understanding mechanically and creatively. Hillsdale, NJ: LEA (1986)

33. Schank, R. C., Kass, A., Riesbeck, C. K.: Inside case-based explanation. Hillsdale, NJ: LEA (1994)

34. Stroulia, E., Goel, A.: Functional representation and reasoning for reflective systems. Applied Artificial Intelligence (to appear)

35. Sussman, G. J.: A computer model of skill acquisition. New York: American Elsevier (1975)

36. Tate, A.: Project planning using a hierarchic non-linear planner (Tech. Rep. No. 25). Edinburgh, UK: University of Edinburgh, Department of Artificial Intelligence (1976)

# On the Limitations of Memory Based Reasoning

Pádraig Cunningham *, Barry Smyth **, Tony Veale **

**Department of Computer Science, Trinity College Dublin, Ireland

**Hitachi Dublin Laboratory, Trinity College Dublin, Ireland

**Abstract.** Memory-Based Reasoning (MBR) represents a radical new departure in AI research. Whereas work in symbolic AI is based on inference and knowledge representation MBR depends on using a large memory of examples as a reasoning base. The MBR methodology is empirical so a typical system does not contain an explicit domain model. This means that MBR systems are quick to set up so the methodology shows considerable promise for knowledge based systems development. Indeed some impressive full scale systems have been demonstrated. In this paper we argue that despite this initial success there are considerable limitations to what can be achieved with MBR. We believe that the absence of a domain model means that MBR will not succeed in complex applications. We illustrate problems in natural language processing and planning that will require access to domain theories in their solution. Our conclusion is that the memory oriented philosophy of MBR has advantages but, for truly intelligent systems, this philosophy is better realised in the CBR paradigm where it can be integrated with a strong domain theory.

## 1. Introduction

This paper is prompted by concern about some of the claims made in research on Memory-Based Reasoning (MBR). The motivation behind the MBR movement is that the advent of massively parallel computing radically changes the way AI should be done. The argument is that intelligent performance can be based on a large empirical database of examples and in particular the requirement that the symbolic AI paradigm has for a strong domain model is avoided (Stanfill & Waltz, 1986; 1992), (Kitano, 1993), (Creecy et al., 1992). In this paper we will attempt to illustrate the unavoidable requirement of domain models and inference mechanisms for more complex tasks. We will use examples from planning and natural language processing to illustrate situations where empirical analysis is not adequate and inference based on a strong domain model is required.

MBR uses similarity metrics to find examples in memory that are similar to the problem in hand and then uses the actions associated with these examples to deal with the current situation. This is similar to the methodology used in Case-Based Reasoning (CBR) with the important difference that CBR systems incorporate some domain theory to guide the case matching and adaptation processes (see Kolodner, (1991); Veloso & Carbonell,(1991); Smyth & Cunningham, (1992), for descriptions of representative CBR systems). Thus MBR is a significant departure from the physical symbol system hypothesis of traditional AI. Instead it is memory centred, depending on a large content addressable memory of examples quickly accessible on parallel hardware. This means that MBR systems are easier to set up than symbolic

AI systems as the knowledge engineering task is largely avoided (see Creecy et al., (1992) for example).

Advocates of the MBR idea have argued for the advantages of MBR over techniques based on knowledge representation and inference; the contention being that MBR techniques take better advantage of massively parallel architectures. This argument is a performance argument, whereas we believe that the crucial drawback with MBR is the lack of domain semantics. It is clear that MBR is a powerful methodology for some tasks for example; phrase translation (Kitano & Higuchi, 1991), classification (Creecy et al., 1992), or information retrieval (Stanfill & Waltz, 1992). However, there is reason to doubt that this impressive performance on what are essentially 'entry level' intelligent tasks will be manifest in tasks of greater complexity. In this paper we will describe problems in natural language processing and planning/design where it is clear that MBR will not succeed without an adequate domain model that captures the causal interactions between domain elements.

Our conclusion is that the memory oriented philosophy of MBR has advantages but, for truly intelligent systems, this philosophy is better realised in the CBR paradigm where it can be integrated with a strong domain theory.

Before elaborating on these arguments a brief introduction to MBR will be presented in the next section.

## 2.  MBR and Massively Parallel AI

Before examining the MBR methodology it is worth reflecting on the problems with the conventional AI paradigm that MBR wishes to avoid. The case outlined here is as presented by Kitano (1993). 'The traditional AI approach' is based on the physical symbol system hypothesis. He argues that it has the following characteristics:-

- Formal Representations

- Rule driven inferencing

- Strong Methods: domain theory must be understood

- Hand-Crafted Knowledge Base

This approach has had considerable success with 'toy systems' but has had problems scaling up to larger applications. Kitano uses the diagram in Figure 1 to contrast the approach of traditional AI with that in MBR.

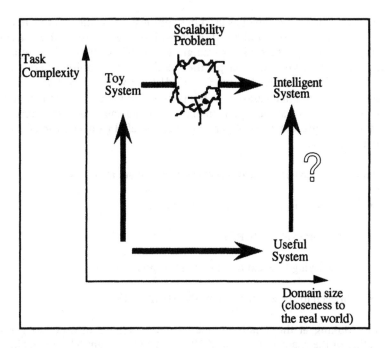

(based on (Kitano, 1993))

*Figure 1: Approaches for building intelligent systems*

The techniques of traditional AI have been successful in developing 'Toy Systems' that exhibit competence in limited domains. There is a widely recognised problem in scaling up this competence to a more broadly based intelligence. The approach in MBR is different. MBR focuses on performance from the start, concentrating on useful full scale systems for simple tasks. This performance on simple tasks has been illustrated in useful systems (see Creecy et al., (1992) for instance) however it is not clear that this methodology can be extended to cover more complex tasks.

The basic idea in MBR is to found intelligence on a large memory of examples. Nearest match computation is used to find the items in memory most similar to a current situation and then the actions associated with these items are used to deal with the current situation. Kitano emphasises three characteristics that are essential to the success of the MBR idea. These are; massive power, massive data resources and sophisticated modelling. He emphasises the importance of this modelling acknowledging that results will be poor if the modelling is not appropriate (Kitano, 1993). For the simple tasks tackled to date this sophisticated modelling involves structuring examples in a manner that allows useful remindings to be generated using statistical techniques. We believe that for more complex tasks this sophisticated modelling will be every bit as complex as the knowledge engineering that MBR wishes to avoid.

One of the major advantages of MBR is that it is a technique that takes full advantage of massively parallel hardware. Proponents of MBR argue that this is in contrast to logic based or rules based techniques used in traditional AI. While it is true that MBR can take full advantage of parallelisation there has been considerable success in transferring the symbolic reasoning paradigm to parallel systems [Evett et al. '93]. Evett and Co. have shown that on parallel hardware recognition queries can be performed on a large knowledge base in $O(d)$ time where $d$ is the depth of the knowledge base. This is in contrast to $O(B^d)$ (where B is the average branching factor in the network), the worst case performance on serial machines. This research is important in that it illustrates that AI on massively parallel hardware can be based on symbolic inferencing.

Some examples of areas of application of MBR to date are as follows:-

- Pronouncing English words (MBRTalk)

- Text retrieval (CMDRS)

- Classifying free text questionnaire responses (PACE)

- Speech to speech translation ($\Phi$DMDIALOG)

It is worth looking at the details of one of these systems in order to get some understanding of the characteristics of MBR. The PACE system (Creecy et al., 1992) is a typical MBR system for classifying US Census Bureau long forms. These forms contain free-text responses to questions on occupation, company, duties and industry type. These responses have to be classified into predetermined categories; 232 industry categories, and 504 categories in the case of the occupation response. PACE uses a database of 132,000 manually classified returns as its reasoning base. The responses under consideration are compared with these using nearest neighbour techniques to determine the best classification. Similarity is normally determined based on features and in this task the features are the words in the responses. One of the main contributions of the PACE work has been the analysis of the reasoning base that determines the features that are most predictive in classification. Evidently, these features are weighted in the nearest neighbour classification. PACE runs on a CM2 Connection Machine so it meets the three criteria of, massive power, massive data resources and sophisticated modelling for MBR emphasised by Kitano. It is also a wholly empirical system.

In terms of the structure presented in Figure 1 this is a 'Useful System'; it tackles a full scale but simple problem. In the next few sections we will argue that this architecture will not be adequate for addressing more complex tasks. In particular we will argue that a system lacking a domain model will not be able to detect useful similarity in **retrieval** and will not be able to perform the required **adaptations** on retrieved solutions. We will conclude that domain knowledge must be available for effective retrieval and adaptation as is the case in CBR.

## 3  MBR in NLP: A Case of Performance Vs. Competence?

Inasmuch as strong MBR proponents seek to overturn the apple cart of traditional rule-based AI, they necessarily also part company with established formal linguistics on the complementary issues of competence and performance in language comprehension, and in particular, translation. Formal linguistics traditionally seeks to account for performance data, the actual use of language by a native speaker, in terms of a rule-based grammar of linguistic competence which generatively models the language ability of the speaker. In contrast, proponents of MBR-based translation claim that a rich example-base, in effect a highly-structured corpus of performance data, tied to a sophisticated statistical model of matching and retrieval, provides a sufficient basis for translation *without* the need for an explicit model of competence.

To commence the argument against this latter view, it is useful to first highlight those aspects of translation in which a performance-based approach reaps strong results. One such boon occurs in the treatment of language *aberrations* such as metaphor and metonymy, in which conceptual transpositions are performed, for reasons of eloquence or conciseness, in violation of default semantic constraints (see Veale & Keane 1992). For example "boiling the kettle" is quite a different action to "boiling an egg", the former usage employing a metonymic shorthand for "the water in the kettle". Likewise, "to play Mozart" and "to play the Jupiter symphony" both use the verb "play" in isomorphic syntactic constructs, but with differing conceptual intent. The conventional rule-based approach to metonymy is to bolster the model of language competence with additional rules of construal (see Jackendoff 1991), or metonymic coherence rules (see Fass 1988). In contrast, the MBR approach does not place a dependence upon explicit *fixit* rules but instead relies upon a preponderance of performance data to provide a nearest-neighbour match. When translating to another language, the MBR system is thus not required to either resolve the metonymy in advance, or determine whether the metonymy will hold in the target language; it is enough (and indeed, from the point of preserving the style of the original statement, often preferable) to retrieve a similar usage from memory and modify the corresponding translation.

By choosing to emphasise linguistic performance over competence, an MBR treatment of language is essentially statistical rather than semantic, the aspiration being that given enough performance data and a sufficiently sophisticated stochastic model, an implicit model of competence will emerge. As argued above, this often is indeed the case, but it is vital to note here that such implicit competence is inherently dependent upon the *chunk* size employed by the statistical model. As the sentences processed by a translation system will be of a varying (and indefinite) size, the past examples stored in memory will have to be partitioned, or chunked, at some level of detail if the obvious combinatorial nightmare is to be avoided, and the utility of the example-base is to be maximised. Consider the following example:

(1) Neville Mariner played Mozart for a hollywood film that has garnered great reviews.

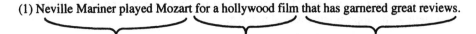

This sentence is simply too long to expect the case base to contain a complete match. More realistically, the sentence needs to be chunked into several semantically viable components, each of which can be matched and modified independently. But while an MBR model demonstrates a semantic competence comparable to a rule-based system on an *intra*-chunk basis, its reliance upon a *reduction to statistics* philosophy leaves it poorly positioned to reason at an *inter*-chunk level. This sentence also exhibits some subtle, but very interesting, effects of real world language usage. First, the speaker has used the word "for" rather than "in" to indicate Mr. Mariner's involvement with the Amadeus project, though both forms are adequate. This reflects the deep cognitive topology that structures our language use, and grounds our concepts in everyday experience (see Brugman & Lakoff 1988), for to employ "in" is suggestive that Mariner actually appears in the film, when in reality he contributes the music "for" the film. This latter form thus represents a weaker commitment to Mariner's role in the project, and is slightly suggestive that he is somehow "outside" the actual film. This in turn is a subtle cue that Mariner is not to be viewed as an actor of the piece, and therefore that the intended sense of "play" is the musical rather than the thespian reading. The daunting task facing an MBR system without recourse to such an explicit cognitive topology is to relate the usage of "for" in one chunk with the usage of "played" in another.

Of course, an intelligent, model-based system might just as easily use the information that Neville Mariner is a world renowned concert conductor to resolve the ambiguity. Consider for instance the following sentence, which is isomorphic with (1) above:

(2) Tom Hulce played Mozart in a film that garnered seven oscars.

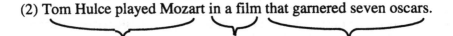

In example (2) the verb "play" is used in quite a different sense to that employed in (1); however, unless the system possesses (and utilises) prior knowledge that Tom Hulce is an actor, this distinction can only become apparent at an inter-chunk level of processing. Ultimately, without a deep conceptual analysis of each individual chunk, performed against a strong conceptual model of the world, a translation system is unable to adequately characterise how different chunks inter-relate and combine to produce a coherent whole. Because of a reliance on statistics over semantics, an MBR system is unable to meet either of these requirements.

But what of the traditional and well-proven disambiguation methods that successively employ statistical analysis, whether explicitly, or in a connectionist guise (see for instance Cottrell & Small, 1982) - surely such strategies can *mine* the surrounding lexical context to discover which readings of each polysem are more semantically primed than others? For example, in sentence (2) above, the terms "film" and "oscars" will strongly prime the thespian reading of "play", both terms providing a more solid evidential basis than that provided by the single term "Mozart" for the musical reading. However, by the same argument then, the thespian reading should also be incorrectly primed in sentence (1) above, the terms "hollywood" and "film" blinding the system to the appropriate musical reading.

As further demonstration of the inadequacy of such a strategy, consider sentence (3) below:

(3) Clint Eastwood played a piano in a musical scene from "In the Line of Fire."

The unfortunate statistical possibilities inherent in this sentence are left as an exercise for the reader.

# 4 MBR & Planning

Before focusing on the role MBR has to play in planning it is worth considering some of the early work on the notion of "plan reuse". The basic idea in MBR of the replacement of a domain model with a extensive but shallow example-base is in direct contrast with the lessons that have been learnt from this early research. One of the first instances of plan-reuse was the work of Fikes, Hart, and Nilsson, (1972). To improve planning efficiency, the STRIPS planner was extended to facilitate the storage and retrieval of plan segments (Macrops). The nature of these stored segments is comparable to the type of examples stored in an MBR system's memory in that they were shallow packets of plan exemplars. It was soon recognised however that there were inherent problems with retrieving a suitable Macrop. Without a complex description language, Macrops were selected on the basis of surface features resulting in unforeseen instantiation problems due to bad interactions. As we shall see, we can expect similar problems within the MBR framework.

While there is a general acceptance of the advantages of "reuse" for many planning tasks, we will argue that it has the effect of redistributing rather than reducing domain knowledge requirements. In a reuse-based planning system a domain model is required to fulfil not only the needs of the adaptation task (which is similar in nature to traditional first-principles planning) but also the needs of the retrieval task.

We will consider these issues using examples taken from Déjà Vu, a case-based reasoning system for the design of Plant-Control software.[1] The problem domain of Déjà Vu has already been introduced in (Smyth & Cunningham, 1992) and so will only be described in outline here. Plant-Control software is concerned with the control of autonomous vehicles within a factory environment. An important class of Plant-Control tasks is aimed at the control of vehicles during the loading and unloading of metal coils in a steel mill. Déjà Vu's cases are software modules for controlling vehicles and other devices performing such tasks. An example of the type of code is shown in the Solution section in Figure 2.

---

[1] This software design task is essentially a planning problem.

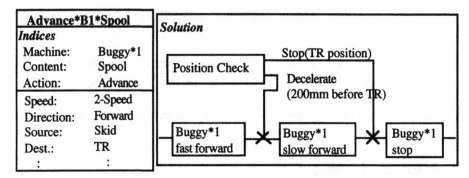

*Figure 2. An example case from Déjà Vu.*

The code is expressed in this network representation that is compilable into and executable form. This sample case controls the movement of a buggy carrying an empty spool. Buggy*1 is a two speed buggy, so stopping is a two stage process with the buggy switching to its slower speed 200mm from its destination.[2]

## 4.1   Retrieval

It seems clear that if MBR systems are to enjoy their stated advantage of ease of set-up then the stored examples must be readily described in terms of shallow, easily observable, surface features. The analytical expense of deep thematic feature descriptors outlaws their use in a pure MBR system. However, surface features are not sufficiently powerful to capture the causal dependencies that exist between plan steps. Consequently, the retrieval mechanism has the potential to generate *false remindings*. That is, it is likely that example plans will be selected whose measurable similarity does not accurately reflect their *true* similarity to the target specification. In computing an accurate measurement of plan similarity one must consider not only surface features (such as the goals), but also deeper causal features that capture dependency configurations within plan structures. The result is the retrieval of a base example which exhibits strong surface commonalties to the target but is at best, difficult to adapt and at worst completely unsuitable.

For example, in Figure 2 we have presented the two-speed motion scenario where a buggy travels from one floor position to another. A behaviourally very similar task is that of controlling the motion of a lifter (a speed controlled lifting platform). This lifter is used to adjust the height of the load for loading and unloading. Like the buggy, the lifter can be a one or two speed device and a component case for a two speed lifter is shown in Figure 3. It can be seen that the solution for the two speed lifter has the same structure as the buggy case described above so it should be possible to reuse the solution from one in designing the other. However, this is problematic because these two cases do not share important surface features. So if this

---

2 It should be noted that Déjà Vu uses a hierarchical reasoning technique and cases are arranged into partonomies that represent complex software designs. As such, the case here is a sub-component of a number of more sophisticated designs.

lifter case were a target case, the useful Advance*B1*Spool case may not be retrieved using similarity based on surface features.

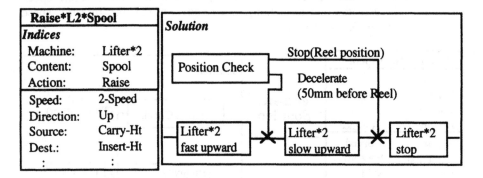

| **Raise*L2*Spool** | |
|---|---|
| *Indices* | |
| Machine: | Lifter*2 |
| Content: | Spool |
| Action: | Raise |
| Speed: | 2-Speed |
| Direction: | Up |
| Source: | Carry-Ht |
| Dest.: | Insert-Ht |
| : | : |

*Figure 3. A two-speed lifter case.*

The current example from Déjà Vu has attempted to describe two cases in terms of surface features, indicating the ACTION, MACHINE, and CONTENT of the cases. The problem is that the observed difference in ACTION types means that the cases are superficially different, even though both behaviourally and structurally the cases are very similar.

It is difficult to see how the MBR paradigm could cope with such problems without moving towards more knowledge intensive and computationally expensive similarity-based retrieval models; for example, using abstract features or feature transformation techniques.

## 4.2  Adaptation

The shortcomings of pure MBR do not stop with retrieval. Probably the most compelling and obvious argument against the shallow knowledge ideal of MBR has to do with the post-retrieval task; an example has been retrieved, it differs from the target in terms of a number of criteria, how can it can be adapted to provide the desired target solution? Without an elaborate "fixing" of representation it should be apparent that this adaptation process will not be adequate in an MBR system tackling a complex task.

Without domain knowledge of any form, adaptation is driven solely on the basis of the mappings generated during the matching stage of retrieval. These mappings are nothing more than correspondences between "similar" base and target features. Differences are captured in the form of base and target features that have failed to be associated with a  matching partner.  The limited inferencing power of this similarity/dissimilarity information can be used only to guide a straightforward substitution of target features with their matching base features.  The hope presumably being that such a superficial modification of the base example will yield the desired target solution. This will of course only work in simple domains.

Let us consider the problem of designing a single speed motion module in Déjà Vu as specified by Figure 4. The retrieval of the Advance*B1*Spool case means that the adaptation process must transform the two-speed structure into a single speed structure. The essential transformation is the removal of the "fast forward" speed control and the "deceleration" check.

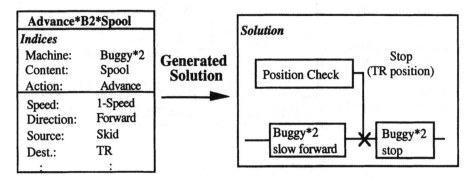

*Figure 4. Designing a single speed motion solution.*

This sort of modification is impossible without having domain knowledge available during the adaptation process. This is further illustrated with many more complex examples from Déjà Vu which rely of far more sophisticated adaptation; for example, arbitrary speed changes may effect a vehicle's fuel supply or particular routes while working for one vehicle may not work for another, due to size restrictions perhaps.

# 5   Conclusion

It this paper we have presented some examples of tasks for which we believe the pure MBR methodology will not be appropriate. For complex tasks in NLP and in planning an MBR system will not always be able to retrieve useful examples from memory nor will it be able to adapt solutions that are retrieved. In the first case, abstract features and domain knowledge are required to assess similarity. In the second case, a model of causal interactions is required in manipulating retrieved solutions.

These problems are not manifest in MBR systems presented to date because the comparatively simple domains chosen do not manifest the complex inter-dependencies that occur in more complex tasks.

We conclude that MBR can work well in situations where solutions are *atomic*, where solutions are expressible as a single symbol. MBR is less likely to perform well in situations where solutions have complex structure such as in the Déjà Vu example. MBR may be made to work in such situations by composing several components into a complex solution. However if the interactions and dependencies between the components are complex then an MBR approach will not be reliable as shown in the NLP examples in section 3.

Despite these criticisms we believe that MBR (or CBR systems without much domain knowledge) will have a significant impact in AI applications. For many tasks MBR does have tremendous advantages over traditional AI techniques—primarily because it does overcome many knowledge engineering problems. However MBR on its own is not an architecture for general intelligence. The idea of reasoning from examples stored in memory is valid but for more complex tasks it needs to be augmented with domain knowledge—like in CBR.

## References

Brugman, C. & Lakoff, G. 1988. "Cognitive Topology and Lexical Networks", in *Lexical Ambiguity Resolution*, edited by S. Small, G. Cottrell and M. Tanenhaus. San Mateo, CA: Morgan Kaufmann Publishers.

Cottrell, G. W. & S. Small. (1982). A Connectionist Scheme for Modelling Word-Sense Disambiguation. In *Cognition and Brain Theory* 6, pp 89-120.

Creecy R.H., Masand B.M., Smith S.J., Waltz D.L., (1992) "Trading MIPS and Memory for Knowledge Engineering: Automatic Classification of Census Returns on a Massively Parallel Supercomputer", *Communications of the ACM,* pp48-64, Vol. 35, No. 8, August 1992.

Evett M.P., Andersen W.A., Hendler J. A., (1993) "Massively Parallel Support for Efficient Knowledge Representation", In *Proceedings of IJCAI-93.*

Fass D., (1988). "An Account of Coherence, Semantic Relations, Metonymy, and Lexical Ambiguity Resolution", *Lexical Ambiguity Resolution: Perspectives from Psycholinguistics Neuropsychology and Artificial Intelligence* Small, S. I, G. W. Cottrell & M. K. Tanenhaus, eds., Morgan Kaufmann, San Mateo, CA.

Fikes, R. E., Hart, P. E., Nilsson, N. J. (1972). Learning and Executing Generalised Robot Plans, *Artificial Intelligence, 2,* 251-288

Jackendoff, R. (1991). Parts and Boundaries, *Lexical and Conceptual Semantics*, B. Levin and S. Pinker, eds. Elsevier Science Publishers, Amsterdam.

Kitano H., (1993) "Challenges of Massive Parallelism", Proceedings of the 13th. International Joint Conference on Artificial Intelligence, Chambery France, Morgan Kaufmann, pp813-834.

Kitano H., Higuchi T., (1991) "Massively Parallel Memory-Based Parsing", Proceedings of the 12th. International Joint Conference on Artificial Intelligence, Sydney Australia, Morgan Kaufmann, pp918-924.

Kolodner J.L, (1991), "Improving Human Decision Making Through Case-Based Decision Aiding", *AI Magazine*, Vol. 12, No. 2, Summer 1991, pp52-68.

Stanfill C., Waltz D., (1992) "Statistical Methods, Artificial Intelligence, and Information Retrieval", in *Text-Based Intelligent Systems*, P. Jacobs ed., pp215-225, Lawrence Earlbaum Associates, Hillsdale, New Jersey.

Stanfill C., Waltz D., (1986) "Toward Memory-Based Reasoning", *Communications of the ACM*, pp1213-1228, Vol. 29, No. 12, December 1986.

Smyth B., Cunningham P., (1992) "Déjà Vu: A Hierarchical Case-Based Reasoning System for Software Design", in *Proceedings of 10th. European Conference on Artificial Intelligence*, Vienna, Austria, ed. Bernd Neumann, Wiley & Son, pp587-589, 1992.

Veloso M., Carbonell J.G., (1991), "Learning by analogical replay in PRODIGY: first results", *European Working Session on Learning*, Y. Kodratoff, ed., pp375-389, Porto, Portugal, Springer Verlag.

Veale T., Keane M.T., (1992), "Conceptual Scaffolding: A Spatially Founded Meaning Representation for Metaphor Comprehension", *Computational Intelligence, 8*, 494-519.

# A Criterion of Comparison between two Case Bases

Jean Lieber

RFIA group
CRIN CNRS – INRIA Lorraine
B.P. 239 – 54506 Vandœuvre-lès-Nancy Cedex – France
(e-mail: lieber@loria.fr)

**Abstract.** This paper presents a criterion of comparison between two case bases for a case-based system for which the retrieval process is done thanks to a similarity metric. Such a criterion can be useful for at least two things. First, it allows to define what a better case base of a given size can be. Second it enables us to build a "forgetting criterion" which aims at answering the question "What are the $p$ cases that can be lost from the base that conduct to a minimal loss of performance?" The definition of case-based reasoning given in this paper stresses the fact that the goal of the similarity measure is to give an *a priori* estimation of the performance of the adaptation process. With an introducing example –the "locksmith's problem"– and then more generally, the criterion is defined thanks to a number associated with each case base; this number is characteristic of the mean performance of the system working with this base. It seems that very few results can be demonstrated without hypothesis on the representation of problems. For this reason, we have performed a study for two different types of representation of these problems (or on their associated indices). Finally we solve the locksmith's problem.

## 1 Introduction and Motivations

Most studies on case-based reasoning (Riesbeck & Schank, 1989; Kolodner, 1993) have concentrated on the processes of case-based reasoning systems (indexing techniques, case retrieval, case adaptation, etc.). Very few have worked on the construction of the case base. In (Porter, Bareiss, & Holte, 1990) an interactive process of construction of classes is described, but that is the expert who chooses which cases are to be given to the system. In (O'Leary, 1993), the author points out that the quality of a case base is linked to the diversity of the cases, which is linked to the similarities between cases of the base, but he does not detail any link between case base quality and similarity. In (Bradtke & Lehnert, 1988), the problem of how building an *effective* case base is raised.

In this paper a criterion of comparison of two case bases is described. This criterion only takes into account the measure of similarity –also called for the sake of simplicity a similarity[1]– between cases; that means that the only knowledge used here is this similarity.

---

[1] In fact, for technical reasons, a dissimilarity is used instead of a similarity, but this does not change anything since the change from one form to the other is very simple to make.

In most case-based systems with an adaptation process, the retrieval process gives as output the *best* case for the problem given in input. It is expected that this *best* case will give the best possible performances[2] for the adaptation module and for a given case base. For this reason we say that the notion of proximity underlying the retrieval process is a measure of the *a priori* performance of the adaptation.

Given this, for a case base $B$, a number $\Phi(B) \geq 0$ which is characteristic of the mean performance of the system can be defined,[3] and we have:

$$B_1 \text{ is said to be } better \text{ than } B_2 \text{ iff } \Phi(B_1) \leq \Phi(B_2). \tag{1}$$

In this paper, "case base" is synonymous with "finite set of cases": we do not take into account the structures of the base. More precisely, we assume that the role of such structures is to make a faster retrieval, and since we are not concerned with the running time of the retrieval, the notions linked to the organization of case bases are not needed in this paper.

This criterion of comparison between two case bases raises several interests. First, this criterion allows to define what a *best* case base of cardinal $n \in \mathbb{N}^*$ is. If this best case base can be computed, the system designer can encode it and he will obtain the most efficient system (for everything but the case base fixed), if $n$ is well-chosen.[4] In the following, such a case base is noted $B_n^*$. More generally, if a case base $B$ has been implemented, and if the implementer can make an effort of acquisition of $p$ cases, then the cases $c_1, c_2, \ldots c_p$ to be acquired are the ones realising the minimum of $\Phi(B \cup \{c_1, c_2, \ldots c_p\})$.[5] Second, this criterion allows to build a "forgetting criterion": given a case base $B$ of cardinal $N$, if we want to keep of $B$ only a subpart $b^*$ of cardinal $n < N$, then the best way to do it is to take among the subparts $b$ of $B$ of cardinal $n$, the subpart $b^*$ which minimizes $\Phi$. For instance, for a case base $B$, if the system has built a new case $c_0$ and if we want to keep a constant size of the case base, then the calculation of the $\Phi((B \cup \{c_0\}) - \{c_i\})$ for $c_i \in B \cup \{c_0\}$ enables us to make the best choice (i.e. the argument of $\Phi$ which gives a minimum value). This forgetting criterion belongs to the general framework of information filtering as defined in (Markovitch & Scott, 1993); more precisely it is an approach of selective retention. Among these two problems, we have more studied the first one.

Before defining this criterion, we give a model of the case-based reasoning process oriented to our purpose. An introducing example close to problems we want to solve follows. In this section, the criterion is given for this specific example. Then the criterion of comparison between two case bases is immediatly

---

[2] What we call performance depends on the nature of the system. For example, it can be the time necessary to reach a valid solution (see for instance (Veloso, 1994)).

[3] See Sect. 4 for a definition of $\Phi$.

[4] We assume that the time performance of the retrieval depends only on the size of the case base.

[5] This is possible because $\Phi$ only uses the "problem parts" of the cases for its calculation, not their solutions.

obtained by generalisation. Some theoretical and empirical results are given, and finally we discuss our work from the point of view of its scope.

## 2  A Way to Model Case-Based Reasoning

In this section, we give a general definition of case-based reasoning oriented to our purpose which aims to stress what is the meaning of the dissimilarity used for the case retrieval. This definition does not take notions such as multiple cases and loops in the algorithm into account, since these notions are not used in this article. Moreover, we assume a case to be splitted up into two parts: one containing the problem to be solved, and the other a solution to this problem.[6] Therefore, a case can be seen as a pair (problem, solution).

Let $\mathcal{P}$ be the set of all possible problems. Let $S$ be the set of all possible solutions (i.e. $S$ contains every solution of each problem of $\mathcal{P}$, and maybe more). Let $\mathcal{A} \subseteq \mathcal{P}^2$ be a set of binary relations containing $\Delta_{\mathcal{P}^2}$, the relation of equality on $\mathcal{P}$. An element $\alpha \in \mathcal{A}$ is said to be an analogical relation. Intuitively, if we have the relation $p \, \alpha \, p_k$ for $p, p_k \in \mathcal{P}$ and $\alpha \in \mathcal{A}$ then a reason why $p$ and $p_k$ are close is given by the semantics of $\alpha$. Moreover, we assume we have a mapping $\alpha \in \mathcal{A} \mapsto F_\alpha$ where $F_\alpha$ is a computable mapping from a subset of $\mathcal{P} \times (\mathcal{P} \times S)$ into $S$. We assume we have a mapping $M : \alpha \in \mathcal{A} \mapsto M(\alpha) \in \mathbb{R}_+$, such that: $M(\alpha) = 0$ iff $\alpha = \Delta_{\mathcal{P}^2}$, and, for $\alpha_1, \alpha_2 \in \mathcal{A}, \alpha_1 \subseteq \alpha_2 \Rightarrow M(\alpha_1) \leq M(\alpha_2)$. We assume also that the semantics of the mapping $M$ is the estimation of the performances of the mappings $F_\alpha$: the performance of $F_\alpha$ is measured *inversely* by $M(\alpha)$ (a high performance is measured by a low number). Then the different steps of a case-based reasoning process are the following ones:

- **Input:** a problem $p \in \mathcal{P}$ and a case base $\mathcal{B} = \{(p_1, s_2), (p_2, s_2), \ldots (p_n, s_n)\}$
- **Case retrieval:** Among the relations $\alpha \in \mathcal{A}$ realising: $\exists \, (p_k, s_k) \in \mathcal{B}, p \, \alpha \, p_k \wedge Conditions(p, p_k, s_k)$, where $Conditions$ is a domain-dependent predicate, choose $\alpha$ which makes $M(\alpha)$ minimal.[7] The output of the case retrieval is such an $\alpha$ with an associated $(p_k, s_k)$.
- **Case adaptation:** $s = F_\alpha(p, (p_k, s_k))$ is computed and given as output of the adaptation process.
- **Tests and corrections:** The solution $s$ is tested and corrected to give a *good* solution $s^*$.
- **Case storage:** $(p, s^*)$ is stored in the case base
- **Output:** the solution $s^*$

With such a definition of case-based reasoning, we introduce the dissimilarity[8]

---

[6] We assume that the indications of the trace leading to a solution are contained in this solution.

[7] The assumption made here is that such a minimal element exists and can be found.

[8] According to (Diday, Lemaire, Pouget, & Testu, 1982), a dissimilarity on a set $\Omega$ is a mapping $d : \Omega^2 \to \mathbb{R}_+$ which is symmetric and such that $\forall (x, y) \in \Omega^2, [d(x, y) = 0 \Leftrightarrow (x = y)]$. In this paper we do not assume a dissimilarity to be symmetric: as mentioned in (Jantke & Lange, 1993), this is not a valid hypothesis in general for case-based systems.

$d$ defined for $(p_1, p_2) \in \mathcal{P}^2$ by:

$$d(p_1, p_2) = \min\{M(\alpha) \mid \alpha \in \mathcal{A} \land p_1 \; \alpha \; p_2\} \qquad (2)$$

Then if we have $p \in \mathcal{P}$ and $(p_k, s_k) \in \mathcal{B}$, with the semantics of $M$ given above, and if $Conditions(p, p_k, s_k)$ holds, then the *a priori* estimation of the performance of the adaptation process is $d(p, p_k)$; this is the most important point of this definition of case-based reasoning.

In the following we will concentrate on the systems for which this dissimilarity does not change during time, which means that $\mathcal{A}$ and $M$ do not change during time. Moreover we assume that $Conditions(p, p_k, s_k)$ is true for each $(p, p_k, s_k) \in \mathcal{P} \times \mathcal{P} \times \mathcal{S}$.

More generally we will concentrate on the case-based systems for which the retrieval is done thanks to a nearest neighbor matching such that it is expected that most of the time if a case $C^1$ is closer to a given problem $p$ than a case $C^2$ according to this nearest neighbor matching, then the adaptation of $C^1$ to $p$ will be *better* (in computing time or from the point of view of the result) than the adaptation of $C^2$ to $p$. This does *not* necessarily mean that the retrieval is an adaptation guided retrieval (as described in (Smyth & Keane, 1994)): it can be a more classical case retrieval using a similarity measure (or a dissimilarity). If the dissimilarity $d$ can be parameterised by a set of weights, then these weights can be learned by the system to provide a better retrieval in the above sense and that will conduct to a better behavior of the system (in term of performance). If the adaptation module is not implemented, then we assume that the user does such an adaptation.

## 3　An Introductory Example

This example aims at illustrating the notions of the next section with the model of the previous section. The problem is the following. A locksmith wants to create keys for his customers. In order to do that, he uses several key moulds which gives him precisely dimensioned keys. If a customer asks him for a key of given dimensions, he makes a bigger key using his moulds and then removes some matter to obtain the desired key.

For our purpose, we assume a key to be an object in the three real-world dimensions, as described in Fig. 1, with characteristics $x$ and $y$. Since the depth is considered to be constant, a key $\gamma$ can be represented by a pair $(x, y) \in \{1, 2, \ldots 5\} \times \{1, 2, \ldots 10\}$ (in millimeters, for instance).[9] For the locksmith, the inputs are the characteristics of a key $\gamma$, the retrieval process gives a mould $\gamma_k$ and the adaptation process aims at giving the desired key. The work to be done is measured by the quantity of matter to be removed if the desired key can be obtained by matter removal. If it is not possible to obtain the desired key, then

---

[9] We have chosen discrete dimensions of the keys because that conducts to an easier way to calculate what follows.

the measure of this work is $+\infty$. Therefore the work to be done is:

$$d(\gamma, \gamma_k) = \begin{cases} x_k(x_k + 4y_k) - x(x + 4y) \text{ if } \gamma \subseteq \gamma_k \\ +\infty \qquad\qquad\qquad\qquad \text{else} \end{cases} \tag{3}$$

We assume that the unit of work is chosen such that the work is exactly measured by this formula. Two keys –or moulds– $\gamma_1$ and $\gamma_2$ satisfy $\gamma_1 \subseteq \gamma_2$ iff $\gamma_1$ can be made with matter removal from $\gamma_2$, i.e.: $x_1 \leq x_2$ and $x_1 + 2y_1 \leq x_2 + 2y_2$.

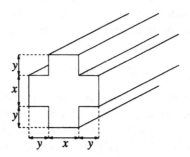

**Fig. 1.** A key defined by its characteristics $x$ and $y$ (the depth is constant)

With the notations of the preceding section, we have:

$$\mathcal{P} = \mathcal{S} = \{1, 2, \ldots 5\} \times \{1, 2, \ldots 10\} \tag{4}$$

$$\mathcal{A} = \{\alpha \mid \alpha = \{(\gamma_1, \gamma_2)\}, (\gamma_1, \gamma_2) \in \mathcal{P}^2, \gamma_1 \subseteq \gamma_2\} \tag{5}$$

$$\forall \alpha \in \mathcal{A}, M(\alpha) = d(\gamma_1, \gamma_2) \text{ for } \alpha = \{(\gamma_1, \gamma_2)\} \tag{6}$$

The dissimilarity $d$ defined by (3) and the definition of $M$ in (6) is consistent with their definitions in Sect. 2. The predicate *Conditions* is here always true.

Now we consider a locksmith who wants to have $n$ moulds $\gamma_1, \gamma_2, \ldots \gamma_n$ in order to make his keys with $n$ a given integer. He assumes that the requests of his customers can be modeled by a random variable $\Gamma$ defined by the mapping $p :$ $\mathcal{P} \to [0, 1]$, with $p(\gamma)$ the probability that the next key requested by a customer will be $\gamma$. Let $\mathcal{B} \subseteq \mathcal{P}$ be a base of moulds. The retrieved case $\gamma_k$ realises $d(\gamma, \gamma_k) \leq$ $d(\gamma, \gamma_j)$ for each $\gamma_j \in \mathcal{B}$, $\gamma$ being the input. Consequently the adaptation work will be $d(\gamma, \gamma_k)$. With the classical notation $\delta(x, F) = \min\{\delta(x, y) \mid y \in F\}$ for a dissimilarity $\delta$, we have then: $d(\gamma, \mathcal{B})$ is the adaptation work. With this we can define the random function $d(\Gamma, \mathcal{B})$, for each $\mathcal{B} \subseteq \mathcal{P}$. The expectation of this function defines $\Phi$:

$$\forall \mathcal{B} \subseteq \mathcal{P}, \Phi(\mathcal{B}) = E[d(\Gamma, \mathcal{B})] \tag{7}$$

The locksmith wants to have exactly $n$ moulds (he is ready to buy exactly $n$ moulds, and the cost of one mould does not depend on its dimensions). He also wants to have the minimum of work to do for adapting a key. The expectation of his work is $\Phi(\mathcal{B})$, and then the locksmith's problem is to find $\mathcal{B}_n^* \subseteq \mathcal{P}$ such that:

$$|\mathcal{B}_n^*| = n \wedge \forall \mathcal{B} \subseteq \mathcal{P}, |\mathcal{B}| = n \Rightarrow \Phi(\mathcal{B}_n^*) \leq \Phi(\mathcal{B}) \tag{8}$$

In 5.2 several solutions for specific values of $n$ are given.

# 4  Criterion of Comparison of two Case Bases

In this section, as in Sect. 2, we assume we have a case-based system with the retrieval of a best case done thanks to a dissimilarity $d$. Moreover we assume that for $p \in \mathcal{P}$ and for a case $(p_k, s_k) \in \mathcal{P} \times \mathcal{S}$, $d(p, p_k)$ gives a inverse measure of the performance of the adaptation process for the input $(p, (p_k, s_k))$, i.e. for a low $d(p, p_k)$ we have a high performance. We want to have an expectation of the performance of the system. For this we assume that the user can be modeled by a random variable $X$ which is known. Then, as in previous section, the random function $d(X, \mathcal{B})$ gives the performance of the system and its expectation defines the mapping $\Phi$, for each case base $\mathcal{B}$:

$$\Phi(\mathcal{B}) = E[d(X, \mathcal{B})] \tag{9}$$

And the criterion of comparison of two case bases is given by (1).

The assumption made here is that $d(x, \mathcal{B})$ is a *good* estimation of the performance of the case-based system. Indeed for some strictly increasing functions $\theta : [0, +\infty[ \to [0, +\infty[$, $\theta \circ d(x, \mathcal{B})$ gives also an estimation of the performance of the system, but it can be the case that: $E[d(X, \mathcal{B}_1)] < E[d(X, \mathcal{B}_2)]$ and $E[\theta \circ d(X, \mathcal{B}_1)] \geq E[\theta \circ d(X, \mathcal{B}_2)]$. In other words, the criterion depends on the function $\theta$ (and on other parameters not mentioned here), and we assume that we have chosen $d$ such that we have a *good* criterion.

# 5  Some Results

Given this criterion, our goal is to find a best case base of cardinal $n$, $\mathcal{B}_n^*$. Since this criterion does not take solutions to the problems into account, a case base can be considered, for simplifying reasons, as a subset of $\mathcal{P}$. In practice, only the finite subsets of $\mathcal{P}$ are to be considered, but this is not theoretically necessary. Therefore the set of case bases is $2^{\mathcal{P}}$.

## 5.1  Theoretical Results

After a brief study of the general case, we make assumptions on the representation of the problems. First we assume that every problem can be represented by vectors of reals, and then by vectors of booleans. An outline of the proofs of these results is given in appendix.

**General Results.** Few results can be given in a very general case. We give two of them.

The first result is the decreasing of $\Phi$:

$$\forall \mathcal{B}_1, \mathcal{B}_2 \in 2^{\mathcal{P}}, [\mathcal{B}_1 \subseteq \mathcal{B}_2 \Rightarrow \Phi(\mathcal{B}_1) \geq \Phi(\mathcal{B}_2)] \tag{10}$$

This result means that if we do not take the performance of the retrieval process into account, and if we assume that the processes do not change during case-based reasoning, then the system improves itself when the case base grows.

The second result is the following:

$$\Phi(\mathcal{P}) = 0 \tag{11}$$

This result simply means that if the system knows the solution of each problem it is likely to be asked, then the performance of the adaptation process is the highest (there is nothing to adapt !).

**When $\mathcal{P}$ is a Subset of a Vectorial Space on $\mathbb{R}$.** It seems to be difficult to give more interesting results while staying at the highest level of abstraction, that is why restricting ourselves to more specific cases appears to be necessary. In this paragraph, we assume that $\mathcal{P}$ is a subset of a vectorial space $\mathcal{E}$ of finite dimension $m$ on $\mathbb{R}$. The random variable $X$, defined in Sect. 4, is there characterized by the measure $\mu$ on $\mathcal{E}$ which values can be positive reals or distributions (e.g. Dirac distribution), and such that $\mu(x) = 0$ for all $x \in \mathcal{E} - \mathcal{P}$. This representation with real numbers and distributions makes it possible to work either on continuous or on discrete sets of cases with the same mathematical representation. Thus for $\mathcal{B} \in 2^{\mathcal{P}}$:

$$\Phi(\mathcal{B}) = \int_{\mathcal{E}} d(x, \mathcal{B}) \cdot d\mu(x) = \int_{\mathcal{E}} d(x, \mathcal{B}) \cdot \mu(x) \cdot dx \tag{12}$$

With these hypotheses two results have been demonstrated, but first we have to introduce the notion of *retrieval zone*. For a case base $\mathcal{B}$ and for $y_0 \in \mathcal{B}$, what we call the retrieval zone of $y_0$ for the case base $\mathcal{B}$ is defined by:

$$\mathcal{Z}(y_0, \mathcal{B}) = \{x \in \mathcal{E} \mid \forall y \in \mathcal{B} - \{y_0\}, d(x, y_0) \le d(x, y)\} \tag{13}$$

$\mathcal{Z}(y_0, \mathcal{B})$ contains all the problems for which $y_0$ is retrieved among the elements of $\mathcal{B}$. Since some $x \in \mathcal{E}$ are shared by (at least) two retrieval zones, such an $x$ belongs to both retrieval zones. Such an $x$ corresponds to a problem for which the dissimilarity cannot establish which is the nearest case in the case base. These retrieval zones are also called Voronoi cells and the union of the boundaries of these cells is called the Voronoi diagram of $\mathcal{B}$ (see e.g. (Evans & Stojmenović, 1989)). We define also the notion of *strict retrieval zone* $\overset{\circ}{\mathcal{Z}}(y_0, \mathcal{B})$ by replacing "$\le$" by "$<$" in (13).

The first result is the following. We assume that $\mu$ is uniform on $\mathcal{P}$ and is null elsewhere with $\mu(\mathcal{P}) \ne 0$, we assume that $d$ is a distance defined thanks to a norm, and that there is some $r > 0$, some $\mathcal{B}_0 \in 2^{\mathcal{P}}$, $\mathcal{B}_0$ being a finite set of cardinal $n$, such that each $\overset{\circ}{\mathcal{Z}}(y, \mathcal{B}_0)$ for $y \in \mathcal{B}_0$ is an opened ball of $\mathcal{E}$ centered in $y$ of radius $r$ for the distance $d$. Then $\mathcal{B}_0$ is a best base of cardinal $n$. Moreover if the conditions of this result are satisfied for a distance $d$, then we have the same result with a dissimilarity $\theta \circ d$ with $\theta$ any strictly increasing function $[0, +\infty[ \to [0, +\infty[$ such that $\theta(0) = 0$.

An example can be useful to understand this result. Suppose we have $d$ defined by: $d(x, y) = \max_{i=1,2,\dots m} |y_i - x_i|$, the $x_i$ (respectively the $y_i$) being the coordinates of $x$ (respectively $y$) in a given base of the vectorial space. A property of this distance is that $\mathcal{E}$ can be covered by closed balls with the same radius, such that the intersection of two different balls has a measure null. Then, with some more hypotheses on $\mathcal{P}$ and $X$, a best case base can be found. Figure 2 gives an example of such a case base.[10]

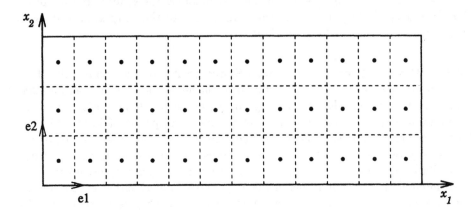

**Fig. 2.** A best base of cardinal 36 for $d$ defined by $d(x,y) = \max_{i=1,2} |y_i - x_i|$ with $x = x_1 \cdot e1 + x_2 \cdot e2$ and $y = y_1 \cdot e1 + y_2 \cdot e2$ (the big points are the cases of the base and the dashed lines constitute the Voronoi diagram of this base with such a distance)

The second result[11] takes as hypothesis that $d$ is defined by $d(x,y) = [\delta(x,y)]^2$ with $\delta$ an Euclidian distance on $\mathcal{E}$. We make no assumption on $\mu$ (its values can be reals or distributions). Let $n \in \mathbb{N}^*$, and $\mathcal{B}^* = \{y_1, y_2, \ldots y_n\}$ a best case base of cardinal $n$ (it can be proved that such a base exists). First, it can be shown that the boundaries of the $\mathcal{Z}(y_i, \mathcal{B}^*)$ are of measure null:

$$\forall i = 1, 2, \ldots n, \mu(\mathcal{Z}(y_i, \mathcal{B}^*) - \overset{\circ}{\mathcal{Z}}(y_i, \mathcal{B}^*)) = 0 \tag{14}$$

Second, it can be shown that $\mathcal{B}^*$ follows the following fix point equation, with $Z_i = \mathcal{Z}(y_i, \mathcal{B}^*)$:

$$\forall y \in \mathcal{B}^*, y = \frac{1}{\mu(Z_i)} \cdot \int_{Z_i} x \cdot d\mu(x) \tag{15}$$

in other words: if $\mathcal{B}^*$ is a best case base of cardinal $n$, then each $y \in \mathcal{B}^*$ is the gravity center of $\mathcal{Z}(y, \mathcal{B}^*)$.

**When $\mathcal{P}$ is $\{0,1\}^m$.** The assumption made in this paragraph is that the representation of the problems used to make case retrieval is a $m$-dimension

---

[10] More things could be said about the possible values of $n$ and the conditions required on $\mathcal{P}$ to make this possible, but we think that such a study would be beyond the scope of this paper.

[11] This result is extracted from the work Jean-Pierre Deschaseaux did on this subject.

boolean vector, $m \in \mathbb{N}^*$. That does not involve that the complete representation of a problem is so simple, but that means that the problem is indexed in this simple way, and for simplifying reasons, we do not use a different notation for a problem and for its index. The semantics of the dissimilarities used in case-based systems are often linked with notions of sharing of informations. For this reason, the dissimilarity we use here is the Hamming distance:

$$d(x, y) = \sum_{k=1}^{m} x_k \oplus y_k \tag{16}$$

where $\oplus$ is the exclusive or on $\{0, 1\}$.

A case base $\mathcal{B}$ of cardinal $n$ can be represented by a $m \times n$ matrix $Y = [y_{ij}], i = 1, 2 \ldots m, j = 1, 2, \ldots n$, with $y_{ij} \in \{0, 1\}$. An element of $\mathcal{B}$ is noted $y_{.j}$, $\Phi(\mathcal{B})$ is noted $F(Y)$, and we have:

$$F(Y) = \Phi(\mathcal{B}) = \sum_{x \in P} \min_{j=1,2,\ldots n} d(x, y_{.j}) \cdot p(x) \tag{17}$$

Let $\mathcal{M}$ be the set of $m \times n$ matrices, and let $D$ be the distance on $\mathcal{M}$ defined by:

$$D(A, B) = \sum_{j=1,2,\ldots n} d(a_{.j}, b_{.j}) = \sum_{(i,j) \in \{1,2,\ldots m\} \times \{1,2,\ldots n\}} a_{ij} \oplus b_{ij} \tag{18}$$

For this distance, the smallest sphere of center $A \in \mathcal{M}$ different from $\{A\}$ is constituted by the matrices obtained by changing exactly one component of $A$. For this reason, we introduce the mappings $t_{ab} : \mathcal{M} \to \mathcal{M}$, such that $t_{ab}(A)$ is the matrix obtained by changing the component of the $a^{th}$ line and $b^{th}$ column in $A$, and keeping the values of the other components.

We try to search a matrix $Y^*$ which minimizes $F$. For this we use a hill-climbing method: we start with a matrix $Y_0$ chosen randomly, and we choose among the nearest matrix (that is $Y_0$ and the $t_{ab}(Y_0)$) the one which has the smallest $F(Y)$. Let $Y_1$ be such a matrix. If $Y_1 = Y_0$ then it is terminated, else, the process continues.

What must be calculated at each step is $F(t_{ab}(Y)) - F(Y)$. Since the change between $t_{ab}(Y)$ and $Y$ is local, this can be calculated without calculating $F(t_{ab}(Y))$ and $F(Y)$ (which may be very expensive). With $\widehat{Y} = t_{ab}(Y)$ we have:

$$F(\widehat{Y}) - F(Y) = \sum_{x \in P} \left[ \min_{j=1,2,\ldots n} d(x, \widehat{y_{.j}}) - \min_{j=1,2,\ldots n} d(x, y_{.j}) \right] \cdot p(x) \tag{19}$$

It can be shown that a necessary condition on $x$ for having a non-zero term in the sum above is that $x \in \mathcal{Z}(y_{.b}, Y)$, with $\mathcal{Z}(y_{.b}, Y)$ defined by (13).[12] As $\mathcal{Z}(y_{.b}, Y)$ does not depend on $a$, this set has to be calculated only one time for the different values of $a$ (for instance by testing each $x \in P$, but there are maybe

---

[12] In fact, we should have written $\mathcal{Z}(y_{.b}, \mathcal{B})$, $\mathcal{B}$ being the case base associated with $Y$.

better ways to do it). Moreover, for $x \in \mathcal{Z}(y._b, Y)$, the term $T$ under the sum can be calculated by:

$$\text{if } x \in \overset{\circ}{\mathcal{Z}}(y._b, Y) \text{ or } d(x, \widehat{y._b}) < d(x, y._b)$$
$$\text{then (if } x_a = y_{ab} \text{ then } T = p(x) \text{ else } T = -p(x))$$
$$\text{else } T = 0 \qquad (20)$$

Since $F(Y_{p+1}) < F(Y_p)$, and $\mathcal{M}$ is finite, the process reach a matrix $Y^*$ in finite time. Unfortunately, $Y^*$ is only a local optimum. That involves that $Y^*$ depends on the choose of $Y_0$.

## 5.2 Empirical Results

This subsection deals with solutions to the locksmith's problem defined in Sect. 3.
For this problem and for a base of moulds $\mathcal{B}$, we have:

$$\Phi(\mathcal{B}) = E[d(\Gamma, \mathcal{B})] = \sum_{\gamma \in \mathcal{P}} d(\gamma, \mathcal{B}) \cdot p(\gamma) \qquad (21)$$

We assume that $p$ is uniform on $\mathcal{P}$.
A simple program computes for several values of $n$ what are the best case bases $\mathcal{B}_n^*$. The results are given by Table 1. Figure 3 represents the best set of moulds for $n = 6$.

| $n$ | $\mathcal{B}_n^*$ | $\Phi(\mathcal{B}_n^*)$ |
|---|---|---|
| 1 | $\{(5, 10)\}$ | 148 |
| 2 | $\{(3, 9); (5, 10)\}$ | 87.52 |
| 3 | $\{(2, 10); (5, 5); (5, 10)\}$ | 59.6 |
| 4 | $\{(2, 10); (5, 2); (5, 6); (5, 10)\}$ | 47.34 |
| 5 | $\{(1, 10); (3, 10); (5, 3); (5, 6); (5, 10)\}$ and $\{(1, 10); (3, 10); (5, 3); (5, 7); (5, 10)\}$ | 39.36 |
| 6 | $\{(1, 10); (2, 10); (4, 9); (5, 2); (5, 5); (5, 10)\}$ | 32.36 |
| 7 | $\{(1, 10); (2, 9); (3, 10); (5, 2); (5, 4); (5, 7); (5, 10)\}$ | 28.2 |
| 8 | $\{(1, 10); (2, 10); (3, 9); (4, 2); (4, 10); (5, 3); (5, 6); (5, 10)\}$ | 24.58 |

**Table 1.** Best bases of moulds of cardinal $n$ ($n = 1, 2, \ldots 8$) for the locksmith's problem

The algorithm used to compute these results was not designed to be efficient: for a given $n$, $\Phi(\mathcal{B})$ was calculated for each $\mathcal{B}$, base of cardinal $n$ containing the key $(5, 10)$, and only the best bases were kept. What we expect to study is the complexity in time of the search of a best case base without using complicated methods. Of course, the time taken grows with $n$. In order to give an idea, the running time for $n = 8$ was about three days on a Sun 4-20 station.

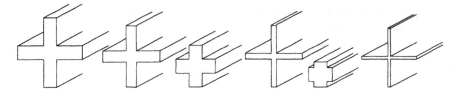

**Fig. 3.** $\mathcal{B}_6^*$: the best base of 6 moulds

## 6 Discussion

In this section, we discuss the scope of our work. First we present several limitations of it, then we outline some ideas about this scope.

The most obvious limitation of this criterion lays in the difficulties of calculation it involves. For problems that cannot be indexed in a simple way, this criterion can be very difficult to implement. Fortunately, the representation of problems themselves and the representation of their solutions can be very complex, what is important is only that the structures on which the retrieval is made are simple. Even for a simple representation like the ones proposed in 5.1, if we have a method to solve the problem, its naïve implementation can be very time-consuming. One way to bypass this problem is to make some simplification hypotheses. In fact, this is what has been done for the locksmith's problem: we could have assumed that the set of keys (or moulds) was the continuous – and infinite– set $[0, 5] \times [1, 10]$, the discrete –and finite– set taken giving only a simplification of the continuous set.

An other limitation is linked to the hypothesis that the dissimilarity enables to build a *good* estimation of the performance of the case-based system. This point is discussed at the end of Sect. 4. More generally, the hypotheses made while building this criterion limit its scope.

The next limitation is linked to the hypothesis that a case base is a "flat" set of cases. Indeed, for most case-based reasoning systems a case base is given by a set of cases and by a hierarchy on this set. Not taking into account such hierarchies means that the retrieval made thanks to the dissimilarity $d$ gives the same result than a retrieval using such a hierarchy, the only difference being at the level of the computing time.

The fact that the criterion is built on a global mark of a case base involves an other limitation: when two case bases are compared, the criterion gives a way to decide which is the better one but it does not explain why.

The last limitation we have noticed is linked with the fact that each case is considered equally. That means that the amount of reusable information is considered as being the same for each case.

It seems difficult to characterize simply what systems are well-suited for this criterion. A simple representation (e.g. vector of reals, vector of booleans) of the part of the problem used for case retrieval seems to give a more easily computable criterion. Indeed, without more theoretical results, it seems that calculating this criterion for complex structure such as graphs is difficult. The simplest thing to do while handling such knowledge representation is to change their representation into a simpler one (with loss of information) and to work on this simpler representation. In fact, that is sometimes what is done when an index is calculated from a case.

## 7 Conclusion

In this paper we have proposed a criterion to compare two case bases from the point of view of the behavior of the adaptation process in a case-based reasoning system: the better base from two bases is the one which will maximize the a priori estimation of this process performance. This criterion gives first a definition of what is a best case base of a given size and second what are the $p$ cases that can be forgotten from a base with a minimal loss of performance. We have presented some theoretical results and have discussed the scope of this work.

This criterion can be seen as a dispersion criterion: it measures how a case base is dispersed while taking the probability of a problem to be asked to the system into account. In that view, what we could call a *good example* (or a *good case*) is an example that is not too close to the other examples.

The search of a best case base of a given cardinal when the set of cases or indices is a vectorial space (see 5.1) can be seen as a problem of vector quantisation (see e.g. (Huang, Ariki, & Jack, 1990)).

This criterion is based on an expectation about the behavior of the system: we want the system to have a good behavior in the average. We could also have wanted the system to have a regular behavior. For instance if we take as performance of the system an estimation of the time taken by the system to reach a solution, it can be appreciated to have an almost constant time. For doing this, in the definition of $\Phi$ ((9) in Sect. 4), instead of using an expectation, one can use a variance. We can also have a composite criterion using both expectation and variance.

As one can see, the problems presented in this paper are far from being completely solved. In fact, the main aim of this paper is to present some problems that are usually not taken into consideration, and some possible ways to solve them.

## Appendix: Outline of the Proofs

In this appendix, we give some indications to build the proofs of the results given in Sect. 5.

The proofs of the general results in 5.1 are very simple to build just by applying the definitions and using the two following properties of an expectation:

$$\text{if for all } x, \ f(x) \leq g(x), \text{ then } E[f(X)] \leq E[g(X)] \qquad \text{and} \qquad E[0] = 0 \quad (22)$$

$\square$

The hypothesis of the first result in the paragraph of 5.1 concerning the case when $\mathcal{P}$ is a vectorial space on $\mathbb{R}$ can be given as follows: $X$ is uniform on $\mathcal{P}$, $\mu(\mathcal{P}) \neq 0$, $d$ is defined by $d(x, y) = \theta(\|y - x\|)$ for $x, y \in \mathcal{P}$, for a norm denoted by

$\| \cdot \|$ and for a given increasing function $\theta : [0, +\infty[ \to [0, +\infty[$ realising $\theta(0) = 0$. Moreover it is assumed that there is a case base $B_0$ and a number $r > 0$ such that for each $y \in B_0$, $\overset{\circ}{Z}(y, B_0) = \beta(y, r)$, with $\beta(\omega, \varrho)$ the opened ball of $\mathcal{E}$ centered in $\omega$ with radius $\varrho$. To prove that $B_0$ is a better case base (of cardinal $n = |B_0|$), we first prove:

$$\text{for each case base } B, \Phi(B) = \sum_{y \in B} \int_{\overset{\circ}{Z}(y, B)} d(x, y) \cdot dx \qquad (23)$$

(this is true because $X$ is uniform on $\mathcal{P}$). Then using the notation $F_{y,Z}(\varrho) = \int_{Z \cap \sigma(y, \varrho)} 1$, with $\sigma(\omega, \varrho)$, the sphere centered in $\omega$ with radius $\varrho$, we prove that for $Z \subseteq \mathcal{P}$, $y \in B_0$ and $\varrho > 0$:

$$\int_Z dx = \int_{\beta(y, \varrho)} dx \quad \Rightarrow \quad \int_Z d(x, y) \cdot dx \geq \int_{\beta(y, \varrho)} d(x, y) \cdot dx \qquad (24)$$

(this can be proven by writing $\int_Z d(x, y) \cdot dx = \int_0^R \varrho \cdot F_{y,Z}(\varrho) \cdot d\varrho$). Let $B$ be a case base of cardinal $n = |B_0|$. Let for $y \in B$, $r_y > 0$ such that $\int_{\beta(y, r_y)} dx = \int_{\overset{\circ}{Z}(y, B)} dx$. Using (23) and (24), it is easy to show that $\Phi(B) \geq \sum_{y \in B} \int_{\beta(y, r_y)} d(x, y) \cdot dx$. Then with $F(\varrho) = F_{\omega, \mathcal{E}}(r)$ (for any $\omega$) it can be shown:

$$\Phi(B) - \Phi(B_0) \geq \sum_{y \in B} \left( \int_0^{r_y} \varrho \cdot F(\varrho) \cdot d\varrho - \int_0^r \varrho \cdot F(\varrho) \cdot d\varrho \right) \qquad (25)$$

Finally it can be shown that the term in the sum in the above expression is greater or equal to $r \cdot \int_r^{r_y} F(\varrho) \cdot d\varrho$, and since $\sum_{y \in B} \int_r^{r_y} F(\varrho) \cdot d\varrho = \int_{\mathcal{P}} 1 - \int_{\mathcal{P}} 1 = 0$ that ends the proof.
$\square$

The second result[13] of this paragraph of 5.1 takes as assumption that $d$ is the square of an Euclidian distance. Let $B^*$ be a best case base of cardinal $n$. Let $y \in B^*$ and $U$ such that $\overset{\circ}{Z}(y, B^*) \subseteq U \subseteq Z(y, B^*)$. Let $\omega$ be the gravity center of $U$. According to Huygens theorem, we have:

$$\int_U d(x, y) \cdot d\mu(x) = \int_U d(x, \omega) \cdot d\mu(x) + \mu(U) \cdot d(y, \omega) \qquad (26)$$

Using the fact that $\mu(U) \cdot d(y, \omega) \geq 0$ and making the sum for $y \in B^*$ we obtain: $\Phi(B^*) \geq \Phi(\{\omega_1, \ldots \omega_n\})$ the $\omega_i$ being the gravity centers of the $U$s. Since $B^*$ is optimal, we can deduce from (26) that for each $y$ and for each $U$ such that $\overset{\circ}{Z}(y, B^*) \subseteq U \subseteq Z(y, B^*)$, $\mu(U) \cdot d(y, \omega) = 0$. Then either $y = \omega$ or $\mu(U) = 0$. Hence, in each case: $\mu(Z(y, B^*) - \overset{\circ}{Z}(y, B^*)) = 0$, and this shows (14). Then using an equality analogous to (23), it can be shown that the gravity centers $\omega$ (calculated for instance for $U = Z(y, B^*)$) are equal to their corresponding

---

[13] due to Jean-Pierre Deschaseaux

$y \in \mathcal{B}^*$ and this is (15).

□

The result given by (19) and (20) is easy to prove just by using the definitions.

□

## Acknowledgements

The author would first like to thank Jean-Pierre Deschaseaux who accepted with the enthousiasm that characterizes him to examine this work from a mathematical point of view. Several results are due to him (the only thing quoted there is the result given by (14) and (15)). The author would also like to thank Stéphane Durand, Jean-Paul Haton, Jean-François Mari, Pierre Marquis, Amedeo Napoli and Olivier Siohan for their encouragements, advices and corrections, and the referees whose suggestions and comments greatly contributed to improve the preliminary versions of this paper. Finally, acknowledgments are due to the *Institut de Recherches Servier* for its financial support.

## References

Bradtke, S., & Lehnert, W. G. (1988). Some Experiments With Case-based Search. In *Proceedings of the Seventh National Conference on Artificial Intelligence (AAAI'88)*, Vol. 1, pp. 133–138 Saint-Paul (Minnesota).

Diday, E., Lemaire, J., Pouget, J., & Testu, F. (1982). *Éléments d'analyse de données*. Dunod.

Evans, D. J., & Stojmenović, I. (1989). On parallel computation of Voronoi diagrams. *Parallel Computing*, *12*, 121–125.

Huang, X. D., Ariki, Y., & Jack, M. A. (1990). *Vector Quantisation and Mixture Densities*, chap. 4, pp. 111–135. Edinburgh University Press.

Jantke, K. P., & Lange, S. (1993). Case-Based Representation and Learning of Pattern Languages. In *Proceedings of the first European Workshop on Case-Based Reasoning*.

Kolodner, J. (1993). *Case-Based Reasoning*. Morgan Kaufmann, Inc.

Markovitch, S., & Scott, P. D. (1993). Information Filtering: Selection Mechanisms in Learning Systems. *Machine Learning*, *10*, 113–151.

O'Leary, D. E. (1993). Verification and Validation of Case-Based Systems. *Experts Systems With Applications*, *6*, 57–66.

Porter, B. W., Bareiss, R., & Holte, R. C. (1990). Concept Learning and Heuristic Classification in Weak-Theory Domains. *Artificial Intelligence*, *45*, 229–263.

Riesbeck, C. K., & Schank, R. C. (1989). *Inside Case-Based Reasoning*. Lawrence Erlbaum Associates, Inc., Hillsdale, New Jersey.

Smyth, B., & Keane, M. T. (1994). Retrieving Adaptable Cases. In Wess, S., Althoff, K.-D., & Richter, M. (Eds.), *Topics in Case-Based Reasoning – First European Workshop (EWCBR'93), Kaiserslautern*, Lecture Notes in Artificial Intelligence 837, pp. 209–220. Springer Verlag, Berlin.

Veloso, M. M. (1994). *Planning and learning by analogical reasoning*. Lecture Notes in Artificial Intelligence. Springer Verlag, Berlin.

# An Average Predictive Accuracy of the Nearest Neighbor Classifier

Seishi Okamoto and Ken Satoh

Fujitsu Laboratories Limited
1015 Kamikodanaka, Nakahara-ku, Kawasaki 211, Japan
E-Mail: {seishi, ksatoh}@flab.fujitsu.co.jp

**Abstract.** The definition of similarity between cases is a key issue on case-based reasoning. The nearest neighbor method represents a basic mechanism for defining the similarity in the case-based reasoning system. In this paper, we perform an average-case analysis of the nearest neighbor classifier for conjunctive classes. We formally compute the predictive accuracy of the nearest neighbor classifier. The predictive accuracy is represented as a function of the number of training cases and the numbers of relevant attributes for classes. We also plot the predictive behavior of the classifier by substituting actual values into the parameters of the accuracy function. The graphs by plotting the predictive behavior help us to understand the relationships between the parameters of the accuracy function and the predictive accuracy of the nearest neighbor classifier. Our investigation focuses on how the numbers of relevant attributes for classes affect the predictive accuracy.

## 1 Introduction

Case-Based Reasoning (CBR) is one of the most attractive research areas in Artificial Intelligence at present, and many CBR systems have already been developed. The definition of similarity between cases is a key issue on CBR and is represented as the mechanism for both the organization and retrieval phases in the CBR system. However, the definition of similarity in most of these CBR systems is strongly dependent on the problem domain. This dependency creates the following problems when we construct a new CBR system.

- It is difficult to reuse the definition of similarity.
- It is difficult to evaluate the adequacy of the definition of similarity.

These difficulties not only make it costly to define the similarity, but also make the system unreliable. We believe that the theoretical analysis for the similarity between cases is indispensable to solve these crucial problems.

In this paper, we deal with the nearest neighbor method. The method represents a basic mechanism for the definition of similarity between cases in the CBR system. That is, this method consists of the flat memory and the static similarity function. We can find the origin of the nearest neighbor method in the field of pattern recognition [5]. Cover and Hart [5] showed that the error probability of the nearest neighbor classifier is bounded from above by twice the Bayes error rate for an infinite number of training samples. However, the assumption of an infinite number of the training samples is not applicable for the practical problem domain.

In recent years, the remarkable results for the nearest neighbor method or its variants have been presented by both empirical [1, 4, 6] and theoretical analyses [2, 3, 8, 10]. Aha [1] proposed a method that changes the weighting incrementally based on the success or failure of classification. Creecy et al. [6] proposed a weighted $k$-nearest neighbor method based on statistical information and discussed the optimization of $k$. Cardie [4] showed the usefulness of eliminating attributes using a decision tree to increase the performance of the $k$-nearest neighbor method. Aha et al. [2] gave a theoretical result concerning the PAC (Probably Approximately Correct) learnability for the nearest neighbor method. Albert and Aha [3] generalized the results in [2] to the $k$-nearest neighbor method. Langley and Iba [8] performed an average-case analysis for the nearest neighbor method under the assumption that the target concept is conjunctive. We [10] showed PAC-learnability for weights from qualitative distance information which is related to the weighted nearest neighbor method.

In this paper, we make an average-case analysis of the nearest neighbor classifier. Average-case analysis is well known to be a useful framework to understand the behavior of the learning algorithm. Some people performed average-case analyses of several learning algorithms [7, 8, 9]. Our analysis is closely related to that of Langley and Iba [8]. Their paper gave a mathematical predictive accuracy function for the nearest neighbor classifier under the assumption that a target concept is conjunctive. Moreover, they suggested the sensitivity of the classifier to the number of irrelevant attributes. This means that the accuracy of the classifier decreases gradually with an increase in the number of irrelevant attributes. However, the effect on the accuracy of the number of relevant attributes to define the class essentially has not yet been clarified.

We perform a deeper analysis of the nearest neighbor classifier for relevant attributes in this paper. Our analysis focuses on how the difference between the numbers of relevant attributes for classes affects the accuracy of the classifier. For clarification of the analysis, we assume that there are no irrelevant attributes. We also assume that the number of classes is two, all attributes have a noise-free Boolean value, and that all instances belonging to either class are drawn from an instance space with the same probability and no instance belonging to neither will appear. The last assumption is clarified to analyze the effect on the accuracy of the difference between the numbers of relevant attributes for classes. Therefore, this paper focuses on the following two issues.

1. We compute a mathematical predictive accuracy function of the nearest neighbor classifier making the above assumptions.
2. We clarify the effect on the accuracy of the number of relevant attributes for classes on the accuracy by substituting actual values into the parameters of the mathematical predictive accuracy function.

## 2    Problem Description

Throughout this paper, we deal with only relevant attributes in order to clarify the relationship between the accuracy and the number of relevant attributes. That is, we assume that there are no irrelevant attributes. We let $F$ be a set consisting of all attributes, and we assume that every attribute has a noise-free Boolean value. We denote $F_1$ and $F_2$ as non-empty disjoint sets such that $F_1 \cap F_2 = \emptyset$ and $F_1 \cup F_2 = F$. And, we let $f_1, f_2, \ldots, f_{r_1}$ be the members of $F_1$, and $f_{r_1+1}, f_{r_1+2}, \ldots, f_{r_1+r_2}$ be the members of $F_2$. Here we assume $r_1 \leq r_2$ without loss of generality. Then, the instance space $\mathcal{H}$ is defined as follows.

$$\mathcal{H} = \{ (a_1, \ldots, a_{r_1}, a_{r_1+1}, \ldots, a_{r_1+r_2}) \mid a_j \in \{0, 1\} \quad (j = 1, 2, \ldots, r_1 + r_2) \},$$

where $a_j (j = 1, 2, \ldots, r_1 + r_2)$ is the value of attribute $f_j$. We also assume that there exist two classes $C_1$ and $C_2$, and these classes are defined by relevant attributes as follows.

$$C_1 = \{ (a_1, \ldots, a_{r_1+r_2}) \mid a_1 \cdot a_2 \cdot \ldots \cdot a_{r_1} = 1 \text{ and } a_{r_1+1} \cdot \ldots \cdot a_{r_1+2} \cdot a_{r_1+r_2} = 0 \},$$

$$C_2 = \{ (a_1, \ldots, a_{r_1+r_2}) \mid a_1 \cdot a_2 \cdot \ldots \cdot a_{r_1} = 0 \text{ and } a_{r_1+1} \cdot a_{r_1+2} \cdot \ldots \cdot a_{r_1+r_2} = 1 \},$$

where the center dot '·' represents multiplication. We call the members of $F_1$ and of $F_2$ the relevant attributes for $C_1$ and $C_2$, respectively. Moreover, we assume that the discrete probability distribution over the instance space $\mathcal{H}$ is defined by the following probability function $f(I)$ for an arbitrary instance $I \in \mathcal{H}$.

$$f(I) = \begin{cases} \dfrac{1}{2^{r_1} + 2^{r_2} - 2} & \text{if } I \text{ belongs to } C_1 \text{ or } C_2, \\ \\ 0 & \text{otherwise.} \end{cases}$$

That is, all instances belonging to either class $C_1$ or $C_2$ is drawn from the instance space $\mathcal{H}$ with the same probability, and no instance belonging to neither $C_1$ nor $C_2$ will appear. This restriction is made in order to clarify the effect on the accuracy of the difference between the numbers of relevant attributes for two classes.

Under the above assumptions, we deal with the following nearest neighbor classifier throughout this paper.

We store all training cases drawn from the instance space $\mathcal{H}$ into the case base $\mathcal{CB}$. When a test instance $T$ is given, we select the nearest case $N$ to $T$ in $\mathcal{CB}$ by Hamming distance, and classify $T$ in the same class as $N$. If there exists more than one nearest case, we select one randomly among them.

# 3   Mathematical Predictive Accuracy

In this section, we would like to compute a mathematical predictive accuracy of the nearest neighbor classifier under the assumptions in the previous section. The predictive accuracy will be represented as a function of the numbers of given training cases and the numbers of relevant attributes for two classes.

Let $P(C_i)$ $(i = 1, 2)$ be the probability that an arbitrary instance from $\mathcal{H}$ belongs to $C_i$. We straightforwardly hold

$$P(C_1) = \frac{2^{r_2} - 1}{2^{r_1} + 2^{r_2} - 2}, \quad P(C_2) = \frac{2^{r_1} - 1}{2^{r_1} + 2^{r_2} - 2}.$$

Let $A_n$ be the predictive accuracy after $n$ training cases . Then, we have

$$A_n = P(C_1)A(C_1)_n + P(C_2)A(C_2)_n,$$

where $A(C_1)_n$ and $A(C_2)_n$ are the respective predictive accuracies for test instance $T$ belonging to $C_1$ and $C_2$ after $n$ training cases. Because $r_1 \leq r_2$, we compute $A(C_1)_n$ and $A(C_2)_n$ separately.

We compute $A(C_1)_n$ and $A(C_2)_n$ by using the prototype method [8]. That is, we select some instance as the prototype, then we compute each predictive accuracy according to the distance $d$ of the test instance from the prototype instance. Although we can choose an arbitrary instance as prototype, we select the one bellow to simplify computation:

$$P_0 = (\overbrace{1, 1, \ldots, 1}^{r_1}, \overbrace{1, 1, \ldots, 1}^{r_2}).$$

Then we get $A(C_1)_n$ and $A(C_2)_n$ by summarizing the predictive accuracies according to $d$.

## 3.1   Computation of $A(C_2)_n$

Let $T_2^d$ be a set of the test instances belonging to $C_2$ at distance $d$ from $P_0$. Then, we have $1 \leq d \leq r_1$ and each test instance in $T_2^d$ has the same predictive accuracy clearly. Therefore, let $B(C_2)_{d,n}$ be the predictive accuracy for one test case $T_2^d \in T_2^d$ after $n$ training cases, we have

$$A(C_2)_n = \sum_{d=1}^{r_1} \frac{\binom{r_1}{d}}{2^{r_1} - 1} B(C_2)_{d,n},$$

where the first term in the sum denotes the probability that an arbitrary instance belonging to $C_2$ has the distance $d$ from $P_0$.

Let $I_2^e$ be a set of the nearest cases in case base $\mathcal{CB}$ to the test instance $T_2^d$ at distance $e$, then clearly $0 \leq e \leq d + r_2$. As we show in Figure 1, we divide this region three according to $e$, for the following reasons.

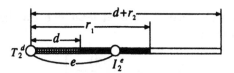

**Fig. 1.** The three regions divided according to $e$.

The shaded region $(0 \leq e \leq d)$ in Figure 1 represents the region in which no training case belonging to $C_1$ exists at distance $e$ from $T_2^d$. Hence, if there is at least one nearest training case at distance $e$ from $T_2^d$ in this region, then the test instance $T_2^d$ will be classified correctly into $C_2$. We let $F_2(e_0^d)_n$ be the predictive accuracy when the nearest training cases in $CB$ to the test instance $T_2^d$ appear in this region.

The black region $(d + 1 \leq e \leq r_1)$ in Figure 1 represents the region in which training cases could belong to either class. We let $G_2(e_{d+1}^{r_1})_n$ be the predictive accuracy when the nearest training cases among $CB$ for the test instance $T_2^d$ appear in this region.

The white region $(r_1 + 1 \leq e \leq d + r_2)$ in Figure 1 represents the region in which no training case belonging to $C_2$ exists at distance $e$ from $T_2^d$. Hence, if the nearest training cases to $T_2^d$ exist in this region, then the test instance $T_2^d$ will be classified incorrectly into $C_1$. The predictive accuracy is therefore zero when the nearest training cases in $CB$ to the test instance $T_2^d$ appear in this region.

As we mentioned above, we can divide $B(C_2)_{d,n}$ into

$$B(C_2)_{d,n} = F_2(e_0^d)_n + G_2(e_{d+1}^{r_1})_n .$$

First, we compute $F_2(e_0^d)_n$. Let $S_2(e_0^d)$ be the number of instances which can appear at a distances from 0 to $d$ from $T_2^d$. Then, we have

$$S_2(e_0^d) = -1 + \sum_{j=0}^{d} \binom{r_1}{j} ,$$

where the first term on the right side represents excluding the situation where the instance is identical to $P_0$ when $e = d$. The probability that there exists a training case in $CB$ at a distance greater than $d$ from $T_2^d$ is

$$1 - \frac{S_2(e_0^d)}{2^{r_1} + 2^{r_2} - 2} .$$

The probability that all $n$ training cases in $CB$ have a distance greater than $d$ from $T_2^d$ is

$$\left[ 1 - \frac{S_2(e_0^d)}{2^{r_1} + 2^{r_2} - 2} \right]^n .$$

Therefore, the probability that there is at least one training case in $CB$ at a distance from 0 to $d$ from $T_2^d$ is

$$1 - \left[1 - \frac{S_2(e_0^d)}{2^{r_1} + 2^{r_2} - 2}\right]^n .$$

If there exists at least one nearest case in this region, then $T_2^d$ is correctly classified into $C_2$. Hence, we have

$$F_2(e_0^d)_n = 1 - \left[1 - \frac{S_2(e_0^d)}{2^{r_1} + 2^{r_2} - 2}\right]^n .$$

Next, we compute $G_2(e_{d+1}^{r_1})_n$. Let $g_2(e)_n$ be the predictive accuracy according to $e(e = d+1, d+2, \ldots, r_1)$, and then we compute $G_2(e_{d+1}^{r_1})_n$ by summing $g_2(e)_n$ over $e$:

$$G_2(e_{d+1}^{r_1})_n = \sum_{e=d+1}^{r_1} g_2(e)_n ,$$

where $G_2(e_{d+1}^{r_1})_n = 0$, when $d = r_1$. We let $M_2(e)_{k,n}$ be the probability that there exist, out of $n$, $k$ training cases in $CB$ at distance $e$ from $T_2^d$ and another $n - k$ training cases in $CB$ at a distance greater than $e$ from $T_2^d$. We let $N_2(e)_k$ be the predictive accuracy for this situation. Then, in terms of $M_2(e)_{k,n}$ and $N_2(e)_k$, $g_2(e)_n$ can be given as

$$g_2(e)_n = \sum_{k=1}^{n} M_2(e)_{k,n} N_2(e)_k .$$

Let $J_2^1(e)_d$ and $J_2^2(e)_d$ be the number of instances belonging to $C_1$ and $C_2$ respectively which can appear at a distance $e$ from the test instance $T_2^d$. Then, we hold

$$J_2^1(e)_d = \binom{r_2}{e - d} , \quad J_2^2(e)_d = \binom{r_1}{e} .$$

Moreover, if we let $K_2(e)$ be the number of instances belonging to either $C_1$ or $C_2$ at a distances from 0 to $e$ from $T_2^d$, then

$$K_2(e) = S_2(e_0^d) + \sum_{j=d+1}^{e} \left(J_2^1(j)_d + J_2^2(j)_d\right) .$$

Therefore, we have

$$M_2(e)_{k,n} = \binom{n}{k} \left[\frac{J_2^1(e)_d + J_2^2(e)_d}{2^{r_1} + 2^{r_2} - 2}\right]^k \left[1 - \frac{K_2(e)}{2^{r_1} + 2^{r_2} - 2}\right]^{n-k} .$$

In this situation, the probability that there exist, out of $k$, $j$ training cases belonging to $C_2$ and $k - j$ training cases belonging to $C_1$ is

$$\binom{k}{j} \left[\frac{J_2^2(e)_d}{J_2^1(e)_d + J_2^2(e)_d}\right]^j \left[\frac{J_2^1(e)_d}{J_2^1(e)_d + J_2^2(e)_d}\right]^{k-j} .$$

As our nearest neighbor classifier selects one nearest case randomly when there exists more than one nearest case to the test instance, we have

$$N_2(e)_k = \sum_{j=1}^{k} \frac{j}{k} \binom{k}{j} \left[ \frac{J_2^2(e)_d}{J_2^1(e)_d + J_2^2(e)_d} \right]^j \left[ \frac{J_2^1(e)_d}{J_2^1(e)_d + J_2^2(e)_d} \right]^{k-j}.$$

We can rewrite $N_2(e)_k$ as below using the binomial theorem.

$$N_2(e)_k = \sum_{j=1}^{k} \binom{k-1}{j-1} \left[ \frac{J_2^2(e)_d}{J_2^1(e)_d + J_2^2(e)_d} \right]^j \left[ \frac{J_2^1(e)_d}{J_2^1(e)_d + J_2^2(e)_d} \right]^{k-j}$$

$$= \left[ \frac{J_2^2(e)_d}{J_2^1(e)_d + J_2^2(e)_d} \right] \left[ \frac{J_2^2(e)_d}{J_2^1(e)_d + J_2^2(e)_d} + \frac{J_2^1(e)_d}{J_2^1(e)_d + J_2^2(e)_d} \right]^{k-1}$$

$$= \left[ \frac{J_2^2(e)_d}{J_2^1(e)_d + J_2^2(e)_d} \right].$$

We then have $g_2(e)_n$ as below, using the binomial theorem again.

$$g_2(e)_n = \left[ \frac{J_2^2(e)_d}{J_2^1(e)_d + J_2^2(e)_d} \right] \sum_{k=1}^{n} M_2(e)_{k,n}$$

$$= \left[ \frac{J_2^2(e)_d}{J_2^1(e)_d + J_2^2(e)_d} \right] \left\{ \left[ 1 - \frac{K_2(e) - (J_2^1(e)_d + J_2^2(e)_d)}{2^{r_1} + 2^{r_2} - 2} \right]^n - \left[ 1 - \frac{K_2(e)}{2^{r_1} + 2^{r_2} - 2} \right]^n \right\}.$$

## 3.2 Computation of $A(C_1)_n$

We can compute $A(C_1)_n$ in almost the same way as $A(C_2)_n$. However, the computation of $A(C_1)_n$ is more complicated than $A(C_2)_n$, because $r_1 \leq r_2$.

Let $T_1^d$ be a set of test instances in $C_1$ at distance $d$ from $P_0$. We have $1 \leq d \leq r_2$, and each test instance in $T_1^d$ has the same predictive accuracy. Then we have

$$A(C_1)_n = \sum_{d=1}^{r_2} \frac{\binom{r_2}{d}}{2^{r_2} - 1} B(C_1)_{d,n},$$

where $B(C_1)_{d,n}$ represents the predictive accuracy for one test case $T_1^d \in T_1^d$ after $n$ training cases.

Let $I_1^e$ be a set of the nearest cases among $CB$ for the test case $T_1^d$ at distance $e$. In this situation, we hold $0 \leq e \leq max(d+r_1, r_2)$ as we show in Figure 2 and Figure 3.

When $r_2 \leq d + r_1$, each of the three regions (shown in Figure 2) has the same meaning as the corresponding region in Figure 1. That is, in Figure 2, the shaded region ($0 \leq e \leq d$) represents the region in which no training case in $C_2$ exists at a distance $e$ from $T_1^d$, the black region ($d+1 \leq e \leq r_2$) represents

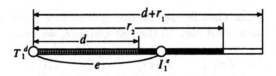

**Fig. 2.** The three regions divided according to $e$ in the case that $r_2 \le d + r_1$.

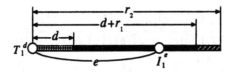

**Fig. 3.** The three regions divided according to $e$ in the case that $r_2 > d + r_1$.

the region in which training cases could belong to either class, and the white region ($r_2 + 1 \le e \le d + r_1$) represents the region in which no training case in $C_1$ exists at distance $e$ from $T_1^d$. When the nearest training cases appear in the white region, the predictive accuracy for $T_1^d$ is zero. Hence, in computing $B(C_1)_{d,n}$, we can ignore the white region.

If $d + r_1 < r_2$, then the three regions (shown in Figure 3) have the following meanings. In Figure 3, the shaded region ($0 \le e \le d$) and the striped region ($d + r_1 + 1 \le e \le r_2$) have the same meanings as the shaded region in Figure 2. That is, no training case in $C_2$ exists at distance $e$ from $T_1^d$ in these regions. The black region ($d + 1 \le e \le d + r_1$) has the same meaning as the black region in Figure 2. That is, training cases in this region could belong to either class.

Let $F_2(e_0^d)_n$ be the predictive accuracy when the nearest training cases to $T_1^d$ appear at a distance from 0 to $d$, $G_1(e_{d+1}^{min(d+r_1, r_2)})_n$ the predictive accuracy when the nearest training cases appear at a distance from $d + 1$ to $min(d + r_1, r_2)$, and $H_1(e_{min(d+r_1, r_2)+1}^{r_2})_n$ the predictive accuracy when the nearest training cases appear at a distance from $min(d+r_1, r_2)+1$ to $r_2$. We assume that $H_1(e_{min(d+r_1, r_2)+1}^{r_2})_n = 0$ when $r_2 \le d + r_1$. Then, $B(C_1)_{d,n}$ can be given as

$$B(C_1)_{d,n} = F_1(e_0^d)_n + G_1(e_{d+1}^{min(d+r_1, r_2)})_n + H_1(e_{min(d+r_1, r_2)+1}^{r_2})_n .$$

First, we compute $F_1(e_0^d)_n$. Let $S_1(e_0^d)$ be the number of instances which can appear at a distance from 0 to $d$. Then, we have

$$S_1(e_0^d) = -1 + \sum_{j=0}^{d} \binom{r_2}{j} .$$

Therefore, we hold

$$F_1(e_0^d)_n = 1 - \left[ 1 - \frac{S_1(e_0^d)}{2^{r_1} + 2^{r_2} - 2} \right]^n .$$

Second, we compute $G_1(e_{d+1}^{min(d+r_1,r_2)})_n$ by summing $g_1(e)_n$ over $e$ ($e = d + 1, \ldots, min(d + r_1, r_2)$) as below.

$$G_1(e_{d+1}^{min(d+r_1,r_2)})_n = \sum_{e=d+1}^{min(d+r_1,r_2)} g_1(e)_n \ ,$$

where $g_1(e)_n$ is the predictive accuracy according to $e$. We let $J_1^1(e)_d$ and $J_1^2(e)_d$ be the numbers defined by replacing $T_1^d$ with $T_2^d$ in the definitions, respectively, of $J_2^1(e)_d$ and $J_2^2(e)_d$. Then, we hold

$$J_1^1(e)_d = \binom{r_2}{e} , \quad J_1^2(e)_d = \binom{r_1}{e-d} .$$

We let $K_1(e)$ be the number defined by replacing $J_2^1(e)_d, J_2^1(e)_d$ and $S_2(e_0^d)$ in the definition of $K_2(e)$ with $J_1^1(e)_d, J_1^1(e)_d$ and $S_1(e_0^d)$, respectively. And we define $M_1(e)_{k,n}$ by replacing $T_2^d$ with $T_1^d$ in the definition of $M_2(e)_{k,n}$. Then, we have

$$M_1(e)_{k,n} = \begin{cases} \left[\dfrac{J_2^1(e)_d + J_2^2(e)_d}{2^{r_1} + 2^{r_2} - 2}\right]^n & \text{if } r_2 - r_1 = d \text{ and } e = r_2, \\[4mm] \binom{n}{k} \left[\dfrac{J_2^1(e)_d + J_2^2(e)_d}{2^{r_1} + 2^{r_2} - 2}\right]^k \left[1 - \dfrac{K_2(e)}{2^{r_1} + 2^{r_2} - 2}\right]^{n-k} & \text{otherwise.} \end{cases}$$

Although the representation of $M_1(e)_{k,n}$ is more complicated than that for $M_2(e)_{k,n}$, we can compute the following $g_1(e)_n$ in the same way for one of $g_2(e)_n$.

$$g_1(e)_n = \left[\frac{J_1^1(e)_d}{J_1^1(e)_d + J_1^2(e)_d}\right] \left\{ \left[1 - \frac{K_1(e) - (J_1^1(e)_d + J_1^2(e)_d)}{2^{r_1} + 2^{r_2} - 2}\right]^n - \left[1 - \frac{K_1(e)}{2^{r_1} + 2^{r_2} - 2}\right]^n \right\} .$$

Finally, we compute $H(e_{d+r_1+1}^{r_2})_n$. As we mentioned above, if there exist nearest cases in the region ($d + r_1 + 1 \leq e \leq r_2$), then the test instance $T_1^d$ is correctly classified into $C_1$. Therefore, we have

$$H(e_{d+r_1+1}^{r_2})_n = \left[\sum_{e=d+r_1+1}^{r_2} \frac{\binom{r_2}{e}}{2^{r_1} + 2^{r_2} - 2}\right]^n .$$

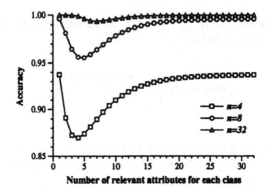

**Fig. 4.** The behavior of the classifier with an equal number of relevant attributes for two classes.

# 4 Predictive Behavior

In the previous section, we formally computed the predictive accuracy of the nearest neighbor classifier as a function of the numbers of relevant attributes for two classes and the number of training cases. In this section, we plot the predictive behavior of the classifier by substituting actual values into the parameters of the function. We can understand the relationships between the parameters of the accuracy function and the predictive accuracy of the classifier by plotting the predictive behavior. Our analysis focuses on the observation of the effect on the accuracy of the difference between the numbers of relevant attributes for two classes.

First, we analyze the predictive behavior of the nearest neighbor classifier in the case where there is no difference between the numbers of relevant attributes for two classes. That is, we assume that the numbers of relevant attributes for the two classes are equal. Figure 4 shows the behavior of the classifier as a function of the number of relevant attributes for each class, when we fix the number of training cases, $n$, at 4, 8 and 32. Figure 4 gives us the following remarkable observations.

- Regardless of the number of relevant attributes, a larger number of training cases results in higher accuracy.
- For each of training cases, as the number of relevant attributes increases, the accuracy decreases monotonously until a pivot number of relevant attributes is reached and afterwards increases monotonously.

Next, we observe the effect on the accuracy of the difference between the numbers of relevant attributes for two classes. Here, we analyze the number of training cases required to achieve 98% accuracy for this observation. Figure 5 shows this required number as a function of the number of relevant attributes for one class when the number of relevant attributes for the other class is fixed at 4, 16 and 32. Let $V$ and $R$ be the former and latter numbers of relevant attributes respectively. Figure 5 gives us the following interesting observations.

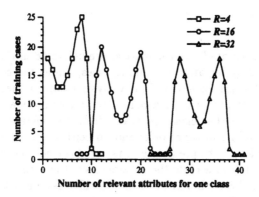

**Fig. 5.** The number of training cases required to achieve 98% accuracy.

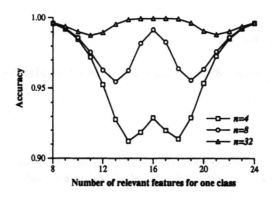

**Fig. 6.** The behavior of the classifier when the number of relevant attributes for one class is fixed at 16.

- For each $R$, the classifier has a similar behavior.
- For each $R$, as the difference between $V$ and $R$ increases, the required number of training cases increases monotonously up to some turning point and decreases monotonously after the turning point as $V$.

We further analyze the behavior of the classifier as a function of $V$ in the each case of $n = 4, 8, 16$ when $R$ is fixed at 16. Figure 6 shows this behavior, with $n$ in the figure representing the number of training cases. From Figure 6, we observe the following behavior of the nearest neighbor classifier for the difference between the numbers of relevant attributes for two classes.

- For each number of training cases, the minimum accuracy appears where $V$ is close to $R$.

# 5 Conclusion

In this paper, we presented a mathematical predictive accuracy function of the nearest neighbor classifier after $n$ training cases, under the condition that all irrelevant attributes are excluded. Our analysis assumed that the number of classes is two, all attributes have a noise-free Boolean value, and that all instances belonging to either class are drawn from the instance space with the same probability and no instance belonging to neither will appear.

Moreover, we plotted the predictive behavior of the nearest neighbor classifier by substituting actual values into the parameters of the accuracy function. First, we analyzed the predictive behavior of the classifier assuming that the numbers of relevant attributes for two classes are equal. Next, we predicted the number of training cases required to achieve 98% accuracy. We also observed the behavior of the classifier for the difference between the numbers of relevant attributes for two classes.

# Acknowledgements

We would like to thank Kazuo Asakawa and Fumihiro Maruyama for support for this research.

# References

1. Aha, D.W.: Incremental Instance-Based Learning of Independent and Graded Concept Descriptions. *Proc. 6th International Workshop on Machine Learning.* (1989) 387–391
2. Aha, D.W., Kibler, D. and Albert, M.K.: Instance-Based Learning Algorithms. *Machine Learning.* **6** (1991) 37–66
3. Albert, M.K. and Aha, D.W.: Analyses of Instance-Based Learning Algorithms. *Proc. AAAI'91.* (1991) 553–558
4. Cardie, C.: Using Decision Trees to Improve Case-Based Learning. *Proc. 10th International Workshop on Machine Learning.* (1993) 25–32
5. Cover, T.M. and Hart, P.E.: Nearest neighbor pattern classification. *IEEE Transactions on Information Theory.* **13** (1967) 21–27
6. Creecy, O.H., Masand, B.M., Smith, S.J. and Waltz, D.: Trading Mips and Memory for Knowledge Engineering. *CACM.* **35** (1992) 48–63
7. Langley, P., Iba, W. and Thompson, K.: Average-Case Analysis of a Nearest Neighbor Algorithm. *Proc. IJCAI'93.* (1993) 889–894
8. Langley, P. and Iba, W.: Average-Case Analysis of a Nearest Neighbor Algorithm. *Proc. AAAI'92.* (1992) 223–228
9. Pazzani, M. and Sarrett, W. A Framework for Average Case Analysis of Conjunctive Learning Algorithms. *Machine Learning.* **9** (1992) 349–372
10. Satoh, K. and Okamoto, S.: Toward PAC-Learning of Weights from Qualitative Distance Information. *Proc. AAAI'94 Workshop on CBR.* (1994) 128–132

# Case-Based Reasoning for Multi-Step Problems and Its Integration with Heuristic Search

Christian Reiser[1] and Hermann Kaindl[2]

[1]Alcatel Austria AG, Scheydgasse 41, A–1210 Wien, Austria, Reiser@aut.alcatel.at
[2]Siemens AG Österreich, Geusaugasse 17, A–1030 Wien, Austria,
kaih@siemens.co.at

**Abstract:** The usual case-based reasoning approach assumes that for each given problem instance it is necessary to retrieve from scratch a similar case from the case base. Therefore, an indexed memory structure or other means of facilitating fast access is typically needed. Moreover, a complete solution is usually stored together with each case, that can be adapted to the given problem. We developed a different approach for *multi-step* problems. It utilizes the information about the relevant case for the last step to quickly find the appropriate case for the current step from only few relevant cases that are connected. Therefore, no special indexing schemata are required. Instead, we store a value for each case and similarity links to other cases, but no solution. For situations outside the scope of the case base we integrated case-based reasoning in several ways with heuristic search. We performed experiments in a game domain, that showed the usefulness of our approach. In particular, we achieved a statistically significant improvement through combination of case-based reasoning with search over pure search or pure case-based reasoning. For multi-step problems, our approach appears to be more useful than the standard approach to case-based reasoning, and we sketch its utility for real-time processing. In summary, we developed a new and promising approach to case-based reasoning for multi-step problems and its integration with heuristic search.

## 1. Introduction

In recent years, case-based reasoning (CBR) has become more and more popular. However, there appears to be a lack of theory of how to apply it best to *multi-step* problems in a real-time environment (such as factory and power plants, railway and network control). The mayor characteristic of multi-step problems is that their solutions consist of several steps. Especially in a real-time environment, a next step has to be chosen before finding a complete solution. Consequently, it is rarely possible to find optimal solutions. However, *complete* solutions to multi-step problems are often not found at all. Therefore, they are unavailable for storage in a case base.

From a planning perspective, this means that plan generation and execution are interleaved. While such problems are common also in single-agent problem solving, we primarily studied case-based reasoning in the context of two-player games with perfect information. In particular, we experimented with a strategic game named Abalone (see Appendix).

Often, access to a case base is done during problem solving in two parts: through an index, and using a similarity metric. Apart from the effort involved in building such an index structure, its compatibility with the similarity metric is an important issue. In our context, the index part can be omitted, since our approach utilizes the information about the relevant case for the last step to quickly find the appropriate case for the current step from only few relevant cases (that are connected). Having a simple and effective mechanism is important for the required predictability in real-time processing.

Moreover, in the classic CBR approaches, a *complete* solution is stored with each case, and this solution is adapted to the given problem. For dealing with multi-step problems in real time, we prefer a different memory organization. We store a value for each case and similarity links to other cases instead of a solution. These values give "hints" for the selection of the next step. Therefore, out new approach described in this paper specially copes with multi-step problems and incomplete solutions. For dealing with situations outside the scope of the case base we show several ways to integrate case-based reasoning with heuristic search.

First, we describe our new approach to case-based reasoning for multi-step problems in a real-time environment. Then we present our concepts for integrating it with heuristic search. Empirical results show the usefulness of our overall approach. Moreover, we sketch the general applicability of our case-based reasoning method for real-time processing. Finally, we discuss its relation to other work.

## 2. Our Approach to Case-Based Reasoning for Multi-Step Problems

### 2.1. Memory Organization of the Case Base

The case base contains a number of states (positions of the game). Each such state is one case. For each case the state information (the board configuration) and the value of the state (from the evaluation function) is stored.

No solution is stored directly with the case (for large problems such a solution may not even be known). However, relations between similar cases are explicitly stored (see the bottom of Figure 1). Hence, information about other relevant cases is available.

In our approach, no further memory organization like indexing schemata is needed. Instead we use a *history pointer* which indicates the relevant case for the current state.

The retrieval and adaptation algorithm described below uses these cases as a hint to the solution for the current case (cf. subgoals in planning). The current case is the case in the base which is one of those most similar to the current state.

### 2.2. The Retrieval and Adaptation Algorithm

A case base of the type described above is the basis of out retrieval and adaptation algorithm. At the beginning of its application, the history pointer is initialized with the start state (of the game). When the start is always the same this poses no problem. However, even if this may take a long time for searching through the whole case base, it is only rarely done. In applications where this is still critical, an appropriate indexing mechanism may be employed here. During the application of our algorithm, the history pointer always points to the case used for the last retrieval. When the next retrieval occurs, the relevant case for the current state is either the case to which the history pointer points

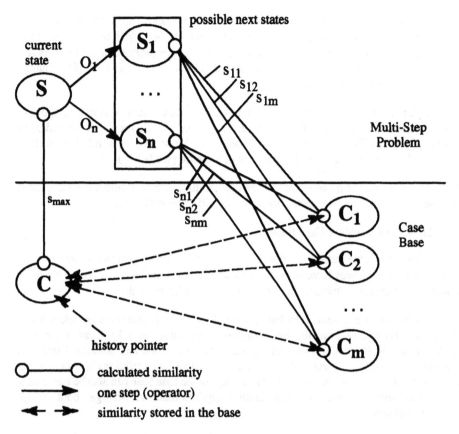

current state

possible next states

Multi-Step Problem

Case Base

history pointer

○——○ calculated similarity

——▶ one step (operator)

◀-- --▶ similarity stored in the base

**Figure 1:** Interplay between the multi-step problem and the case base.

or, one of the cases to which a similarity relation exists in the case base from this case. So the search for the relevant case is reduced to a limited number of cases.

The adaptation algorithm calculates all states reachable from the current state and checks which of them is the "best". For each of these states both the similarity to a case in the base and the value of this case (from an evaluation function) are taken into account, because a more similar case is easier to reach and a high value should be found.

Figure 1 shows the interplay between the multi-step problem (above the line) and the case base (below). The retrieval and adaptation algorithm can be sketched as follows:

1. Locate the case referred to by the history pointer and all cases directly related to this one in the case base, and determine among these the case C that is most similar to the current state S ($s_{max}$).
2. Generate all states $S_i$ which are reachable from S in one step by applying the operators $O_i$ defined in the domain (e.g., possible moves).
3. Calculate the similarities $s_{ij}$ between the states $S_i$ and the cases $C_j$ for which similarity relations with C are stored in the case base.

4. Combine the similarities $s_{ij}$ with the values of the cases $C_j$ with a function, which weights the similarity versus the value, and select the step which leads to one of the states $S_i$ with the best result. This step is selected and performed in the real world.

5. Check, if the new state is more similar to one of the cases $C_j$ than to C. If so, change the history pointer to this case.

The similarity metric — which also exists in classical case bases — is more important in this approach, since together with the history pointer it also replaces the indexing mechanism normally used to find the relevant case. Moreover, the similarity relations stored in the case base can also be based on this metric (see below).

The adaptation algorithm introduced here uses multiple cases to find a solution, but it does not split the cases. It selects a step by comparing several ones.

### 2.3. How to Generate a Case Base

When there is a large number of possible states, it is hard to generate a case base by hand. All relevant states have to be found and additional states in between have to be generated, so that the similarity between the cases is high enough.

When case bases are generated by hand, parts of earlier step sequences are taken, some of the states are removed and the remaining ones are used as cases. Each case has a similarity relation to its predecessor and successor in a sequence and additional relations are introduced between parts of different step sequences. (The relations between the cases of a step sequence are a useful optimization, but the case base can also be based only on the similarity metric.) Such a generation requires much knowledge about the application domain.

Less sophisticated but more easily achievable case bases were generated automatically for the game used for our experiments as follows. With the algorithm described below, 100 different realistic game positions (states) were generated. An iterative $\alpha\beta$ search played against itself, and the records of these games were used to generate case bases. Depending on the target size of the case base every nth position was converted into a case with similarity relations to its predecessor and successor. These cases were added together, where each new case was linked with a similarity relation to the most similar case already in the base, using the similarity metric. The values of the cases are the static values of the positions assigned by the static evaluation function that is also used by the search heuristic (see below). These case bases are independent of human skill and can be used for an objective comparison of different algorithms.

## 3. Integration of Case-Based Reasoning with Heuristic Search

When following the case base as described above, states may occur that are not sufficiently similar to any case in the case base used. In such a situation, it is possible to switch to another problem-solving method: heuristic search. For two-player games with complete information, there exists a well-developed theory about using heuristic search (for a review see, e.g., [11]). The standard approach is to perform iterations of deeper and deeper minimax searches. These can be performed using several algorithms (for a comparison see [13]). The best-known of these is the $\alpha\beta$ algorithm.

Sometimes it may be known a priori that in certain situations the case base is inappropri- ate. In the game-playing context this applies to "tactical" situations, where large differ- ences in the evaluation may occur (cf. the concept of *quiescence* in [12]). Cases repre- senting such situations can be labeled. Whenever a given state is most similar to such a labeled case, heuristic search is used instead of case-based reasoning. In some sense, these labels represent *metaknowledge* about the case base itself, i.e., its (in-)compe- tence.

Another useful possibility for switching to the search mode occurs in situations where a tactical move is possible. This means that the case base is considered incompetent in all such situations (or at least it is safer to use search here). In this variant the decision to switch is based on the actual problem, not on the case base.

These approaches represent an integration of case-based reasoning with heuristic search, but a rather loose one. Tighter integrations are possible when using the knowl- edge in the case base for *guiding* a search. One possibility is to search branches deeper that contain favorable steps according to the case base. This leads to *variable-depth* search (see, e.g., [10]).

When the branching degree of the given domain is high (as in the game we used for our experiments), an old approach called *forward pruning* becomes of interest. While it turned out to be not the first choice in highly tactical domains like chess, we investigated its integration with the case base in one of our variants. With the exception of steps that lead to material change (in order to cope with tactics), the search prunes away all the moves that are not considered useful according to the case base.

## 4. Experiments

### 4.1. Evaluation Environment

All the experiments were performed on a Sparc 1 Sun 4/40 workstation with 28 MB memory running SunOS 4.1(UNIX) and OpenWindows. The times reported in this work refer to the UNIX system time of this configuration.

The algorithms were implemented in C++ using the gnu g++ 2.3 compiler. The algo- rithm independent parts needed for the game (Abalone) were the same in all algorithms. The procedure to statically evaluate a position (the heuristic evaluation function) was used both in the $\alpha\beta$ algorithm and to assign a value to the cases in the base. In this way, the same domain knowledge about the quality of positions is available both for the search approach and for case-based reasoning. This static evaluation function (for Ab- alone) takes into account the material balance, the distance of the balls from the border, and their compactness.

### 4.2. Similarity Metric

The similarity metric is an essential part of our case base and the appropriate retrieval and adaptation algorithm. We defined and used one that compromises between exact- ness and run-time cost. In order to use the value 0 for identical positions, actually the difference rather than the similarity is expressed by this metric. Low values indicate similar states and high values dissimilar ones.

The difference between states (board configurations) is computed in our approach based on distances between balls. Due to the chosen internal representation of the board it is easy to calculate, how many steps it takes to move a single ball from one hole to another, assuming there were no other balls. We call this *One-Ball-Distance* (OBD). The average distance of all the balls of one color in one position to all the balls of the same color in the other position, and the sum of these values for both colors is calculated.

Let $OBD(b_1, b_2)$ be the distance in single steps between the balls $b_1$ and $b_2$ as described above. If the balls belong to different positions, we assume for this calculation that they are on the same board. Moreover, let $B_c(P)$ be the set of all balls of color c where c is either white or black in the position P, and $N_c(P)$ the number of balls of color c in the position P, i.e., $N_c(P)=|B_c(P)|$. Then the average distance $DS_c(b, P)$ of a single ball b to all balls in the other state P of color c can be given as

$$DS_c(b, P) = \frac{1}{N_c(P)} \sum_{x \in B_c(B)} OBD(b, x) \quad .$$

The average distance of all balls of color c between two positions $D_c(P_1, P_2)$ is

$$D_c(P_1, P_2) = \frac{1}{N_c(P_1)} \sum_{x \in B_c(P_1)} DS_c(x, P_2) \quad .$$

Finally, the difference between two positions $D(P_1, P_2)$ is defined for $P1 \neq P2$ as

$$D(P_1, P_2) = D_W(P_1, P_2) + D_B(P_1, P_2)$$

and for $P_1 = P_2$ as $D(P_1, P_2) = 0$. $D_W$ and $D_B$ are the distances for the white and the black balls, respectively. A proof that this is a metric in the mathematical sense can be found in [20].

## 4.3. Experiment Design

For the experiments with our approach we had to develop a special design, since we wanted to gather statistical data with the deterministic algorithms to be compared. We had to define a method for guaranteeing fair games between them. Therefore, the games in the tournaments between the algorithms were started with automatically generated start states. 200 different states were generated as described below.

1. The algorithm for iterative $\alpha\beta$ search was changed so that it does not use the best but randomly 1 of the 5 best steps.
2. Using a random number generator, 5 – 40 steps were played with this changed algorithm.

3. The resulting state was statically evaluated and rejected if the absolute value was larger than a certain limit, i.e., the advantage of one of the colors was decisive.
4. The colors of the states were exchanged to get another position.

Since the automatically generated case bases provide different information for different colors, it is not possible to compare our algorithm with another one by having it play once as black and once as white on the same start position. This is compensated by exchanging the colors of the position as described in step 4.

We were interested in comparing different sizes of case bases. Therefore, we generated several case bases of different size from the same "training" games. This was achieved by inserting only every 4th, 5th, ... 8th or 16th position into the case base.

Moreover, we wanted to compare different approaches of integrating our case-base algorithm with heuristic search. Instead of playing all of them against each other, we chose to have them only play against a reference algorithm. We compared all our algorithms using the case base with an iterative $\alpha\beta$ search with variable search depth. Since all our algorithms were tested against the same opponent, comparing them is possible.

## 4.4. Empirical Results

We performed experiments according to this design and achieved empirical results that are summarized below. The difference in size of case bases generated from the same set of games showed no statistically significant difference in their results (according to the *sign test*) when at least every 16th position is inserted in the case base. We used the case base containing every 4th position for the experiments of comparing several variants of case-based reasoning (integrated with search) against the pure iterative $\alpha\beta$ search.

A small selection of the most interesting results of our experiments is summarized in Table 1. (More details can be found in [20].) This table shows the results of three variants playing against pure (iterative) $\alpha\beta$ search. The first column gives the percentage of wins for each variant in these games. The data in the *Significance* column are based on the sign test. The *null hypothesis* is that the algorithms are equally good. These data signify the probability that the result is from chance fluctuation. "Forward Pruning" wins 83.33%, but this result is less significant than that of "Fastness" (77.78%) because more games were drawn. The third column gives the time consumption relative to the pure search approach.

The "Switch" algorithm used here is an instantiation of the one described above that switches to the $\alpha\beta$ search whenever a tactical move is possible. More precisely, it does so whenever a pushing move is possible in the actual position. It wins in 58.33% of the cases versus the pure search approach, though using less time.

"Forward pruning" only searches the steps with immediate material change, and those recommended by the case base. The latter ones are all steps where the product of similarity and value of the case is higher than for the current position, i.e., improvements according to the knowledge in the case base. The highly significant win of this approach vs. pure search indicates the potential of such combinations of case-based reasoning with search.

| Algorithm | wins n % | Significance | needs n % of time |
|:---:|:---:|:---:|:---:|
| Switch | 58.33 | 0.06332 | 81.8 |
| Forward Pruning | 83.33 | 0.01046 | 100.0 |
| Fastness | 77.78 | 0.00921 | 40.82 |

**Table 1:** Selected Results of our Experiments.

The table entry "Fastness" shows the result of having the pure case-based algorithm play vs. the pure search algorithm, when the latter may only use 2 seconds instead of 10 seconds as in all the other experiments. Still, the case-based algorithm is faster in our environment. The highly significant result indicates the power of our case-based reasoning approach in situations with small and strict time limits.

## 5. General Applicability for Real-Time Processing

Of course, we are also interested in applying our approach to multi-step problems of the real world that involve real-time processing (such as in factories, power plants, railway and telecommunication systems). In the context of this work (in contrast to [6] and [19]) real-time processing does not mean responding fast to an external request, e.g., by the user. "Real time" as defined in [21] or [3] means guaranteeing to deliver the right result before a certain point of time. This does not necessarily mean having to be fast, but being able to determine, when a calculation will be ready. The approach by [15] satisfies this requirement using bounded look-ahead search (see also [12]). We show how to achieve this type of real-time behavior using our case-based reasoning approach.

From the description of the case-base algorithm a realistic upper bound for the calculation time can be estimated. Let o be the maximum number of operators (steps) applicable in one situation (state), $T_o$ the time to apply an operator, s the maximum number of similarity relations for one case, and $T_s$ the time needed to calculate the similarity between two states. Then the worst-case execution time (WCET) for one retrieval-adaptation cycle can be estimated as

$$WCET = o \cdot (T_o + s \cdot T_s) + a,$$

where a is the fixed amount of administrative overhead.

Another research approach is currently in progress analyzing the real-time behavior of this method. The navigational task of an autonomous mobile robot is investigated to apply our case-based reasoning approach to a real-world problem. The domain has hard intrinsic constraints such as the time to recognize and to avoid obstacles. Missing such deadlines would inevitably lead to a collision with the consequence of damage or injury. Additionally continuous operation is required as in a changing environment there is no time to stop and think. To demonstrate the predictability of our approach will be the main focus of this ongoing work.

The applicability of this approach in real-time systems, e.g. on top of a real-time process server as described in [17] and [16] is subject to further investigations.

# 6. Related Work

Well-known CBR Systems use flat memory (HYPO [2]), shared feature network (Mi-croMOPs [14]), priorized discrimination nets (CHEF [8]) or redundant discrimination nets (JULIA [9]) as memory organization for the case library together with some sort of indexing for retrieval. In these kinds of case-base organization all cases can be equal-ly reached.

Work done for multi-step problems in the current case-based reasoning research can be found, e.g., in [23]. This paper introduces multi-cases as memory (space) optimization of micro-cases (see [7]). Both micro and multi-cases are designed for "procedural knowledge" (as multi-step problems are called there). Every case is reachable in re-trieval for every problem.

Our case-base memory organization is problem oriented. In multi-step problems it is not necessary to reach all cases, but using the similarity relations and the history pointer, relevant cases can be found easily with less effort.

In CBR Systems where multiple cases are used for one request (e.g., [22]) the problem of splitting these cases for adaptation exists. We reason from multiple cases, but no splitting is done. The cases have weights and the step is selected which leads to the state most similar to the worthiest case.

Time is introduced to case-based reasoning in [5], where time-extended cases are used to deal with the change of the load on a telephone network over time. This system called NETTRAC helps the operator to decide about load balancing strategies. Since NET-TRAC helps a person, the notion of real time is — equally to the one in the work of [6] and [19] — limited to "fast enough for a human".

The real-time aspects in our work do not aim for fastness (even though our algorithm is fast), but for guaranteeing to be in time. With the simple structure of our retrieval and adaptation algorithm a realistic worst-case execution time can be given. This estimate can be used in any appropriate real-time system. Therefore, a new application area is opened for CBR.

CBR integrated with heuristic search can be found in [18] and [4]. Case bases organized in discrimination nets and equivalence classes are used there for forward pruning. In our work, where the cases are connected by similarity links, forward pruning is one of several possibilities to use the case base and similarity metric. We developed a pure case-based algorithm and combined it with other ways of performing heuristic search. Since we use a similarity metric instead of equivalence classes, the density of the case base is less important, and by combining the similarity value with the value of the case we have the possibility of explicitly representing the importance of certain cases. In [4] neither a possibility of assigning "importance" to the cases can be found nor a possible use of the case base for other algorithms than heuristic search. Furthermore, it is not described, how a case base is designed. Our case-based algorithm can also work by it-self, and the case base used was generated automatically.

# 7. Conclusion

We developed a new approach for applying case-based reasoning to multi-step problems. In particular, we designed a new memory organization for this class of problems. Our approach avoids the compatibility issue of index structure and similarity metric in only using a similarity metric. Although it may be possible to view our approach as a form of *caching*, the use of a similarity metric and the combination of similarity value and case value makes it a form of reasoning based on cases.

Moreover, we integrated case-based reasoning in several ways with heuristic search. The results of our experiments show a statistically significant improvement through combination of case-based reasoning with search over pure search or pure case-based reasoning.

Our approach does not even require knowledge about complete solutions. In real-world problems, complete solutions are often unavailable, and just an appropriate next step is selected. Our algorithm selects such a step based on knowledge about preferable cases and their similarity to the achievable states in the given situation.

Similarity links and values organize the case base in a kind of subgoal structure, that is used for the selection of the next step. However, the cases are not subgoals in the usual sense of planning. They are more like prototypes of desirable states.

We primarily studied case-based reasoning in the context of two-player games. However, the approach appears to be general enough to be also applicable to single-agent problem solving. In particular, we propose it for real-time processing. For the required predictability in such applications, the rather simple structure of the case base in our approach is especially well suited. In summary we developed a new and promising approach to case-based reasoning for multi-step problems and its integration with heuristic search.

## Acknowledgments

We would like to thank Wilhelm Barth, Atilla Bezirgan, Helmut Horacek, Christian Koza, Stefan Kramer and Markus Robin for comments on earlier versions of this paper.

## Appendix: The Game Abalone

Abalone is a two-player game with perfect information like, e.g., chess or checkers, developed by the French computer scientists Michel Lalet and Laurent Levi. It focuses on the idea of synergy.

### Rules

1. The player who first pushed 6 balls of the opponent out of the board wins.
2. Each player performs one step in turn.

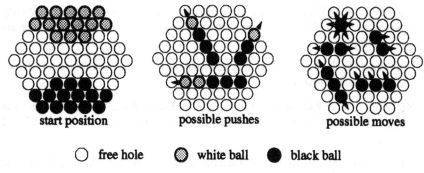

○ free hole     ◉ white ball     ● black ball

**Figure 2:** Abalone.

3. In one step 1, 2, or 3 balls of the player may be moved according to Figure 2 "possible moves".

4. In one step 1 or 2 opponent's balls may be pushed if they are in one line with the player's balls, the player has more balls in the line and the hole behind the opponent's ball(s) is empty, or the ball is pushed out of the board (see Figure 2 "possible pushes").

5. The opponent's balls do not necessarily have to be pushed or pushed out of the board.

For a detailed description of the rules of Abalone see [1].

**Special Characteristics**

Two special characteristics of the game Abalone are important for our experiments. The "branching degree" of the game in a typical position is between 50 and 120 different moves, and "strategy" is more important than "tactics".

# References

[1] Abalone s. a. (1990). *The game Abalone: Rules.* Abalone s. a., Z. I. de la Bonde, 91300 Massy, France.

[2] Ashley, K. D. & Rissland, E. L. (1988). Compare and Contrast, A Test of Expertise. In *Proceedings of a Workshop on CBR (DARPA)*, Morgan Kaufmann Publishers Inc., (pp 31–36).

[3] Bhattacharyya, A. (Ed.) (1990). *Real-Time Systems (Specific Closed Workshop).* Esprit PDCS Workshop Report W6, Department of Computer Science, University of York, United Kingdom, Sep.

[4] Bradtke, S. & Lehnert, W. G. (1988). Some Experiments With Case-Based Search. In *Proceedings of a Workshop on CBR (DARPA)*, Morgan Kaufmann Publishers Inc., (pp 80–92).

[5] Brandau, R., Lemmon, D. & Lafond, C. (1991). Experience with Extended Episodes: Cases with complex Temporal Structure. In *Proceedings of a Workshop on CBR (DARPA)*, Morgan Kaufmann Publishers Inc., (pp 233–243).

[6] Fertig, S. & Gelernter, D. H. (1991). FGP: A Virtual Machine for Acquiring Knowledge from Cases. In *Proceedings of the 12th International Conference on AI (IJCAI-91)*, (pp 796–808).

[7] Goodman, M. (1991). A case-based, inductive architecture for natural language processing. In *AAAI Spring symposium on Machine Learning of Natural Language and Ontology*.

[8] Hammond, K. J. (1989). *Case-Based Planning, Viewing Planning as a Memory Task*. Academic Press, Inc.

[9] Hinrichs, T. R. & Kolodner, J. L. (1991). The Roles of Adaptation in Case-Based Design. In *Proceedings of the 11th National Conference on AI (AAAI–91)*, (pp 28–33).

[10] Kaindl, H. (1983). Searching to Variable Depth in Computer Chess. In *Proceedings Eighth International Joint Conference on Artificial Intelligence (IJCAI–83)*, Karlsruhe, Los Altos, Calif.: Kaufmann, (pp 760–762).

[11] Kaindl, H. (1990). Tree Searching Algorithms. In *Computers, Chess, and Cognition* (T. A. Marsland and J. Schaeffer, Eds.), New York: Springer-Verlag, (pp 133–158).

[12] Kaindl, H. & Scheucher, A. (1992). Reasons for the Effects of Bounded Look-Ahead Search. *IEEE Transactions on Systems, Man, and Cybernetics* SMC–22(5), (pp 992–1007).

[13] Kaindl, H., Shams, R. & Horacek, H. (1991). Minimax Search Algorithms with and without Aspiration Windows. *IEEE Transactions on Pattern Analysis and Machine Intelligence PAMI–13(12)*, (pp 1225–1235).

[14] Kolodner, J. & Riesbeck, C. (1989). Case-Based Reasoning. *Tutorial Notes at the 11th International Joint Conference on Artificial Intelligence (IJCAI–89)*.

[15] Korf, R. E. (1990). Real-Time Heuristic Search. *Artificial Intelligence* 42, (pp 189–211).

[16] Koza, C., Pottendorfer, M. & Reiser, C. (1994). An Application Programming Model for the AEOS Real-Time Process Server based on a Flexible Precedence Graph Model. *Proceedings of the Real-Time Systems Conference RTS '94*, Jan. 11–14, Porte Maillot – Paris.

[17] Koza, C. & Reiser, C. (1992). Real-Time Process Server for the Micro-Kernel Based Alcatel Elin Operating System Testbed (AEOS). In *Proceedings of the IEEE Real-Time Systems Symposium*, IEEE Computer Society Press, (pp 231–234).

[18] Lehnert, W. G. (1987). *Case-Based Reasoning as a Paradigm for Heuristic Search*. COINS 87–107, Department of Computer and Information Science, University of Massachusetts at Amherst, Amherst, MA.

[19] McCartney R. & Wurst C. R. (1991). DEFRAGE: A Real-time Execution Monitor for a Case-Based Planner. In *Proceedings of a Workshop on CBR (DARPA)*, Morgan Kaufmann Publishers Inc., (pp 233–243).

[20] Reiser, C. (1994). *Case-Based Reasoning für mehrstufige Probleme und die Integration mit heuristischer Suche*. Doctoral Dissertation, Technical University of Vienna, Vienna, Austria, April.

[21] Stankovic, J. A. (1988). *Misconceptions about Real-Time Computing: A Serious Problem for Next-Generation Systems*. IEEE Computer Society Press, Washington, D.C., USA.

[22] Sycara, K. P. & Navinchandra, D. (1991). Influences: A Thematic Abstraction for Creative Use of Multiple Cases. *Proceedings of a Workshop on CBR (DARPA)*, Morgan Kaufmann Publishers Inc., (pp 133–145).

[23] Zito-Wolf, R. & Alterman, R. (1993). A Framework and an Analysis of Current Proposals for the Case-Based Organization and Representation of Procedural Knowledge. *Proceedings of the 11th National Conference on AI (AAAI-93)*, (pp 73–78).

# Qualitative Models as a Basis for Case Indices[*]

Bradley L. Richards

Artificial Intelligence Laboratory, Swiss Federal Institute of Technology,
EPFL-Ecublens, CH-1015 Lausanne, Switzerland, bradley@lia.di.epfl.ch

**Abstract.** Two issues are central to effective case-based reasoning: deriving good indices for retrieving cases and effectively using those cases. A number of straightforward methods for using cases, such as interpolation, can provide good results. However, effective indexing strategies have proven more elusive. This paper presents a new and effective approach based on qualitative modelling. We build a partial or complete qualitative model of a physical system, and use this model to derive the minimal sets of parameters relevant to each of the desired inputs. This reduces the number of attributes used for indexing, thereby increasing the density of cases in the parameter space. We present results showing the effectiveness of the approach on a simplified sewage treatment plant.

## 1 Introduction

Controlling complex physical systems is difficult, particularly if feedback information is sparse or difficult to obtain. For example, in process control, feedback may come only from periodic laboratory tests of product output. Hence, incorrect settings may not be detected before large quantities of defective product have been produced.

One possible solution is to take a case-based approach, and calculate settings based on past experience with the production process. However, case-based systems are only effective if they are able to do effective matching to historical cases. Complex systems may have dozens or hundreds of parameters; indexing on all of these parameters would mean that even a large library of historical cases will provide only very sparse coverage of the parameter space. To overcome this, we must substantially reduce the number of indices, and do so in a way that maximizes the usefulness of the available historical data.

Our approach to this problem is to derive indices appropriate to each input parameter that the user wishes to set; hence, if the user has a problem which requires settings for three parameters, three different indices are produced. This multiple indexing allows the setting of each parameter to be more precise than when a single index is used. The indices are derived from a qualitative model of the target system. Using qualitative models, we are able to identify the minimal

[*] This work has been funded jointly by Swiss National Science Foundation grant #5003-034269 and by Nestle York RECO, England. Particular thanks to Prof. Boi Faltings (EPFL) and Mr. Peter Duxbury-Smith (Nestle) for their help and inspiration.

set of parameters which are relevant to any particular input. This can substantially reduce the number of parameters appearing in an index, thereby increasing the density of cases in the parameter space and improving the accuracy of the case-based matches.

The remainder of this paper is divided into the following sections: Section 2 defines the problem we are addressing, and introduces the example we will use throughout the paper. Sections 3, 4, and 5 describe the three stages in our approach: building a qualitative model, deriving indices from the model, and using the indices in a case-based system. Section 6 presents test results comparing our approach to other standard index-derivation approaches. Section 7 discusses related work in the field, and Section 8 discusses our plans for the future. Finally, Section 9 presents our conclusions.

## 2 Controlling a Physical System

When working with physical systems to achieve some desired goal, the parameters of the system may generally be divided into three categories: input, observable, and hidden parameters. Input parameters can be controlled directly by the user, observable parameters can be measured but not directly controlled, and hidden parameters can be neither directly controlled nor directly observed. The observable parameters include, as subsets, fixed parameters whose values are considered constant for a particular control problem, and output parameters in terms of which the user's goal is expressed. Hence, the control problem may be stated as follows:

- **Given:**
  - The values of all fixed parameters.
  - Desired values for all output parameters.
- **Find:**
  - Settings for the input parameters which will produce the desired output parameter values.

Throughout the remainder of this paper, we will refer to the example shown in Figure 1. The figure shows a simplified two-stage sewage treatment plant, and portrays the problem of treating sewage during rainfall. Normally, runoff from the streets is added to domestic waste and all of the wastewater is fully treated by the plant. However, during periods of heavy rainfall, there is too much volume to treat all of the runoff. As much as possible is fully treated, but some is added only during the second stage of treatment, and the rest is passed on untreated.

In this example, *Domestic-waste* is the sewage waste flowing into the treatment plant, *Runoff-A* is the amount of runoff which can be fully treated, and *Runoff-B* is the additional quantity of runoff added at the second stage. *Amount-A* and *Amount-B* represent the amount of waste water present in the two stages in the treatment plant; if the capacity of either stage is exceeded then untreated sewage will overflow and escape. Finally, *Partially-treated* and *Fully-treated* are the flows out of the two treatment stages.

Our goal, during rainfall, is to treat as much runoff as possible without causing an overflow. We will treat *Domestic-waste* as a fixed parameter, and *Partially-treated* and *Fully-treated* as observables. *Amount-A* and *Amount-B* are output parameters, which we want to hold near the capacity of the plant by setting the input parameters *Runoff-A* and *Runoff-B* appropriately.

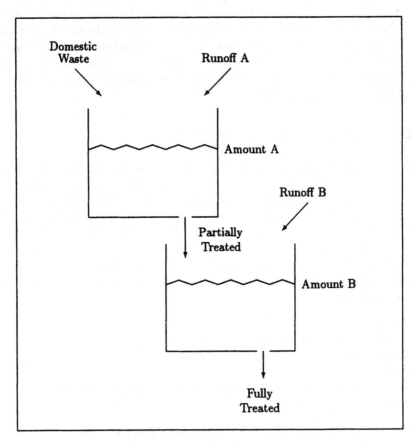

**Fig. 1.** Simplified sewage plant.

## 3   Building a Qualitative Model

In order to build a qualitative model of a system, we have used the MISQ algorithm described in [9]. MISQ takes a set of numerical behaviors of a system, ideally direct sensor logs, and uses these to construct a qualitative model. If MISQ is able to construct a complete model of the target system, then the system is completely understood and the index parameters we derive will be the minimal set required. If MISQ is unable to develop a complete system model, then it will have some number of model fragments. Each of these can be analyzed to provide one or more index parameters, and the combined set will be used as the final index.

The qualitative model derived for our simple sewage plant, stated as a QSIM model, is:

```
add(Runoff_A, Domestic_waste, Inflow_A)
add(Net_change_amount_A, Partially_treated, Inflow_A)
derivative(Amount_A, Net_change_amount_A)
m_plus(Amount_A, Partially_treated)
add(Runoff_B, Partially_treated, Inflow_B)
add(Net_change_amount_B, Fully_treated, Inflow_B)
derivative(Amount_B, Net_change_amount_B)
m_plus(Amount_B, Fully_treated)
```

The symbols *add*, *derivative*, and *m_plus* are qualitative constraints which stand for families of possible quantitative functions. For example, *m_plus* states that a strictly monotonically increasing function holds between its two arguments. From this we know that the directions of change of the two variables must always be the same, and further that each value of one variable corresponds to a unique value for the other (the definition of a function). The new variables *Net_change_amount_A*, *Net_change_amount_B*, *Inflow_A*, and *Inflow_B* are hidden variables in the system.

The MISQ approach is a general one which can be applied to any physical system whose normal operation can be described in terms of continuous parameters. Where transitions are required, MISQ must be applied separately to each operating region. Automatically handling region transitions is the subject of current research, described in [8].

## 4  Deriving the Indices

Our goal in controlling the system is to adjust the input variables so that, as long as the fixed parameters remain constant, the output parameters will reach equilibrium at the desired values[2]. We wish to extract appropriate settings for the input variables from a historical case base; to do this, we need suitable indices.

Since the goal is to reach an equilibrium, we can set all derivatives in the model to zero, thereby eliminating them. We can also eliminate any variable which has an *m_plus* or *m_minus* relationship to a derivative. The reason that this is valid is that such a variable will have the same value at *any* equilibrium point. Since all of our cases represent equilibrium points, its value is qualitatively unimportant. After eliminating these variables, we are left with a reduced set of constraints:

---

[2] In some cases there may be several paths to a given equilibrium condition. Although our current implementation does not address this, it is in principle possible to restrict intermediate parameter values and thereby control which path is followed.

```
Set derivatives to zero
Propagate zeroes through M+ and M- constraints
Eliminate zeroes

Convert equations to sets

Eliminate intermediate variables which appear in exactly two sets
For each equation with input parameters
     Find all solutions
          Repeat
               For all intermediate variables present
                    Substitute for the variable in all equations
               End for
          Until no more intermediate variables
     Choose smallest set found
End for
```

**Fig. 2.** Index derivation algorithm.

```
add(Runoff_A, Domestic_waste, Inflow_A)
m_plus(Partially_treated, Inflow_A)
m_plus(Amount_A, Partially_treated)
add(Runoff_B, Partially_treated, Inflow_B)
m_plus(Fully_treated, Inflow_B)
m_plus(Amount_B, Fully_treated)
```

Note that, in addition to deleting the derivative constraints, we have also simplified constraints where derivative variables previously appeared. We can further simplify matters by anticipating our goal, namely, we want to use the qualitative model to identify which variables are interrelated. This means that we can view the arguments to each constraint as a set. Since qualitative constraints represent functions, if values for all but one of the members in a set are known, they uniquely determine the value of the remaining member.

For example, the last constraint states that a function relates *Amount_B* and *Fully_treated*. Hence, if either value is known, the other is determined by the function. Although we don't know the function, we can use the case-index to approximate it. So, if we want to predict a value for *Amount_B*, the last constraint tells us that we need only index the case-base on the variable *Fully_treated*.

Unfortunately, we cannot directly use the sets above for this purpose. Our goal is to determine values for input variables by indexing on fixed parameters and output parameters. This means that we need to derive sets that contain no other variables. Moreover, when possible, we would prefer to have only one input variable in each such set. Annotating the sets by underlining the input variables and italicizing the fixed and output parameters yields:

{Runoff_A, *Domestic_waste*, Inflow_A}
{Partially_treated, Inflow_A}

{*Amount_A*, `Partially_treated`}
{<u>`Runoff_B`</u>, `Partially_treated`, `Inflow_B`}
{`Fully_treated`, `Inflow_B`}
{*Amount_B*, `Fully_treated`}

We eliminate the undesired intermediate variables by successive substitutions. Since the sets represent variables in qualitative equations, a substitution consists of taking the union of two sets with a common member, and then deleting that member from the union.

The first series of substitutions eliminates all intermediate variables which appear in exactly two equations. Such substitutions are determinate, and it is more efficient to eliminate them at the beginning than to perform them many times during the search that follows. Making these determinate substitutions typically results in a dramatic simplification; in our example we are left with:

{<u>`Runoff_A`</u>, *Domestic_waste*, `Partially_treated`}
{*Amount_A*, `Partially_treated`}
{<u>`Runoff_B`</u>, `Partially_treated`, *Amount_B*}

The next step is to perform substitutions to eliminate the remaining intermediate variables (in this case, only *Partially_treated*). Complex systems may allow several possible substitutions, but the search space is normally quite small, and the finite number of intermediate variables guarantees termination. Hence, we simply perform exhaustive search with a few enhancements such as pruning hopeless search branches. In our example, the preference for sets with only one input variable leaves only one possibility, namely, using the second equation to substitute for *Partially_treated* in the first and third equations. This leads to the final sets:

{<u>`Runoff_A`</u>, *Domestic_waste*, *Amount_A*}
{<u>`Runoff_B`</u>, *Amount_A*, *Amount_B*}

From these sets, we can derive our indices. To determine *Runoff_A*, we will index the cases on *Domestic_waste* and *Amount_A*. To determine *Runoff_B*, we will index the cases on *Amount_A* and *Amount_B*. Since these indices were derived from a model which completely describes the system, we know that they represent the minimum sets of variables sufficient to uniquely determine values for the input parameters.

# 5 Case-Based Indexing

Performing case-based reasoning involves two steps, which are essentially independent: developing the indices to use, and deriving values from the cases retrieved by the indices. Since we only wish to demonstrate the effectiveness of our index-selection scheme, we use a simple nearest neighbor approach to deriving values [3], i.e., we retrieve the case which has the smallest root-mean-square distance from the specified index values, and directly use the values contained in that case. While better results could be obtained by using interpolation or other techniques, these gains would apply to any index-derivation method.

Percent

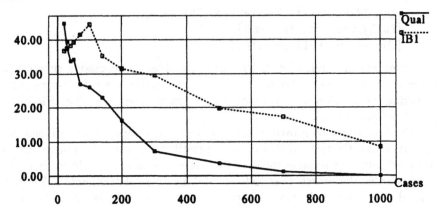

**Fig. 3.** Overflow rates for the sewage plant example.

Percent

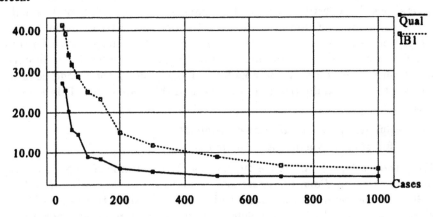

**Fig. 4.** Error rates for the sewage plant example.

## 6  Evaluation

To evaluate the gain of using the qualitatively derived indices, we created a simulation for the simplified sewage plant which, all too much like real sewage plants, is prone to overflowing. We then tried to control the simulation using two sources for the case-based indices. The first source is our qualitative-modelling approach. The second source is the indexing algorithm IB1, described in [1]. The IB1 algorithm indexes on all fixed and output parameters, in this case, the three parameters *Domestic_waste*, *Amount_A*, and *Amount_B*.

We also tried to compare our approach to the work presented in [2]. She used C4.5 to build decision trees, and used the attributes which appeared in the decision trees as case indices. In our test domain, however, the "class" of an instance is a real number. This means that we were unable to use C4.5 to build the decision trees. Instead, we used the tree-building capabilities in Remind[3]. Unfortunately, the resulting decision trees were severely overfitted, with most leaf nodes containing only a single training instance[4]. The indices derived from the trees referenced all possible attributes, and were therefore the same as those used by IB1.

The historical case bases were randomly generated for each test run, and were restricted to non-overflowing equilibria with both treatment stages at least half full. The test cases were also randomly generated, but with the treatment stages 80-95% full. Figures 3 and 4 show, respectively, the percentage of overflows generated by each indexing method, and the percentage of error in the desired amount present in the treatment stages for non-overflowing cases. The solid lines show the performance of the qualitative-indexing approach, and the dashed lines show the results of IB1. Each data point represents the average of 400 test cases (20 for each of 20 different case-bases). Except where the lines cross in Figure 3, all data points are statistically significant ($p < 0.01$).

As can be seen, model-based indexing provides much better results than IB1 for all sizes of case-bases. With more than 700 cases, qualitative indexing reduces the overflow rate to near zero, while its error rate is about half that of IB1. The only surprise in the test results is the drop in IB1's overflow rate for very small case-bases. On inspection, it appears that IB1 is choosing very conservative settings in these cases, resulting in fewer overflows at the expense of a much higher error rate.

# 7 Related Work

A good introduction to instance-based learning can be found in [1]. The IB1 algorithm was taken from this paper. We did not compare our work with the IB2 algorithm and its derivatives, since their motivation is to reduce the storage requirements of IB1 at the expense of accuracy. However, [1] notes that one of the problems with techniques for reducing storage space is that it increases the sparsity of cases in the parameter space. Hence, applying our indexing technique in conjunction with methods for reducing storage space should prove very profitable.

If we view the equation solving as graph traversal, then our method of solving for fixed and output parameters attributes is somewhat similar to the "footprint" method employed in the planning domain by [10]. In both cases, graph traversal

---

[3] Remind is a commercial case-based reasoning system distributed by Cognitive Systems, Inc..

[4] [4] presents current work which uses statistical significance testing to prune the decision trees produced by Remind.

is employed to identify the subset of attributes that are considered to be relevant indices.

An alternate approach to combining model-based and instance-based learning can be found in [7] Quinlan uses a quantitative model to correct the values retrieved by a normal case-based system, by applying the model both to the target instance and to the retrieved instance. His supposition is that, if the model is correct, it should be possible to calculate a corrective factor to apply to the retrieved instance. This approach works well if one has a good quantitative model. In domains with weak models, however, the corrective factors proved counterproductive. Our approach, on the other hand, requires only a qualitative model, and uses the model, not to correct the cases, but only to increase their relative density in the parameter space. Where a qualitative model cannot be developed, or can only partially be developed, our approach degrades gracefully to providing indices equivalent to IB1.

Perhaps the most similar work appears in [2], which uses decision trees to derive indices for case-based reasoning. In this approach, C4.5 [6] is given the case-base and induces a decision tree for each input parameter. Rather than using the decision trees directly to provide values for the inputs, the attributes which appear in the nodes of the trees are used to construct case-based indices. However, since our domain uses a real-valued "class" attribute, we were unable to produce decision trees that improved on the indices used by IB1 (see Section 6).

## 8  Future Work

We are currently applying our approach to a real process control problem. To deal with the inevitable complexities this introduces, we are enhancing MISQ in two ways:

- Robust numerical filtering. The input to MISQ is raw sensor information, which it converts to qualitative behaviors in order to construct a model. Hence, MISQ must be able to deal with data problems such as noise and missing values.
- Initial model. Accepting an initial model will allow MISQ to take advantage of what the user already knows about the operation of a system. This is helpful either when the sensor information is ambiguous (and, hence, subject to several alternate interpretations), or if the system contains hidden variables which are known to the user.

Farther in the future, we may consider lifting the assumption that the control problem seeks to produce an equilibrium condition, albeit one that only lasts as long as the values of the fixed parameters remain unchanged. To do this, we would allow the user to specify both the values and desired directions of change for the output variables. However, a great deal of power is gained by knowing that all derivatives are zero, so lifting the equilibrium assumption is likely to substantially increase the number of parameters appearing in the indices.

Finally, recent work in [5] extends Cardie's approach by working directly with the information gain used in constructing decision trees. We expect that this work will provide more competitive results than those obtained using Remind. We will be testing our indexing technique against [5] in the near future.

# 9 Conclusions

Case-based reasoning provides a good technique for working in weak-theory domains. Its effectiveness, however, depends on a good indexing scheme into the historical cases. This paper has presented a method for deriving good indices from qualitative models of physical systems.

This approach is particularly promising for process control problems. It is often not possible to develop a good quantitative model of a process control system, and hence there is no basis but experience for setting control parameters. In these cases, if historical information is available, our approach is a natural one to take. The historical information provides the necessary case-base, and the normal level of instrumentation present in most process control systems provides the data MISQ needs to build a qualitative model. The result, a qualitative understanding of system behavior plus actual historical experience, provides an effective way to determine accurate settings for control parameters.

# References

1. D. W. Aha, D. Kibler, and M. K. Albert: Instance-based learning algorithms. Machine Learning 6 (1991) pp 37–66.
2. C. Cardie: Using decision trees to improve case-based learning. Proceedings of the Tenth International Conference on Machine Learning (1993) pp 25–32.
3. T. H. Cover and P. E. Hart: Nearest neighbor pattern classification. *IEEE Transactions on Information Theory* 13 (1967) pp 21–47.
4. M. Goodman: Results on controlling action with projective visualization. *Proceedings of the Twelfth National Conference on Artificial Intelligence* (1994) pp 1245–1250.
5. J. J. Parry and C. X. Ling: Deciding Weights for IBL Algorithms using C4.5. unpublished draft (1994).
6. J. R. Quinlan: *C4.5: Programs for Machine Learning* 1 (1992).
7. J. R. Quinlan: Combining instance-based and model-based learning. *Proceedings of the Tenth International Conference on Machine Learning* (1993) pp 236–243.
8. S. Ramachandran, R. Mooney, and B. Kuipers: Learning Qualitative Models for Systems with Multiple Operating Regions. *Proceedings of the Eighth International Workshop on Qualitative Reasoning about Physical Systems* (1994) pp 212-223.
9. B. L. Richards, I. Kraan, and B. Kuipers: Automatic abduction of qualitative models. *Proceedings of the Tenth National Conference on Artificial Intelligence* (1992) pp 723-728.
10. M. M. Veloso: *Planning and Learning by Analogical Reasoning*, Springer-Verlag Lecture Notes in Artificial Intelligence (1994).

# Using gestalten to retrieve cases

Jörg Walter Schaaf, Michael Nowak, Angi Voß

Artificial Intelligence Research Division
German National Research Center for Computer Science (GMD)
P.O. Box 1316 D-53757, Sankt Augustin, Germany
phone: +49-2241-142855
fax: +49-2241-142384
e-mail:Joerg.Schaaf@gmd.de

**Abstract.** Design and construction of buildings is a most expensive enterprise. CAD plans of architects and civil engineers contain thousands of layout fragments (cases) which could be helpful for later use. In FABEL[1] we try to find those fragments which are useful for a problem, to evaluate them and adapt them to the current context.

The present approach helps to support a CAD system with case based reasoning (CBR). As usual in CBR we reduce the notion of *usefulness* of cases to the one of *similarity*. We describe a similarity criterion that is based on detection of gestalten. Gestalten try to catch the main topological properties and spatial relations of an object constellation. To detect them, focused object groups of a CAD plan are represented as sketches and compared with a set of sketches of predefined gestalten. Gestalt recognition yields an index for the determination of similarity between a plan to be elaborated and a plan stored in a conventional case base. In this article we focus on the aspects of gestalt acquisition, representation and recognition, and their integration in the FABEL prototype.

## 1 What are gestalten good for?

*The problem: how to find reusable cases in CAD plans of buildings?* The CAD system our domain experts use is called A4 (Hovestadt, 1993). It is specialized to architectural design with a focus on the conceptual phase. Objects are placed in the three spatial dimensions. They have different types and are presented as ellipses or rectangles. Rectangles are projections of precise bounding boxes while ellipses are more abstract space reservations. A problem is a piece of an object oriented CAD plan (in the following "plan") that is to be refined or augmented. In their work, architects often encounter problems that remind them of similar situations in previous designs. Adapting the former solution may be easier than solving their problem from scratch. However, searching for the old cases in all

---

[1] This research was supported by the German Ministry for Research and Technology (BMFT) within the joint project FABEL under contract no. 01IW104. Project partners in FABEL are German National Research Center for Computer Science (GMD), Sankt Augustin, BSR Consulting GmbH, München, Technical University of Dresden, HTWK Leipzig, University of Freiburg, and University of Karlsruhe.

the old plans may be very time consuming. It would be a great help if a problem could be passed as a query to the retrieval of similar pieces of plans, called cases, and solutions could be made available in seconds.

So our first task is how we can find cases in a case base which are similar to the current problem.

The retrieval of reusable, similar pieces of CAD plans is a new and interesting research problem. In the FABEL project different approaches have been developed (Voß, 1994b), (Voß, 1994a). Some of them ignore geometry and calculate similarity using the type of objects and their number. These approaches calculate results fast but the precision is low. Others focus on the topology of the objects in detail, but are too slow to deal with bigger case bases.

In this article we will introduce a new method of how to catch the main topological properties of a case in very short time. We first describe the concept as introduced in (Schaaf, 1994b) and (Schaaf, 1994a) and then its integration in FABEL and its evaluation.

*The idea to use gestalten for indexing* To catch the main topological features of a case we want to focus on a few constellations that catch one's eye instead of thoroughly examining all relationships between all objects. Often there are typical patterns that the architect recognizes, remembers and reuses. We symbolize them by icons like fishbone, comb, quadrangle etc. Because they are only patterns in our mind, emergent shapes (Soufi & Edmonds, 1994) that are never explicitly included in the plans, we call them *gestalten*. From our architects we learned that they use such gestalten to remember similar problems and their solutions. Gestalten are surface features of CAD plans, but meaningful ones. This is the reason why the gestalten shall be used in FABEL to retrieve similar cases. We try to recognize gestalten fast and use them in quick-time retrieval methods like associative memories.

Although knowing how useful indexing by gestalten would be, it is not realistic to ask architects to index the plans by hand because there are sometimes more than hundreds of cases in the plans of a building. We have to ask how we can index cases automatically, which means how we can automatically recognize gestalten.

So, the problem of how to find reusable cases specializes to the problem of how to find gestalten in plans.

*Which gestalten are relevant?* In working with experts, we identified a set of gestalten. We gave the architect fragments of plans to which he should attribute gestalten given on cards. Besides these gestalten, he had empty cards on which he could draw new ones. From all the gestalten we finally had, only those which were really used are included in figure 4. This initial set can be extended by the architect while working with our system. The acquisition of gestalten will be the topic of section 4.

*How to recognize gestalten automatically?* We considered two possibilities of how to search for gestalten in plans.

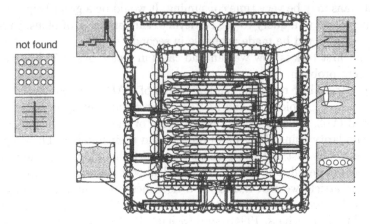

not found

**Fig. 1.** An Plan with gestalt labels

- First possibility: For each gestalt an algorithm is given that searches for the gestalt within the plan. In the worst case, this approach must check the position and constellation of hundreds of CAD objects. If a feature of a gestalt is found, the search for other gestalten may become necessary. Because the feature tests have to be done redundantly for each gestalt, in the worst case we need time depending on the product out of the number of predefined gestalten, the number of features of each gestalt and the number of objects in the whole group.

- Another way: On the other hand, we may find an abstract representation of object groups which matches the equivalent representations of gestalt examples[2]. In this manner, each object would only be examined once. The identification of an object group is then only a comparison of abstract representations. We have to be careful that this comparison will not become too expensive. Because architects only accept response times below a few seconds, it is important to keep the time for representation and comparison as short as possible. For this reason we decided on the second method. It will be detailed in section 7.

But first of all, we have to clarify what must be represented, what can be neglected and what representations are easy to compare.

## 2 How to represent gestalten?

### 2.1 Sketches as economical representations of gestalten

The main idea is to sketch a group of objects in the same manner as we sketch a stick person: the constellation of head, body, arms and legs of a human. Perhaps

---

[2] You find the idea that humans transform pictures for a comparison into an abstract form e.g. in (Marr, 1982)

the challenge of this approach is to find sketches that represent groups of the same gestalt equally and those of different gestalt unequally.

Figure 2 shows the origin of the idea and how it was developed.

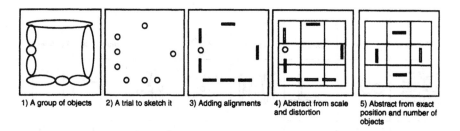

1) A group of objects  2) A trial to sketch it  3) Adding alignments  4) Abstract from scale and distortion  5) Abstract from exact position and number of objects

**Fig. 2.** How a group of objects can be sketched

**Object group:** Part 1 of figure 2 shows an arrangement of rooms on a floor. Ellipses indicate the approximate position of objects in the conceptual phase. It is a typical object group that is often found in plans. We call this gestalt a quadrangle.

**Trial to sketch it:** The second subfigure shows how a sketch would look if only the centers of objects were represented. The problems are that on the one hand, too much information gets lost while on the other hand, this way we get different sketches for constellations of the same gestalt. (E.g. if two quadrangles differ in size.)

**Adding alignments:** To avoid too much loss of structure, we decided to take the alignment of an object into account. The alignment is represented as a short line of the same orientation. A small circle indicates an object without preferential axis (Subfigure 3 in fig. 2).

**Abstract from scale and distortion:** If the scale and the distortion of a gestalt were considered, it would be impossible to classify gestalten correctly. Humans also neglect these attributes while sketching things and in recognizing gestalten. Subfigure 4 shows a sketch which abstracts from scale (by scaling a grid) and abstracts from distortion (by distorting the grid the same way).

**Neglect exact position and number of objects:** In the previous sketches, the exact number of objects is noticed. To abstract from similarly aligned objects, we defined a way to merge objects into one element. Subfigure 5 shows the result of this merging.

Thus we constructed a sketch that may be developed out of many occurrences of the gestalt quadrangle.

These considerations gave rise to the set of sketch elements shown in fig. 3. Since the grids used in the plans allow to arrange elements only orthogonally, it is sufficient to express horizontal and vertical alignments.

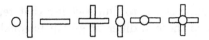

**Fig. 3.** Possible elements of a sketch

| fishbone | row | bug leg | comb | regulary filled | H | dragon-fly | quadrangle |
|---|---|---|---|---|---|---|---|
| | | | | | | | |
| | | | | | | | |

**Fig. 4.** Examples of object groups and their sketches

## 2.2 The sketching algorithm

The sketching algorithm accepts a group of CAD objects and returns one or two sketches of that group. The algorithm coinsists of the following steps:

**Bounding box:** Set a bounding box around the given object group. *This serves to place the grid.*

**Grid:** Scale a grid of 3*3 equally sized fields so that it fills out the bounding box. *Scaling and distorting the grid we abstract from scale and distortion of the object group.*

**Alignments:** Sketch each object in its center as a line with the alignment of the object. If the object has no detectable orientation we represent it as a circle. *This keeps information needed to distinguish the gestalten.*

**Inner merge:** Merge equally oriented objects within the same grid field. *This reduces the number of sketch elements and abstracts from the exact position of each one.*

**Objects without orientation:** If there are only objects without orientation within one field, compute the orientation of the whole group.

**First sketch:** Center all symbols of one field. *So we get only one of the elements shown in fig. 3 in each grid field.* This is the first sketch to be returned.

**Outer merge:** Try to apply the rules of the inner merge to objects in neighboring grid fields. *The outer merge is crucial because it abstracts very much from the exact position of objects and depends on calculation order.*

**Second sketch:** Center again all symbols of one field and return the result as the second sketch.

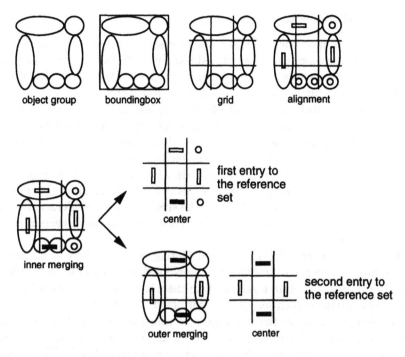

object group   boundingbox   grid   alignment

first entry to
the reference
set

center

inner merging

second entry to
the reference set

outer merging   center

**Fig. 5.** Steps of the sketching algorithm illustrated by means of the gestalt quadrangle.

In section 4 we will show how for each gestalt a set of sketches is acquired as examples. These sets are called reference sets. Although ideal, it is not realistic to have one sketch for each gestalt. Therefore we allow different sketches in the reference set of the same gestalt. The reference sets must contain enough examples so that many occurrences of a gestalt can be recognized.

## 3 How to recognize gestalten?

For retrieval, the case base (once for all) and the query have to be indexed by gestalt names. For this purpose, sketching is applied to the current problem (that means to an incomplete plan) as well as to the cases. Because the same mechanism (sketching) is used to represent groups of objects in cases and in problems, the recognition of the gestalten is insensitive toward the quality of the representation through the sketching.

The new question is now, how those groups of objects that possibly constitute a gestalt can be focused? An answer is deferred to section 3.2. For the time being, we assume that an interesting object group has already been chosen and describe the indexing of a problem situation.

## 3.1 Which sketches to compare?

According to our intuition, sketches are representations which make similar things equal. If these sketches are reduced too much, dissimilar things may possibly be equally represented. To prevent this, we check if the gestalt can already be found prior to a further abstraction during outer merging.

- **First, try to find the gestalt after completing the inner merge.** We first sketch the object group (as in 2.2) until the inner merge is completed. We now try to find[3] the generated sketch in one of the reference sets. If a sketch is found, the name of the gestalt is one of the indices for retrieval.

- **Second, try to recognize a gestalt after the outer merge.** If an identification after inner merging fails, we merge between neighboring grid fields (outer merging) and check again to see if the sketch under consideration is contained in the reference set of any gestalt. Otherwise, we have encountered a missing reference.

- **Third, try to repair the sketch.** During retrieval, there is no time to solve the missing reference problem in a principled way. The sketch should be ignored if it does not contain a gestalt. Else there is at most time for a fix. That means, a best fitting gestalt has to be determined. For that purpose we have to find that sketch within all the reference sets which is most similar to the one we generated. This task can be performed by an associative memory. We may accept the resulting superficial classification, or else rationalize it. That means, for each difference between the generated sketch and the most similar gestalt sketch, we have to find a justification to eliminate it. We find arguments for this in early stages of the merging process or in the object group itself by answering questions like: *Is it possible to find an object close to field 5, which was only by chance represented in field 4? Is there a good reason to represent it alternatively in field 5? Can this object be represented by a horizontal line? If so, then this was the sketch of an abnormal comb.* The example in fig. 6 shows how we can repair a misbuilt sketch of the gestalt comb.

In repairing the sketch, the point of view changes. During sketching, objects are abstracted from. During repair, the original objects are examined to find justification for demanded changes of sketches. In this way, the repair is a form of expectation driven recognition. The expectation is that the focused and sketched object group is a representative of a predefined gestalt. Accordingly, the conditions positioning an object in certain boundaries can be relaxed without leading to an insufficient discrimination. So the recognition of gestalten is supported by a repairing that couples the data driven representation with an expectation driven interpretation.

If one of the three attempts was successful, a gestalt within a group of objects was recognized and the plan can be indexed by its name. In FABEL, two retrieval methods were extended to use gestalt indices.

Figure 7 summarizes the major steps in gestalt recognition. We now turn to focusing.

---

[3] This search is not a major problem because a sketch is only made up of 9 fields and each field can only contain one of 8 possible elements.

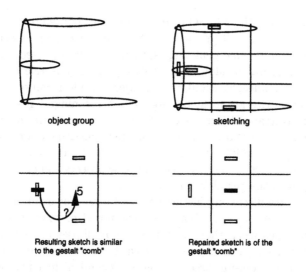

object group          sketching

Resulting sketch is similar          Repaired sketch is of the
to the gestalt "comb"                gestalt "comb"

**Fig. 6.** An object is interpreted as a comb tooth

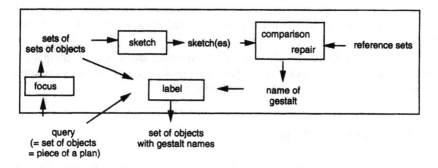

**Fig. 7.** Data flow between focusing, sketching, and comparison during gestalt recognition

## 3.2 Focusing

Focusing is the step before sketching the cases and the query. Only for the reference sets, the expert has a priori specified isolated object groups as examples for each gestalt (section 8). But cases and queries may contain any number of gestalten. The problem is which subsets of objects possibly constitute a gestalt?

Focusing is a challenging problem and active area of research. Gestalt psychology (Helson, 1933) or (Zusne, 1970) suggests to group objects by similarity or spatial proximity. The research of Treisman (Treisman, 1982) und (Treisman, 1985) confirms the cognitive relevance of this approach. Gestalt laws were applied for instance in the MAX system (Rome, 1992) and (Rome, 1993)) developed at GMD within the TASSO project. Others suggested to take into account temporal proximity as well (Yang, Garrett, Shaw, & Rendell, 1994).

Since gestalten are emergent shapes, their constituents need not be designed in the same temporal window. But spatial proximity is relevant because the constituents are connected. Similarity of objects would mean objects with identical types. This criterion must be modified. A meaningful gestalt may not be composed of arbitrary objects. We still have to acquire the knowledge about what combinations of types may make up the constituents of a gestalt. With that knowledge, we can filter the CAD plan by the admissible types ((Treisman, 1982), (Treisman, 1985)) identify spatially close objects and check them for type compatibility wrt. the gestalt's constituents.

Besides, we are discussing hierarchical gestalten. For example, a quadrangle is composed of four rows, fishbones are composed of rows, and bug legs are part of dragon flies when they are refined from ellipses to rectangles. Assume we could construct a hierarchy of gestalten, then we could use this knowledge for top-down or bottom-up directed context-dependent focusing: we could look whether a row is part of a quadrangle or whether a quadrangle is made up of rows.

In addition, focusing could be controlled by the objects. In accordance with the model of pattern recognition in the visual cortex, specific regularities in the image could lead to a synchronization of the related objects (cf. (Reitböck, 1993)).

On the other hand, we discuss using sketching itself for the focusing. The idea is to sketch the whole case or problem (as described) and to examine only those parts in more detail, where structure strikes.

## 4   How to acquire gestalten?

In practice, gestalten will be acquired incrementally. In working with the system the architect identifies pieces of his current plan as queries. As we have seen, interpreting a query may indicate missing references, sketches that cannot be associated to a gestalt. During retrieval, there is time for quick superficial reactions, only. Later on, the missing references must dealt with in a principled way, namely as follows:

*How to cope with the missing reference problem?* Missing references may have several causes.
- Focusing was wrong: the sketch has no gestalt. The sketch should be ignored.
- Comparison was not good enough: This is handled by repairing the sketch during retrieval.
- A reference set is incomplete: the sketch should be included later on in a separate acquisition phase.
- A gestalt is missing: the sketch is to be included in a new reference set for a new gestalt. This, too, should be done later on, not during retrieval.

If during acquisition, two object groups for different gestalten are represented by the same sketch (c.f. the lightning-bolt line in figure 8), we have encountered a collision problem.

Training sets of gestalt occurrences     Reference sets of sketches

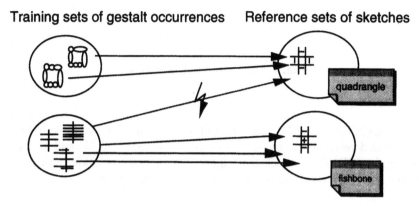

**Fig. 8.** Sketches are associated as representatives of gestalten (here quadrangle and fish-bone)

*How to cope with the collision problem?* If the number of collisions increases too much, we have to refine the classification. This can be accomplished as follows:
  - By expansion of the alphabet. (See fig. 3)
- By refinement of the grid, e.g. from 3*3 to 5*5 fields.
- By changing the layout of the grid (e.g. like a honeycomb).
- By statistical methods during the calculation of a "balanced bounding box"
- By changing the merging rules.
- By renunciation of the grid, using a sort of compass card to locate the elements.

Such important modifications are not performed automatically, only collision detection is automatically performed. Figure 9 summarizes the data flow during gestalt acquisition. Even though it is desirable to distinguish the gestalten carefully, we have to take into account that it does not matter to FABEL if an object group – in question – is annotated with all possible interpretations. Even humans do not always manage to make a clear classification. Instead, they say that something almost looks like X but at the same time has similarities to Y.

## 5   Integration in FABEL

To make the gestalt approach operational, algorithms for sketching, comparison and repair, focusing, and acquisition have to be implemented. In the context of

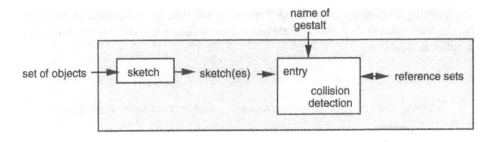

**Fig. 9.** Data flow during acquisition

FABEL, gestalten are to be used as additional features by two already existing feature-based retrieval methods: an associative memory (ASM) and a distance-based method (FAV) (Voß, 1994b). Figure 10 shows the data flow between these components and the gestalt recognition module from figure 7.

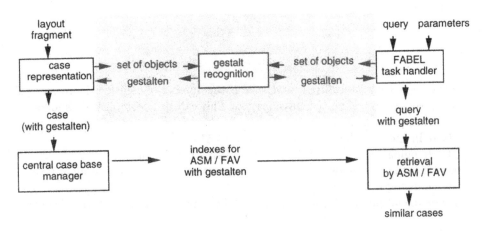

**Fig. 10.** Dataflow between gestalt recognition and ASM or FAV retrieval in FABEL

To check very quickly whether indexing and retrieving CAD plans with gestalten was a good idea at all, the first thing we did was to extend the retrieval methods ASM and FAV to take into account user-detected gestalten. This is shown in the part of figure 10 with the white background.

The architect was offered a menu with the eight initially predefined gestalten (c.f. section 1), which he could attach to any of the cases and to the query. He was very enthousiastic and manually marked a 100 of the 126 cases in our test base with gestalten. The cases are labeled with up to 6 occurrences of gestalten.

In total we have 157 examples of user-detected gestalten.

The features used so far by ASM and FAV (e.g. types and number of objects) mainly ignored topological and geometric information. By including the gestalt features, we expected to increase selectivity. In detail, the following turned out:

- **FAV** represents the exact number of gestalten and (in our experiment) weighs this feature with 0.113. FAV retrieves cases beyond a minimal similarity threshold. If the treshold is high, gestalten can have a minor overall effect, only. If the threshold is lowered, they may have more impact. But it is doubtful whether FAV will often be invoked with such a low threshold. Otherwise, the weight 0.113 for gestalten should be increased.

- **ASM** generates two kinds of indices, vague ones with the gestalt names only and exact ones with the number of occurrences of each gestalt (c.f. (Voß, 1994b)). ASM can operate with exact and vague indexes and for both compute an exact and a partial match. Exact match retrieves only cases with the same features, partial match allows significant overlaps. Invoking ASM with (exact or vague) gestalten as additional features affects retrieval with partial match in a way hard to predict – less or more or the same number of cases may be retrieved. But for exact match, it augments selectivity. Therefore, if retrieval shall be fast but selective, we recommend to take geometry and topology into account and use ASM with vague or exact gestalten and exact match.

In particular this latter option was enough motivation to go on implementing the gestalt algorithms (the grey part in figure 10). By now, at the end of 1994, the sketching algorithm is complete. Acquisition, comparison, and a simple form of repair are straightforward, while focusing still needs some conceptual work and will be implemented in the first half of 1995.

# 6 Evaluation of sketching

The sketching algorithm is implemented in C++. Together with a visualization component for a single step mode it has a size of 60KB. On a SUN 20 it processes our examples, which consist of about a dozen objects, in about 0.2 seconds. As some are very similar, we selected 50 sufficiently different ones for evaluation: 9 bug legs, 2 combs, 22 dragon flies, 4 regular fillings, 46 rows and 7 quadrangles. By chance, there are no Hs and no fish bones. There are combinations of dragon flies with bug legs and with rows. In our sample, all gestalt occurrences consist of objects of the same type. All 50 examples were processed with the sketching algorithm.

The algorithm produced 11 new sketches beside the ones shown in figure 4. All of them were new examples of existing gestalten and could be added to their reference sets without any collisions. So we could extend our initial reference sets by 5 new sketches of bug legs, 3 new dragon flies, 1 new rectangle, 2 new rows. Figure 11 shows a group recognized as a comb and two groups suggesting new sketches of bug legs.

The reference sets will surely grow further. We then expect collisions, in particular between Hs and bug legs. We will be able to avoid them by filtering

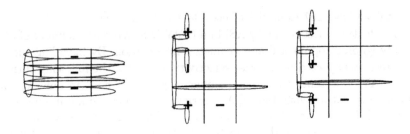

**Fig. 11.** Sketch of a comb and two bug leg sketches

the object groups by their types of objects. Although both bug legs and Hs are or can be composed of bounding boxes for supply air connections, they differ in scale. This is already the most intricate differentiation we expect. Thus, our initial choices for sketching gestalten have turned to be out nearly perfect.

## 7  Scope

Although largely tailored to the requirements of FABEL, the present approach can certainly be used beyond this domain. It indexes plans in accordance with the gestalten contained in a plan. In FABEL, this index is used to determine similarity and finally to select cases. In other domains gestalten could be used e.g. for focusing attention or recursive image reduction.

In order to determine the scope of the approach, input and sketching algorithm are to be examined.

- The input should be an image. The image should be composed of objects since the central idea of producing a sketch depends on the alignment and topology of objects. The presented approach is not limited to the A4 world though the defined alphabet for sketching is specialized. It can be replaced changing the type of plans it should work on. If the image consists of pixels, an appropriate preprocessing is to be performed. Several realistic examples of the gestalten to be recognized should be available to generate powerful reference sets.

- The suggested representation algorithm sketches object groups in CAD plans in the domain of architecture. If two object groups are of similar gestalt they are sketched equally (or the sketches are in the same reference set). The comparison of sketches is fast. If gestalten should be recognized in other domains, the set of the representation elements may have to be modified.

The presented approach should not be mixed up with the tasks of pattern, image feature or character recognition. It is more comparable with watching the stars on firmament, finding the constellation[4] "scorpion" than finding which one of the 2965 japanese kanji characters ( e.g. (Kawamura, T., Yura, & Tanaka, 1992)) can be identified. We try to name characteristic constellations that were never created as items. Nevertheless we use some common techniques of pattern recognition such as finding a bounding box, scaling grids or representing alignments.

**Acknowledgment** We would like to thank the FABEL team, especially Barbara Schmidt-Belz for her cooperation in knowledge acquisition and integration with the FABEL prototype. Also thanks to Wolfgang Gräther and Bernd Linowski who extended the ASM and FAV retrieval methods wrt. gestalten, and to Barbara Schmidt-Belz and Friedrich Gebhardt for their comments on this paper. Special thanks also to Merinda Johnson for the support she gave in editing this paper.

# Reference

Helson, H. (1933). The Fundmental Propositions of Gestaltpsychologie. *Psychological Review, 40,* 13–32.

Hovestadt, L. (1993). *A4 – digitales bauen: Ein Modell für die weitgehende Computerunterstützung von Entwurf, Konstruktion und Betrieb von Gebäuden.* Ph.D. thesis, Institut für industrielle Bauproduktion der Universität Karlsruhe.

Kawamura, A., T., M., Yura, K., & Tanaka, A. (1992). On-line Recognition of Freely Handwritten Japanese Characters. In *Pattern Recognition Methodology and Systems,* Vol. II, pp. 183–186 Los Alamitos, California. 11th IAPR International Conference on Pattern Recognition, IEEE Computer Society Press.

Marr, D. (1982). *Vision - A Computational Investigation into the Human Representation and Processing of Visual Information.* W.H. Freeman and Company, New York (NY).

Reitböck, H. J. (1993). Mechanismen der Mustererkennung im Sehsystem. In Herzog, O., Christaller, T., & Schütt, D. (Eds.), *Grundlagen und Anwendungen der Künstlichen Intelligenz,* pp. 90–106 Berlin. 17. Fachtagung für Künstliche Intelligenz, Springer-Verlag.

Rome, E. (1992). Wahrnehmungspsychologie, Bilderkennung und der Grafikdesigner. Tech. rep. TASSO 36, GMD.

Rome, E. (1993). Max, ein maschinelles Gestalt-Erkennungssystem. *KI – Künstliche Intelligenz, 7*(Sonderheft), 70–71.

Schaaf, J. W. (1994a). Detecting Gestalts in CAD-plans to be used as Indices for Case-retrieval in Architecture. In Nebel, B., & Dreschler-Fischer, L. (Eds.), *KI-94: Advances in Artificial Intelligence,* Lecture Notes in Artificial Intelligence 861, pp. 154–165 Berlin. Springer-Verlag.

---

[4] The most similar approach we found was (Tuceryan, Jain, & Ahuja, 1992)

Schaaf, J. W. (1994b). Gestalts in CAD-plans, Analysis of a Similarity Concept. In Gero, J., & Sudweeks, F. (Eds.), *AI in Design'94*, Kluwer Academic Publishers, pp. 437–446 Dordrecht.

Soufi, R., & Edmonds, E. (1994). Perceptual interpretation and representation of emergent shapes. In Damski, J., & Woodbury, R. (Eds.), *Workshop notes: Reasoning with Shapes in Design*, No. 1, pp. 39–45 Lausanne, Switzerland. AID, Swiss Federal Institute of Technology.

Treisman, A. (1982). Perceptual Grouping and Attention in Visual Search for Features and for Objects. *Journal of Experimental Psychology: Human Perception and Performance, 8*(2), 194–214.

Treisman, A. (1985). Preattentive Processing in Vision. *Computer Vision, Graphics and Image Processing*, pp. 156–177.

Tuceryan, M., Jain, A., & Ahuja, N. (1992). Supervised Classification of Early Perceptual Structure in Dot Patterns. In *Pattern Recognition Methodology and Systems*, Vol. II, pp. 88–91 Los Alamitos, California. 11th IAPR International Conference on Pattern Recognition, IEEE Computer Society Press.

Voß, A. e. a. (1994a). Retrieval of similar layouts – about a very hybrid approach in FABEL. In Gero, J., & Sudweeks, F. (Eds.), *AI in Design'94*, Kluwer Academic Publishers, pp. 625–640 Dordrecht.

Voß, A. (1994b). Similarity concepts and retrieval methods. FABEL-Report 13, GMD, Sankt Augustin.

Yang, D., Garrett, J., Shaw, D., & Rendell, L. (1994). An intelligent symbol usage assistant for CAD systems. *IEEE Computer Society*, 32–41.

Zusne, L. (1970). *Visual Perception of Form*. Academic Press, Inc., New York (NY).

# A Comparison of Incremental Case-Based Reasoning and Inductive Learning

Barry Smyth[1] and Pádraig Cunningham[2]

[1]Hitachi Dublin Laboratory, Trinity College, Dublin 2, IRELAND
{E-mail: barry.smyth@hdl.ie}

[2]Department of Computer Science, Trinity College, Dublin 2, IRELAND

**Abstract.** This paper focuses on problems where the reuse of old solutions seems appropriate but where conventional case-based reasoning (CBR) methodology is not adequate because a complete description of the new problem is not available to trigger case retrieval. We describe an information theoretic technique that solves this problem by producing focused questions to fill out the case description. This use of information theoretic techniques in CBR raises the question of whether a standard inductive learning approach would not solve this problem adequately. The main contribution of this paper is an evaluation of how this incremental case-based reasoning compares with a pure inductive learning approach to the same task.

## 1 Introduction

The CBR strategy described in this paper is incremental in the sense that the target case description is built up during the case retrieval process. This incremental strategy is motivated by the fact that there are many potential CBR applications for which it is expensive to determine the predictive features of the target case. Our system produces focused questions for the user, only requesting those features that are useful in retrieving good matches from the case-base.

This work was motivated by an attempt to re-engineer a model-based reasoning (MBR) fault diagnosis system as a case-based reasoning system. One of the great strengths of the model-based system was that the main part of its reasoning mechanism was goal driven so the operator was only asked to perform tests that would contribute to a particular diagnosis. In this problem domain the data used in diagnosis seems naturally to fall into two categories, free data and expensive data. The model-based system only requested such expensive data as was needed.

So our CBR implementation has free case features and expensive case features. In this paper we describe an information theoretic approach to incremental case retrieval where only a subset of the expensive features are requested from the user. In an earlier paper [1] we have compared this incremental CBR method with the model-based approach and found that less data was required for correct diagnoses than with the model-based system; on average the CBR version asked 30% fewer questions than did the MBR system.

The information theoretic criteria used in incremental CBR (I-CBR) bear the hallmark of inductive learning techniques. However there is an important distinction in the manner in which I-CBR manipulates its training data and the manner in which conventional inductive learning methods treat their data sets. This distinction is made in the literature by referring to conventional methods (such as ID3 [2] and COBWEB [3]) as performing *eager generalisation*, whereas I-CBR performs *lazy generalisation*. Very briefly, eager generalisation involves the compilation of the training data into abstractions, during the training process, often throwing away the raw data after training. In contrast, lazy generalisers delay this process and represent the concept descriptions directly with the data itself. There are a number of advantages offered by lazy approaches like I-CBR from both a knowledge representation viewpoint and a performance viewpoint.

In this paper we evaluate our incremental CBR by comparison with a pure inductive learning approach; this performance evaluation is presented in section 4. But first we start in section 2 with a look at tasks that require incremental CBR. Then in section 3 we describe the incremental CBR strategy itself.

## 2 Problems Requiring Incremental CBR

Our experience with CBR applications, particularly in the area of diagnosis, convinces us that there is an important class of problems for which it is difficult to determine the predictive features of the target case in advance of case retrieval. In these situations some features may be readily available while others are more expensive to collect. In the rest of this paper we will use the following notation for these sets of features:

**F**   is the set of all features that can describe a case

**F** $= \mathbf{I} \cup \mathbf{E}$ where

**I** $= \{I_1, ..., I_i\}$ the set of inexpensive or *free* features

**E** $= \{E_1, ..., E_f\}$ the set of features that are expensive to determine

The importance of this observation is that, of the features that are expensive to obtain, only some may be needed to determine a suitable case (or cases) for retrieval. Machine learning research distinguishes *characteristic descriptions*[1] from *discriminant*[2] *descriptions* [4] and we argue that where features are expensive to determine a discriminant description is sufficient for case retrieval. If the case representation is a good one then **F** is a characteristic description. However, some subset of **F** may be adequate as a discriminant description. In particular, **I** plus some subset of **E** may be

---

[1]A characteristic description is a description of a class of objects that states facts which are true about all objects in the class. It is usually used to discriminate objects in the given class from *all other possible* classes.

[2]A discriminant description is a description of a class of objects in the context of a *fixed* set of other classes of objects. It states only those properties of the objects in the given class that are necessary to distinguish them from objects in the other classes.

adequate for retrieval. The challenge for incremental CBR is to generate queries that will require the user to provide a minimal subset of **E**.

Before introducing our mechanism for incremental CBR we will describe some potential CBR applications that fit this characterisation.

## 2.1 Diagnosis

Much of the work on incremental CBR described here focused on the re-engineering of a model-based system (called NODAL) for fault diagnosis of power-supplies [5,6]. The main components of this system are shown in Figure 1.

NODAL is designed to operate in a repair shop so the initial input data in the diagnosis are the results from the test equipment on which it was confirmed that the unit was faulty. These function tests are performed on the unit as a 'black box', and measure outputs associated with test inputs. The tests will number between twenty and forty depending on the complexity of the circuit. However, because the internals of the unit are not being examined, the amount of diagnostic information in these tests is limited. The test results are processed by the Function Test Rules (a shallow reasoning component in NODAL) and a set of candidate faulty modules is produced. In the CBR implementation of NODAL these function test results make up the free features in the case description.

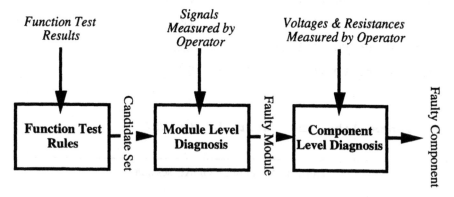

**Fig. 1.** The main components in the NODAL fault diagnosis system.

In order to further isolate the fault it is necessary to perform some internal measurements on the unit modules. These measurements are taken at internal nodes in the circuit; evidently these are expensive features. Measurements may involve estimating the goodness of a signal, or measuring voltages and resistances. A typical circuit will have about 20 nodes at the module level and approaching 100 nodes altogether. Consequently there is a large number of measurements that can be taken during the diagnosis. The advantage of this goal-driven diagnosis is that it requests only measurements that contribute to its current hypothesis. In a typical session only about 20% of the total possible measurements are actually requested. A typical dialogue with the system is shown below in Table 1.

Even by NODAL's standards this dialogue is particularly short as the first module to be examined proves to be the faulty one. Nevertheless, it serves to illustrate how the goal-directed reasoning focuses the requests for measurements from the operator.

This clarifies the requirements of a CBR implementation of NODAL. Since there is a cost associated with determining the inputs to the diagnosis it is important that the CBR system should not need to have all the inputs in advance. Moreover, it should be able to direct the operator as to what measurements are important just as the goal-driven system does.

---

**Setup for Test Vector 1**

What is the SIGNAL of NODE-2?  <u>Good</u>

What is the SIGNAL of NODE-3?  <u>Bad</u>

*It looks like the fault is in the LOCAL-POWER-SUPPLY module*

**Switching to component level analysis...**

What is the VOLTAGE of NODE-2?  <u>23.4</u>

What is the VOLTAGE of LPS-1?  <u>18.79</u>

What is the VOLTAGE of NODE-3?  <u>18.12</u>

What is the VOLTAGE of NODE-9?  <u>0</u>

*It looks like the fault is in CR2*

---

**Table 1.** A sample NODAL session.

## 2.2 Incremental CBR in Classification

In order to evaluate the merit of our incremental CBR mechanism we implemented a simple classification system using this approach. Two different domains were examined. One domain is credit risk assessment using the Japanese credit screening data taken from the UCI repository of machine learning databases. This domain provides 125 cases and the task is to determine whether an individual's credit assessment should be positive or negative. The second domain is a property valuation domain containing 65 cases gathered in the Dublin area. The object of this system is to set an asking price for the target property. Sample cases from these domains are shown in Figure 2. The free features are shown in italics.

In these classification problems the imperative for the distinction between free and expensive features is not as strong as it is in diagnosis situations. Nevertheless, there is still a benefit in performing case retrieval without requiring all the case features.

**Credit Assessment Case**     **Property Valuation Case**

| | | | | |
|---:|:---|---:|:---|
| *Gender* | *Female* | *Location* | *loc4* |
| *Purchase Item* | *PC* | *No-bed-rooms* | *5-bed-room* |
| Jobless | No | No-rec-rooms | 2 |
| Unmarried | Yes | Kitchen | Modern |
| Problematic Region | No | Structure | detached |
| Age | 18 | No-floors | 2-floors |
| Deposit | 20 | Condition | excellent-condition |
| Monthly Payment | 2 | Age | mature-age |
| No. of Months | 15 | Facilities | facilities-near |
| No. of Years in Company | 1 | Price | 88000 |
| Credit Screening | Pos | | |

**Fig. 2.** Sample cases for credit assessment and property valuation.

# 3 Incremental CBR

Incremental CBR is a two stage case retrieval mechanism. Stage one exploits free features in the domain to select relevant candidate cases from the case-base. Stage two uses an information theoretic criterion and the candidate set to request additional target features to discriminate between the available candidate cases and select a single one for retrieval. The key to the success of I-CBR lies in the criterion used to suggest additional relevant target features. A good criterion is one which is capable of selecting a minimal set of features.

In this section, after detailing the I-CBR algorithm and selection criterion we discuss a worked example from the property valuation domain and demonstrate how in this example I-CBR performs considerably better that ID3, a comparable inductive learning algorithm.

## 3.1 The Incremental CBR Algorithm

The two central features of I-CBR are the ability to initiate case retrieval without a complete case description and a facility to request useful extra information. The I-CBR algorithm is shown below in Algorithm 1. The main objective is to provide added information about the target case that will allow the system to reduce the set of relevant cases to a single case for retrieval. The key issue here is the process in Step 1 where the system determines the test to perform next.

---

**Step 0:**    Generate a **candidate set** of cases based on initial free features available. The **candidate set** is made up of cases that match on these features.

**Step 1:**    Select the most discriminating expensive feature in the candidate set.

**Step 2:**    Query the operator for the value of that feature in the target case.

**Step 3:**    Narrow down the candidate set based on this information (i.e. eliminate cases that *cannot* match this feature)

**Step 4:**    Repeat from 1 until a unique classification/diagnosis remains.

---

**Algorithm 1.** The I-CBR Algorithm

## 3.2 Discriminatory Power

The selection of a minimal set of features with which to discriminate against a set of cases amounts to building a decision tree with internal nodes corresponding to feature queries and leaf nodes corresponding to the different solution classes; the leaf nodes contain the cases that fall into these classes. A good rule of thumb in building an efficient decision tree is that features that provide the most information should appear high up in the tree (close to the root). Information theory provides us with a means of measuring the information content or discriminatory power (DP) of case features with respect to a set cases; this is similar to ID3 [2, 7] and also related to the work of Wess, Altoff and Derwand [8]

The mechanism of selecting discriminating features is best explained in terms of building a decision tree that will have leaf nodes corresponding to the different classifications/diagnoses **D** and the set of cases **C** will be located, or classified, on these nodes. The process of selecting discriminating features used in I-CBR is similar to that in ID3 except that the semantics of the branching in the decision tree is slightly different because of the possibility of unknowns in the case features. A brief explanation of how the discrimination works is as follows:-

| | |
|---|---|
| $D=\{D_1,...,D_d\}$ | the set of possible classes or classifications |
| $C=\{C_1,...,C_c\}$ | the set of cases to classify |
| $F=\{F_1,...,F_f\}$ | the set of features, one of which is selected at each decision point (In I-CBR these are all expensive, that is $F = E$). |

We can view the decision tree as an information source producing one of $d$ messages from the set **D**. Let $|D_j|$ represent the number of cases with diagnosis $D_j$. Then the expected information needed to generate the appropriate message, for some case, using the tree is:-

$$I\left(\frac{|D_1|}{|D_1|+...+|D_d|},....,\frac{|D_d|}{|D_1|+...+|D_d|}\right) = -\sum_{j=1}^{d}\left(\frac{|D_j|}{|D_1|+...+|D_d|}\bullet\log_2\left[\frac{|D_j|}{|D_1|+...+|D_d|}\right]\right) \qquad (1)$$

Consider the root decision node of the tree (see Figure 3). Assume this node tests the feature $F\in F$ and this feature has possible values $V=\{V^1,....,V^n\}$. Then $V$ partitions $C$ into $n$ groups of cases, $G^1,....,G^n$; where $G^i$ contains those cases that have value $V^i$ for feature $F$.

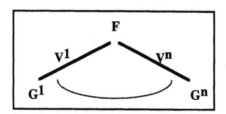

**Fig. 3.** The root classification of the cases in **C**.

Let $G^i$ contain $|D^i_j|$ cases with diagnosis $D_j$, that is $|D^i_j|$ instances of class $D_j$. The probability of a case belonging to $G^i$ is (i.e. the probability of a case having the $i$th. value for attribute $F$) :-

$$\frac{|D^i_1|+,....,+|D^i_d|}{|D_1|+...+|D_d|} \qquad (2)$$

So after testing $F$ the remaining information associated with the subtrees, $G^1,....,G^n$ is:-

$$Remainder(F) = \sum_{i=1}^{n}\left(\frac{|D^i_1|+,....,+|D^i_d|}{|D_1|+...+|D_d|}\right)\bullet I\left(\frac{|D^i_1|}{|D^i_1|+...+|D^i_d|},....,\frac{|D^i_d|}{|D^i_1|+...+|D^i_d|}\right) \qquad (3)$$

The weight of the $i$th. branch is the proportion of cases in $C$ that belong to $G^i$. The information gained from using $F$, or the *discriminatory power* of $F$, is:-

$$DP(F) = I\left(\frac{|D_1|}{|D_1|+...+|D_d|},....,\frac{|D_d|}{|D_1|+...+|D_d|}\right) - Remainder(F) \qquad (4)$$

Thus the feature that leaves the smallest Remainder is the most discriminating. So, at each stage in the reduction of the set of cases, the most discriminating feature is selected using this criterion. The user is requested to determine the value of this feature for the target case. The cases in the candidate set that *cannot* match on this feature are removed from the candidate set. This process is repeated until the set reduces to one diagnosis or the target case proves to be dissimilar to all the retrieved cases. It is important to emphasise that, in I-CBR, a discrimination tree for the set of cases is not being produced, instead local discriminations are determined at run-time. This technique has proved remarkably successful for retrieving good matches while requiring a minimum number of expensive feature values.

## 3.3 An Example Classification Session

To illustrate more clearly the operation of I-CBR we provide the following classification session example from the property valuation domain. The task is to provide an asking price for a new target property by classifying it in terms of the selling prices of the properties in the case-base.

---

**Tree Building**


Features : (NR-BED-ROOMS LOCATION NR-REC-ROOMS KITCHEN

STRUCTURE NR-FLOORS CONDITION AGE FACILITIES)


[Internal Nodes : 16    Leaf Nodes : 29]


**Following Decision Path**

What is the value for LOCATION ?      LOC3

What is the value for AGE ?       NEW-AGE

What is the value for NR-BED-ROOMS ? 5-BED-ROOMS

What is the value for FACILITIES ?   FACILITIES-MEDIUM


Retrieved : (CASE12)    **Asking Price : £90,000**

---

**Table 2.** An ID3 session for Property Valuation

Table 2 shows a classification session using ID3, a traditional inductive learning algorithm. As you can see the first thing that ID3 does is build a decision tree from all of the available cases (there are 65 cases and a tree of 16 internal nodes and 29 leaf nodes is built). Next starting at the root of the decision tree, target information is requested from the user that will lead to a unique classification at a leaf node of the tree. Such a classification is found after 4 feature queries, on the location, age, number of bedrooms, and facilities features of the target property. In fact, two of these features are deemed to be freely available, location and number of bedrooms. This means that ID3 makes 2 costly feature requests, one for the age feature and one for the facilities feature.

Table 3 shows how the same target property is valuated by the I-CBR algorithm. Again the free features are location and number of bedrooms. Using these free features to filter the case-base only two candidate cases are found. Building a decision tree over these candidate cases is much simpler than building a decision tree over all of the cases in the case-base. Indeed, only one feature is needed to discriminate between these two candidates. This feature is the structure of the property (detached or semi-detached). So I-CBR reaches the same conclusion as ID3 but after only a single expensive feature query.

---

**Base Filtering**

```
Indices    : (NR-BED-ROOMS LOCATION)        {Free Features}

Candidates : (CASE36 CASE12)
```

**Following Decision Path**

```
What is the value for STRUCTURE ?  SEMI

Retrieved :  (CASE12)  Asking Price :  £90,000
```

---

Table 3. An I-CBR session for Property Valuation

# 4 Incremental CBR *vs.* Pure Inductive Learning

In this section we investigate, in detail, the application of incremental CBR to the credit risk assessment and property valuation problems. We provide experimental evidence to support the hypothesis that, for such tasks, incremental CBR does exhibit performance advantages over inductive learning. In particular, these advantages are readily shown in domains where the accumulation of relevant data is costly and where some initial data is provided free in the form of a set of free features; for example, in the credit risk assessment domain the free features may be the purchase item whereas the costly unknown data may be such things as the employment status or social history of the applicant.

The first set of experiments is designed to compare the performance characteristics of inductive learning and incremental CBR and demonstrate that the CBR approach provides a very definite performance gain. The second set of experiments investigatesthe sensitivity of this gain to variations in the available free features.

## 4.1 Performance Experiments

These experiments compared the performance of a pure inductive learning approach (ID3) and an incremental CBR approach over a set of problems from the property valuation and credit risk assessment domains. The performance measure used is the number of queries made in solving a particular target problem; our assumption being that performance is primarily influenced by the cost of gathering expensive data during the solution process. Moreover, it assumed that every expensive query has the same cost.

To test the pure inductive learning approach a decision tree was built from the available training cases. Each case then served as a target problem and the total number of questions asked during their solution was accumulated; of course questions relating to the free features were not counted during these tests. Similarly, to test the incremental CBR approach each available case served as a target problem. For each run the free features were used during base filtering and a partial, local decision tree was constructed over the selected candidates. Again the number of questions asked during the traversal of these local trees was accumulated.

**Property Valuation**

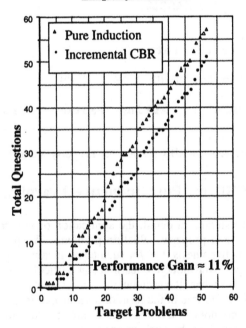

**Fig. 4.** Property Valuation Performance Experiments
Free Features = {Location, No-Bed-Rooms}

The results of these experiments can be seen in Figures 4 and 5. Figure 4 plots the results for a set of 52 target problems from the property valuation domain, and Figure 5 shows the results for a set of 125 problems from the credit risk assessment domain.

In each graph the total number of questions asked during the solution of all the target problems is plotted against the number of target problems solved. It is clear that the incremental CBR approach provides a consistent reduction in the number of questions needed to solve each set of targets. Indeed, for each domain we can obtain an average value of the *performance gain* (the percentage reduction in questions asked) for the chosen set of free features; 11% for the property valuation tests and 38% for the credit risk assessment tests.

The incremental CBR gain is due to the fact that the construction of a decision tree specific to some target problem (that is, over some reduced set of cases) tends to result in a considerably more efficient (compact) tree than if a global decision tree was constructed over the entire case-base. In particular, certain features necessary in the global tree are unnecessary in the local tree as there are fewer cases to discriminate against.

Thus it is the fact that the retrieval mechanisms have access to the raw case data that supports the ability to generalise with respect to the actual target situation (lazy generalisation). This target specific generalisation produces more efficient decision structures (shallower decision trees) that those produced by eager generalisation..

**Credit Risk Assessment**

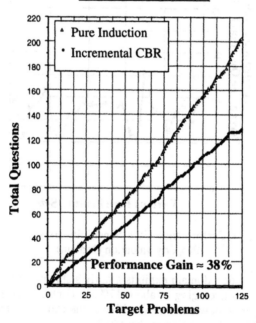

**Fig. 5.** Credit Risk Assessment Performance Experiments
Free Features = {Purchase-Item, Gender}

## 4.2 Sensitivity Experiments

In this set of experiments we investigate the relationship between the performance gain and the available free features. Modelling the precise nature of this relationship is beyond the scope of this paper but we can at least gain an impression of the range of potential performance gains for different sets of free features in different types of problem domains.

Again the property valuation and credit risk assessment domains were investigated. For each domain the experiments of the previous section were re-run 25 times, each time with a different set of free features, and each time the average performance gain was noted; for these experiments each free feature set comprised of two randomly selected features from the list of available features.

Figures 6 and 7 show our results for the property valuation and credit risk assessment experiments respectively, plotting the performance gain against the different sets of free features.

## Property Valuation

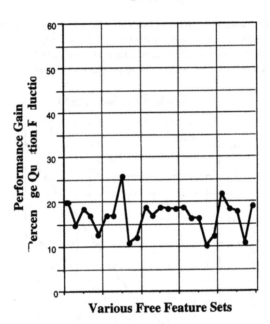

**Fig. 6.** Performance Gain Sensitivity Experiments
(Property valuation Domain)

The property valuation domain exhibits a fairly stable performance gain, ranging from 26% to 10% and averaging at about 17%. In contrast, the gain in credit risk assessment domain is somewhat more sensitive to the choice of free feature, ranging from only 1% to 52% and averaging at about 23%.

Clearly, the available free features are important. The best case scenario for incremental CBR can result in substantial performance gains over pure induction methods (witness the 52% maximum gain in the credit risk assessment domain), but even the worst case situation resulted in marginal improvements.

We believe that the discriminatory power of the free features contributes to the observed performance gain. In particular, free features with very low DP values result in very low gains as the impact of base-filtering is minimal and the resulting local decision tree is essentially the same as the global one produced by a pure inductive learning approach. At the other extreme, free features with high DP values tend to result in much greater performance gains. Unfortunately the precise relationship between the DP values of each free feature and how they combine to produce different performance gains is not clear at this time and further analyses and experiments are needed.

**Credit Risk Assessment**

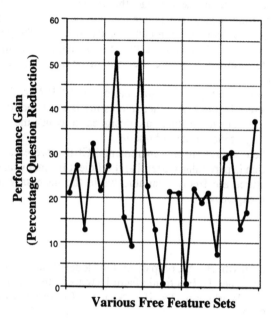

**Fig. 7.** Performance Gain Sensitivity Experiments
(Credit Risk Assessment Domain)

# 5 Conclusion

We have described a technique, incremental CBR, that borrows from inductive learning research to solve a problem in case-based reasoning. In addition, we have described a common class of problem tasks that can benefit from this technique instead of a more traditional inductive learning approach. This class is characterised by the fact that many relevant problem features are expensive to procure while a small set of initial features are freely available. The key components of the incremental CBR approach are: firstly, the identification of a subset of relevant candidate cases by using the free features to eliminate many incompatible cases; secondly, the formulation of a minimal set of features from the remaining cases which, when instantiated in the target problem situation, will lead to the appropriate candidate case with which to solve the target problem.

While the immediate result is a CBR technique that has the informational parsimony goal-directed reasoning, the main thrust of this paper was to investigate whether or not incremental CBR would actually exhibit performance improvements over pure inductive learning across a number of problem domains. In our experiments, carried out over two such domains, incremental CBR consistently outperformed traditional induction techniques, exhibiting performance gains (depending on the nature of the free features) from as little as 1% to as much as 52%, and averaging at about 20%.

These results suggest that the lazy generalisation approach offered by I-CBR has definite performance benefits over traditional eager methods (such as those offered by ID3 for example). In particular, the very fact that the training data is directly available at problem solving time means that better use can be made of this data since the context of the target problem situation can directly influence the generalisation and problem solving process. This is exactly what is happening in I-CBR, where irrelevant cases are eliminated before the system begins to look at relevant and discriminating features.

Future work will investigate the application of I-CBR to domain with both continuous and discrete features. Another interesting issue is the idea of introducing query costs so that the selected features are designed to reduce the overall cost of the querying process, not just the number of queries.

In conclusion then, we submit that incremental CBR represents a model of case-based reasoning which is particularly useful and efficient for many tasks where a small set of problem features are freely available while the necessary accumulation of additional features is expensive.

# References

1. Cunningham P., Smyth, B.: A Comparison Of Model-Based And Incremental Case-Based Approaches To Electronic Fault Diagnosis. In D. Aha (Ed.) Case-Based Reasoning Workshop, Twelfth National Conference on Artificial Intelligence. (1994)
2. Quinlan J.R.: Induction of Decision Trees. Machine Learning, 1 (1986) 81-106.
3. Fisher, D. H.: Knowledge Acquisition via Incremental Conceptual Clustering. Machine Learning, 2 (1987) 139-172.
4. Michalski R.S.: A Theory And Methodology Of Inductive Learning. In R.S. Michalski, J.G. Carbonnell, & T.M. Mitchell (Eds.), Machine Learning An Artificial Intelligence Approach. Morgan Kaufmann. (1983)
5. Cunningham P., Brady M.: Qualitative Reasoning In Electronic Fault Diagnosis. In J. McDermott (Ed.), Tenth International Joint Conference on Artificial Intelligence. (1987) 443 - 445.
6. Cunningham P.: Knowledge Representation in Electronic Fault Diagnosis, Ph. D. Thesis, Department of Computer Science, Dublin University, Trinity College, Ireland. (1988)
7. Quinlan J.R.: Learning Efficient Classification Procedures and their Application to Chess End-Games. In R.S. Michalski, J.G. Carbonnell, & T.M. Mitchell (Eds.), Machine Learning An Artificial Intelligence Approach. Morgan Kaufmann. (1983)
8. Wess, S., Althoff, K-D., and Derwand, G: Using k-d Trees to Improve the Retrieval Step in case-Based Reasoning. In S. Wess, K-D Althoff, M. Richter (Eds.) Topics in Case-Based Reasoning. Springer-Verlag (1994) 167-181

# Examples and Remindings in a Case-based Help System

Gerhard Weber

University of Trier, FB I - Psychology, D-54286 Trier, Germany
weber@cogpsy.uni-trier.de

**Abstract.** ELM-PE is an intelligent programming environment aimed at helping beginners in learning a new programming language. The knowledge-based component of this system is based on interpreting, storing, and reusing solutions to programming tasks. For this system, an analogical component has been developed to retrieve structurally similar problem solutions from the case base by an explanation-based retrieval method (EBR). Cases consist of explanations from previous problem solutions, as analysed by a diagnostic component, and are distributed over the knowledge base with respect to the programming concepts captured in the explanation structures. In an empirical study, it has been shown that in many cases the system is able to offer better suited analogies than the students selected by themselves. These results show advantages of a case-based help system supporting complex problem solving and learning tasks.

## 1 Introduction

A "classical" task of a case-based reasoning system is to find similar previous cases that help or allow to analyse new problems or to make new decisions. Most CBR systems start with a rich case base covering a wide range of different cases. In a tutoring or help system, such pre-stored cases can be used as examples that can be offered to the user or learner to help him or her when solving a new and similar problem. For the system itself, these cases can be used to analyse and to classify problem solutions (e.g., the SCENT-Advisor; McCalla & Greer, 1993). A different situation occurs, however, when the system is supposed to monitor the problem solving and learning process of a human user. Then, episodes from the user's own learning history consisting of solutions to problem solving tasks may serve as remindings (Schank, 1982) when solving new problems. The ACT-R theory (Anderson, 1993) too describes learning by analogy as a central and powerful learning mechanism. However, in the CMU-LISP-tutor (Anderson, 1993; Anderson, Conrad, & Corbett, 1989) that is based on the ACT theory, an analogy mechanism is not implemented and example-based learning is not supported.

An example-based learning system that considers not only examples from a text book but also individual remindings from the user's learning history should be able to retrieve, from an individual case base, instances that are structurally and semantically similar to the current problem. To allow for this situation, episodes from the user's problem solving history can be seen as new cases that have to be inserted into the case base in addition to pre-stored cases. Integration of new cases has to be done such that these cases can be indexed and retrieved by the same mechanism that retrieves pre-stored cases.

Similar cases retrieved from the case base play the role of remindings that occur in humans when understanding texts or solving problems. According to Schank, these remindings occur casually when, in processing a new text or a new problem, the same organisational structures are used as before (Riesbeck & Schank, 1989; Schank, 1982). The REMIND system (Lange & Wharton, 1992; Wharton & Lange, 1993) is an example of this approach to retrieve similar episodes and to indicate analogies in text comprehension. In addition to the well known effects of structural and semantic similarity on retrieving cases and analogues (Clement & Gentner, 1991; Gentner, 1989; Gentner & Landers, 1985; Holyoak & Koh, 1987; Ratterman & Gentner, 1987; Thagard, Holyoak, Nelson, & Gochfeld, 1990), organisational similarity (Wolsten-croft, 1989) plays an important role in knowledge-based systems running on computers. That is, the closer new items are stored to already existing concepts in a conceptual hierarchy, the more they are similar to each other. Inserting episodic frames into a hierarchy and building new generalisations and subframes results in a dynamic memory (Schank, 1982). Thus, a case-based learning system allows for retrieving remindings based on organisational similarity.

These ideas of case-based learning, dynamic memory, and retrieving examples as well as individual remindings were the starting points of building the Episodic Learner Model (ELM), a case-based learning model in a knowledge-based help system that supports programming skill acquisition (Weber, 1993). ELM plays the role of an expert who tries to explain how a solution to a programming task may have been produced by a programmer. During diagnosis of program code, information from an individual, episodic learner model is used to shorten the diagnostic process and to adapt to the user. The episodic learner model is updated with information from the diagnostic process.

ELM can be used to present examples and remindings. In this context, examples are solutions to programming problems that are explained in the accompanying text book. Remindings are solutions to programming problems that the individual learner coded during working at exercises. When starting working at a new lesson, the appropriate examples from the text materials are analysed and the resulting derivation trees of these example-episodes are integrated into the individual learner model as if they were solved by the learner. On the one side, this reflects that the learner read and–hopefully–understood the exercises. On the other side, it guarantees that examples are processed in the same way as solutions to exercises and that examples and remindings can be accessed by the same analogy mechanism.

Searching for a best analogue to a given new programming problem works as follows. First, rules that are used by the diagnostic component to analyse program code can be used by a generation component to generate an expected solution to a new programming task (Weber, Bögelsack, & Wender, 1993). Second, this expected solution is diagnosed and the resulting explanation is stored temporarily in the episodic learner model. Third, from computing the organisational similarity to other episodes (examples and remindings) stored with the user model, a best match can be found and offered to the learner as an example solution to a similar programming problem. Fourth, the temporarily stored case is removed. In this paper, this episodic retrieval mechanism will be outlined, and empirical data from testing this component will be reported.

In the following, the episodic learner model and the retrieval mechanism are described in more detail. In the final section, the programmers' selections of examples and remindings during a programming course are compared to selections preferred by the analogical component of ELM.

## 2 Description of ELM

The case-based learning model ELM is the knowledge-based component of the programming environment ELM-PE that supports learning the programming language LISP (Weber & Möllenberg, 1994; 1995). Programming novices participating in an introductory LISP course solve exercises with support from ELM-PE. Programmers can ask for help when they get stuck coding function definitions, or when errors occur that they cannot understand and debug by themselves. On demand, the—possibly incomplete—problem solution is analysed by the diagnostic component. This component uses information from a task description, from the domain knowledge, and from the individual learner model to analyse program code produced by the learner (Fig. 1).

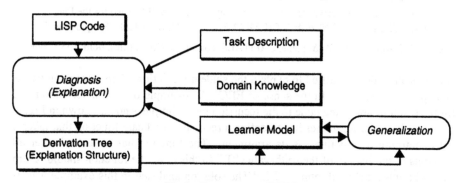

**Fig 1.** Components of ELM

The analysis of program code employs an explanation-based generalisation (EBG) method (Mitchell, Keller, & Kedar-Cabelli, 1986). The explanation step starts with a task description related to higher concepts (general and LISP-specific programming concepts, plans, and schemata) in the knowledge base. Every concept comprises plan transformations and rules describing different ways to solve the goal given by the current plan. Applying a rule results in generating new subplans or in comparing the plan description to the corresponding part of the student's code. This cycle of the diagnosis is called recursively until it matches a function name, a parameter, or a constant. The diagnosis results in a derivation tree built from all

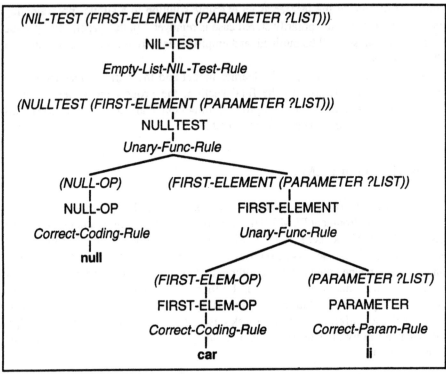

**Fig. 2.** Partial Derivation Tree Explaining the Code (null (car li)) for the Plan (NIL-TEST (FIRST-ELEMENT (PARAMETER ?LIST))) in Task "Simple-And."

Legend: *ITALIC-CAPITALS*: plans, CAPITALS: concepts, *Italics*: rules, **bold**: LISP code.

concepts and rules identified to explain the student's solution. This derivation tree is an explanation structure in the sense of EBG. An example of such a derivation tree for the result of analysing code to the recursion task "Simple-And" is shown in Fig. 2. In this task, the programmer has to define a recursive predicate function that takes a list containing truth-values as its argument. The function has to test whether all elements of the list are of the truth-value "T." In this case, the function should return "T," otherwise it should return "NIL." The solution analysed in this example was as follows:

```
(defun simple-and (li)
    (cond ((null li) t)
          ((null (car li)) nil)
          (t (simple-and (cdr li))))))
```

The part of the code corresponding to the derivation tree in Fig. 2 is printed in bold face.

All concepts mentioned in the derivation tree are the basis for creating episodic frames. Episodic frames contain information about the current subplan to be solved, the rule that was used to solve the plan, and the corresponding part of the analysed code. For instance, for the concept NULLTEST in Fig. 2, an episodic frame

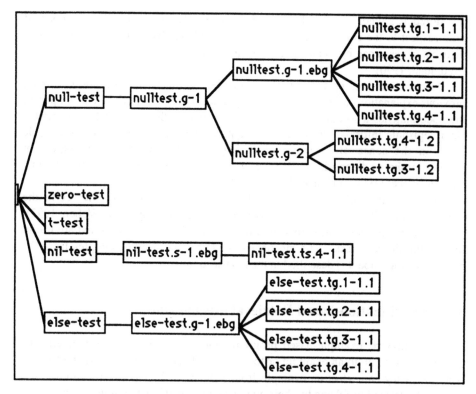

**Fig. 3.** Part of the Concept Hierarchy After Inserting Episodic Frames for three Examples from the Learning Materials and for Task "Simple-And."

NULLTEST.TG.4-1.2 is created containing slots for the current plan *(NULLTEST (FIRST-ELEMENT (PARAMETER ?LIST)))*, for the rule *Unary-Func-Rule* that applied to solve this plan, and for the corresponding code (null (car li)). These frames are integrated into the knowledge base as instances of their concepts. If an episodic frame is the first instance under its concept of the knowledge base, this single case is used to generalise from structural and semantic aspects in the data. This generalisation mechanism is comparable to single-case generalisation in EBG. Additionally, similarity-based generalisation of data and plans can occur. With more and more knowledge about a particular learner, increasingly complex hierarchies of generalisations and instances are built under the concepts of the knowledge base. Fig. 3 shows part of the concept hierarchy after inserting episodic frames for all examples from the first lesson on recursion, and for the analysed solution from the "Simple-And" task. The entire set of episodic instances constitutes the episodic learner model.

The set of episodic frames of a particular episode constitutes a case in the case library, the episodic learner model. Each case is identified by an episode frame that indexes all episodic frames contributing to the episode. Starting from the episode frame, the complete derivation tree can be reconstructed by scanning all episodic frames and re-establishing the old plan contexts and rules. That is, in ELM, cases are not stored as a whole but are divided into *snippets* (Kolodner, 1993) that are stored with respect to the concepts in the system's knowledge base. Related notations of distributed cases can be found in DMAP (Riesbeck & Martin, 1986) and in CELIA (Redmond, 1990).

Information from episodic instances can be used in further diagnoses to reuse previous explanations or to prefer applying previously used rules if the current part of the code matches a solution to a similar plan stored in the episodic learner model. Using episodic information in ELM is a type of *analogical replay* using multiple cases in the sense of *derivational analogy* (Veloso, 1994). This aspect of explanation-based diagnosis and of case-based learning in ELM is described in more detail in Weber (1994) and in Weber et al. (1993).

An advantage of episodic modelling is its potential to predict code the programmers will produce as solutions to new programming tasks (Weber, 1993). These predictions can be used to search for examples and reminders that are useful for solving the new task. The mechanism of retrieving useful examples from the episodic learner model is described in the next section.

## 3 The Explanation-based Retrieval Mechanism

ELM-PE supports example-based programming (Neal, 1989). Programmers can display the solution to an example or to a previously solved problem in an example window. They can select an example from a menu of the names of examples and previously defined problems by their own, or they can ask the system to present the analogue being mostly useful to solve the current problem.

On the basis of explanation structures stored into distributed frames representing steps of the solution path, it is easy to retrieve previous problem solutions similar to the current problem. From the system's knowledge about the problem, a solution can be generated taking into account the individual case memory. On the basis of concepts and rules used to generate the new solution, the case memory can be probed for cases most similar to this solution. Concepts from the resulting explanation structure are inserted temporarily into the existing concept hierarchy of the episodic learner model. All episodic frames that are neighbours to the temporarily inserted frames contribute to computing weights for similar episodes. In Fig. 3, for instance, the episodic frame NULLTEST.TG.4-1.2 (from Episode No. 4) is most similar to the episodic frame NULLTEST.TG.3-1.2 (from Episode No. 2). Due to its shorter distance in the frame hierarchy, the frame NULLTEST.TG.3-1.2 receives a higher weight than the episodic frames NULLTEST.TG.1-1.1, NULLTEST.TG.2-1.1, NULLTEST.TG.3-1.1, and NULLTEST.TG.4-1.1 under the generalisation frame NULLTEST.G-1.EBG. From the point of view of the concept NULLTEST, Episode No. 3 is most similar to Episode No. 4. However, weights from other concepts favour other episodes which is why, at the end, another episode is selected as most useful to the current problem. Stored explanation structures are the basis for retrieving previous cases, so we call it "Explanation-based Retrieval" (EBR). The complete EBR-algorithm is described in Fig. 4.

---

**The Five Steps of the EBR-Algorithm**

*Step 1*: Diagnose the solution of the new problem generated automatically by the system. This will result in an explanation structure of all concepts and rules which may be used to solve the problem.

*Step 2*: Store all elements of the explanation structure as episodic frames temporarily into the hierarchy of already existing episodic frames from the case memory and generalise if possible. All episodic frames $t_i$ created in this way belong to the goal episode $T = \{t_1, ..., t_i, ..., t_n\}$. Accordingly, cases $B(k)$ stored in the case base can be defined as sets of episodic frames: $B(k) = \{b_1(k), ..., b_j(k), ..., b_{m(k)}(k)\}$, where $m$ depends on the number of frames in case $k$.

*Step 3*: Scan all episodic frames of the new (goal) episode, look for similar episodic frames from previous episodes in the hierarchy of episodic frames and assign appropriate similarity weights. Episodic frames subsumed under the same direct generalisation frame are given a similarity weight $h$ that is multiplied by a factor $\delta_d$ for each intervening generalisation. For other similar episodic frames subsumed under higher levels of abstraction assign lower similarity weights ($h$ is multiplied by $\delta_u$ for each intervening parent generalisation frame). The resulting weight $h_{ijk}$ is the organisational similarity weight from the episodic frame $b_j(k)$ with respect to the episodic frame $t_i$ from the goal episode $T$. The similarity weight $w_{ik}$ of episode $b(k)$ with respect to episodic frame $t_i$ of the goal episode $T$ is the maximum of all weights of the episodic frame $b_j(k)$ from episode $B(k)$ that show similar frames corresponding to frame $t_i$ from goal episode $T$.

$$w_{ik} = \max_j (h_{ijk})$$

*Step 4*: Let $\mathcal{B} = \{B(1), ..., B(l), ..., B(n)\}$ the set of related cases found in Step 3. Compute weights $g_{ik}$ for all episodic frames from these cases by dividing the specific similarity weight $w_{ik}$ by the sum of weights from all competing frames according to the choice model (Luce, 1959).

$$g_{ik} = \frac{w_{ik}}{\sum_l w_{il}}$$

*Step 5*: For every episode $B(k)$ considered in Step 3 the weights $g_{ik}$, for all episodic frames computed in Step 4 are summed up and sorted.

$$G_k = \sum_i g_{ik}$$

---

**Fig. 4.** The EBR-Algorithm.

The similarity measure expressed by the EBR-algorithm described above is a special case of the *contrast model* (Tversky, 1977). In the contrast model, the similarity between a target case $T$ (the new problem solution) and a base case $B$ is given by the formula

$$S(T, B) = \theta f(B \cap T) - \alpha f(T - B) - \beta f(B - T)$$

with the intersection $(B \cap T)$ describing the set of features that are common (in terms of the EBR-algorithm organisational similar) to $B$ and $T$, and the complement sets $(T - B)$ and $(B - T)$ describing features observed only in the target and features observed only in the base case, respectively. In the version of the EBR-algorithm described in this paper, $\alpha$ and $\beta$ are 0, $\theta$ is 1, and $f$ is given by the five steps described in Fig. 4. Setting $\alpha$ and $\beta$ to 0 results in the simplest procedure to access episodes sharing features. Searching for organisational similar episodic frames within the hierarchy of episodic instances under a concept frame and dividing weights according to competing episodic frames as described in the EBR-algorithm (Fig. 4) is similar to spreading activation mechanisms used in connectionist systems.

This retrieval method computes organisational similarity. Episodic frames stored under a concept from the knowledge base are semantically similar because they belong to the same concept. This retrieval method reflects semantic similarity that plays the most important role in analogue retrieval (Thagard et al., 1990). However, because structural similarities play an important role in the generalisation of episodic frames, structural consistencies are also considered. Pragmatic aspects are not considered directly in the current version of the EBR-algorithm, but it would be easy to give special pragmatic weights to observed buggy rules and to poorly solved concepts such that corresponding episodic frames from previous cases can dominate the retrieval of these episodes. Thus, tutorial goals could impose pragmatic constraints on the retrieval process.

## 4 Empirical Evaluation of the EBR-Method

Simulation studies and empirical investigations were tried to evaluate the EBR-method. In a first simulation study, we compared our EBR-method to the hybrid-connectionist ARCS-model (Thagard et al., 1990). Results of the simulation study showed that in most cases the EBR method retrieved the same analogues as the ARCS-method (Weber, 1991).

As this first study did not directly test the usefulness and helpfulness of the retrieved examples, we wanted to investigate in a further study whether the EBR-method is able to present useful examples and remindings to programmers and compare these examples with examples chosen by the programmers themselves while working with ELM-PE. This study will be reported in the present paper. Presenting examples by an automatic help system may be helpful to the learner, because in several empirical investigations subjects had difficulties in retrieving structurally similar and useful analogues if there existed competing, superficially similar cases (Gentner & Landers, 1985; Ratterman & Gentner, 1987; Ross, 1987). On the other hand, Faries and Reiser (1988) found that subjects who were learning LISP and were well-trained in this domain were able to retrieve structural remindings, despite the presence of competing surface similarities.

## 4.1 Method

In this study, 21 subjects that participated in an introductory LISP course worked at up to 17 different programming tasks in three lessons on recursion. When starting with a new task, each subject had to select the most useful example from a menu containing the names of all examples and self-defined function definitions from this lesson. The program code was displayed in a separate example window and the subject had to confirm that it was the correct choice. Otherwise, he or she could select another example until the subjectively best one was found. One subject was subsequently excluded from this study because in too many cases he apparently did not select meaningful examples. In most cases, he selected the example from the previous task, but coded the solution to the new task correctly and more similar to another example. The remaining 20 subjects selected 315 examples or remindings.

In simulation runs with data from these subjects, the EBR-method was used to retrieve analogues while subjects had to choose a best example. The episodic learner model was built up gradually from examples from the learning materials and from the programmers' solutions to programming tasks from the exercises. When a new task started, the diagnostic component of ELM generated an expected solution for this task considering individual information from the episodic learner model. This correct function definition was analysed and the resulting derivation tree was integrated temporarily into the learner model. For this new case, the EBR-method searched for a best analogue as described above. The EBR-algorithm (Fig. 4) was run with $h = 1.0$, $\delta_u = 0.8$, and $\delta_d = 1.0$. Subsequently, the temporarily stored case was deleted from the learner model.

## 4.2 Results

For every task the programmers worked at in the exercises, the example chosen by the programmer and the example chosen by the system were categorised into the categories: "Best Example", "Surface Similarity Only", and "Not Useful." The category "Best Example" contained all examples that were rated best by experts in LISP. For some tasks, two different examples were rated best because the new solution could be derived equally from both examples. The category "Surface Similarity Only" contained examples that were similar in some specific aspects, especially similarities from the text of the task description, but a different and better example could have been chosen. The category "Not Useful" combined all examples that were not as useful to the current task as examples from the category "Best Example" or that were not useful at all and the choice could not be put down to apparent surface similarities as its cause. In case of ties, that is the system selected more than one previous case with the same similarity value, the worst case was chosen. That is, if at least one of these selected examples was assigned "Not Useful" then this case was counted into this category even if a potentially better example tied. The same procedure was used when ties occurred in the "Surface Similarity Only" category.

In 67.3 % of all cases, subjects selected an example (from the learning materials) or a reminding (a solution to a task previously defined by themselves) that was judged best (see Tab. 1). However, in 13.7 % of all cases, subjects preferred an example that was most similar in surface features and a better (more useful) example could have been chosen. For the EBR-method, things look different. In 89.5 % of all cases, the automatic selection of an example by the EBR-method resulted in a best choice, and in only 4.4 % of all cases, the example chosen showed surface similarity only. In all other cases (subjects 19.0 % vs. EBR 6.0 %), the example chosen was not the best one or even not useful. Differences in cell frequencies are significant ($\chi^2 = 45.9$, $df = 2$, $p < .0001$).

The relatively large number of less useful examples chosen by the EBR-method are mostly due to one single task where the EBR-method preferred an example from the learning materials with the same number of arguments in the parameter list to another example that would fit better. This is the only case where superficial structural similarities apparently dominated the retrieval process. In no case, this less useful analogue stemmed from the just previous programming episode. Less useful or useless examples chosen by subjects are due to a type of recency effect. In more than half of these cases (38 of 60), subjects preferred the previous function definition coded by themselves. This indicates that programmers, in some cases, tend to proceed programming of a sequence of tasks in such a way that they simply use the solution to the last problem to solve the next problem without checking whether another example may be more helpful. In many of these cases, we observed an error in solving the new task that could be traced back to the misleading example. However, it is not clear from this study whether the poorly chosen example caused the error or whether misunderstanding the problem resulted in choosing the bad example.

## 5 Discussion

Results from this study show that a case-based learning system not only learns to improve and to shorten its own decision or problem solving process (Weber et al.,

**Tab. 1.** Number and Percentage of Examples Categorised as "Best Example," "Surface Similarity Only," and "Not Useful" ($N = 315$).

| Example Chosen | Subjects | EBR |
|---|---|---|
| Best Example | 212 <br> 67.3 % | 282 <br> 89.5% |
| Surface Similarity Only | 43 <br> 13.7 % | 14 <br> 4.4 % |
| Not Useful | 60 <br> 19.0 % | 19 <br> 6.0 % |

1993), but it also models the process of knowledge acquisition and the resulting knowledge of a user in such a way that, based on the dynamic learner model, the system is able to offer examples and remindings from the user's learning history that are judged as being useful for him or her to solve new problems. As discussed above, in many experiments subjects have difficulties finding appropriate and useful analogy (Gentner & Landers, 1985; Ross & Kennedy, 1990). These findings may result from very unrealistic learning and problem solving situations in experimental designs. Our results support the findings from Faries and Reiser (1988) that subjects are able to find structurally useful analogues in a realistic learning situation. In our experiment, the high percentage of "best" examples (67.3 %) is facilitated by the fact that subjects had to select an example from a list of examples and previous solutions from the same lesson only. However, similarities in the wording of task descriptions resulted in 13.7 % of all cases in selections based on superficial similarities. This is about 50 % above the figures reported by Faries and Reiser.

In the present study, the case-based system ELM was even better than subjects in indicating useful examples because the system is not influenced by superficial similarities from wordings of task descriptions. The EBR-method retrieves analogues and remindings based on the organisational similarity of stored explanation structures. These explanation structures represent something like the intention and the meaning of a problem solution and, therefore, serve as an appropriate basis for retrieving useful examples and remindings. This makes the system a good candidate component for tutorial and help systems.

Additionally, storing cases in a dynamic case base and retrieving analogues and remindings based on organisational similarity can be done without too much computational effort. Therefore, it can be used on-line in a help system. In contrast to retrieval methods that compare a new problem to all stored cases according to a similarity index which results in increasing computational effort with an increasing case base, the EBR-method considers only those cases that have components stored directly with components of a proposed new problem solution. The disadvantage with this type of user modelling is the increasing space needed to store all cases during a long period monitoring the user. In the future, this problem may be solved by forgetting specific details from cases and relying more on generalisations built up gradually over time. Further studies will have to show how forgetting in ELM will influence the process of retrieving useful analogues and remindings.

Retrieving examples and remindings from a case base is only a first step in supporting example-based learning and programming. Students learn most effectively when they explain examples to themselves (Chi, Bassok, Lewis, Reimann, & Glaser, 1989). These self-explanations should be supported explicitly by an intelligent learning environment (Linn, 1992). In a next step developing ELM-PE, we will add a mechanism to the system that will explain what the reasons are for similarities and dissimilarities between the new problem on the one side and the old retrieved problem on the other side. Combined with such an explanation mechanism, the system will be able to provide multiple examples to a new problem and will show which parts from the old solutions can be used to solve the new tasks.

# Acknowledgements

This work was supported by the "Deutsche Forschungsgemeinschaft" under Grant We 498/12. I wish to thank Alexander Bögelsack for programming the ELM model and Axel Buchner and three anonymous reviewers for their helpful comments and corrections on an earlier draft of this paper.

# References

Anderson, J. R. (1993). *Rules of the mind*. Hillsdale, NJ: Lawrence Erlbaum Associates.

Anderson, J. R., Conrad, F. G., & Corbett, A. T. (1989). Skill acquisition and the LISP tutor. *Cognitive Science*, *13*, 467-505.

Chi, M. T. H., Bassok, M., Lewis, M., Reimann, P., & Glaser, R. (1989). Self-explanations: How students study and use examples in learning to solve problems. *Cognitive Science*, *13*, 145-182.

Clement, C. A., & Gentner, D. (1991). Systematicity as a selection constraint in analogical mapping. *Cognitive Science*, *15*, 89-132.

Faries, J. M., & Reiser, B. J. (1988). Access and use of previous solutions in a problem solving situation. *Proceedings of the Tenth Annual Conference of the Cognitive Science Society*. Hillsdale, NJ: Lawrence Erlbaum Associates.

Gentner, D. (1989). Finding the needle: Accessing and reasoning from prior cases. In K. J. Hammond (Eds.), *Proceedings of the Second Workshop on Case-Based Reasoning*. San Mateo, CA: Morgan Kaufmann Publishers.

Gentner, D., & Landers, R. (1985). Analogical reminding: a good match is hard to find. *Proceedings of the International Conference on Systems, Man and Cybernetics, Tucson, AR*.

Holyoak, K. J., & Koh, K. (1987). Surface and structural similarity in analogical transfer. *Memory & Cognition*, *15*, 332-340.

Kolodner, J. L. (1993). *Case-based reasoning*. San Mateo, CA: Morgan Kaufmann.

Lange, T. E., & Wharton, C. M. (1992). REMIND: Integrating language understanding and episodic memory retrieval in a connectionist network. *Proceedings of the Fourteenth Annual Conference of the Cognitive Science Society*. Hillsdale, NJ: Lawrence Erlbaum Associates.

Linn, M. C. (1992). How can hypermedia tools help teaching programming. *Learning and Instruction*, *2*, 119-139.

Luce, R. D. (1959). *Individual choice behavior*. New York: Wiley.

McCalla, G. I., & Greer, J. E. (1993). Two and one-half approaches to helping novices learn recursion. In E. Lemut, B. du Boulay, & G. Dettori (Eds.), *Cognitive models and intelligent environments for learning programming*. Berlin: Springer-Verlag.

Mitchell, T. M., Keller, R. M., & Kedar-Cabelli, S. T. (1986). Explanation-based generalization: a unifying view. *Machine Learning*, *1*, 47-80.

Neal, L. R. (1989). A system for example-based learning. In K. Bice & C. Lewis (Eds.), *Proceedings of Human Factors in Computing Systems, CHI'89*. Reading, MA: Addison-Wesley.

Ratterman, M., & Gentner, D. (1987). Analogy and similarity: determinants of accessibility and inferential soundness. *Proceedings of the Ninth Annual Conference of the Cognitive Science Society*. Hillsdale, NJ: Lawrence Erlbaum Associates.

Redmond, M. A. (1990). Distributed cases for case-based reasoning: Facilitating use of multiple cases. *Proceedings of AAAI-90.* Cambridge, MA: AAAI Press/MIT Press.

Riesbeck, C. K., & Martin, C. E. (1986). Direct memory access parsing. In J. L. Kolodner & C. K. Riesbeck (Eds.), *Experience, memory, and reasoning.* Hillsdale, NJ: Lawrence Erlbaum Associates.

Riesbeck, C. K., & Schank, R. C. (1989). *Inside case-based reasoning.* Hillsdale, NJ: Lawrence Erlbaum Associates.

Ross, B. H. (1987). This is like that: the use of earlier problems and the separation of similarity effects. *Journal of Experimental Psychology: Learning, Memory, and Instruction, 13,* 629-639.

Ross, B. H., & Kennedy, P. T. (1990). Generalizing from the use of earlier examples in problem solving. *Journal of Experimental Psychology: Learning, Memory, and Cognition, 16,* 42-55.

Schank, R. C. (1982). *Dynamic memory.* Cambridge, MA: Cambridge University Press.

Thagard, P., Holyoak, K. J., Nelson, G., & Gochfeld, D. (1990). Analog retrieval by constraint satisfaction. *Artificial Intelligence, 46,* 259-310.

Tversky, A. (1977). Features of similarity. *Psychological Review, 84,* 327-352.

Veloso, M. M. (1994). Prodigy/Analogy: Analogical reasoning in general problem solving. In S. Wess, K.-D. Althoff, & M. M. Richter (Eds.), *Topics in case-based reasoning.* Berlin: Springer-Verlag.

Weber, G. (1991). Explanation-based retrieval in a case-based learning model. *Proceedings of the Thirteenth Annual Conference of the Cognitive Science Society.* Hillsdale, NJ: Lawrence Erlbaum Associates.

Weber, G. (1993). ELM: Case-based diagnosis of program code in a knowledge-based help system. In M. M. Richter, S. Wess, K.-D. Althoff, & F. Maurer (Eds.), *Proceedings of the First European Workshop on Case-based Reasoning (EWCBR), Posters and Presentations.* Kaiserslautern (Germany): University of Kaiserslautern, SEKI Report SR-93-12 (SFB 314).

Weber, G. (1994). *Fallbasiertes Lernen und Analogien: Unterstützung von Problemlöse- und Lernprozessen in einem adaptiven Lernsystem.* Weinheim: Psychologie Verlags Union.

Weber, G., Bögelsack, A., & Wender, K. F. (1993). When can individual student models be useful? In G. Strube & K. F. Wender (Eds.), *The cognitive psychology of knowledge. The German Wissenspsychologie project.* Amsterdam: Elsevier (North-Holland).

Weber, G., & Möllenberg, A. (1994). ELM-PE: A knowledge-based programming environment for learning LISP. In T. Ottmann & I. Tomek (Eds.), *Proceedings of ED-MEDIA '94.* Charlottesville, VA: AACE.

Weber, G., & Möllenberg, A. (1995). ELM programming environment: A tutoring system for LISP beginners. In K. F. Wender, F. Schmalhofer, & H.-D. Böcker (Eds.), *Cognition and computer programming.* Norwood, NJ: Ablex Publishing Corporation.

Wharton, C. M., & Lange, T. E. (1993). Case-based retrieval and priming: Empirical evidence for integrated models. In W. Visser (Eds.), *Proceedings of the Workshop of the Thirteenth International Joint Conference on Artificial Intelligence „Reuse of designs: an interdisciplinary cognitive approach".* Le Chesnay Cedex (France): INRIA.

Wolstencroft, J. (1989). Restructuring, reminding, repair: What's missing from models of analogy. *AI Communications, 2,* 58-71.

# Part II
# Applications

# A CBR Knowledge Representation for Practical Ethics

Kevin D. Ashley and Bruce M. McLaren
University of Pittsburgh
Intelligent Systems Program and Learning Research and Development Center
Pittsburgh, Pennsylvania 15260
(email: ashley@vms.cis.pitt.edu, bmm@cgi.com)

**Abstract.** TRUTH-TELLER, a program for testing a Case-Based Reasoning (CBR) knowledge representation in practical ethics, compares cases presenting ethical dilemmas about whether to tell the truth. Its comparisons list ethically relevant similarities and differences (i.e., reasons for telling or not telling the truth which apply to both cases, and reasons which apply more strongly in one case than another or which apply only to one case). The program reasons about reasons in generating context-sensitive comparisons. The reasons may invoke ethical principles or selfish considerations. We describe a knowledge representation for this practical ethical domain including representations for reasons and principles, truth telling episodes, contextually important scenarios, and comparison rules. In a preliminary evaluation, a professional ethicist scored the program's output for randomly-selected pairs of cases. The work contributes to AI CBR efforts to integrate general principles and context-sensitive information in symbolically assessing case similarity and to model comparing problems to paradigmatic cases. It also furthers research on cognitive and philosophical models of ethical judgement and decision-making.

## 1 Introduction

A primary goal for AI CBR research is to identify ways that human reasoners employ cases to evaluate problems comparatively. In a variety of professional domains and in "common sense" reasoning, humans employ techniques to draw inferences about problem situations by comparing them to past cases. Case-based comparative evaluation skills appear to assist human reasoners to deal with weak analytic domain/task models. Such models are too weak to support constructing proofs of the correct answers to problems. Nevertheless, the models do support constructing arguments comparing the problems to past cases and drawing some useful conclusions. We will refer to them as comparative evaluation models.

* This work is supported by The Andrew W. Mellon Foundation. We are grateful to Athena Beldecos for her research on casuistic models and data collection of case comparison protocols. We are also grateful to Ken Schaffner, University Professor of Medical Humanities, George Washington University, for participating in our preliminary evaluation. Vincent Aleven has given us good advice in designing our evaluation.

Practical ethical reasoning is a domain in which a comparative evaluation model supplements a weak analytic model. Although philosophers have explored a variety of techniques for solving practical dilemmas by resolving conflicting ethical principles, the attempts have largely failed. Deductive reasoning does not work, because ethical principles are often inconsistent and their antecedents are not well defined. "No moral philosopher has ever been able to present a system of moral rules free of these kinds of conflicts between principles and exceptions to principles" (Beauchamp & McCullough, 1984, p. 16). If one could assign weights to competing principles, resolving them would simply be a matter of comparing the weights. However, "the metaphor of the 'weight' of a principle of duty has not proven amenable to precise analysis" (Beauchamp & McCullough, 1984, p. 16). More recently, ethicists have proposed alternative case-based (i.e., "casuistic") models in which problems are systematically compared to past or paradigmatic cases that bear on the decision (Strong, 1988; Jonsen & Toulmin, 1988; Schaffner, 1990).

Carson Strong, for instance, has proposed a systematic, five-step Case Comparison Method for justifying decisions in practical ethics. The last three steps involve comparing the problem with relevant paradigmatic cases. The comparison aims to illuminate the factors that favor applying or not applying the principles used in the paradigm (Strong, 1988). Strong's model will strike the AI CBR researcher intuitively as nearly computational:

1. Identify middle-level principles and role-specific duties pertinent to situation.
2. Identify alternative courses of action that could be taken.
3. Identify morally relevant ways in which cases of this type can differ from one another (i.e., factors). Comparing with other cases of the same type also helps identify factors.
4. For each option, identify paradigm case in which option would be justifiable. Paradigms can be actual or hypothetical cases. Identify middle-level principle which would provide that justification.
5. Compare case at hand with paradigm cases. Determine which paradigms it is "closest to" in terms of presence of morally relevant factors (Strong, 1988).

Computationally realizing a model like Strong's is interesting from an AI CBR viewpoint because, while it is similar to various AI CBR models (e.g., HYPO in comparing cases along factors (Ashley, 1990), PROTOS in comparing problems to prototypical or paradigmatic cases (Bareiss, 1989), Veloso's PRODIGY/ANALOGY in comparing cases to select appropriate actions to apply (Veloso, 1992)), it introduces important components of CBR that have not yet been modeled such as: (1) symbolically comparing problems and paradigmatic cases to resolve conflicts among applicable general principles and (2) adequately accounting for a problem's specific contextual circumstances in deciding how to resolve conflicting general principles.

As a first step toward computationally realizing a model like Strong's, we have designed and built a computer program, TRUTH-TELLER, whose task is to draw ethically relevant comparisons between practical ethical problems in the truth telling domain. We have focused on case comparison initially because any casuistic model requires a capacity for symbolic case comparison (see e.g., the last three steps of Strong's process). Like (Edelson, 1992), we represent principles at various levels of abstraction which apply to cases, but our representation is designed for comparing cases in ways other than in terms of the principles' abstraction levels. High level case information (i.e., legal theories) and prototypical cases have been integrated into case retrieval and argumentation in (Rissland, Skalak, & Friedman, 1993). We attempt, however, to elaborate a more comprehensive knowledge representation for a more reflective comparative justification with principles, cases, and actions in a context where cases regularly have more than two possible outcomes. Unlike (Kass, Leake, & Owens, 1986; Edelson, 1992), we do not attempt a narrative representation of the truth telling episodes in terms of either the protagonists' goals and plans or expectation violations.

## 2 The Comparative Evaluation Model in TRUTH-TELLER

TRUTH-TELLER (TT), a program for testing and developing a CBR knowledge representation in practical ethics, compares cases presenting ethical dilemmas about whether to tell the truth. Its comparisons list ethically relevant similarities and differences (i.e., reasons for telling or not telling the truth which apply to both cases, and reasons which apply more strongly in one case than another or which apply only to one case). The reasons may invoke ethical principles or selfish considerations. The knowledge representation for this practical ethical domain includes representations for reasons and principles, truth telling episodes, contextually important scenarios, and comparison rules. Our ultimate goal is to see whether a comparative evaluation model like TRUTH-TELLER's could help drive a tutorial program in practical ethical reasoning. Currently, we are recording protocols of high school students' and ethics graduate students' arguments about the same ethical dilemmas contained in TT's Case Knowledge Base.

Currently, TRUTH-TELLER has 23 cases adapted from a game called Scruples (TM). Two of those cases, Rick's Case and Wanda's Case, are shown at the top of Figure 1, followed by the program-generated comparison of the cases. After reciting the cases, TT lists ethically relevant similarities and differences between the cases, differences it finds or infers using five knowledge sources:

- **Truth telling episodes** including: (a) the actors (i.e., the truth teller, truth receiver, others affected by the decision), (b) relationships among the actors (e.g., familial, seller-customer, attorney-client, student-teacher), (c) the truth teller's possible actions (i.e., telling the truth, silence, telling a lie, or taking some alternative action, and (d) reasons for and against each possible action. The information is represented in a semantic network using the knowledge representation language, LOOM (MacGregor, 1991)(Woods & Schmolze, 1990).
- **Relations Hierarchy:** The relationships among the actors are drawn from the Relations Hierarchy, a taxonomy of approximately 80 possible relationships among the participants in a truth telling episode. Mid-level relationships include familial,

commercial, and acquaintance relations. Higher level relationships include minimal-trust and high-trust relations, authority relations, personal and social relations. Typically, the Relations Hierarchy is used to infer which relationships are "similar" for purposes of identifying the levels of trust and responsibility that apply among the participants (i.e., the applicable scenarios. See below).

- **Reason Hierarchy:** A reason is a rationale for taking an action. We represent reasons as a hierarchy of concepts, the Reason Hierarchy. Reasons have four facets: type, criticality, if altruistic, and if principled; each facet is important to ethical decision-making and is represented as a distinct branch of the Reason Hierarchy. The Reason Hierarchy is used to characterize abstractly the reasons for and against an action according to these facets. Based on the formulation in (Bok, 1989), a reason's type is based on four underlying general principles for telling the truth or not: Fairness, Veracity, Beneficence, and Nonmaleficence (i.e., avoiding harm to others). We also represent a variety of more specific principles.[2]

- **Scenario Hierarchy:** In determining whether or not to tell the truth, contextual information is important. One needs to consider such things as the consequences of an action, the reasonable expectations of truthfulness that apply in different social contexts, and the level of trust or reliance among the actors. We have identified approximately 15 types of contextual information. We call them truthtelling scenarios and have organized them into a Scenario Hierarchy. Our scenarios include context-specific considerations such as: Is there a relationship of authority between the teller and receiver? of trust? Are others affected by the decision to tell the truth? Is the action a matter of telling an out-and-out lie or simply keeping silence? If the action is telling a lie, is it premeditated or not? What is the nature of and how severe are the consequences of the action? Are there alternative actions that obviate the need to tell the lie or disclose the information? Are the participants involved in a game or activity governed by disclosure rules?

- **Comparison rules:** We have defined 58 Comparison Rules for deciding whether one case presents a stronger or weaker justification than another case for taking a course of action such as disclosing information or not telling a lie. From the information contained in the cases' applicable scenarios, actions, reasons, and principles, the rules infer relevant ethical similarities and differences between the cases. The rules' left hand sides employ classified scenarios, actions, reasons and reason-associated principles. The right hand sides make assertions about the relative strength in the two cases of the conclusions that the teller should tell the truth or disclose information (or not).

The goal of TRUTH-TELLER's knowledge representation design is to enable the program to make context sensitive ethical comparisons of cases. To this end,

---

[2] Some of the more specific principles represented include: (a) One must protect ones self and others from grave danger. (b) Individuals have a right to confidentiality. (c) If one knows that others are relying on the disclosure of important information, it should be disclosed. (d) One should make only well-founded accusations. (e) One who has committed a misdeed should be accountable to those affected. (f) The rules of a game should be followed. (g) One should compete fairly. (h) One should admit ones mistakes. Unprincipled reasons include avoiding harm to oneself in terms of emotional distress, financial loss, punishment or damage to ones reputation and accruing benefits such as reduced work loads, possible financial gain, competitive advantages, professional opportunities and future favors.

**RICK's CASE:** "Rick's father is having an affair. Rick's mother is unaware of it. Should Rick tell his mother?"

**WANDA's CASE:** "Wanda's brother, Paul, is a real playboy. He's setting up a young woman, whom Wanda knows casually, for a big disappointment. The young woman asks Wanda if Paul loves her. Should Wanda tell her the truth?"

SIMILARITIES:                                                                    **R17**

Rick and Wanda have a common principled reason for telling the truth, i.e. providing the right to disclosure of information. This reason is supported by the ethical principle: 'When one knows that another person is relying on the disclosure of information, that information should be disclosed.'

Rick and Wanda have a common principled reason for not telling the truth, i.e. avoiding becoming a 'tattle tale'. This reason is supported by the ethical principle: 'One should not 'tattle' on another person.'                                          **R25**

Rick and Wanda have purely altruistic reasons for not telling the truth. To some extent this would excuse each for not telling the truth.

Both of the cases involve someone other than the person who must decide whether or not to tell the truth and the person who will hear the truth. Ricks-father is affected by Rick's decision, and Paul is affected by Wanda's decision.

Both Rick and Wanda have an alternative action that could be taken before making the truthtelling decision. Rick could approach Ricks-father before deciding whether to tell the truth or not, while Wanda could approach Paul before deciding whether to tell the truth or not.

DIFFERENCES:

The stakes for Rick are much higher than for Wanda. Rick's decision is highly important.

Rick has a reason for telling the truth -- providing fairness for a misdeed that has been committed -- that is not shared by Wanda. This reason is supported by the ethical principle: 'When one has committed a misdeed, they should be held accountable to those who have been affected.'

Rick has a reason for not telling the truth that is not shared by Wanda. The reason is avoiding major emotional distress. The ethical principle: 'One should protect themself and others from serious emotional distress.' supports this reason.

Wanda has a reason for not telling the truth that is not shared by Rick. The reason is protecting against a possibly false accusation. The ethical principle: 'One should not make accusations unless they are sure their accusations are well-founded.' supports this reason.

Wanda has a second reason for not telling the truth, i.e. avoiding minor emotional distress, that is not shared by Rick. However, this reason is not supported by any ethical principle.

Ricks-mother has authority over Rick, but Young-woman and Wanda are on a relatively equal basis. Since Rick is subject to this authority, it may increase the pressure to tell the truth.

Rick has a high level of duty to tell the truth to Ricks-mother. However, the duty Wanda has to Young-woman is much lower.

Ricks-mother is likely to have great trust in Rick telling the truth. However, the trust   **R36**
Young-woman has in Wanda is much lower.

Wanda is confronted with telling an outright lie, while Rick must decide whether to remain silent about the truth. This tends to make Wanda's decision more difficult, i.e. it is typically less excusable to lie than to remain silent about the truth.

**Fig. 1.** TRUTH-TELLER's Output Comparing Rick's and Wanda's Cases

we have designed the knowledge representation to enable TRUTH-TELLER, in comparing cases, to go some way beyond matching the reasons listed in the two cases' representations. In effect, TT reasons about reasons in the context of a particular pair of cases in a variety of ways. We will illustrate the ways in an extended example comparing the output text of Figure 1 with the initial lists of reasons in the semantic networks for Rick's and Wanda's cases, shown in Figure 3. Specifically, the example illustrates how TRUTH-TELLER: (1) classifies reasons as principled, self-motivated or altruistic, (2) elicits the principles underlying the reasons, (3) matches reasons to find shared reasons for an action (similarities) and unshared reasons or reasons that apply more strongly in one case than another (differences). In the example, the program tailors the comparison based on (4) differences in criticality of the reasons, (5) differences in the participants' roles, (6) similarity in types of reasons considered in the aggregate, (7) similarities in the presence of untried alternatives and of (8) others affected by an action.

## 3   An Extended Example of Case Comparison

TRUTH-TELLER applies its five knowledge sources in a two-step process illustrated in Figure 2. In the first step, Classification, for each of two selected input cases, TT classifies the case's manually-constructed semantic representation by (1) all applicable scenarios (using the Relations and Scenario Hierarchies), (2) all applicable actions, and (3) an abstract characterization of the reasons for those actions (using the Reason Hierarchy.) In the second step, Comparison, TT attempts to apply all Comparison Rules to the classified cases. The output of this step is a list of relevant similarities and differences which is translated into a comparison text.

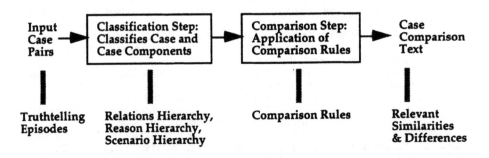

**Fig. 2.** Overview of TRUTH-TELLER's Process

TRUTH-TELLER's process starts with semantic representations of each of the cases. The representation of a case is an interpretation of its language and is filled in manually. Figure 3 depicts the semantic representation of Rick's case on the left. Rick is the truth teller (i.e., it is he who is confronted with the decision to tell the truth or not.) Rick's mother will hear the truth, should Rick decide to divulge it, and thus is the truth receiver. Finally, Rick's father is an affected other, since he is the subject of any truthtelling disclosure, and he would be affected by the disclosure. The relevant roles and relationships between actors in the case are also included in the semantic representation. Some relationships and roles are provided as input (e.g., Rick is the son-of Rick's mother and father) while others are deduced by forward chaining rules (e.g., Rick's mother has-husband Rick's father, since they share a common child).

The semantic representation also contains a set of possible actions that the truth teller could take and reasons supporting each of the actions. One of the possible actions is always to tell the truth and another is some version of not telling the truth, for instance, telling a lie or keeping silent (i.e., not disclosing information). In Rick's case, the choice is between telling the truth about his father's affair or keeping silent. Since the case does not state that Rick was asked whether his father was having an affair, Rick is not confronted with telling an outright lie. Rick also has an alternative action he could take before deciding whether or not to talk with his mother; he could first speak with his father. Actions are supported by reasons; a reason is a rationale for taking an action. For example, a rationale for Rick's telling the truth is to protect his mother's right to the disclosure of information important to her. A rationale for keeping silent is to avoid inflicting serious emotional distress upon his mother.

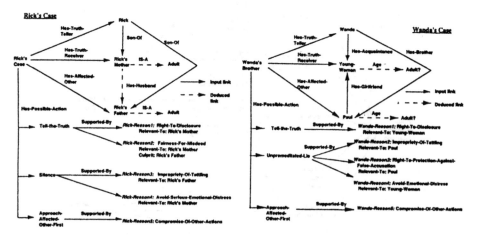

**Fig. 3.** Semantic Network Representation of Rick's Case (left) and Wanda's Case (right)

Given the input representations, TRUTH-TELLER performs the Classification Step; it classifies the cases and case components including the actions and reasons. For purposes of comparing cases, the two most critical classifications are assigning the scenarios and characterizing the reasons.

A case may be classified under any number of scenarios. LOOM's automatic classifier performs the scenario classification. Figure 4 shows a portion of the Scenario Hierarchy with the Rick and Wanda cases classified. The relationships between actors in the case are the key ingredients for scenario classifications. All of the relationships in the truthtelling cases are classified within the Relations Hierarchy (a small portion of which is shown in Figure 5). The Relations Hierarchy represents various types of relationships (i.e., familial, commercial, etc.) as well as important abstract information (i.e., expected level of trust, duty, and authority between the actors). The specific relations in the semantic representation of a case (e.g. son-of and has-husband as in Rick's case) are found at the lowest level of the Relations Hierarchy. Scenarios are defined with respect to relation abstractions (e.g., high trust, authority, etc.) and relation directionality (e.g., truth-teller to truth-receiver, truth-teller to affected-other, etc.) For instance, Rick's case is classified in the Scenario Hierarchy as a high trust scenario due to the relationship between Rick and his mother. Their parent-child relationship is defined, through a series of links, to be a high trust relation. By contrast, Wanda's case is classified as a minimal trust scenario, since the acquaintance relationship between Wanda and the young woman is a minimal trust relationship. Also, notice how Rick's case is classified as an authority scenario due to the parent-child relationship being an authority relationship. The cases do share one relevant scenario, however. They both involve an affected other, Rick's father and Wanda's brother.

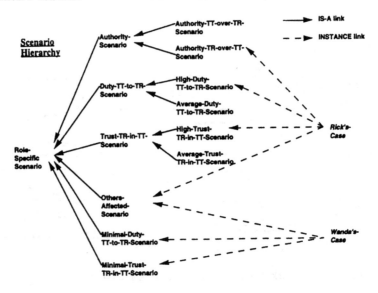

**Fig. 4.** Excerpts from Scenario Hierarchy

TRUTH-TELLER also classifies the reasons associated with cases. Figure 6 shows a small portion of the Reason Hierarchy with two of Rick's reasons and one of Wanda's depicted. The top reason in the diagram – Rick-Reason4 – supports Rick's remaining silent (refer to Figure 3). This reason deals with Rick's sparing his mother emotional distress, should she hear of her husband's extramarital activities. Using classification information contained in the Reason Hierarchy, the program classifies Rick-Reason4 in four ways, according to: (1) Type: Rick-Reason4 is a nonmaleficence type (i.e., intended to avoid harm). (2) Principled or not: Since this particular reason has an associated ethical principle (i.e., one should protect others from serious emotional distress) the reason is also classified as principled. (3) Criticality: qualitatively, an avoid-serious-emotional-distress reason is deemed to be highly important. (4) Altruistic or not: Rick-Reason4 is altruistic, since it is to the benefit of Rick's mother, not to Rick himself. The other two reasons in the diagram show that Rick and Wanda share a rationale

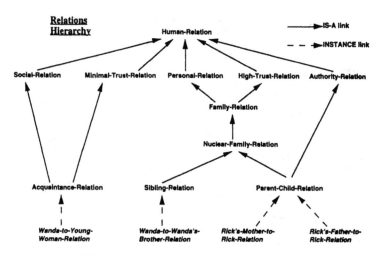

**Fig. 5.** Excerpts from Relations Hierarchy

for telling the truth, namely to preserve the right of the truth receiver to hear important information. This reason is related to fairness, it is principled, and it is considered less critical than Rick-Reason4, although still considered important. Again, the reason is altruistic, as it is to the benefit of the truth receiver in both instances.

TRUTH-TELLER's comparison step attempts to apply the Comparison Rules to the cases as classified in order to draw inferences about their relevant similarities and differences and generate the comparison text as in Figure 1. Figure 7 shows a number of TT's comparison rules. We will focus on three rules that generated the text circled in Figure 1: Rules 17, 25 and 36. (The LOOM form of the rules is paraphrased for readability.) Rule 17 says, "IF CASE-1 and CASE-2 have a common principled reason for telling the truth THEN they are similar re telling truth." Here, the two cases shared the principled reason that the truth receivers had a right to the disclosures as discussed above and depicted in Figure 6. Rule-25 says, "IF CASE-1 and CASE-2 have only altruistic reasons for not telling the truth THEN they are similar re not telling truth." Since Rick and Wanda have solely altruistic reasons for not telling the truth, they both have a stronger justification for taking this action. This is an example of a comparison rule that abstracts from individual classifications and views the reasons supporting an action in the aggregate. Rule-36 says, "IF CASE-1 is a high duty scenario and CASE-2 is not THEN they are different; CASE-1 has a stronger reason to tell truth." It employs the Scenario Hierarchy (see Figure 4) to identify this important distinction between the cases. The duty between Rick and his mother is much higher than between Wanda and the young woman; this is shown by the classification of the cases within the Scenario Hierarchy. This point is important as it indicates that Rick's duty to tell the truth is higher than Wanda's. Other rules pick out the differences in criticality of consequences and similarities in the presence of untried alternatives and of others affected by the actions.

To summarize, the extended example illustrates how TRUTH-TELLER reasons about the reasons that apply in each case's particular facts and draws

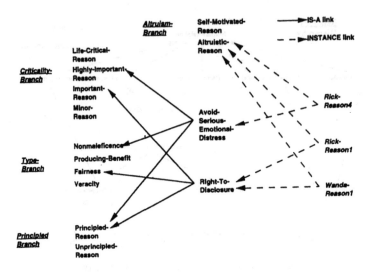

**Fig. 6.** Excerpts from Reasons Hierarchy

inferences that reflect the ethically significant differences implicit in the cases' facts. Figure 8 summarizes all the ways that TT reasons about reasons, most of which are illustrated in the example. We have seen how TT classifies reasons as principled, self-motivated or altruistic, elicits the principles underlying the reasons, matches reasons to find shared reasons for an action (similarities) and unshared reasons or reasons that apply more strongly in one case than another (differences). The differences may be related to differing criticalness, differences in the participant's roles, differences in the aggregate types of reasons, and the presence of untried alternatives or of others affected by an action. TT's methods for qualifying reasons, items four through eight in Figure 8, make use of these distinctions and enable TT to take context into account in analyzing a case and comparing it to another case.

## 4 The Evaluation

We designed TRUTH-TELLER to reason about reasons so that it could tailor its comparisons to the particular context of the cases compared. We claim its ability to point out differences based on unshared compelling reasons not to tell the truth, life critical consequences of an action, varying levels of duty to tell the truth associated with particular roles and relationships among the participants, untried alternative actions and the existence of affected others enables it to make context sensitive comparisons.

We undertook a preliminary evaluation to test our claim, in particular, to test how robustly the program compared cases and how well the program's outputs took context into account. Adopting an approach from the Intelligent Tutoring Systems literature, we conducted a formative evaluation (Littman & Soloway,

R17: IF CASE-1 and CASE-2 have a common principled reason for telling the truth THEN they are similar re telling truth

R25: IF CASE-1 and CASE-2 have only altruistic reasons for not telling the truth THEN they are similar re not telling truth

R36: IF CASE-1 is a high duty scenario and CASE-2 is not THEN they are different; CASE-1 has a stronger reason to tell truth

R18: IF CASE-1 has principled reason for telling the truth that CASE-2 does not have THEN they are different; CASE-1 has a stronger reason to tell truth

R21: IF Both CASE-1 and CASE-2 have an alternative action THEN they are similar in having a compromise alternative

R28: IF CASE-1 has a reason that is higher in criticality than any reason associated with CASE-2 THEN they are different; CASE-1 has a stronger reason to tell the truth [or not to tell truth]

R30: IF CASE-1 is an authority scenario (truth receiver over truth teller) and CASE-2 is not THEN they are different; CASE-1 has a stronger reason to tell truth

R40: IF a possible action in CASE-1 is LIE, but SILENCE is a possible action in CASE-2 THEN they are different; CASE-1 has a stronger reason to tell the truth

R41: IF CASE-1 has a Life-Critical Reason supporting telling the truth [or not telling truth] and CASE-2 does not THEN they are different; CASE-1 has a stronger reason to tell the truth [or not to tell truth]

**Fig. 7.** Sample Comparison Rules

1. **Classify reasons:** The Reason Hierarchy classifies reasons as principled, self-motivated, altruistic.
2. **Elicit principles underlying reasons:** The Reason Hierarchy follows links from reason type to principles.
3. **Match reasons:** Comparison rules identify reasons for a particular action shared by cases and reasons not shared. The matches are based on a literal comparison of reason types.
4. **Qualify reasons by criticalness of consequences:** The Reason Hierarchy qualifies reasons according to the criticalness of what happens if an action were not taken.
5. **Qualify reasons by participant's roles:** The Relations Hierarchy and Scenario Hierarchy detect qualifications on reasons based on the participants' roles (e.g., trust, duty, authority).
6. **Qualify reasons in the aggregate:** Comparison rules note if all [some] reasons supporting an action are principled or unprincipled, altruistic or self-motivated.
7. **Qualify reasons by alternative actions:** Comparison rules qualify reasons based on the existence of untried alternative actions in the case representation.
8. **Qualify reasons based on how others affected by action:** The Scenario Hierarchy notes how others in the case representation are affected by an action and the comparison rules qualify the reasons accordingly.
9. **Order reasons for action by importance:** If a case has multiple reasons favoring one action, they are ordered locally in terms of whether the reasons are principled or not, altruistic or self-motivated.
10. **Group reasons:** Reasons that deal with related issues are grouped.

**Fig. 8.** TRUTH-TELLER's Ways of Reasoning about Reasons

1988). Our goals were to validate the program-generated comparison texts along three dimensions: reasonableness, completeness, and context sensitivity, and to identify specific misconceptions and/or missing conceptions in our representation. Our approach was to have a human expert grade TT's output along each of the three dimensions for four types of case comparisons: very similar cases, very dissimilar cases, cases from the original knowledge base, and cases from an extended knowledge base.

Of the 23 cases in TRUTH-TELLER's CKB, thirteen original cases were used to develop the program. The thirteen cases were employed in an initial series of interviews in which a graduate student studying medical ethics and the first author were asked to analyze, compare and contrast the cases. This information formed the basis of the knowledge representation. The remaining ten cases (i.e., the extended knowledge base) were added after the program had been designed and the knowledge representation had become settled.

In this preliminary experiment, we submitted fifteen pairs of cases and comparison texts (like the one in Figure 1) to an expert on moral philosophy. Thirteen of the comparison texts were generated by the TRUTH-TELLER program. The pairs were drawn from five categories. See the Table in Figure 9 for a description of the categories. Two of the comparison texts were extracted from the original interviews with the ethics graduate student (pair no. 3) and the first author (pair no. 7) and formatted and edited to look like the other comparison texts. (These pairs are marked with an "H" in the table.) The pairs of cases for the thirteen program-generated texts were selected as follows: five pairs of cases selected at random from the ten subsequent cases (category T4), five pairs of cases selected randomly consisting of one case from the initial set and one from the subsequent set (category T3), two pairs of very similar cases selected by us from the initial thirteen (category T1) and one pair of clearly distinguishable cases selected by us, one from the initial set and one from the subsequent set (category T2). The expert was not informed which texts were generated by humans and which by computer program, but he did know that some texts were generated by computer.

Of the thirteen pairs of cases for which the program generated texts, we selected three pairs and asked the expert "briefly and in writing to compare the cases in each pair from an ethical viewpoint", listing the ethically relevant similarities and differences as defined above. This task was performed before the expert saw any of the fifteen comparison texts. Then we asked the expert to "evaluate the [fifteen] comparisons as you might evaluate short answers written by your students." We asked him to assign to each text three grades on a scale of 1 to 10 for reasonableness (R score: 10 = Very reasonable, sophisticated; 1 = Totally unreasonable, wrong-headed), completeness (C score: 10 = Comprehensive and deep; 1 = Totally inadequate and shallow), and context sensitivity (CS score: 10 = Very sensitive to context, perceptive; 1 = Very insensitive to context). For each point of similarity or difference in the comparison text, we asked him also to mark the point as follows: "$\sqrt{}$" if the point is reasonable and relevant, "$\sqrt{+}$" if the point is especially good or perceptive, "$\sqrt{-}$" if the point

| Pair No. | 1 | 2 | 3 | 4 | 5 | 6 | 7 | 8 | 9 | 10 | 11 | 12 | 13 | 14 | 15 | Avg.* |
|---|---|---|---|---|---|---|---|---|---|---|---|---|---|---|---|---|
| Category | T1 | T4 | H | T2 | T4 | T3 | H | T3 | T4 | T1 | T4 | T3 | T3 | T3 | T4 | |
| R Score | 8 | 8 | 10 | 9 | 6 | 7 | 8 | 8 | 7 | 7 | 8 | 7 | 7 | 8 | 9 | 7.6 |
| C Score | 9 | 8 | 10 | 9 | 8 | 5 | 8 | 7 | 9 | 6 | 7 | 5 | 7 | 8 | 8 | 7.4 |
| CS Score | 8 | 8 | 10 | 8 | 4 | 2 | 7 | 3 | 6 | 3 | 7 | 4 | 3 | 7 | 6 | 5.3 |
| | | | | | | | | | | | | | | | | %** |
| √ 's | 6 | 7 | 3 | 7 | 3 | 8 | 3 | 5 | 7 | 9 | 4 | 9 | 7 | 7 | 8 | 51 |
| √ +'s | 1 | 3 | 4 | 1 | 2 | 2 | 1 | 2 | 1 | 1 | 3 | 1 | 0 | 3 | 2 | 13 |
| √ -'s | 2 | 3 | 1 | 1 | 4 | 2 | 0 | 3 | 1 | 1 | 2 | 1 | 1 | 3 | 0 | 14 |
| X 's | 2 | 2 | 0 | 1 | 3 | 4 | 2 | 5 | 3 | 4 | 2 | 4 | 5 | 1 | 1 | 22 |
| Tot. Sim & Dif | 11 | 15 | 8 | 10 | 12 | 16 | 6 | 15 | 12 | 15 | 11 | 15 | 13 | 14 | 11 | |

←— Rick's and Wanda's cases

**Categories Key**
T1: TT output; similar cases picked by us from initial 13
T2: TT output; clearly distinguishable cases picked by us,
 1 from initial 13, 1 from subsequent 10
T3: TT output; randomly chosen, 1 from initial 13, 1 from
 subsequent 10
T4: TT output; randomly chosen, 2 from subsequent 10
H: Prepared by humans

**Key re Individual Similarities & Differences**
√ = point is reasonable and relevant
√+ = point is especially good or perceptive
√- = point is irrelevant
X = point is plain wrong

**Score Key**
R score (Reasonableness):
 10 = Very reasonable, sophisticated;
 1 = Totally unreasonable, wrong-headed
C score (Completeness):
 10 = Comprehensive and deep;
 1 = Totally inadequate and shallow
CS score (Context Sensitivity) :
 10 = Very sensitive to context, perceptive;
 1 = Very insensitive to context

\* Average score computation excludes
 pairs 3 and 7 (humans' output)

\*\* % of total number of similarities and
 differences generated by TT (170)

**Fig. 9.** Evaluation Table

is irrelevant, and "X" if the point is plain wrong.

The results are presented in tabular form in Figure 9. The grader treated only one text as a perfect ten, the one prepared by the medical ethics graduate student (suggesting, arguably, that context sensitive case comparison is a learned expert skill). The program-generated text scores for reasonableness ranged from a high of nine to a low of six. The completeness scores ranged from a high of nine to a low of five. The scores for context sensitivity were lower, ranging from eight to two and averaging 5.3. The comparison text shown in Figure 1, for instance, which was the subject of the extended example (regarding pair no. ten, Rick's case and Wanda's case) was judged by the expert as one of the poorer comparisons in terms of context sensitivity. Interestingly, the expert graded a number of program-generated texts higher than or nearly the same as the text generated by the first author. As to the 170 points of comparison which the program drew in total for the thirteen pairs, the expert regarded 64% as either reasonable and relevant or especially good or perceptive, 14% as irrelevant, and 22% as plain wrong.

# 5 Discussion of Results

The evaluation suggests that the program displays a capacity for intelligently comparing truth telling episodes. The knowledge representation was general enough to enable TRUTH-TELLER to draw reasonable comparisons of randomly selected pairs of cases from beyond the initial set used to build the representation.

The knowledge representation also was robust enough to enable comparison of the same cases in different contexts. Seven of the cases were used in more than one comparison. The program was able to draw a comparison in each context in which those cases appeared. The contexts must have been fairly different because the expert expressed difficulty working through the some of the comparisons, "[p]erhaps because the focus is on comparison, and the cases kept appearing in new comparison contexts."

While the program's context sensitivity scores were lower than the other scores, three of its CS scores were higher than and two tied one of the human's CS scores. Since being sensitive to context in ethical judgments is one of the hardest things to get the program to do (it's also hard for humans), the lower scores are, perhaps, to be expected.

Since the expert assigned a mark to each point of similarity and difference generated by the program, we have been able to evaluate how well specific Comparison Rules functioned. For each of 58 rules, we assigned scores based on the expert's marks (i.e., $X = 0$, $\sqrt{-} = 1$, $\sqrt{} = 2$ $\sqrt{+} = 3$). We found that the expert scored highly TRUTH-TELLER's ability to point out differences based on: unshared compelling reasons not to tell the truth, life critical consequences of an action, varying levels of duty to tell the truth associated with particular roles and relationships among the participants, and untried alternative actions. The latter two are very significant because reasoning about roles, relationships, and alternative actions helps TT make context sensitive comparisons.

On the other hand, the expert did not seem satisfied with the program's ability to point out differences based on: unshared reasons to tell the truth or not (the rule fired a lot of times but did not always make a sensible contribution) and the existence of affected others. In particular, the program lacked a robust ability to explain an action's effects on the participants and was not successful in tying the existence of the affected others to a specific argument for or against an action. According to the expert, a better comparison would describe how actors are affected by telling the truth or not: "If the alternative actions and the affected others included information about how telling the truth or not influenced them, then the program's contextual comments would be better. For example, in case 10, [a better comparison would explain], 'Why are the stakes higher for Rick than Wanda?'"

Another "missing conception" has to do with the program's inability to consider alternative interpretations of a case's facts. As the expert pointed out, Rick's parents' marriage could have been an "open" one. Our case representation captures only one stereotypical interpretation of the facts of the case. We recognize this failing, but have not devised any general way to deal with exceptions to default expectations. At best, the links in the semantic networks representing cases may provide "hooks" on which to "hang" specific exceptions that have already been encountered in a domain or are likely to be. It remains to be seen whether implementing that kind of limited capacity for alternative interpretations will suffice for some real applications such as tutoring practical ethical decision making.

Finally, the expert criticized the program for having no way to compare the importance of reasons across cases in general. TRUTH-TELLER has only local measures for assessing the relative importance of reasons within a case or across pairs of cases. Strong's casuistic methodology, discussed above, is one attempt at stating a general method for assessing the importance of reasons in light of their supporting principles and applications in paradigmatic or hypothetical cases or in past dilemmas. So far, we have tackled only part of the comparison step required by Strong's method.

The evaluation has been conducted at an early stage of development of the TRUTH-TELLER program. A more formal evaluation would require obtaining other experts' evaluations of the same data. Since we are at a preliminary stage, we have focussed instead on how this expert's evaluation and comments can lead to improvements in the knowledge representation. One area where we have made improvements concerns "marshalling." The expert commented generally that the comparison texts lacked an "organizing roadmap" and a recommended final decision "which could guide thinking and in terms of which the similarities, differences, and ethical principles could be marshalled." Marshalling entails presenting reasons as part of a coherent argument for a specific conclusion. As per his suggestion, we are reorganizing the comparison text around specific conclusions and experimenting with various techniques for formulating more pointed arguments supporting a conclusion. Our initial attempts at marshalling immediately pointed out an interesting aspect of the salience of differences: If cases are really different, you do not need to recite each difference, only the important ones. Consequently, we are developing a typology for characterizing the overall similarity between cases in order to frame TT's selections of which similarities and differences to emphasize.

# 6  Conclusions

In conclusion, TRUTH-TELLER compares cases presenting ethical dilemmas about whether to tell the truth. Its comparisons list ethically relevant similarities and differences in terms of shared and unshared reasons. The program reasons about reasons in generating context-sensitive comparisons; it qualifies reasons in light of the participants' relationships, consequences of actions, alternative actions, others affected, and by considering reasons in the aggregate. We have described a knowledge representation for this practical ethical domain including representations for reasons and principles, truth telling episodes, contextually important scenarios, and comparison rules. In a preliminary experiment, a professional ethicist scored the program's output for randomly-selected pairs of cases. The experiment confirmed that the comparative evaluation model enables the program to make comparisons robustly and with some degree of context sensitivity, at least for 23 cases in the field of truth telling. We anticipate a final case base of between 50 and 75 cases.

The evaluation shows that we have developed an AI CBR knowledge representation which can very nearly simulate intelligent comparisons of practical ethical problems. We plan to use this knowledge representation for a cognitive science investigation of the differences between novice and experienced reasoning about ethical dilemmas. As previously noted, we are collecting and analyzing protocols of high school and ethics graduate students' arguments about the same cases as in TRUTH-TELLER's database. We hope to use our knowledge representation to duplicate and explain some of the observed differences in novice and experienced reasoning and to model some of the arguers' specific differences of opinion. We also hope to model arguments that a proposed resolution is inconsistent with an arguer's previous arguments about similar cases. This investigation will lead, we hope, to a realistic model of ethical decision-making or, at least, of reasonable ethical case-based argumentation upon which to base a tutoring system to improve novices' abilities to recognize and analyze practical ethical dilemmas.

From a philosophical viewpoint, the new casuistic models developed by Carson Strong and others may or may not amount to a process for justified ethical decision making. We believe, however, and hope this work will ultimately demonstrate, that case-based comparative evaluation models in practical ethics offer cognitive benefits. An AI CBR program that helps novices gain practice comparing cases may encourage better ethical decision making. Comparing cases may help ethical reasoners recognize important aspects of a dilemma: the issues presented, morally relevant factors, applicable principles and useful paradigmatic examples, the players' interests and viewpoints, and important missing facts. Case comparison may even facilitate building consensus by focusing on context and specifics rather than abstract moral principles, basing decisions on practical judgements and moral sentiments in similar cases rather than on abstract moral justifications, and leading reasoners to consider creative alternative solutions.

# References

Ashley, K. D. (1990). *Modeling Legal Argument: Reasoning with Cases and Hypotheticals*. MIT Press, Cambridge. Based on Ashley's 1987 PhD. Dissertation, University of Massachusetts, COINS Technical Report No. 88–01.

Bareiss, E. R. (1989). *Exemplar-Based Knowledge Acquisition - A Unified Approach to Concept Representation, Classification, and Learning*. Academic Press, San Diego, CA. Based on PhD thesis, University of Texas, 1988.

Beauchamp, T., & McCullough, L. B. (1984). *Medical Ethics: The Moral Responsibilities of Physicians*. Prentice-Hall, Englewood Cliffs, NJ.

Bok, S. (1989). *Lying*. Random House, Inc. Vintage Books, New York.

Edelson, D. C. (1992). When Should A Cheetah Remind You of a Bat? Reminding in Case-Based Teaching. In *Proceedings AAAI-92*, pp. 667–672. American Association for Artificial Intelligence. San Jose, CA.

Jonsen, A. R., & Toulmin, S. (1988). *The Abuse of Casuistry A History of Moral Reasoning*. University of California Press, Berkeley.

Kass, A. M., Leake, D., & Owens, C. C. (1986). Swale: A Program that Explains. In Schanck, R. C. (Ed.), *Explanation Patterns: Understanding Mechanically and Creatively.* Lawrence Erlbaum Associates, Hillsdale, NJ.

Littman, D., & Soloway, E. (1988). Evaluating ITSs: The Cognitive Science Perspective. In Polson, M. C., & Richardson, J. J. (Eds.), *Foundations of Intelligent Tutoring Systems.* Lawrence Erlbaum Associates, Hillsdale, NJ.

MacGregor, R. (1991). The Evolving Technology of Classification-Based Knowledge Representation Systems. In Sowa, J. F. (Ed.), *Principles of Semantic Networks: Explorations in the Representation of Knowledge*, pp. 385–400. Morgan Kaufmann, San Mateo, CA.

Rissland, E. L., Skalak, D. B., & Friedman, M. T. (1993). BankXX: A Program to Generate Argument through Case-Base Search. In *Fourth International Conference on Artificial Intelligence and Law* Vrie Universiteit, Amsterdam.

Schaffner, K. F. (1990). Case-Based Reasoning in Law and Ethics. Presentation at the "Foundations of Bioethics" Conference. Hastings Center.

Strong, C. (1988). Justification in Ethics. In Brody, B. A. (Ed.), *Moral Theory and Moral Judgments in Medical Ethics*, pp. 193–211. Kluwer Academic Publishers, Dordrecht.

Veloso, M. M. (1992). *Learning by Analogical Reasoning in General Problem Solving.* Ph.D. thesis, Carnegie Mellon University. Technical Report No. CMU-CS-92-174.

Woods, W. A., & Schmolze, J. G. (1990). The KL-ONE Family. Tech. rep. TR-20-90, Center for Research in Computing Technology, Harvard University, Cambridge, MA.

# Case-Based Spatial Design Reasoning

Bharat Dave[1], Gerhard Schmitt[1], Shen-Guan Shih[1], Laurent Bendel[1],
Boi Faltings[2], Ian Smith[2], Kefeng Hua[2],
Simon Bailey[3], Jean-Marc Ducret[3] and Kim Jent[3]

[1] Architecture and CAAD
Swiss Federal Institute of Technology, 8093 Zürich, Switzerland
[2] Artificial Intelligence Lab
Swiss Federal Institute of Technology, 1015 Lausanne, Switzerland
[3] Steel Structures- Department of Civil Engineering
Swiss Federal Institute of Technology, 1015 Lausanne, Switzerland

**Abstract.** Case-based design reasoning provides support for design of buildings and products. This paper describes a computer based system that uses case-based reasoning for design of spatial aspects of buildings. We describe the processes of case adaptation where an existing design case is dimensionally and topologically adapted to suit a new design problem, and case combination where parts of more than one design case are combined to develop a new design solution.

## 1 Introduction

Case-based design (CBD) reasoning is based on a more general paradigm of case-based reasoning (CBR) where previous situations are represented as cases and are used to solve a new problem. This project is an exploration of CBD concepts and techniques in the domain of building design. The ideas are explored and tested using a computer based system called CADRE (CAse-based Design Reasoning Environment). CADRE supports two ways of utilizing previous design cases, case adaptation and case combination. Case adaptation is the process of using a design case and modifying it to solve a new design problem. Case combination is the process of using parts of one or more cases and combining them to solve a new design problem. Both these processes require computation of dimensional or topological modifications. CADRE emphasizes two additional concerns: integration between multiple abstractions of design, e.g., architectural and structural, and providing interactive support to designers.

### 1.1 Design Cases in Architecture

The pedagogic tradition in architectural education relies heavily upon the use of cases as a vehicle of discourse between teachers and students; the hope being that the particulars in a given case offer a holistic view of design issues. Many issues are difficult to articulate or view if they are taken up separately. This mode of example-based teaching and learning entails developing a facility for making generalizations as a function of new examples that are encountered. The dialectical process of using past knowledge to solve new design problems also continues into professional practice.

There are two approaches in architectural design that are of interest to us: case adaptation and case combination. The campus of the University of Texas (UT) at El Paso (Figure 1, left) shows an adpatation of the elements of the architecture of Bhutan. An example of case combination is the Royal Pavilion in Brighton (Figure 1, right). It was designed by John Nash and combined elements from architectural styles as diverse as Chinese, Saracenic and Indian. Other examples of reuse of design cases can be found in colonial architecture, and many building reuse and extension projects.

**Fig. 1.** Case adaptation (left) and combination (right) in architecture.

These examples point out why and how cases may be reused in design. Cases are adapted or combined in a design for the efficiency obtained when compared with generation and search processes during design development. An objective of our work is to develop computational techniques to support case-based spatial design reasoning.

## 1.2 Related Studies

Research into case-based reasoning originated from ideas on human memory structure (Kolodner, 1984) and was thus motivated by research into cognitive psychology. Application of CBR techniques to design began during the end of the last decade. Some of the notable CBD systems reported so far and some key aspects in which our work differs from these systems are as follows.

CYCLOPS (Navinchandra, 1987) addressed a different set of issues than CADRE. The area of application (i.e., placing of buildings), results obtained (i.e., there is no geometric reasoning about shapes or locations), and the reasoning mechanism (i.e., rule-based) are different from our approach. CADRE reasons about the design of objects at a more detailed level and attempts generalization of a case when needed in a new design context.

Archie-II (Goel and Kolodner, 1991) is a system developed to aid in the design of office buildings. It incorporates a large case library of design fragments, organized by a number of descriptors. Given a new design problem, it can retrieve similar cases with annotated justifications and alternatives in a hyper-media environment. FABEL (Group, 1992) also provides a rich set of features for case representation and retrieval. SEED (Flemming et al., 1994) represents a CBD system that is still in its developmental phase. Archie-II, FABEL and SEED do not provide any computational support for reuse of the retrieved information. In this regard, CADRE does not emphasize case indexing and retrieval like the other systems do but it provides computational techniques to adapt or combine selected case(s) or their fragments for a new design problem.

CADSYN (Zhang and Maher, 1993) decomposes building design problems into subproblems, deal with each of those separately, and then recomposes part solutions into a final solution. CADRE avoids partitioning of various abstractions and maintains simultaneously requirements of diverse abstractions using the dimensionality reduction process (Faltings et al., 1991).

## 2  CADRE: System Architecture and Processes

### 2.1  Components of CADRE

The architecture of CADRE (Figure 2) comprises representation of cases, case library, and constraints, and procedures for constraint solving to carry out case adaptation and combination.

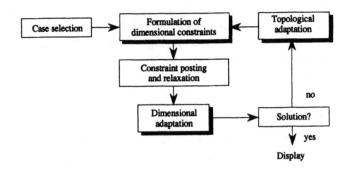

**Fig. 2.** CADRE: System architecture.

**Representation of Cases**  Building designs involve multiple abstractions, e.g., architectural, structural, mechanical, each of which is related to other abstractions. CADRE currently integrates two abstractions of design cases: architectural and structural, both of which are specialized symbolic representations of a common three- dimensional geometric model.

The architectural issues of a case are specified by elements such as partitioning walls, windows, doors and spaces. Each element is described in terms of its properties such as location, size and function, which is primitive information that can be directly derived from a raw model of the case. A graph-based data structure is used to make such information accessible and to simplify reasoning processes concerning spatial relationships.

The structural information in a case is primarily in the form of element dimensions. Constraints used during dimensional adaptation are generated automatically by generic processes within the CADRE system. For structural engineering design criteria, these constraints are valid for any structure of a given type. Structural information stored in a case is therefore limited to a minimum; cases are created from building plans. A higher level representation of the geometric model is used during the topological structural adaptation process. The structure is represented by a grid and structural modules. A structural module comprises a combination of columns, primary and secondary beams and a slab. It is characterised by the type of structural system, and contains domain knowledge for its instantiation as a function of the size of the grid.

**Case Library** The case library is a collection of design cases represented using the information described above: geometric and symbolic pertaining to both architectural and structural issues. At present, the case library in CADRE contains a relatively small case base. Nevertheless, we have selected cases that are complex, large-scale and diverse. For developing and testing case adaptation techniques, we have primarily used residential designs and an educational building, i.e., the Computer Science Building, at EPF Lausanne. For developing and testing case combination techniques, the case library in CADRE contains four architectural schools as shown in Figure 3. The design of the architecture school at the University of Houston is an example of an historical adaptation. The school at the Rice University is an example of a new design that is adapted to blend in with its existing surroundings. The school at the Arizona State University incorporates a number of design elements such as a courtyard that are recurring themes in architectural designs, whereas the school at the Harvard University exemplifies a completely different design approach. Taken together, these four cases represent different design intentions and offer a range of solutions for testing our ideas.

Although most other CBR systems treat classification of features and indexing of cases as one of the central issues, we have selected not to address these issues for the following reasons. First, a classification of features in the architectural design is meaningful and useful only with respect to a specific purpose at hand. Second, the case base will require modification the moment a new feature is proposed in the future. Third, since we do not know in advance how various characteristics of design cases are to be used in either case adaptation or case combination, it is not very useful to classify or index any one characteristic. It is useful to know how cases will be changed before we decide on how they should be classified and stored. Similar views are also gaining acceptance by other researchers (Smyth and Keane, 1994) in this area.

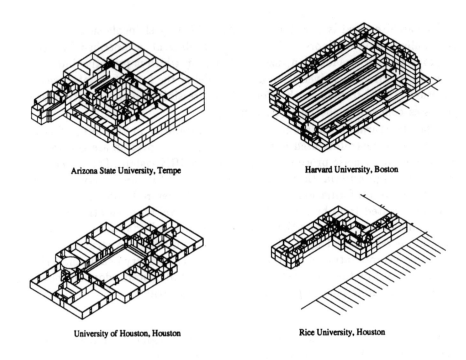

Arizona State University, Tempe         Harvard University, Boston

University of Houston, Houston         Rice University, Houston

**Fig. 3.** Cases of the architectural schools in the CADRE case library.

**Representation of Constraints** Constraints related to architectural requirements, e.g., desired dimensions and areas, are interactively posted by a user. Structural constraints are automatically introduced based on the design of a structural grid and the selected structural system.

*Architecture.* Constraints are the fundamental element for building generalised models of cases on which the adaptation and combination of spatial layouts are based. Each constraint introduces restrictions to one or more spaces regarding their geometric properties and relations. In CADRE, constraints (Figure 4) are used to control case adaptation and combination so that the spatial integrity of the cases is not destroyed after that process. Each spatial constraint is defined with disjunctive and conjunctive combinations of mathematical equalities and inequalities on variables that define spaces. This concept has been elaborated in (Baykan, 1991) for solving spatial layout problems. Primitive constraints, such as the minimum and maximum dimensions of a space, can be defined with one single or a conjunctive combination of some equalities and inequalities. More complex constraints can be defined by combining such primitive constraints.

*Engineering.* For dimensional adaptation, structural constraints are represented as equations which link building dimensions and element spans to sectional

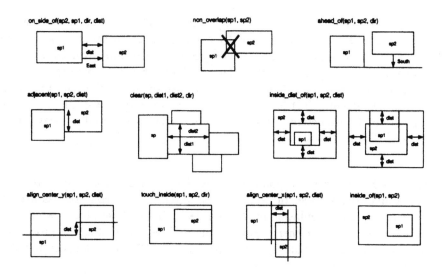

**Fig. 4.** Example architectural constraints.

dimensions of elements. These constraints are formulated according to safety and serviceability criteria and are generic for any structure having the same type of structural system. As a result of structural topological adaptation, a set of dimensional constraints linking the position of structural elements to room sizes is generated. These constraints are expressed in terms of room dimensions only and ensure that there is no conflict between structural elements and certain defined architectural spaces.

**Constraint Solving: Dimensionality Reduction** Design parameters in the parameterization of a geometric structure are connected by constraints. Therefore, most design parameters are not independent. When the set of constraints is under-constrained, it defines an adaptation space $R^{n-m}$ embedded in design space $R^n$, where $m$ is the number of non-reducible constraints. The process which determines the adaptation space $R^{n-m}$ is called *dimensionality reduction*.

The concept of dimensionality reduction originates from the recoding method in the reduction of dimensionality of multivariate data in statistics Krishnaiah and Kanal, 1982). This idea was developed further by Saund (1989, 1992) in image recognition. In general, dimensionality reduction is the process of finding a computational mapping between locations in an n-dimensional feature space and locations on an m-dimensional constraint surface embedded in the n- dimensional feature space.

The concept of dimensionality reduction was first introduced to case-based design in (Faltings et al., 1991). This method is aimed at simplifying dimensional adaptation of cases by finding the exact degrees of freedom that can be changed for the case in a new situation and by defining all the other design variables with a small set of adaptation parameters. Since constraints involved in dimensionality reduction include many different types, processes for dimensionality reduction can be categorized as follows: (i) Gaussian elimination, (ii) algorithms for computer algebra, (iii) local elimination for bijective constraints, and (iv) organization of parameters. These issues are discussed in detail in (Dave et al., 1994) and (Schmitt et al., 1994).

**Interface** The various components of CADRE described above are integrated into a graphical interface. In designing the interface, our concern has been to provide a direct manipulation mode to a designer for those phases where user intervention or input is either required or desired. For other stages in processing, a visual and understandable feedback about the specific task being computed by CADRE is provided.

Most of the interaction with CADRE takes place in a main working window. Pulldown menus provide access to various operations, e.g., calling up a case browser. A case may be brought up and viewed using various operations such as zooming or rotating in the case browser. Once a case is selected, it is inserted in the main working window where it may be viewed and operated upon using either its architectural or structural information, in either geometrical or topological representations.

At this stage, a designer posts additional constraints to specify how the selected case needs to be modified with regard to a new design problem. Typically it involves specification of changes on the areas or dimensions of spaces, their topological relations, or specifying new spaces and their relations with others. The constraints are posted using property sheets attached to each element in the model (Figure 5). The default information is derived from what is explicitly represented in each case whereas some other information is derived by CADRE from information implicit in the models.

If the constraints posted require only dimensional changes, CADRE attempts to compute a solution by dimensionality reduction. If topological adaptation is required, CADRE will generate possible topological alternatives which are shown in pop-up windows. When a designer selects one alternative, structural grids for that alternative are shown, followed by identification of suitable structural systems, followed by the process of dimensionality reduction to fix dimensions. If there are free variables, these are shown on the interface and a designer is free to interactively fix such variables in the indicated range of values.

## 2.2 Case Adaptation

Depending on the design problem at hand and the constraints posted, CADRE computes either dimensional adaptation or topological adaptation followed by dimensional adaptation.

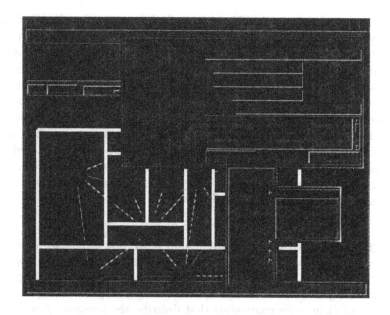

**Fig. 5.** CADRE: Constraint specification.

**Dimensional Adaptation** Dimensional adaptation involves the solution of a set of linear and non- linear constraints on the parameters used to describe the building. This kind of adaptation produces integrated solutions because constraints from all abstractions are considered simultaneously. Dimensionality reduction is used to identify key parameters for adaptation. This is different from prototypical design because the parameters we consider are identified at run-time.

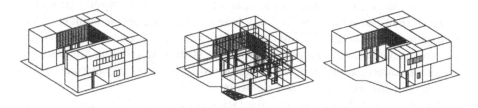

**Fig. 6.** Axonometric views: Original case (left), its parameterisation in new site (middle), and dimensional adaptation (right) by CADRE.

An example of the case adaptation by CADRE is illustrated in Figure 6. The original case is a U-shaped residential design on a rectangular site (Figure 6, left). It is inserted in a new site which is truncated on one side. CADRE evaluates the case in its original and new environments to find discrepancies. This leads to the identification of constraints related to the corner of the case that now needs to be dimensionally adapted so that it lies inside the new site (Figure 6, middle). Next, the process of dimensionality reduction identifies only those adaptation parameters that need to be changed in the constraints identified earlier. These parameters are dimensionally varied by CADRE and any changes are propagated to related variables inside relevant areas of the building (Figure 6, right). Once the dimensional adaptation is carried out, it may be necessary, as in this example, to also undertake topological adaptation, e.g., to resolve problems caused by the shortened wing. By focusing on only what needs to be adapted, i.e., a local generalization of a case, CADRE is able to find design solutions in a manner that is more efficient than other approaches.

**Topological Adaptation** In the event that a solution cannot be found by dimensional adaptation, a topological adaptation is attempted. Topological relations of spaces are expressed with disjunctive constraints. Valid topological variations of a given case are found by enumerating all possible ways to satisfy the system of disjunctive constraints that describe the necessary conditions for maintaining the spatial quality of the case. The enumeration is realized by adapting the branch-and-bound method in integer programming so that all possible design layouts, instead of only the optimal ones, are found.

Given a design layout, the structural gridding process searches for possible grids upon which columns could be placed whilst avoiding conflict between structural elements and architectural spaces. The search begins with the grids used in the original case, and iterates by alternatively increasing and decreasing the number of bays in each direction. A rule based approach is used to identify suitable structural systems for each possible grid. Rules are based on the feasibility of certain systems for given grid sizes. Constraints governing the dimensions of elements as a function of the grid size are generated based on: (i) live loads from the original cases, (ii) dead loads from the given structural system, (iii) structural safety criteria, and (iv) long and short term serviceability criteria.

More than one solution is generally found, depending on the number of possible grids and suitable structural systems for each. Once the user makes a choice, the dimensional constraints generated during structural gridding are passed to the dimensional adaptation process together with the relevant constraints governing the dimensions of structural elements.

An example of the topological adaptation is illustrated in Figure 7. It shows the Computer Science Building at EPF Lausanne. The building has a column structure that is the same for all the floors except that the room layout changes from floor to floor. The free-standing columns in the middle of some lecture rooms, e.g., on the second floor, obstruct the proper usage of these spaces. CADRE was used to adapt this case with a constraint that the free-standing columns should be coincident with the walls. Initially, CADRE attempts to change the dimensions of spaces since the structural system is fixed. Since no solution could be found that satisfies all the constraints, CADRE attempts a topological

original case

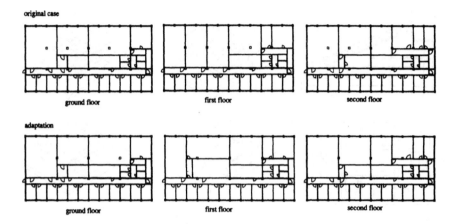

adaptation

Fig. 7. Case adaptation: original case (top) and its adaptation (bottom) by CADRE.

adaptation of the structural system. The topological adaptation, i.e, a new structural grid, followed by a dimensional adaptation produces a result for the second floor. This creates a problem on the first floor where there is a free-standing column in the laboratory. There is no dimensional adaptation possible for this situation. CADRE remedies this by a topological adaptation of the first floor layout which makes the walls and the columns coincident (Figure 7, bottom).

## 2.3 Case Combination

An alternative to the topological adaptation of one case is a combination of parts of several cases. Subsets of rooms may be selected from different cases to be combined during the adaptation process. A new room layout is produced by searching for new topologies that obey a set of constraints defining the desired room adjacencies. These constraints can be derived from the original geometrical model and can also be defined by the user. More than one alternative is generally found and the user chooses the layout with which to continue the adaptation. Dimensional constraints on the geometry of rooms for this layout are eventually passed to the dimensional adaptation process. A default geometric model of the chosen layout is generated using simplified linear architectural dimensional constraints, and is subsequently passed to the structural gridding process.

Two cases of the architectural schools are selected (Figure 8, left), for demonstrating case combination in CADRE. The cruciform volume with a central atrium of the the Houston building (Figure 8, bottom-left) is to be combined with the terraced studios of the Harvard building (Figure 8, top-left). In the process of combination, the four wings, the roof, the atrium and the lantern of the Houston building are represented with rectangular volumes.

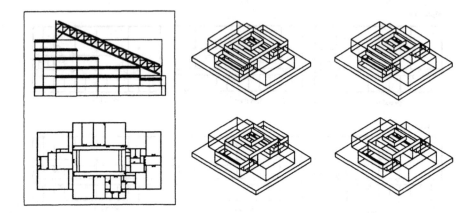

**Fig. 8.** Original cases (left) and example combination solutions (right) by CADRE.

Constraints are defined to maintain the proportion and the relation of these volumes so that formal characteristics of the Houston building are preserved. The spatial continuity of the terraced studios in the Harvard building is constrained by linking studios with open spaces. The studios are then inserted into the Houston building by asserting constraints that force the studios to fit in two of the four wings of the Houston building. Figure 8 (right) shows four alternatives generated in one of our experiments for case combination. Constraints can be added or taken out for more restricted or more flexible results. Subsequently, CADRE carries out the design of structural system for each generated alternative.

## 3 Evaluation

### 3.1 Contributions

This project has made a number of contributions towards the paradigm of case-based reasoning in general and to design computation in particular.

- CADRE exemplifies an approach to design of shapes with continuous variables using the paradigm of case-based reasoning.
- Multiple abstractions of designs are integrated and maintained at the dimensional level using a technique called dimensionality reduction. At the topological level, a process called structural gridding is used.
- CADRE represents a distinct kind of a CBD system that supports transformation of retrieved design case(s) to derive a design solution with a higher degree of detail than other systems.
- The role of the designer in design development is recognized and supported with a graphical interface that enables a designer and the system to exercise their mutual strengths in the design process.

## 3.2 Limitations and Challenges

As in all research projects, our results have limitations as follows: (i) better mechanisms for topological adaptation are needed, (ii) general models of integration of architecture and engineering activities need to be developed, (iii) efficient resolution of non-linear constraints, and look-ahead strategies to detect dimensional- topological adaptation cycles need to be identified.

# 4 Conclusion

A case-based design system, CADRE, was presented that enables case adaptation and case combination of design cases to generate new design solutions more efficiently. The implementation of CADRE and its application to a number of test design contexts demonstrate the usefulness of our approach. Although the development of computational techniques to support reuse of design cases is a hard problem, our work uniquely contributes to this research area by the implementation of CADRE.

*Acknowledgement.* This research project has been funded by the Swiss National Science Foundation under the program NFP 23: Artificial Intelligence and Robotics. This paper is based on an extended paper presented at the Swiss National Science Foundation Symposium, held on 28-29 September, 1994, Lausanne.

# References

Baykan, C. (1991). Formulating Spatial Layout as a Disjunctive Constraint Satisfaction Problem. Ph.d. thesis, Dept. of Architecture, Carnegie-Mellon University, Pittsburgh.

Dave, B., Schmitt, G., Faltings, B., and Smith, I. (1994). Case-based Design in Architecture. In Artificial Intelligence in Design-94, Lausanne, 145–162.

Faltings, B., Hua, K., Schmitt, G., and Shih, S. (1991). Case-based Representation of Architectural Design Knowledge. In DARPA Workshop on Case-Based Reasoning Workshop, Washington, 307–316.

Flemming, U., Coyne, R., and Snyder, J. (1994). Case-Based Design in the SEED System. In Computing in Civil Engineering. Proceedings of the first ASCE Congress, Washington, 446–453.

Goel, A. K. and Kolodner, J. L. (1991). Towards a Case-based Tool for Aiding Conceptual Design Problem Solving. In DARPA Case-based Reasoning Workshop, 109–120.

Group, T. F. (1992). FABEL: Integration von modell- und fallbasierten Entwicklungsansätzen für wissensbasierte systeme. Technical report, Verbundvorhaben des BMFT (01IW104) unter der Leitunge der Gesellschaft für Mathematik und Datenverarbeitung, Bonn.

Kolodner, J. L. (1984). Retrieval And Organizational Strategies in Conceptual Memory: A Computer Model. Lawrence Erlbaum Assoc.

Krishnaiah, P. and Kanal, L. (1982). Handbook on Statistics, Vol. 2. North-Holland, Amsterdam.

Navinchandra, D. (1987). Exploring Innovative Designs by Relaxing Criteria and Reasoning from Precedent Knowledge. Ph.d. thesis, Dept. of Civil Engineering, MIT, Cambridge, MA.

Saund, E. (1989). Dimensionality-reduction using connectionist networks. IEEE Trans. PAMI, 11, 304–314.

Saund, E. (1992). Putting Knowledge into a Visual Shape Representation. Artificial Intelligence, 54, 71–81.

Schmitt, G., Dave, B., Shih, S., Faltings, B., Smith, I., Hua, K., Bailey, S., Ducret, J., and Jent, K. (1994). Case-based Spatial Design Reasoning. In Swiss National Science Foundation Symposium, Lausanne.

Smyth, B. and Keane, M. (1994). Retrieving Adaptable Cases. In Topics in Case-Based Reasoning: Lecture Notes in Artificial Intelligence 837. Springer Verlag, Berlin Heidelberg, 209–220.

Zhang, D. M. and Maher, M. L. (1993). Using case-based reasoning for the synthesis of structural systems. In Knowledge-based systems in civil engineering. IABSE Colloquium, Beijing, 143–152.

# Case-Based Support for the Design of Dynamic System Requirements*

define a service's desired behaviour (see figure 1) as input and produces transition rules (called partial rules) that cover the same behaviour as the input examples. These partial rules are then used in a matching process to identify similar, previously formalised services and transition rules, which have already been tested and integrated

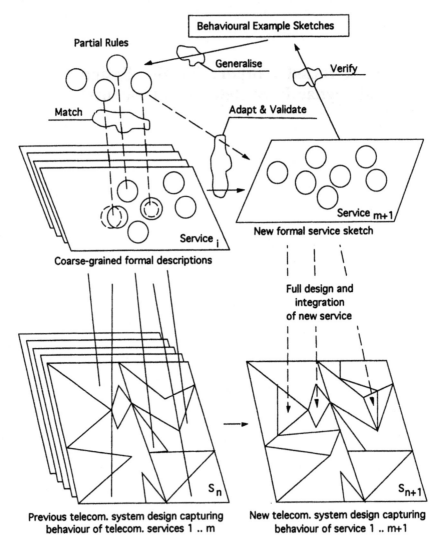

**Fig. 1.** Behavioural example, services and the full design of the system.

with other services. By reusing them, we should reduce the time needed to develop, test and integrate the new service requirements with the other services it has to interact with. This allows us at an early stage to provide the customer and supplier with the ability to explore the dynamic behaviour of the new service (by simulation of the formalised requirements), before any time and effort has been spent on design and implementation. It is very beneficial to clarify and correct any disagreement on functionality at this stage.

Each sheet in the bottom left corner of the diagram represents a collection of previously designed and integrated services, composed of very complex configurations of system components. The new service requirements (of which the formalised requirements is a small but important part) has also to be designed and integrated. Formalised requirements can be used in a variety of ways to enhance the traditional software development process [4], e.g., as a reference by which to guide design, to generate test cases [24], and to map onto design components [22], etc. If we have access to the relation between all previously designed and implemented parts, and their originating coarse-grained service requirements, we may assist the designers in choosing parts for reuse, by pointing out where modifications have to be made, when producing a design of the new service (thus taking us to our end point in the bottom right corner of figure 1). We do not address the task of producing a final design.

The main objective of this paper is to give an overview of our approach, which involves combining case-based reasoning with formal methods in order to benefit from the reuse of previously formulated requirements in the design of large systems. Section 2 briefly describes CABS relations to formal methods. Section 3 examines CABS in its context of case-based reasoning. Section 4 gives a brief overview and some examples of the logic used for representing cases in the case library. Section 5 gives an example of input to CABS, and explains how transition rules are generated from it. Section 6 examines how input cases are matched to cases stored in the case library. This section also offers illustrations of the set theoretical approach as well as the pseudo code for the matching algorithm. Section 7 gives a brief account of how specifications are adapted and tested. Section 8 explores some related work. Finally, section 9 summarises the research.

## 2. Requirements Specifications

Much effort has been made over many years to bring formal methods into use in industry. The fact that they are nevertheless not widely used may indicate that they are not yet mature, or that they are misunderstood by industry, or that industry has difficulty integrating them into current software development processes [15]. Although individual elements of a reactive system's behaviour may be amenable to representation and verification using formal methods, scaling up this approach to the specification of large complex systems appears to be difficult.

If we are to specify the complete behaviour of a large reactive system in detail in a single formalism, we may end up needing sophisticated logics and sets of axioms that can handle concurrency, time constraints, indeterminism, asynchronism, statistics, etc. The resulting complexity of proving theorems and simulating dynamic behaviour can be difficult to handle. In addition, many of the formalisms used for complex specifications are not "executable", and therefore do not allow developers to explore the dynamics of the specifications.

However, if we simply wish to outline the original requirements, as opposed to providing a complete formal specification (including error handling, odd cases, unusual interactions, etc. [28]), it is usually sufficient to consider a simplified view. We call such a view a requirements specification, since these are the original requirements, not a complete specification. We note in passing that these are not the only possible requirements which one might collect for such a system – they are merely a particular type of functional requirement.

## 3. Case-Based Reasoning for Requirements Capture

CABS is closely structured accordingly to the four REs (Retrieve, Reuse, Revise, Restore, [1]) in the case-based reasoning cycle (see figure 2). CABS uses a simple predicate logic to represent, in the case library, only the coarse-grained behaviour of functional elements that have already been designed and implemented. This logic is able to represent stimuli, facts, responses and simple transition rules (as shown in section 4). A case in the case library is a set of transition rules (a service). The logic

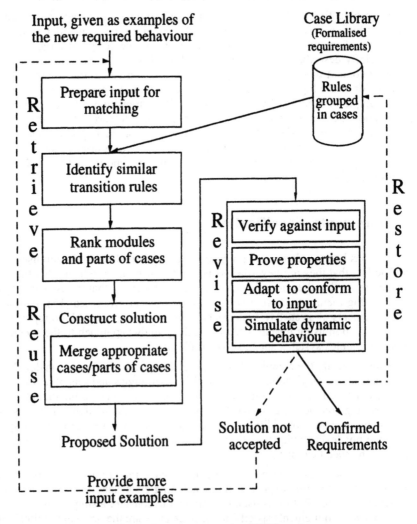

**Fig. 2.** Overview over the CABS system

used to represent the dynamic behaviour of cases gives us access to the coarse-grained, dynamic behaviour of each case – which provides the basis for choosing fully specified indexes [19] and for testing new cases.

The designer provides input to the system in the form of examples of the new required behaviour and the first task (upper left box in figure 2) is to prepare the input for the matching. CABS translates the input examples to a set of transition rules, which are under-specified since they do not give all details and only describe parts of the behaviour and hence the produced transition rules are called partial rules (see section 5 and 6).

The partial rules enable us to determine the similarity between the behaviour of a case in the case library and the behaviour of the new case outlined by the designer (and to indicate where the differences lie). The system identifies the cases that exhibit behaviour most similar to the new behaviour and uses them to construct a proposed solution. In addition, behavioural elements inside cases are accessible in this notation and so elements of a case can be used to construct a new solution.

The revision phase relies on the simulator and theorem prover (see section 7). By using a simulator, we automatically verify whether the proposed solution covers the behaviour exemplified in the input. If CABS discovers any discrepancies at this semantic level, it makes an attempt to adapt them, or points out where the differences lie, and requests further refinement of the input. The theorem prover may also be used to identify parts that need adaptation.

Finally the user can use the simulator and the theorem prover to explore whether the new formalised service meets his intention. If not, he provides more input examples, or, if his idea of the behaviour has changed, he modifies the previously given input examples. A confirmed solution is then stored in the case library (if it has been successfully designed and implemented), which bring us back up in the right upper corner of figure 2.

## 4. A Simple Case Description Logic

To represent cases, we have chosen a simple logic based on first-order predicate logic extended with a frame axiom [10,7,13]. Note that since we are using our coarse-grained specifications only as a means of identifying the appropriate designed and implemented services rather than modelling all the details of services, it is sufficient to use a comparatively simple logic. Simplification gives us further advantages by making the specification more accessible to users. For example, it is easier to state behavioural sequences because we ignore problems arising from asynchronous events. It is also possible to provide tractable methods for interfacing to the logic via natural language and/or graphical systems (see e.g. [8, 5, 6, 25, 9]). The behaviour sequences may also be used to test the final specification and for test generation for the final implementation, in addition to tests generated form the specifications [24].

The logic represents transition rules that handle changes, and intra-state rules that handle domain knowledge inside states, i.e. facts true at time $t_i$ (see figure 3). A frame axiom moves all unchanged facts from the previous state T, to the next one, T+1. A transition rule is constructed using two types of term:

o(T, E)  denotes that an event, E, occurred at time T.

p(T, P)  denotes that the property, P, holds in the state of the system at time T.

Preconditions of transition rules must contain a single, triggering event and may also contain a conjunction of system properties (or their negation) which determines whether the transition rule can apply to the current system state. The conclusion of a transition rule contains a conjunction of properties (or their negation) which will hold in the succeeding state after the transition rule is applied. An example of a transition rule is given below, where offhook is the stimulus signalling that the user has lifted his/her receiver:

> Transition Rule: normal_offhook
> ∀ SubscA
> o(T+1, offhook(SubscA)) &
> p(T, idle(SubscA)) &
> ¬p(T, ∃ SubscB calling(SubscB,SubscA))
>     →    ¬p(T+1, idle(SubscA)) &
>           p(T+1, dialtone(SubscA)).

Stimuli are sequenced in order to simplify the logic: we do not attempt in this high-level specification to specify what should happen when signals are competing (e.g. if two users call a third user at exactly the same time), and we suggest that the decision of how to resolve such situations is not necessarily a requirements choice, and can be dealt with in the design process. Figure 3 shows the model used in the formal requirements specifications of telecommunications services. Sequences of stimuli which are provided by users of telephones are used to activate appropriate

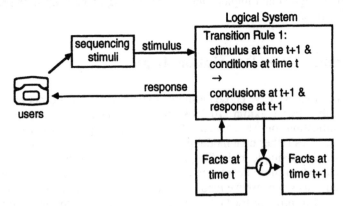

**Fig. 3.** Model of the dynamic behaviour of telecommunications network.

transition rules. As a consequence, a sequence of states is generated, containing sets of facts that describe the system after each event (*f* represents the frame axiom, which transfers unaltered facts from the previous time *t* to the current time *t+1*).

Because of the simplifications which we have made in our high-level specification language, we are able to simulate the behaviour obtained from these specifications by using a fairly simple theorem prover and simulator (see section 7). The theorem prover and simulator have been implemented in Prolog, together with a basic environment which allows the designer to test the specification and refine it in accordance with her ideas. It is necessary that this process be manual since we cannot know what the designer has in mind. We cannot require that she make a complete formal and correct description of her ideas in one step. Most likely, she will refine her ideas and give them a formal representation after she has simulated the formalised behaviour.

## 5. Assigning Behavioural Features to Cases

In the telecommunications domain, it is natural for users to describe new services by giving examples of the behavioural sequences that they should produce. The task of our case-based system is to locate existing services which most closely match these behavioural examples, based on their high-level specifications [17]. Since our case library consists of sets of transition rules, we must provide a means of matching these rules to behavioural examples. The behavioural examples may be given in a variety of notations, such as restricted natural language, graphical notations, scenarios etc., as long as they can be translated to a set of partial transition rules. We have chosen an intermediate formal representation, used as a starting point in producing a set of transition rules capturing the behaviour. The following is a behavioural example in its intermediate notation accompanied by a translation into English:

| | |
|---|---|
| phoneNumber(A,111) & | A´s phone number is 111. |
| phoneNumber(B,222) & | B´s phone number is 222. |
| idle(A) & | Subscriber A is idle. |
| idle(B) | Subscriber B is idle. |
| – | then |
| offHook(A) | A lifts his receiver. |
| -> | and as a consequence |
| dialTone(A) | A hears a dial tone. |
| – | then |
| dials(A,222) | A dials 222. |
| -> | and as a consequence |
| ringTone(A)& | A hears a ringing tone. |
| ringSignal(B)& | B hears a ringing signal. |
| .. | .. |

**Table 1.** Intermediate notation and translation to English.

A behavioural example starts with a conjunction of terms denoting the main features classifying exemplified states in which the following event (after the symbol "–") occurs. Thereafter a sketch of some of the terms outlining the main characteristics of the resulting state are given (after the symbol "->"). The last two steps may be repeated.

It is easy to generate a set of rules that precisely covers the behaviour given in a behavioural example. However, what we want is a set of rules that covers general behaviour, without excluding all other behaviour. Since humans often leave out obvious statements, we may wish to add some of the assumed domain knowledge. For this and for handling instances and variables we need some heuristics. This is acceptable, since the transition rules generated from the input are mainly used as indexing features in the matching process. The original input examples are also kept in their initial form, to be used later in validation and verification.

## 6. Re-Using and Finding the Best Matched Case

In section 5 we described how to put behavioural examples into rule form in preparation for the matching process. We shall now sketch the matching algorithm itself. Our aim is to reuse as much as possible of previously specified formal requirements, which is possible if the new demands on the system are semantically similar to previous demands and the previous demands are adaptable [26].

We treat the stimulus, condition and conclusion elements of the transition rules as sets of atomic terms. With this approach it is easy to identify matching rules. Figure 4 gives examples of different matches of elements from transition rules in the case library, and partial rules.

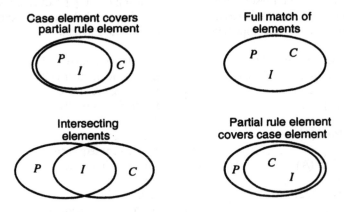

**Fig. 4.** Examples of different matches of transition rule elements.

An element in a rule is either a stimulus, condition or conclusion element. An element is a set of terms (a stimulus element is always a set with only one term). $P$ denotes an element in a partial transition rule. $C$ denotes the corresponding element of the case library rule. $I$ stands for the intersecting terms in these two sets of terms. The relation between $P$, $C$ and $I$ is used as a basis for the final scoring. An example of two condition elements from two transition rules are:

Condition element in rule $P_i$: p(T,idle(X)),  p(T,last_diald(X,Nr))
Condition element in rule $C_j$: p(T,redirect(X,Nr)),  p(T,idle(X))

The intersection $I$ is in this match a set containing one term, {p(T,idle(X))}. The following is an example of the process from behavioural example to a scored match:

Behavioural example (the notation for which bears similarities to signalling schemes for informal telephone service examples, see e.g. [18]):

idle(A) – offHook(A) -> dialTone(A) & idle(B) – dials(A,222) -> ringTone(A) & ringSignal(B).

Translating this into two partial rules gives:

Partial Transition Rule P1: ∀ A

$$o(T+1,offHook(A)) \&$$
$$p(T,idle(A))$$
$$\rightarrow \quad p(T+1,dialTone(A)).$$

Partial Transition Rule P2: ∀ A NR B

$$o(T+1,dials(A,NR)) \&$$
$$p(T,idle(B))$$
$$\rightarrow \quad p(T+1,ringTone(A)) \&$$
$$p(T+1,ringSignal(B)).$$

In most cases this translation is a straightforward process, but in some situations heuristics are used to make an assumption about what the user means or to keep the partial rules within the restrictions opposed on transition rules. This can be accepted since we mainly use the partial rules to index the case library. One heuristic is used to avoid introducing unbound variables in a transition rules conclusion. In the above example this is noted by the fact that idle(B) in the behavioural example is only used as a precondition in P2. If it had also been used as a conclusion in rule P1, we would have introduced an unbound variable in the conclusions, which would conflict with our restrictions.

C1 and C2 are two transition rules (oversimplified to focus the attention on matching) belonging to the case "standard telephone call":

Transition Rule C1: call busy

∀ SubscA NR SubscB
$$o(T+1,dials(SubscA,NR)) \&$$
$$p(T,answers\_on\_number(SubscB,NR)) \&$$
$$\neg p(T,idle(SubscB))$$
$$\rightarrow \quad p(T+1,busy\_tone(SubscA)) \&$$
$$p(T+1,call\_busy(SubscA,NR)).$$

Transition Rule C2: normal call

∀ SubscA NR SubscB
$$o(T+1,dials(SubscA,NR)) \&$$
$$p(T,answers\_on\_number(SubscB,NR)) \&$$
$$p(T,idle(SubscB))$$
$$\rightarrow \quad p(T+1,ringTone(SubscA)) \&$$
$$p(T+1,ringSignal(SubscB)) \&$$
$$p(T+1,last\_called\_nr(SubscA,NR)).$$

Only the matching of P2 is illustrated. We start by comparing P2 with C1. Some parts of the rules so standardised that they can be excluded in the matching process (e.g. time information and quantifiers). All three elements (stimulus, condition, conclusion) are to be matched, we start with the stimulus element:

Stimulus element in P2:   dials(A,NR)
Stimulus element in C1:   dials(SubscA,NR)

This gives a full match (identifying appropriate variables in the two terms).

Condition element in P2:  idle(B)
Condition element in C1:  answers_on_number(SubscB,NR),
                          ¬idle(SubscB)

The condition element in the rule C1, from the case library, has a negated form of an expression in P2. At this stage we simply conclude that the two sets do not have any common terms and contain one negation (used later when elements are finally ranked). The intersection of the conclusion element in C1 and P2 does not contain any elements, hence P2 and C1 only have a full match in their stimuli.

We now continue by matching P2 with C2, where again their stimuli match fully. We then compare their conditions.

Condition element in P2:  idle(B)
Condition element in C2:  answers_on_number(SubscB,NR),
                          idle(SubscB)

The condition of rule C2, from the case library, covers the condition of P2, hence the condition of C2 is more restricted than P2. Similarly the conclusion element of C2 contains one additional conclusion term.

Conclusion element in P2: ringTone(A),  ringSignal(B)
Conclusion element in C2: ringTone(SubscA),
                          ringSignal(SubscB),
                          last_called_nr(SubscA,NR)

Finally we employ a heuristic scoring algorithm to produce a numerical triple for each match and sort the matching rules in the case library, 'best first'. The approach taken is to give a percentage figure to each matching element in the rules (compare figure 4 with table 2).

P2 matching C1:

The intersection I is 100% of C1-stimulus and 100% of P2-stimulus.
The intersection I is 0% of C1-condition and 0% of P2-condition.
A negation of a term exists.
The intersection I is 0% of C1-conclusion and 0% of P2-conclusion.

P2 matching C2:

The intersection I is 100% of C2-stimulus and 100% of P2-stimulus.
The intersection I is 50% of C2-condition and 100% of P2-condition.
The intersection I is 67% of C2-conclusion and 100% of P2-conclusion.

**Table 2.** Coverage percentage of intersection for C1 and C2.

The fact that there exists a negation of a term in the match of the P2-condition and the C1-condition indicates that it is a mismatch, hence C1 may be excluded from further calculations. In CABS the user can decide whether or not to apply this filtering criterion to negation. Comparison of the scores for the three individual elements of the match provides us with a final ranking of each rule.

The pseudo-code for the matching algorithm appears below (all the domain-specific parameters have been omitted):

For all partial transition rules generalised from the input $P_n$:
 For all transition rules in the case library, $C_m$:
  For p in {stimulus element, condition element, conclusion element}:
   Calculate the intersection, $I_p$ for $P_{np}$ and $C_{mp}$
   Calculate the coverage percentage of $I_p$ on $P_{np}$,
   Calculate the coverage percentage of $I_p$ on $C_{mp}$.
  Determine the final score for $C_m$ by:
   Apply filtering criterion to negation (if a negated term exists, we may either choose to ignore it or to weight the result, depending on how the user has parameterized the system) in order to get a final score for $C_m$ as a match for $P_n$.
For all cases (requirements specifications), S:
 For all partial rules $P_n$:
  Take the score from the rule in S which has the best score as a match for $P_n$ and use it in order to score S in total.

## 7. Revising the Proposed Solution

CABS performs four steps of revision (see figure 2): test proposed solution against input (simulator) and against general domain knowledge (theorem prover); adapt any differences or ask user for clarification (by providing or refining input examples); finally the user explores the proposal with the simulator and theorem prover and confirms the behaviour or refines/modifies his input examples.

To perform a verification between the input examples and the proposed solution, we simulate the proposed solution and use the intermediate input as input to the simulation. If the proposed solution covers the behaviour of the input, the next step is to prove general domain properties about the solution. Examples of such properties in telephone services may be:

1. A subscriber cannot be in speech connection with himself.
2. In all situations a subscriber should be able to request to leave the current service (on_hook).

For the purpose of refining and testing the requirements specifications, a user interface is provided for the simulator and theorem prover. The simulator allows the user to give sequences of stimuli and evaluate whether the response exhibited by the formal specification corresponds to his intentions. This step is important in refining the designer's idea of how the service should behave in its final state. If the service does not correspond to his intention, the user has to provide more input examples, or refine previous given input examples. One other advantage of simulation, compared with theorem proving, is that it is more resistant to inconsistency in the formalised requirements, which is to be expected during the refinement process.

An example of a simulation is given in figure 5. We first display the initial facts in our simulation. If we want to simulate subscriber a1 going off-hook at time 1, we type O(1,offhook(a1)). The simulator triggers all the rules with offhook as their triggering condition and with all their conditions true, and thereafter shows the result (facts at time 1). To check if our set of transition rules behaves as expected if subscriber a1 is calling herself, we give the stimulus O(2,dialling(a1,111)). If a term is crossed out, it is not true at this time, but was true in the previous state. If a term is shown in bold face, it is a new term that has been added.

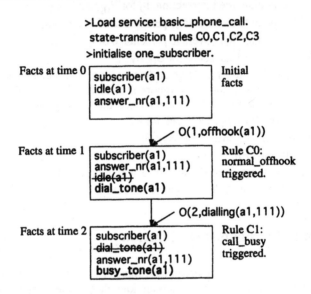

**Fig. 5.** Example of a simulation

The simulation system is highly interactive with the designer because full expansion of all possible states would require a huge amount of memory in any non-trivial specification. Fortunately, expanding the search space interactively by only a limited number of steps at a time is already of value in our domain since phone users are not usually expected to take part in any complex sequence of actions before returning to the initial state (hook on). Proving that a particular state cannot be reached in any sequence of, say, 8 steps will therefore be desirable for the user and will help him to validate his formal requirements specifications.

# 8. Related Work

Producing formal requirements from informal ones is an active research area. Much research in formal methods aims at producing detailed specifications of software, and the level of detail and difference in abstraction between the specification and the software to be produced is often small. We have adopted the approach of highly restricting the formalism and only outlining the main behaviour in our requirements specifications. With this approach we avoid some of the problems of using formal specification. There are similarities between the CABS approach and systems such as ARISE [6], AIR [20] and WATSON.

WATSON [17] is in essence based on the same ideas as CABS and has influenced our research. WATSON also starts with scenarios (similar to behavioural example sketches) which are used in a variety of different ways to produce formal requirements of telephone services. WATSON uses extensive domain knowledge (about telephone hardware, network protocols, preferred styles of control skeleton design, etc.) in the process. The user is consulted to resolve problems that the system cannot resolve itself. One of the key differences is that CABS takes the approach of using examples to generate features in order to identify and reuse previously specified services. WATSON has proved to be difficult to scale up for realistic use [24]. Our belief is that case-based reasoning and extensive reuse of previous requirements may help to bridge the gap between informal requirements and formal requirements and aid in the task of updating a previous implementation to capture the new requirements.

There has been much research in the area of applying case-based reasoning to the domain of design. Examples of systems using case-based reasoning to tackle such complex tasks are CADET [27], BOGART [21], DEJAVU [2], KRITIK [14] and SUPPORT [23]. A number of different approaches are used, such as multi-level representations, verifying results by qualitative simulations, and derivational analogy (i.e. the storing and reuse of design plans). In particular, case-based planners explore the use of formal logical representations. NETTRACK (Network Traffic Management Using Cases) [3] is a system which uses formal logic and which originally used a representation similar to situation calculus related to the representation used in CABS. CABS narrow focus on a particular class of specifications allows us to automate the case-based reasoning process considerably, compared with more general systems.

## 9. Conclusions

We have presented a system that produces formalised requirements, capturing the dynamic behaviour of a particular class of requirements (sequential, non distributed, deterministic). Given an outline of a required behaviour, the system produces a formal requirements specification capturing certain dynamic aspects of the requirements, constructed from previous cases and parts of cases. Selecting the way in which cases should be represented is an essential aspect of providing case-based support for specification of system requirements. A case should be able to represent the dynamic behaviour that the specification calls for. In our approach, the requirements designer has only to give examples of a new service's behaviour. The input is translated to a representation, more suitable for matching, and a set of generalised partial transition rules is produced. These rules are then used in the matching process, and modules with similar behaviour are identified by means of a simple and sufficient matching algorithm based on set theory.

The logic used for the representation of cases contains transition rules, terms (stimuli, responses, facts) and a frame axiom handling change of time (discrete time steps). This logic has proved to be sufficient for outlining and testing (by simulation and theorem proving) the behaviour of some telecommunications services' coarse-grained behaviour [12]. The combination of simple representation and a case-based approach that we advocate can be successfully applied in order to reuse elements of earlier requirements. Because the older cases describe the behaviour of existing services that have been fully tested, integrated and implemented, the effort required to integrate a new service with these other services - or to test it - is considerably reduced.

If the behaviour of a case does not fully conform to the behavioural examples, the missing elements of behaviour can be filled in by using the rules, generalised from the examples. This will produce a naive solution - which the user may subsequently refine and test - that conforms to the behavioural examples. Since the logic is comparably simple, it is easy to verify by simulation that the identified service and its transition rules correspond to the behaviour in the input examples. The user can also simulate the system's behaviour to examine other behaviour which he may not have stipulated in the original examples, but which may have arisen as a result of reuse (such as interaction with other services).

# References

1. A. Aamodt, E. Plaza, Case-Based Reasoning: Foundational Issues, Methodological Variations, and System Approaches. *AI Communications*, vol. 7 no. 1, 39-59, 1994.

2. T. Bardasz, I. Zeid, Dejavu: A Case-Based Reasoning Designer's Assistant Shell. *Artificial Intelligence in Design '92*, J.S. Gero (ed.), Kluwer Academic Publishers 477-496, 1992.

3. R. Brandau, A. Lemmon, C. Lafond, Experience with Extended Episodes: Cases with Complex Temporal Structure. *Workshop on case-based reasoning*, Morgan Kaufmann, 1-12, 1991.

4. A. Bundy: Tutorial notes: reasoning about logic programs. *Second International Logic Programming Summer School, LPSS '92. Proceedings,* G. Comyn, N.E. Fuchs, & M.J. Ratcliffe (eds.), Springer-Verlag, 232-277, 1992.

5. H. Dalianis: Aggregation in the NL-generator of the VIsual and Natural Language Specification Tool. *The Sixth International Conference of the European Chapter of the Association for Computational Linguistics, EACL-95,* Dublin, Ireland, 1995.

6. E. Davis: *Representations of Commonsense Knowledge,* chapters 2 and 3. Morgan Kaufmann, 1990.

7. J.-P. Echarti, G. Stålmarck: A logical framework for specifying discrete dynamic systems. *Technical Report,* Ellemtel Telecommunication Systems Laboratories, 1988.

8. M. Engstedt: A Flexible Specification Language using Natural Language and Graphics. *MSc thesis,* University of Edinburgh, 1991.

9. N. Fuchs, R. Schwitter, Specifying Logic Programs in Controlled Natural Language. *Workshop on Computational Logic for Natural Language Processing,* Edinburgh, 1995.

10. P.J. Funk: Development and Maintenance of Large Formal Specifications Supported by Case-Based Reasoning. *Technical Report TP026.* University of Edinburgh, 1993.

11. P.J. Funk, D. Robertson: Requirements Specification of Telecommunication Services Assisted by Case-Based Reasoning. *The 2nd International Conference on Telecommunication Systems, Modelling and Analysis,* Nashville, 160-169, 1994.

12. P.J. Funk, S. Raichman, ROS, an Implementation Independent Specification for ISDN. *Technical Report,* Ellemtel Telecommunication Systems Laboratories, 1990.

13. M. Gelfond, V. Lifschitz: Representing action and change by logic programs. *Logic Programming,* 301-321, 1993.

14. A.K. Goel, Representation of Design Functions in Experience-Based Design. *Intelligent Computer Aided Design*, Elsevier Science Publishers, 283-303, 1992.
15. A. Hall: Seven Myths of Formal Methods. *IEEE Software*, September, 11-18, 1990.
16. W.L. Johnson, K.M Brenner, Developing Formal Specifications from Informal Requirements. *IEEE Expert*, vol. 8, no. 4, 1993.
17. V.E. Kelly, U. Nonnenmann: Reducing the Complexity of Formal Specification Acquisition. *Automating Software Design*, M. Lowry, & R. McCartney (eds.), 41-64, 1991.
18. S. Klusener, B. Vlijmen, A. Waveren: Service Independent Building Blocks-I; Concepts, Examples and Formal Specifications. *Technical Report P9310*, University of Amsterdam, 1993.
19. J.L. Kolodner: *Case-Based Reasoning*. Morgan Kaufmann (1993).
20. N.A.M. Maiden, A.G. Sutcliffe, Requirements Engineering by Example: an Empirical Study. *Proceedings of IEEE International Symposium on Requirements Engineering*, 104-111, 1995.
21. J. Mostow, M. Barley, T. Weinrich, Automated reuse of design plans. *Artificial Intelligence in Engineering*, vol. 4, no. 4, 181-196, 1989.
22. K. Nakata: Behavioural Specification with Nonmonotonic Temporal Logic. D. Finn (ed.), *Preliminary Stages of Engineering Analysis and Modelling Workshop*, AID '92, 41-45, 1992.
23. Y. Nakatani, M. Tsukiyama, T. Fukuda, Engineering Design Support Framework by Case-Based Reasoning. *ISA Transaction*, vol. 31, no. 2, 235-180, 1992.
24. U. Nonnenmann, J.K. Eddy, KITSS - A functional Software Testing System Using a Hybrid Domain Model. *IEEE*, 136-142, 1992.
25. S. Preifelt, M. Engstedt, Results from the VINST Project (In Swedish). *Technical Report*, Ellemtel Telecommunication Systems Laboratories, 1992.
26. B. Smyth, M.T. Keane: Retrieving Adaptable Cases. In: S. Wess, K.-D. Althoff, & M.M. Richter (eds.), *Topics in Case-Based Reasoning*, Springer-Verlag, 1994.
27. K. Sycara, D. Navin chandra, R. Guttal, J. Koning, S. Narasimhan, CADET: A Case-Based Synthesis Tool for Engineering Design. *International Journal of Expert Systems*, vol. 4, no. 2, 167-188, 1992.
28. P. Zave, Feature Interactions and Formal Specifications in Telecommunications. *Computer*, vol. 26, no. 8, 1993.

# A Maintenance Approach to Case Based Reasoning

Byeong Ho Kang and P.Compton

School of Computer Science and Engineering
University of New South Wales,
Sydney NSW 2052, Australia 2033
(E-mail: kang@cse.unsw.edu.au)

**Abstract.** The motivation for CBR is that knowledge comes mainly from experience, from dealing with cases. The goal of CBR is not to find knowledge in the knowledge base that applies to the present problem, but to find a case similar to the current case in a database of cases. This paper describes a methodology, ripple down rules (RDR), which allows a CBR system to be built without either induction or knowledge engineering and is well suited to maintenance. In essence, when the system fails to find the proper case to match with the present problem case, it asks the expert to identify the important features which differentiate the incorrectly retrieved case and the problem case. The problem case is added to the database and is indexed to be retrieved using the identified features only after the same incorrectly retrieved case is reached. This simple approach allows large systems to be easily built by unaided experts. RDR has been used for a large medical expert system (PEIRS) which is in routine use in a major teaching hospital's chemical pathology laboratory, providing clinical interpretations of data for diagnostic reports. PEIRS uses 2000 cases(rules), covers 20% of chemical pathology and is 95% accurate to date. It was built by pathologists without knowledge engineering assistance or skills.

## 1. Introduction

Case Based Reasoning is a method of building knowledge based systems (KBS) using past cases to solve new problems [33]. It is based on the philosophy that real expertise comes from the experience of the expert and that the appropriate memory to model to produce expertise, is episodic memory [29, 30]. CBR is appropriate when there is no formalised knowledge in the domain or where it is difficult for the expert to communicate a body of expertise. In general an expert is good at judging cases, their job as an expert, but not good at providing knowledge in the abstract [22].

RDR is based on a similar philosophy. From a long experience of knowledge base maintenance [6] it was clear that experts never provide information on how they reach conclusions, rather, they justify that their conclusions are correct [5, 7]. These justifications are dependent on context and will vary depending on whether the expert is dealing with another expert, a trainee, a layperson etc. A common feature is that the justification will always be in terms of the present case and why the judgement the expert is giving is to be preferred over some other judgement. The justification will always concern features that are absent or present in the case that discriminate between the two judgements [21]. This same viewpoint, that human expertise is concerned with identifying differences between cases rather than defining concepts, also underlies personal construct theory and repertory grid knowledge acquisition [12].

The ripple down rule methodology is essentially a way of storing and retrieving cases. The cases and associated justifications or rules are added incrementally when a case is misclassified. This is a similar to "Failure-driven memory" which was introduced by Schank [27]. No case or rule is deleted, and the structure of the tree is not reorganised so that the accumulated cases and justifications do represent an accumulation of experience. It seems, in fact, that the particular historical way in which the experience develops can be used by the system to critique its own judgements [18].

Both CBR and RDR reject the Platonic assumption underlying much KBS development that knowledge is something mined or extracted from experts [11] and that if only one perseveres one can extract from the expert the knowledge the expert uses to solve the problem. In contrast, CBR emphasises that expertise comes largely from the experience [29] which leads on to the notion that experience is largely determined by the cases seen.

However, more than just cases are involved in a CBR system. Domain knowledge specifies how the case data is to be used. For example, if in a problem case the data includes the information that an emergency light is flashing it is probably more relevant to retrieve a case that also has the emergency light flashing rather than one that is similar in other regards. The system must include some indices to organise matching the cases in terms of the most important features first and therefore must know what the important features are. Another major area in CBR is analogical reasoning; retrieving cases where the similarity between the cases lies in the similarity of the relationship between separate features in the cases. That is, the relationship between features is itself a feature which should be used to recognise similarity. This again requires domain knowledge to identify such features. This domain knowledge may be developed inductively or be provided by experts via knowlege engineering.

## 2. Aim

Cases cannot be separated from knowledge; experience involves both cases and knowledge about what is important in the cases. The aim of this paper is to discuss how the knowledge that is essential to the functioning of a case based reasoning system may be accumulated in a way that is closely consistent with the case based philosophy rather than as an add-on that is required to make the approach work. In such a system an expert without any training or support in knowledge engineering, CBR or induction should be able to develop a system.

## 3. Case Based Reasoning

Designing a CBR system can be abstracted into three parts: the design of the domain model, the design of operations to adapt the conclusion, the design of operations on the case database. These distinctions help clarify the domain dependent and domain independent requirements of a CBR system.

### 3.1 Designing the Case Representation

The major question in designing a domain model in CBR is how to represent cases to identify important features in the cases. Many different representations can be considered. For example, representation in single vs multiple problem spaces and symbolic vs integration of symbolic and numeric data [32]. However, there is no best solution for all domains. The best representation is tailored to the characteristics of the domain. These problems may seem less apparent in KBS since an expert's knowledge appears to translate directly into rules. This is not true, since for any real application where the KBS has to deal with cases (i.e. any real application), the cases must be appropriately represented for the KBS to deal with them. For example, in KADS, the modelling process for KBS can be divided into two parts, modelling the problem-solving structure and the domain of application [34]. The representation problems are a function of the types of features that must be reasoned about, either with rules or by matching cases.

### 3.2 Design of Operations to Adapt the Conclusion

When a case is retrieved as being most like the problem case, the desired solution will not necessarily be stored as part of the case data, but may have to be calculated. In a classification system [3], the classification will be part of the case data, but in a system without enumerated solutions the system must extrapolate from the case retrieved. For example, with a differential equation solver, for a case $(X^3)'$ one may retrieve the case $(X^2)' = 2X$ and the system will need to extrapolate to the solution $(X^3)' = 3X^2$. The possibility of this type of extrapolation arises much more naturally and is therefore of more interest in CBR than in rule based systems. The ability to carry out such manipulations reduces the number of cases required [16]. However, this is again an area where domain knowledge and representation of features are the relevant issues. A CBR system cannot make such a match between cases unless it has the appropriate knowledge about the domain. In this methodology our concerns are with finding the relevant case given that the representation of features is appropriate for the domain.

### 3.3 Design of Operations for the Case Database

Operations for the case database (memory) can be divided into 2 parts – retrieving a case using the index, and adding a case and updating the index. Cases are retrieved to produce a conclusion and cases are added to correct errors and omissions. Memory in CBR is identified with episodic memory [30] with perhaps many thousands of cases recorded. There are several design issues such as retrieving single or multiple cases, successful cases vs(or) unsuccessful cases vs(or) default cases and whole cases vs parts of cases etc [32]. However, the indexing of the cases and "retrieval and adding" mechanisms are of fundamental importance in any large scale system and performance depends on these mechanisms [26, 31].

If we assume that the important features in cases are already well represented, then the issue is whether to add the case and index it manually, or to use an automated method. Automated methods are generally more attractive since machine learning strategies can be applied to the problem fairly readily. However, a problem with machine learning is that generally a large training set is required. Also, the training set must be fairly consistent, have sufficient examples of the various types of cases and the representation must be suitable. The representation can make a considerable difference to the quality of the learned concepts and the number of examples required. In other words, there are a number of "knowledge engineering" considerations in successfully using machine learning.

Adding a case to correct a mistake, i.e. maintenance, is of central importance in a large system used in a real application [6, 7]. A major problem with conventional KBS is that is very difficult to add knowledge to a KBS without affecting the systems prior performance [15]. Verification and validation are required to ensure changes to the KBS are incremental. CBR has the same requirement but one hopes that problems will be minimised because of the use of cases.

## 4. Ripple Down Rules

RDR can be characterised as a machine learning method of building an index, but where the expert rather than an algorithm is used to identify the salient features in a case to use in the index. The task for the expert is to identify features that distinguish cases. When a case is misclassified the expert is asked how it differs from the case that was incorrectly retrieved. The index is refined on the basis of the differentiating features. The closest CBR system to RDR is probably PROTOS, not only in being a classification system but in its emphasis on difference links where the expert selects important differences as part of its indexing scheme [1].

Ripple down rules grew out of a philosophical analysis of the experience of maintaining an early medical expert system for a number of years [6, 7]. Observation of experts during maintenance suggests that experts never provide information on how they reach a specific judgment. Rather, the expert provides a justification that their judgement is correct. The justification they provide varies with the context in which they are asked to provide it [6, 7]. This is closely related to ideas coming from a "situated cognition" critique of current approaches to KBS [4]. Ideally the knowledge provided by the expert should only be used in the same context in which it was provided. Where an expert is attempting to correct a trainee's mishandling of a particular case, essential components of the context are the case in hand and the experts' surmise as to what led the trainee to the wrong conclusion. In RDR the expert's knowledge is only used in the context of the same mistake being made and the knowledge provided must differentiate the case from cases the trainee (or CBR system) incorrectly retrieved. This last part is of course easier with a CBR trainee than a human trainee.

## 4.1 RDR Structure

The RDR index structure can be viewed as a decision tree or as a decision list with refinements to decisions which are also decision lists (Figure 1). The decision list view best represents the system, as real systems tend to be flat with the average depth of refinement being 2–3. Each node in the representation in Figure 1 consists of two parts, salient features used for the index and a case (called a cornerstone case). Only conjunctions of features are allowed, no disjunctions.

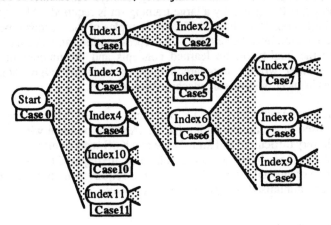

**Figure 1** RDR structure. Each node consists of an index part (conjunction of salient features) and a cornerstone case ( a case on which an error had been made previously).

## 4.2 Retrieving a Case to Match an Unknown Case

The retrieving process searches from a first case in the cornerstone case database. The system moves down the first decision list until it finds the case whose index features match the test case. It then moves to the decision list that refines the first match. If a further match is found it moves to the next level of refinement and so on. The system finally returns the last case matched.

In Figure 2, if the system is asked to retrieve a case for {rain, cold, meeting}, it tests the index feature "sunny,hot" of Case 1 {sunny, hot}. Since there is no match, it next tests Case 3. In this case there is a match so that the system goes to Case 5 and Case 6 which are the corrections of Case 3. Since the index features of 5 & 6 do not match the current case, the system finishes the searching process and retrieves the last matched case, Case 3 {rain,meeting,hot} and produces the conclusion "Take an umbrella" from Case 3.

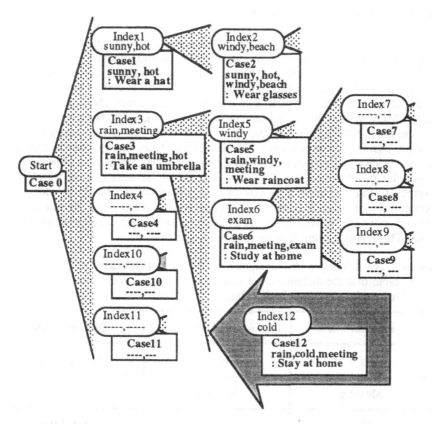

**Figure 2.** When a case, {rain,cold,meeting} is presented, the system tries to match it with cases in level 1. Case 3 is matched so the system moves to the cases in the level 2 list which can be reached from Case 3. When there is no matching case in level 2 the system produces the conclusion, take an umbrella, from Case 3 which is the last matched case in the search. If this conclusion is not correct then the system adds the new case to the bottom of the level 2 list under Case 3 and after 5 & 6 as Case 12. The expert identifies the features for the Case 12 index from a list of the differences between Case 3 and Case 12 {not(hot), cold}. Case 12 will be retrieved only if the same search sequence is followed as when Case 12 was added.

### 4.3 Adding New Cases

If the answer "take an umbrella" needs to be corrected because the correct answer is "Stay at home", the new case is added. The current test case is added at the bottom of cases, refining Case 3 with the index "cold" as Case 12 (Figure 2). Case 12 will only be reached if the same search sequence is followed that led to the wrong conclusion for this case. That is, the knowledge is only used in the same context in which it was added.

## 4.4 Validating the Expert's Justification

When the system adds the case to the data base, the new cornerstone case {rain, cold, meeting} can be considered as an exception to the cornerstone case, Case 3 {rain, hot, meeting}. Therefore, the features to justify that the conclusion "take an umbrella" is wrong and new conclusion "stay at home" is correct must differentiate Case 12 from Case 3, for which "take an umbrella" is correct. The expert is presented with a list of the differences between the two cases (Table 1). The expert must select one or more features from this list, and if required for clarity, may also add features that are common to the two cases. The indexed features, or ripple down rules, added are never changed or deleted. If an expert identifies features as important for a particular conclusion, there will always be some circumstance in which this is correct, so that the addition of refinements will eventually make the scope of the parent rule sufficiently narrow. To cope with clerical error, or blunders, the difference list can be overridden and a further rule added for the previous cornerstone case. This facility is almost never required in practice.

**Table 1** The difference list distinguishing the current test case and the cornerstone case. Note that the difference list can contain negated conditions. These can be useful for attributes with multiple values.

| Cornerstone case | Current test case | Difference list |
|:---:|:---:|:---:|
| Rain | Rain | Not applicable |
| Meeting | Meeting | Not applicable |
| Hot | | not Hot |
| | Cold | Cold |

## 4.5 Experience with RDR

PEIRS is a large medical expert system built using RDR and used to provide clinical interpretations for laboratory reports from the Department of Chemical Pathology at St Vincent's Hospital Sydney [10]. Figure 3 shows the type of case interpreted by PEIRS. The system was put into routine use with about 200 cases, with all later cases added with the system in actual routine use. The 200 initial cases were added off-line while interfacing problems were sorted out, but by the same process of adding cases to correct errors. The system now has over 2000 cases. The experts have built the system without any knowledge engineering or programming assistance or skills.

The laboratory issues about 500 reports per day. PEIRS at present provides comments on about 100 reports. Of these, on average, 4-5 per day require correction and for which cases are added to the data base and indexed. This suggests that the system is running at 95% accuracy in the domains for which it has been trained. On conventional assessment its accuracy is considerably higher as many of the cases in the subdomains it covers do not require an interpretation. The system is thus at least 95% accurate in 20% of chemical pathology, making it a very comprehensive medical expert system, as well as being one of the few in actual use. The experts add the new cases as a minor addition to their normal duties with each case taking about 3 minutes. The system has thus taken about 100 expert hours to develop. It should be noted that the time for each maintenance incident is a constant independent of the size of the developing system, whether it is 10 cases(rules) or 1000.

It should be noted that PEIRS is a good example of the decision list rather than decision tree nature of the index. The average depth of corrections is 2–3, so that, as a tree, the system is very shallow and branchy [25]. Normally 1-2 conditions are selected for a rule, with a maximum of 6. The total number of features used in finding a case is on average 4–5.

```
05-Jul-91                ST. VINCENT'S HOSPITAL              12:58 PM
                     DEPARTMENT OF CHEMICAL PATHOLOGY
                 --------------------------------------------
   Patient ....... : LAIDUP,I.M. Male, 72 years

   A. ........ : 02-62-64  Ward : CH ITU


                                 BLOOD   BLOOD   BLOOD   BLOOD   BLOOD
                                 746406  746573  746590  746986  747004
                                 B.    07:12   08:46   07:14   09:15
   Test          Range   Units   03 Jul  04 Jul  04 Jul  05 Jul  05 Jul
                                 C.    1991    1991    1991    1991
   ----------------------------  ------  ------  ------  ------  ------
   Sodium        137-146  mmol/L  ....    ....    139     ....    140
   Potassium     3.5-5.0  mmol/L  ....    ....    4.0     ....    3.8
   Chloride      95-105   mmol/L  ....    ....    103     ....    104
   Bicarbonate   24-31    mmol/L  ....    ....    23*     ....    22*
   Urea          3.0-8.5  mmol/L  ....    ....    8.7*    ....    8.6*
   Creatinine    0.06-0.12 mmol/L ....    ....    0.14*   ....    0.13*
   Inorg. Phos.  0.70-1.40 mmol/L ....    ....    ....    ....    0.90
   Magnesium     0.85-1.05 mmol/L ....    ....    ....    ....    0.86
   Calcium       2.10-2.60 mmol/L ....    ....    ....    ....    2.16
   Albumin       36-47    g/L     ....    ....    33*     ....    34*
   Tot. Protein  66-82    g/L     ....    ....    62*     ....    65*
   Bilirubin     < 18     umol/L  ....    ....    15      ....    12
   Alk. Phos.    30-100   U/L     ....    ....    52      ....    64
   ALT           < 30     U/L     ....    ....    33*     ....    40*
   GGT           < 35     U/L     ....    ....    46*     ....    55*
   pH            7.35-7.45        7.51*   7.40    ....    7.43    ....
   PCO2          32-45    mmHg    28*     37      ....    34      ....
   PO2           75-105   mmHg    107*    93      ....    68*     ....
   Bicarb.       24-31    mmol/L  22*     23*     ....    22*     ....
   Base Excess   -3-+3            +1      -1      ....    -1      ....
   --------------------------------------------------------------------
   Results consistent with:
   Resolution of respiratory alkalosis.
   Evolving hypoxaemia.
```

**Figure 3** illustrates a typical case interpreted by the expert system. The interpretation of the data directly follows the data. The other abnormalities in this data are not yet covered by the knowledge base.

## 5. RDR as CBR

Ripple down rules have mainly been described in the knowledge acquisition literature [7] as a way of carrying out knowledge acquisition for KBS. We argue here that in fact they blur the distinction between CBR and conventional KBS:

Structure: The tree structure (or decision list with decision list refinements) provides an index for the cases located at each node. This can be used directly to retrieve a case.

Reasoning vs Retrieving: The rules are really an encapsulation of the salient features of a case. In reaching a case, one can view the process as a sequence of rules being fired, or as building up a list of the salient features to uniquely identify one of the cornerstone cases.

Knowledge acquisition vs storing new case: In the RDR framework knowledge acquisition means identifying the salient features that distinguish a case. No other knowledge engineering is required, making the knowledge acqusition component of an RDR at least as small as most CBR. However, no other knowledge engineering or other programming decisions are required when building the index and storing the case. Note also, the knowledge is validated in that only valid rules can be added.

Similarities versus Differences :The underlying major issue in CBR is identifying and adjusting cases [31]. There are many types of indices that are used to match cases, including differences. It is probably reasonable to say that in general a match is made on some type of similarity, and where difference lists are used, they attempt to refine the similarity based match as in PROTOS [1]. In RDR the expert is asked simply to identify the features in the new case which lead him or her to an alternate conclusion to the one presented. The system requires that at least some of these features differentiate the new case from the incorrectly retrieved case. However, the notion of similarity and difference are hidden from the expert on the grounds that since the expert is justifying why the conclusion should be different it will be natural to select differentiating features.

CBR is motivated by the idea that experts are poor at expressing abstract knowledge about their expertise but they are very good at dealing with cases. RDR emphasises that cases are not divorced from expertise, and that in fact experts will very willingly tell one why a case belongs in one class rather than another and that this justification will differentiate two representative cases. This fits closely with the notion of humans being better at identifying differences than giving abstract definitions that comes from Kelly's personal construct psychology [12]. The notion of on–going refinement by differentiating cases seems a useful model for human episodic memory. CBR is motivated by the idea that in conventional KBS too much emphasis is placed on knowledge. Perhaps it is also reasonable to suggest that in CBR too much emphasis is placed on cases. Consequently, although knowledge is essential to a CBR, its proper use is not specified. With RDR we perhaps have a system which emphasises both cases and expert knowledge. In particular it develops the idea that experts are very good at justifying their conclusions about cases in terms of cases differences.

## 6. RDR Problems and Discussion

An obvious problem with the RDR methodology, is that since refinements are local and no effort is made to control the order in which cases are provided to the system, there may be a lot of local repetition of knowledge. In a previous study [23]. it was shown that in fact a manual ripple system was of similar size to decision trees built by ID3 or C4.5[1]. Gaines has developed an inductive algorithm which learn RDR[13]. In this case the KB/CB built is half the size of the manual version. Simulation studies have confirmed these results[9]. A two or even three fold difference would be acceptable in terms of the ease of building ripple down rules. The use of induction depends on a large set of training cases. It can also be used to reorganise a system initially built manually [13]. RDR KBs built inductively tend to be two to three times smaller in size that KBs built by other inductive algorithms [14]. Catlett [2] has argued for RDR as a mediating representation in machine learning while Kivinen [20] has shown they are PAC learnable and Siromoney and Siromoney [28] has argued for their inclusion in inductive logic programming.

The reason why manual RDR produces a fairly compact KB is that the approach allows the expert to focus purely on their expertise. It appears from the very simple rules and the flat structure in PEIRS, that in this environment experts will naturally provide rules which attempt to minimise both false positives covered by the rule and the false negatives not covered because the rule is too specific. This then tends to counteract the repetition that may emerge because of the random order in which cases are presented to the system.

Another problem with the current RDR method is retrieving only a single case. There are two arguments for retrieving multiple cases. Firstly, multiple cases provide choices from which the expert can select the best case. Secondly, multiple cases are needed for multiple types of classification required in some domains. For example, a patient may have multiple independent diseases. RDR adopts the approach that since it is trivial to correct errors there is no point in retrieving alternative cases; if an error is made it can be fixed. However the approach does support the possibility of suggesting that the case retrieved may not be the best possibility. This depends not on simple matching, but using the history of how the knowledge has been corrected [17].

---

[1]It should also be noted that this study provided a perhaps more remarkable demonstration of the advantages of CBR over induction than PROTOS (Porter et al 1990). ID3 applied to a case base of 291 thyroid cases had an error of 74% on 9514 test cases while RDR had an error of 12%. As the size of the training set was increased it was not until 6000 cases were seen that ID3 caught up to the RDR error rate (then 2%). In the process RDR had added about 500 of the 6000 cases to its case base. What this shows is not the advantages of CBR per se., over induction but the advantages of a CBR system that takes advantage of human expertise in a consistent way.

The MCRDR system [18] based on RDR has been introduced to handle multiple independent classifications. In MCRDR, the system uses the same notion of refinement but discards the decision list idea shown in Figs 1 and 2. Instead of finding the first case or rule in the decision list that matches and passing to its refinements, the system evaluates all cases in the first list and then moves to the refinements of all matches. Such a system is probably best understood as an n-ary tree. The interaction with the expert in correcting the system when a case has one or more wrong classifications remains essentially the same in that the expert is asked to select from lists of features that describe and distinguish the case. Hidden from the expert, the process may cycle through a number of cases that have to be distinguished from the new case as in MCRDR other cases in the case base may match with the new case and be thereby misclassified. The various classifications that may be required for the new case are handled one at a time. Evaluation studies to date suggest that although the knowledge acquisition process is longer than with RDR it still only takes a few minutes and is of the same ease [19].

RDR have also been applied to other problems such as configuration, however using Gaines's inductive method to build the RDR system [24]. It has also been proposed that there may be a general RDR method whereby a system that starts by dealing with a problem such as simple classification can evolve into whatever type of RDR system is best suited to the problem as further knowledge and cases are provided [8].

## References

1. Bareiss, E.: Exemplar-Based Knowledge Acquisition: a Unified Approach to Concept Representation, Classification and Learning. Boston Academic Press (1989).

2. Catlett, J.: Ripple-Down-Rules as a Mediating Representation in Interactive Induction, in Proceedings of the Second Japanese Knowlege Acquisition for Knowledge-Based Systems Workshop. Kobe, Japan (1992) 155-170.

3. Clancey, W.J.: Heuristic Classification. Artificial Intelligence 27(3) (1985) 289-350.

4. Clancey, W.J.: A Neuropsychological Interpertation to Vera and Simon. Cognitive Science 17(1) (1993) 87-116.

5. Compton, P.: Insight and Knowledge, in AAAI Spring Symposium: Cognitive aspects of knowledge acquisition. Stanford University, USA (1992) 57-63.

6. Compton, P., Horn, K., Quinlan, J.R., Lazarus, L., and Ho, K.: Maintaining an Expert System, in Application of Expert Systems, J.R. Quinlan, Editor. Addison Wesley London (1989) 366-385.

7.  Compton, P. and Jansen, R.: A Philosophical Basis for Knowledge Acquisition. Knowledge acquisition **2** (1990) 241-257.

8.  Compton, P., Kang, B.H., Preston, P., and Mulholland, M.: Knowledge Acquisition Without Analysis, in Knowledge Acquisition for Knowledge Based Systems, Lectures Notes in AI (723), G. Boy and B. Gaines, Editors. Springer Verlag Berlin (1993) 278-299.

9.  Compton, P., Preston, P., Kang, B.H., and Yip, T.: Local Patching Produces Compact Knoweldge Bases, in A Future for Knowledge Acquisition, L. Steels, G. Schreiber, andW.V.d. Velde, Editors. Springer-Verlag Berlin, German (1994) 104-117.

10. Edwards, G., Compton, P., Malor, R., Srinivasan, A., and Lazarus, L.: PEIRS: a Pathologist Maintained Expert System for the Interpretation of Chemical Pathology Reports. Pathology **25** (1993) 27-34.

11. Forsythe, D.: Engineering Knowledge: the Construction of Knowledge in Artificial Intelligence. Computer Science Department, University of Pittsburgh CS-90-9 (1990).

12. Gaines, B. and Shaw, M.: Cognitive and Logical Foundations of Knowledge Acquisition, in The 5th Knowledge Acquisition for Knowledge Based Systems Workshop. SRDG Publications, Department of Computer Science, University of Calgary, Calgary, Alberta, Canada Banff, Alberta, Canada (1990) 9.1-9.25.

13. Gaines, B.R.: The Sisyphus Problem Solving Example through a Visual Language with KL-ONE-like Knowledge Representation, in Sisyphus'91: Models of Problem Solving. (1991).

14. Gaines, B.R. and Compton, P.J.: Induction of Ripple Down Rules, in AI '92. Proceedings of the 5th Australian Joint Conference on Artificial Intelligence. World Scientific, Singapore Hobart, Australia (1992) 349-354.

15. Grossner, C., Preece, A.D., Chander, P.G., Radhakrishnan, T., and Suen, C.Y.: Exploring the Structure of Rule Based Systems, in The Eleventh National Conference on Artificial Intelligence. MIT Press Washington DC, USA (1993) 704-709.

16. Jones, E.K.: Model-Based Case Adaptation, in The Tenth National Conference on Artificial Intelligence. AAAI Press San Jose, California (1992) 673-678.

17. Kang, B. and Compton, P.: Towards a Process Memory, in AAAI Spring Symposium: Cognitive aspects of knowledge acquisition. Stanford University (1992) 139-146.

18. Kang, B.H. and Compton, P.: Knowledge Acquisition in Context : the Multiple Classification Problem, in Proceedings of the 2nd Pacific Rim International Conference on Artificial Intelligence. Seoul, Korea (1992) 847-853.

19. Kang, B.H., Compton, P., and Preston, P.: Multiple Classification Ripple Down Rules, in Third Japanese Knowledge Acquisition for Knowledge-Based Systems Workshop. Japanese Sociey for Artificial Intelligence Hatoyama, Japan (1994) 197-212.

20. Kivinen, J., Mannila, H., and Ukkonen, E.: Learning Rules with Local Exceptions, in Proceedings Ewo-COLT. (1993).

21. Kolodner, J.L.: A Process Model of Case-Based Reasoning in Problem Solving, in The Ninth Internation Joint Conference on Artificial Intelligence. Morgan Kaufmann Los Angeles, USA (1985) 284-290.

22. Manago, M.V. and Kodratoff, Y.: Noise and Knowledge Acquisition, in The Tenth International Joint Conference on Artificial Intelligence. Morgan Kaufmann Milano, Italy (1987) 348-349.

23. Mansuri, Y., Compton, P., and Sammut, C.: A Comparison of a Manual Knowledge Acquisition Method and an Inductive Learning Method, in Australian workshop on knowledge acquisition for knowledge based systems. Pokolbin, Australia (1991) 114-132.

24. Mulholland, M., Preston, P., Sammut, C., Hibbert, B., and Compton, P.: An Expert System for Ion Chromatography Developed Using Machine Learning and Knowledge in Context, in The Sixth International Conference on Industrial & Engineering Applications of Artificial Intelligence and Expert Systems. Endinburgh, Scotland (1993) 258-267.

25. Preston, P., Edwards, G., and Compton, P.: A 1600 Rule Expert Systems without Knowledge Engineer, in World Congress on Expert Systems. Macmillan New Media License Lisbon, Portugal (1994) 17.1-17.10.

26. Ross, S.P.: Case-Based Reasoning. Department of Computer Science, University College London RN/89/69 (1989).

27. Schank, R.C.: Dynamic Memory : A Theory of Reminding and Learning in Coumputers and People. Cambridge Cambridge University Press (1982).

28. Siromoney, A. and Siromoney, R.: Local Exceptions in Inductive Logic Programming, in The 14th Machine Intelligence Workshop. (1993).

29. Slade, S.: The Yale Artificial Intelligence Project: a Brief History. AI Magazine 8(Winter) (1987) 67-80.

30. Slade, S.: Case-Based Reasoning: a Research Paradigm. AI magazine **12** (1991) 42-55.

31. Stottler, R.H., Henke, A.L., and King, J.A.: Rapid Retrieval Algorithms for Case-Based Reasoning, in The Eleventh International Joint Conference on Artificial Intelligence. Morgan Kaufmann Detroit, Michigan USA (1989) 233-237.

32. Sycara, K.P. and Ashley, K.D.: Case-Based Reasoning : Tutorial Note of the Twelfth International Joint Conference on Artificial Intelligence. IJCAI-91 (1991).

33. Sycara, K.P. and Navinchandra, D.: Index Transformation Techniques for Facilitating Creative Use of Mulitple Cases., in The Twelfth International Conference on Artificial Intelligence. Morgan Kaufmann Darling Harbour, Sydney, Australia (1991) 347-352.

34. Wielinga, B.J., Schreiber, A.T., and Breuker, J.A.: KADS: a Modelling Approach to Knowledge Engineering. Knowledge Acquisition **4** (1992) 5-54.

# Case-Based Evaluation in Computer Chess[*]

Yaakov Kerner

Department of Mathematics and Computer Science
Bar-Ilan University
52900 Ramat-Gan Israel
kerner@bimacs.cs.biu.ac.il

**Abstract.** Current computer-chess programs achieve outstanding results in chess playing. However, there is a deficiency of evaluative comments on chess positions. In this paper, we propose a case-based model that supplies a comprehensive positional analysis for any given position. This analysis contains evaluative comments for the most significant basic features found in the position and a general evaluation for the entire position. The analysis of the entire position is presented by an appropriate Multiple eXplanation Pattern (MXP), while the analysis of each chosen feature is presented by a suitable eXplanation Pattern (XP). The proposed analysis can improve weak and intermediate players' play in general and their understanding, evaluating and planning abilities in particular. This model is part of an intelligent educational chess system which is under development. At present, our model deals only with a static evaluation of chess positions; addition of searching and playing modules remains for future work.

**Keywords:** case-based reasoning , computer chess, explanation patterns

## 1. Introduction

Case-Based Reasoning (CBR) in computers has been successfully employed in several domains like law (Ashley & Rissland, 1987) and medicine (Koton, 1988). Another potentially exciting CBR domain is game playing in general and chess in particular, since human players use extensive knowledge in their playing. However, little research has been done on CBR in game playing in general and in chess in particular. In CBR research on non-chess playing programs, we find treatment in the games of eight-puzzle (Bradtke & Lehnert, 1988) and othello (Callan et al., 1991).

Current game-playing programs use various types of brute-force search, relying on a heuristic evaluation function to evaluate positions. However, most game-playing programs do not make the evaluation process explicit. That is, there is a deficiency of evaluative comments concerning given positions. General evaluative comments

---

[*] This research is in partial fulfillment of the requirements towards the degree of Ph.D. by the author under the supervision of Dr. Uri J. Schild at Bar-Ilan University. It was supported in part by the "Ben-Gurion Fund for the Encouragement of Research" Histadrut - The General Federation of Labour in Israel.

concerning given positions have been supplied by several systems (e.g., Michie, 1981; Berliner & Ackley, 1982; Epstein, 1989; Pell, 1994). Nevertheless, these systems do not supply any detailed evaluative comments about the internal content of the given positions. Moreover, these systems are not case-based systems. We believe that using CBR can contribute to the task of giving detailed evaluative comments about the internal content of the given positions.

Our goal is development of an intelligent educational chess system. In this paper, we propose a case-based model that supplies an analysis for any chess position (except for illegal and mate positions). Our model is not currently useful to strong players since it does not use any search. Instead, we analyze the given position by analyzing the most significant basic features found in the position. The model should be helpful to weak and intermediate players wishing to improve their play. The proposed analysis is mainly directed at teaching chess evaluation and planning.

This paper is organized as follows: Section 2 gives background describing knowledge-based position evaluation and evaluative comments. In Section 3 we present our basic chess patterns. Section 4 describes suitable data structures for evaluation of chess positions. In Section 5 we propose several algorithms for evaluating chess positions. Section 6 presents a short example for evaluation of a position based on one of our case-based algorithms. Section 7 summarizes the research and suggests future directions. In the Appendix we give a glossary of the main chess concepts mentioned in the paper.

## 2. Background

### 2.1. Position Evaluation in Chess

The quality of the player's evaluation capability is one of the most important factors in determining his strength as a player. Evaluation of a position allows a chess player to work out plans and to decide which specific variations to calculate. Evaluation combines many different factors, each factor with its own weight, depending upon the factor's relative importance (Samuel, 1967).

A psychological study by de Groot (1965) shows that chess players base their evaluations of chess positions on patterns (typical positions) gained through experience. The player's patterns guide him either in deciding which move to play or rather, which strategy to choose in a given position. Simon (1974) estimates that a master has an estimated repertoire of between 25,000 and 100,000 patterns.

### 2.2. Case-Based Position Evaluation in Computer Chess

Chess playing programs do not involve case-based evaluation in the sense of retrieving a similar position and adapting its evaluation to the position at hand. These programs use hash tables. Hash tables are optimization tables that store positions that have already been evaluated in previous searches (Zobrist, 1970).          However, hash tables are used only to prevent recalculations of the same positions and different kinds of symmetric positions, such as: white and black symmetric, vertical symmetric, horizontal symmetric and diagonal symmetric. These tables cannot pertain to analogous positions.

A pseudo-CBR evaluation process is proposed by Levinson and Snyder (1991). Their system, called Morph, splits the given position into several chosen patterns that have been already evaluated and computes the evaluation value of the entire position based on the values of the chosen patterns. However, Morph is restricted to lower level tactical or piece position patterns with only limited ability to abstract from these. MorphII (Levinson, 1994) has addressed these concerns, by abstracting new and wider patterns from the rules of the domain and additional patterns from those. However, MorphII's patterns may not really coincide with the way human would classify the position and thus only have limited explanatory use.

To sum up, Morph and MorphII do not supply any detailed evaluative comments about the given position. Moreover, they do not use CBR in the sense of retrieving a similar position and adapting its evaluative analysis to the position at hand.

## 2.3. Evaluative Comments

Chess experts have established a set of qualitative evaluation measures. Each chess position can be evaluated by one of these measures. Table 1 presents a few qualitative measures, their equivalent quantitative measures and their meanings. These measures are based on the common relative values of the queen, rook, bishop, knight and pawn which are 9, 5, 3, 3 and 1 points, respectively (Shannon, 1950).

**Table 1.** A few qualitative measures (LMs) in chess, their equivalent quantitative measures (NMs) and their meanings. The LMs are intervals of NMs, which are numbers based roughly on positional evaluations.

| Qualitative measures | Quantitative measures | Meaning |
|---|---|---|
| +− | $3 < NM$ | White is winning |
| ± | $1 < NM <= 3$ | White has a big advantage |
| ± | $0 < NM <= 1$ | White has a small advantage |
| = | $NM = 0$ | The game is even |
| ∓ | $-1 =< NM < 0$ | Black has a small advantage |
| ∓ | $-3 =< NM < -1$ | Black has a big advantage |
| −+ | $NM < -3$ | Black is winning |

Little research has been done concerning the task of giving detailed evaluative comments for game positions. Most game-playing programs do not make the evaluation process explicit, but rather give only one evaluative score. A chess student is not always capable of understanding why the specific chess program he is working with, evaluated the position the way it did. In order to increase his evaluating ability effectively, he needs to receive explanatory evaluative comments. However, there are programs that can supply a more detailed explanation concerning an evaluated position. A few such programs are presented below.

A theory of evaluative comments has been proposed by Michie (1981). In addition to the construction of the classical minmax game tree, Michie has developed a model of fallible play. His theory assigns to each position two values: "game-theoretic value" and "expected utility." Based on combinations of these values, his theory supplies short comments on chess positions, e.g., "Black has a theoretical win but is likely to lose." However, his theory does not supply any comments about the internal content of the evaluated positions, e.g., the pawn-structure. Moreover, this theory does not suggest any plans for the continuation of the game.

Another explanation mechanism has been constructed by Berliner and Ackley (1982). Their system, called QBKG, can produce critical analyses of possible moves for a backgammon position using a hierarchical knowledge tree. It gives only two kinds of comments. The first is a general evaluation of the discussed position. The second is an answer to the question: "Why did you make that move, as opposed to this move?" In addition, Berliner and Ackley admit that their system is only able to produce comments on about 70% of positions presented to it.

In the last years, a few additional programs that can explain their positions, have appeared (e.g., HOYLE (Epstein, 1989); METAGAMER (Pell, 1994)). HOYLE and METAGAMER view a feature as an advisor that encapsulates a piece of advice about why some aspect of the position may be favorable or unfavorable to one of the players. Using these advisors, these programs can comment generally on positions.

To sum up, little research has been done concerning case-based detailed evaluations of game positions in general and case-based detailed evaluations of chess positions in particular. Michie, Berliner and Ackley, Epstein and Pell contribute to the task of giving general evaluative comments concerning game positions. Nevertheless, their models and, to the best of our knowledge, other existing models do not supply any detailed evaluative comments concerning the internal content of the given positions. In this paper, we propose an initial framework for a detailed case-based evaluation model for computer chess programs.

## 3. Basic Chess Patterns

A basic chess pattern is defined as a certain minimal configuration of a small number of pieces and squares which describes only one salient chess feature. In order to discover as many different basic chess patterns as possible, we, with the help of strong chess masters, have constructed a hierarchical tree structure that includes most basic positional features concerning evaluation of chess positions.

This tree is a hierarchical classification of most common chess features at different levels of abstraction. At the root of the tree, we have the concept of "static evaluation." Each leaf (a node at the last level) in this tree represents a unique basic pattern (e.g., "one isolated pawn in the endgame stage"). Each basic pattern has two suitable explanation patterns (one for White and one for Black) that contain several important comments concerning the discussed pattern.

Most of the concepts were collected from a variety of relevant chess books (Nimzowitsch, 1930; Fine, 1952; Pachman, 1973; Pachman, 1976; Kotov, 1978). The highest level concepts of this tree are shown in Fig. 1. Figures 2 and 3 illustrate the sub-trees describing the pawn and king concepts, respectively. A few important concepts mentioned in these trees are defined in a chess glossary in the Appendix.

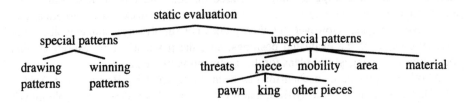

**Fig. 1.** The evaluation tree

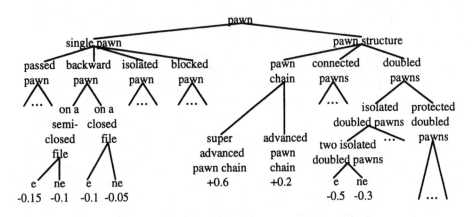

**Fig. 2.** The evaluation sub-tree for the pawn concept

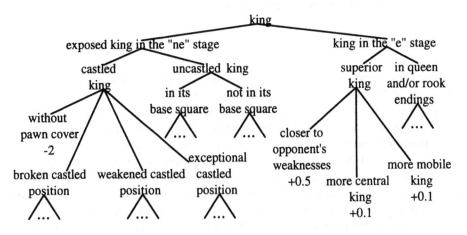

**Fig. 3.** The evaluation sub-tree for the king concept

Each leaf which represents a unique basic chess pattern has its own evaluative value. For example, the pattern "two isolated doubled pawns in the endgame stage" has an evaluative value of -0.5. It is important to mention that the evaluative value given to each basic pattern is only a general estimate that represents its value in the majority of the positions that include this pattern.

In addition, often when evaluating a chess pattern, we consider the stage in the game in which the pattern takes place. This distinction is important since the same pattern can be evaluated differently in the "e" and "ne" stages (the endgame stage and not the endgame stage respectively). For example, the pattern "isolated pawn" becomes a greater weakness in the "e" stage, since the importance of a pawn becomes greater.

This tree is used primarily for two main tasks: (1) searching the tree to find all basic patterns included in a given position and (2) determining pattern similarity in the adaptation process in our model (details in Section 5). The structure of our evaluation tree is similar in some ways to the E-MOP, the memory structure introduced by Kolodner (1981). Our chess concepts resemble Kolodner's generalized information items and our basic chess patterns can be viewed as her "events."

At present, the tree contains 613 nodes where 403 of them are leaves (i.e., basic patterns). In the next section we describe suitable data structures for evaluating any given chess positions.

## 4. Data Structures for Evaluation of Chess Positions

### 4.1. XPs

XPs are explanation patterns (Schank, 1986). Kass (1990, p. 9) regards XPs as "*variablized explanations that are stored in memory, and can be instantiated to explain new cases.*" The XP, according to Schank (1986, p. 39), contains the following slots: (1) a fact to be explained, (2) a belief about the fact, (3) a purpose implied by the fact, (4) a plan to achieve purpose, and (5) an action to take.

The XP structure has been applied to criminal sentencing (Schild & Kerner, 1993). We find this structure also appropriate for the domain of evaluation of chess positions. While the judicial XP describes a specific viewpoint of a judge concerning a sentence, the chess XP describes a specific viewpoint of a chess position from either White's point of view or Black's point of view.

In the case of chess, since we are concerned with the evaluation of the given position, we use an evaluation slot instead of an action slot. The evaluation slot contains two kinds of evaluative values: a quantitative measure (NM) and a qualitative measure (LM) (which are demonstrated in Table 1).

In our model, each basic pattern in the evaluation tree has two *general XPs* (one for White and one for Black). Six different examples of XPs are presented in Figures 6 and 7. For the sake of convenience, we use some abbreviations: W for White, B for Black, K for king and Q for queen. Without loss of generality, our examples will be evaluated from White's viewpoint, assuming that it is White's turn to move.

In summary, the XP-structure seems to be a convenient data-structure for describing and explaining a specific chess pattern of a given position. However each chess position usually includes more than one important pattern. Thus, the XP-structure does not suffice to explain an entire chess position.

## 4.2. MXPs

The MXP (Multiple eXplanation Pattern) structure (Schild & Kerner, 1993) was first introduced to assist judges in deciding which sentence to hand down in a new case. The MXP is a detailed graphical explanation to a given case and its outcome. In general, the MXP is defined as a collection of XPs and an outcome slot. Each XP represents a unique important viewpoint concerning the given case and carries its weight in its evaluation slot to the outcome slot of the entire case. In our model, each important chess viewpoint regarding the given position is explained and evaluated by a suitable XP, and the general evaluation for the entire position is represented in the outcome slot.

In order not to overload the user with too much information, we stipulate that the chess MXP is composed of the three most important XPs (those with the highest absolute evaluation values) suitable to the discussed position. At present, our evaluation function is a summation over the evaluation values of these XPs. We use this simple rough function to enable the user to understand how the system reached its general evaluation. Nevertheless, the summation is meaningful since each XP included in the MXP describes only one unique independent basic pattern. That is, the quantitative measure of the "general evaluation" slot is a summation over its XPs' quantitative values. Its qualitative measure is dependent on its quantitative measure according to Table 1.

Figures 4 and 5 present two chess positions. Figures 6 and 7 describe the MXPs that analyze these positions, respectively. The most important chess concepts mentioned in these MXPs are defined in a glossary in the Appendix.

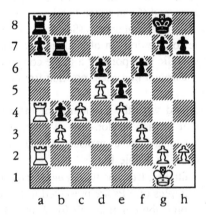

**Fig. 4.** Chess position 1

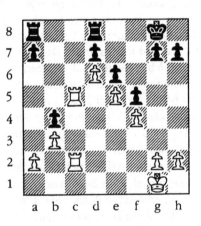

**Fig. 5.** Chess position 2

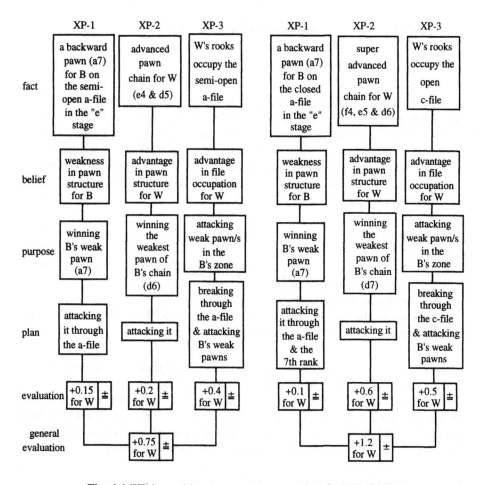

|  | XP-1 | XP-2 | XP-3 | XP-1 | XP-2 | XP-3 |
|---|---|---|---|---|---|---|
| fact | a backward pawn (a7) for B on the semi-open a-file in the "e" stage | advanced pawn chain for W (e4 & d5) | W's rooks occupy the semi-open a-file | a backward pawn (a7) for B on the closed a-file in the "e" stage | super advanced pawn chain for W (f4, e5 & d6) | W's rooks occupy the open c-file |
| belief | weakness in pawn structure for B | advantage in pawn structure for W | advantage in file occupation for W | weakness in pawn structure for B | advantage in pawn structure for W | advantage in file occupation for W |
| purpose | winning B's weak pawn (a7) | winning the weakest pawn of B's chain (d6) | attacking weak pawn/s in the B's zone | winning B's weak pawn (a7) | winning the weakest pawn of B's chain (d7) | attacking weak pawn/s in the B's zone |
| plan | attacking it through the a-file | attacking it | breaking through the a-file & attacking B's weak pawns | attacking it through the a-file & the 7th rank | attacking it | breaking through the c-file & attacking B's weak pawns |
| evaluation | +0.15 for W ± | +0.2 for W ± | +0.4 for W ± | +0.1 for W ± | +0.6 for W ± | +0.5 for W ± |
| general evaluation | | +0.75 for W ± | | | +1.2 for W ± | |

**Fig. 6.** MXP for position 1      **Fig. 7.** MXP for position 2

Our MXP structure fits the way Steinitz (the first formal world chess champion between 1886-1894) taught players. "*Steinitz taught players most of all to split the position into its elements. Naturally they do not play the same role in a given position, they do not have the same importance. Once, he has worked out the relationship of the elements to each other, the player moves on the process of synthesis which is known in chess as the general assessment*" (Kotov 1978, p.24).

We believe that the MXP structure provides a better framework for explaining a given position than those given by other systems, because we supply comments on the internal content of the position, and our comments are more detailed. Moreover, the application of the MXP structure for evaluating chess positions shows that the MXP structure is an appropriate knowledge structure not only for sentencing criminals. These findings lead us to believe that the MXP should be examined as a suitable tool for other CBR domains where there is need to evaluate or to solve complex problems.

# 5. Algorithms for Evaluation of Chess Positions

## 5.1. A Simple Evaluation Algorithm

We aim at evaluating any given chess position by constructing a suitable MXP for it. We search our evaluation tree in order to find all basic patterns included in the position. We choose only the most important basic patterns (i.e., the patterns with the highest absolute evaluation values). We retrieve the stored XPs of these patterns and combine them into a new MXP. The retrieved XPs are analogical to the snippets (portions of cases) used in other CBR domains by Kolodner (1988), Redmond (1990) and Branting (1991).

A description of this algorithm, *Algorithm-1*, is given here. Given a New Chess Position (NCP):
  (1) Find the evaluation values of all basic patterns (features) included in the NCP.
  (2) For the most important patterns retrieve their XPs.
  (3) Combine all these adapted XPs into a MXP.
  (4) Compute the general evaluation of the MXP of the NCP using a simple summation over the evaluation values of the retrieved XPs.

This algorithm has been used primarily in the establishment of the original data base of positions and their MXPs. We use this data base for evaluating new given chess positions in our case-based evaluation algorithms described in the next sub-section. At present, we have 12 representative positions. These positions have been slightly adapted from positions taken from different relevant chess books (e.g., Pachman, 1976; Kotov, 1978; Shereshevsky, 1985; Averbakh, 1986).

## 5.2. Case-Based Evaluation Algorithms

Case-based algorithms, more creative than Algorithm-1, can be proposed. These algorithms use the data base of positions and their MXPs. Controlled learning of new positions with their MXPs enlarges the extent of this data base and improves the explanation ability of the evaluation algorithms. General descriptions of two algorithms are given below.

*Algorithm-2*, given below, uses only the MXP most suitable to the NCP. Given a NCP, the algorithm is as follows:

*Retrieval of suitable MXPs and Selection of the best MXP*
  (1) Find the evaluation values of all basic patterns included in the NCP.
  (2) Choose the most important patterns according to their absolute evaluation values.

(3) Retrieve all positions that their MXPs include at least one XP whose fact-slot is either one of the patterns found in step (2) or a "brother" of one of them (according to the evaluation tree). In case of failure, jump to step (8).

(4) For each retrieved position compute its similarity measure relative to the NCP.

(5) Choose the most suitable MXP (i.e., with the highest similarity measure).

*Adaptation and System Evaluation*

(6) Keep exactly matched XP.

(7) Adapt suitable XPs of the chosen MXP to the NCP using the evaluation tree and suitable general XPs.

(8) Explain other important facts of the NCP by general XPs.

*Construction of the solution, Real World Evaluation and Storage*

(9) Combine all exactly found and adapted XPs into a new MXP.

(10) Compute the general evaluation of the new MXP by summing the evaluation values of its XPs.

(11) Test the proposed MXP by a chess expert and make optional improvements by hand where needed.

(12) If the proposed MXP is found appropriate for acquisition then store it according to the fact-slots of its XPs.

*Algorithm-3* can use several MXPs suitable to the NCP. The difference between it and Algorithm-2 is step (8). In Algorithm-3 step (8) is as follows: For all important facts of the NCP not found in the facts of the MXP nor adaptable to the XPs of the MXP, select the next MXP suitable to the NCP, and return to step (6).

In the next sub-sections of Section 5 we shall give a detailed description of the most important CBR stages of *Algorithm-2*.

## 5.2.1. Retrieval of suitable MXPs and Selection of the best MXP

Given a NCP, we retrieve all MXPs that include at least one XP whose fact-slot is either one of the patterns found in step (2) or a "brother" of one of them (according to the evaluation tree). The MXP with the highest similarity measure ($sm$) to the NCP is chosen for the next stage of our CBR algorithm. Our similarity function has the following form: $sm = a*ifs + b*ps$ where $sm$ is the computed similarity measure, $a$ and $b$ are specific constants, $ifs$ is the important features' similarity, and $ps$ is the position's similarity. The $ifs$ is similar to the *contrast measure* of Tversky (1977) and the $ps$ is similar to the *nearby measure* of Botvinnik (1984). Intuitively, the $ifs$ and $ps$ can be regarded as a semantic similarity and a structural similarity, respectively.

The $ifs$ function is the computed similarity measure between the important facts (basic patterns) found in the NCP and the retrieved MXP. It is defined as follows: Let S1 be the set of all facts found both in the NCP and in the retrieved MXP. Let S2 be the set of all facts of the NCP for which we found near-neighbors patterns to them in the retrieved MXP (according to the evaluation tree). Let S3 be the set of all facts found in the NCP but without near-neighbor facts in the retrieved MXP. Let S4 be the set of all facts found in the retrieved MXP but without near-neighbor facts in the NCP. Then, $ifs = \alpha * \sum_{i \in S1} W_i + \beta * \sum_{i \in S2} (W_i * d_i) - \gamma * \sum_{i \in S3} W_i - \delta * \sum_{i \in S4} W_i$ where $\alpha$, $\beta$, $\gamma$ and $\delta$ are specific constants, $w$ (weight) is the evaluation value of every discussed fact, whether it is an important fact found in the NCP or it is a fact-slot of a XP of the discussed MXP, and $d$ a near-neighbor factor that measures the distance between each pair of facts.

The $ps$ function measures the similarity between two positions: the NCP and the position related to the retrieved MXP. It is defined by: $ps = c*ips + d*wms + e*bms$ where $c$ and $d$ are specific constants, $ips$ is the identical pieces' similarity, $wms$ is White's material similarity, and $bms$ is Black's material similarity. $ips$ is defined as the number of the exact pieces found on the same squares of the two positions divided by the number of pieces found in the NCP. The $wms$ and $bms$ are defined as follows:

$wms = 1- abs((wpm(NCP)-wpm(RP))/ wpm(NCP))$ and
$bms = 1- abs((bpm(NCP)-bpm(RP))/ bpm(NCP))$

where $abs$ is the absolute function, $wpm$ is the calculated material value of White's pieces (except the king) according to Table 1, $bpm$ is the same function for Black's pieces, $NCP$ is the new chess position, and $RP$ is the retrieved position.

### 5.2.2. Adaptation and System Evaluation

After choosing the most suitable MXP we adapt its XPs in order to construct a MXP for the NCP. In step (6), for the facts found both in the NCP and in the retrieved MXP, we take exactly the XPs of these facts from the retrieved MXP.

In step (7), for the facts of the retrieved MXP found as near-neighbors (according to the evaluation tree) using suitable general XPs, we process a learning process on each XP of the MXP (call each in its turn XP-1) in order to adapt XP-1 to its matching fact in the NCP. To validate the proposed adaptation we use some chess tests (e.g., a limited search). These tests are partly a simulation of the proposed adaptation and serve as the system evaluation to its own solution.

In step (8), for all important facts of the NCP that are neither found in the facts of the chosen MXP nor could be adapted reasonably to the XPs of the chosen MXP, using chess tests, we adapt suitable general XPs.

### 5.2.3. Construction of the solution, Real World Evaluation and Storage

A MXP for the NCP is proposed after combining all exactly found and adapted XPs and computing the general evaluation slot of the MXP, using a summation over the evaluation values of the XPs of the new MXP. A chess expert will either approve or disapprove of this MXP. In case of disapproval, at present, potential improvements are inserted by hand. In case of approval, a potential learning process is executed.

We have constructed a learning mechanism that is able to enlarge our data base of MXPs. A new MXP will be added to the data base of MXPs only if at least one adapted XP is learned (step 7 or 8). Such a MXP is inserted in the flat data base of MXPs. The indexes that enable any kind of access (insertion or retrieval) to a MXP in this data base are the fact-slots of the XPs of the MXP.

## 6. A Short Example

In this section, we illustrate a use of Algorithm-2. Assuming the NCP is position 2 (Fig. 5), we retrieve the MXP presented in Fig. 6 (which is the MXP of position 1 that is presented in Fig. 4) as the best MXP for explaining position 2.

The adaptation process constructs the MXP presented in Fig. 7 as an explanation for the NCP. Due to the lack of space, we will only explain the construction of the XP relates to Black's backward pawn (a7) on the closed a-file in the "e" stage (i.e., XP-1 in Fig. 7 ) from White's viewpoint.

The fact slot of XP-1 of the NCP relates to a closed file while the fact slot of XP-1 of the retrieved MXP relates to a semi-open file. These facts are close neighbors in the evaluation tree. Therefore, we choose XP-1 of the retrieved MXP for the adaptation process. In addition, we retrieve a suitable general XP according to the discussed fact of the NCP. Using these two retrieved XPs, we construct XP-1 of the new MXP.

In the fact slot we write exactly the discussed fact of the NCP. Since the belief and purpose slots are the same in both retrieved XPs, we take them as they are. The plan slots in the two retrieved XPs are different. The plan slot of the general XP proposes to attack the weak pawn through its rank (i.e., the 7th rank). The plan slot of the XP-1 of the retrieved MXP proposes to attack the weak pawn through its file (i.e., the a-file). Utilizing an elaboration strategy, we refine the plan slot of these two retrieved XPs and construct a new plan slot, which is to attack the weak pawn through both the a-file and the 7th rank.

By using simple limited searching, we ensure that the new plan can be theoretically made on the board. We find a way to switch the White rook on c5 to the a-file (a5) and to switch the White rook on c2 to the 7th rank (c7). For the evaluation slot we take the evaluation value of the general XP since it relates to the same discussed fact.

Due to the approval of this MXP by our chess expert and to the construction of a new more complex plan slot, we store this MXP in the data base of MXPs according to the facts-slots of its XPs.

To sum up, we think that this controlled learning process will improve the evaluation ability of our algorithms because of the accumulation of new MXPs. These algorithms become more adequate by deriving more creative and better evaluations than those supplied with fewer MXPs.

## 7. Summary and Future Work

We have made a contribution to CBR research by extending its range in the game-playing domain in general and in computer chess in particular. We have developed a case-based model which supplies a comprehensive positional evaluation for any chess position. This model seems to supply better explanations for chess positions than other existing computer game-playing programs. In addition, our model includes a learning mechanism that enables it to supply more adequate evaluations.

We think that this model, in principle, can be generalized for evaluating any game position for any board game. The three highest levels of our evaluation tree are appropriate for game playing in general. While the king and pawn sub-trees are unique for chess-like games, all other sub-trees (e.g., threats and material) fit in general to all board games.

In computer chess, profound understanding has been shown to be inefficient without deep searching. Therefore, to strengthen our model, there is a need to add searching capability. Case-based planning is another important issue which we have to deal with more deeply. The plans we retrieve for each XP of the MXP for the discussed position and adapt to fit the discussed position, may be combined into one complete plan using game tree search. Finally, addition of playing modules will enable our system to, besides play chess, learn in the real world and therefore to improve its evaluating, explaining and planning capabilities.

## Acknowledgments

Thanks to Ofer Bruk (an international master) and Allan Savage (a FIDE master). These two strong players and experienced trainers played a crucial role in the development of the evaluation tree. Thanks also to Sean Engelson, Robert Levinson, Avraham Norin, Barney Pell, Shlomit Zeiger, Sara Zimin and the reviewers for helpful comments on earlier drafts of this paper. Finally, special thanks to my talented students Alon Geri and Danny Moore for implementing a big part of the system described in this paper as their graduation project.

## References

Ashley, K. D. & Rissland, E. L. (1987). Compare and Contrast, A Test of Expertise. In *Proceedings of the Sixth National Conference on Artificial Intelligence* (pp. 273-278). Los Altos: Morgan Kaufmann.

Averbakh, Y. (ed.) (1986). *Comprehensive Chess Endings* (a five-volume set). Translated by Neat, K. P. Oxford: Pergamon Press.

Berliner, H. J. & Ackley, D. H. (1982). The QBKG System: Generating Explanations from a Non-Discrete Knowledge Representation. In *Proceedings of the National Conference on Artificial Intelligence* (pp. 213-216). AAAI Press.

Botvinnik, M. M. (1984). *Computers in Chess: Solving Inexact Search Problems.* Translated by Brown A. A. New York: Springer-Verlag.

Bradtke, S. & Lehnert, W. G. (1988). Some Experiments With Case-Based Search. In *Proceedings of the Seventh National Conference on Artificial Intelligence* (pp. 133-138). San Mateo: Morgan Kaufmann.

Branting, L. K. (1991). Reasoning with Portions of Precedents. In *Proceedings of the Third International Conference on AI and Law* (pp. 145-154). New York: ACM Press.

Callan, J. P., Fawcett, T. E. & Rissland, E. L. (1991). Adaptive Case-Based Reasoning. In *Proceedings of a Workshop on CBR* (pp. 179-190). San Mateo: Morgan Kaufman.

de Groot, A. D. (1965). *Thought and Choice*. Mouton, The Hague.

Epstein, S. (1989). The Intelligent Novice - Learning to Play Better. In D. N. L. Levy & D. F. Beal (Eds.), *Heuristic Programming in Artificial Intelligence - The First Computer Olympiad*. Ellis Horwood.

Fine, R. (1952). *The Middle Game in Chess*. New York: David McKay Company.

Kass, A. M. (1990). *Developing Creative Hypotheses by Adapting Explanations*. Technical Report #6, p. 9. Institute for the Learning Sciences, Northwestern University, U.S.A.

Kolodner, J. L. (1981). Organization and Retrieval in a Conceptual Memory for Events or Con54, Where are You? In *Proceedings of the Seventh International Joint Conference on Artificial Intelligence* (pp. 227-233). Los Altos: William Kaufmann.

Kolodner, J. L. (1988). Retrieving Events from a Case Memory: A Parallel Implementation. In *Proceedings of a Workshop on CBR* (pp. 233-249). San Mateo: Morgan Kaufman.

Koton, P. (1988). Reasoning about Evidence in Causal Explanations. In *Proceedings of a Workshop on CBR* (pp. 260-270). San Mateo: Morgan Kaufman.

Kotov, A. (1978). *Play Like a Grandmaster*. Translated by Cafferty, B. London: B. T. Batsford Ltd.

Levinson, R. & Snyder, R. (1991). Adaptive Pattern-Oriented Chess. In *Proceedings of the Ninth National Conference on Artificial Intelligence* (pp. 601-606). Menlo Park: AAAI Press/The MIT Press.

Levinson, R. (1994). Morph II: A Universal Agent: Progress Report and Proposal. Technical Report UCSC-CRL-94-22, University of California Santa Cruz.

Michie, D. (1981). A Theory of Evaluative Comments in Chess with a Note on Minimaxing. *The Computer Journal, Vol. 24, No. 3*, 278-286.

Nimzowitsch, A. (1930). *My System - A Chess Treatise*. New York: Harcourt, Brace and Company.

Pachman, L. (1973). *Attack and Defence in Modern Chess Tactics*. Translated by Clarke P. H. London: Routledge and Kegan Paul LTD.

Pachman, L. (1976). *Complete Chess Strategy* (Volumes 1 & 2). Translated by Littlewood J. London: B. T. Batsford Ltd.

Pell, B. (1994). A Strategic Metagame Player for General Chess-Like Game. In *Proceedings of the Twelfth National Conference on Artificial Intelligence* (pp. 1378-1385). Seattle: AAAI Press/The MIT Press.

Redmond, M. (1990). Distributed Cases for Case-Based Reasoning: Facilitating Use of Multiple Cases. In *Proceedings of the Eight National Conference on Artificial Intelligence* (pp. 304-309). Menlo Park: AAAI Press/The MIT Press.

Samuel, A. L. (1967). Some Studies in Machine Learning Using the Game of Checkers II- Recent Progress, *IBM Journal of Research and Development, Vol. 11, No. 6*, 601-617.

Schank, R.C. (ed.) (1986). *Explanation Patterns: Understanding Mechanically and Creatively*. Hillsdale: Lawrence Erlbaum.

Schild, U. J. & Kerner, Y. (1993). Multiple Explanation Patterns. In *Proceedings of the First European Workshop on Case-Based Reasoning*, Vol. II (pp. 379-384). Kaiserslautern: Germany. Extended paper in Wess, S.; Althoff, K-D.; and Richter, M. M. (Eds.), *Topics in Case-Based Reasoning - EWCBR'93*, Lecture Notes in Artificial Intelligence 837 (pp. 353-364). Berlin: Springer-Verlag, 1994.

Shannon, C. E. (1950). Programming a Computer for Playing Chess. *Philosophical Magazine, Vol. 41(7)*, 256-277.

Shereshevsky M. I., (1985). *Endgame Strategy*. Translated by Neat, K. P. Oxford: Pergamon Press.

Simon, H. A. (1974). How Big is a Chunk? *Science No. 183*, 482-488.

Tversky, A. (1977). Features of Similarity, *Psychological Review, 84, 4*, 327-352.

Zobrist, A. L. (1970). *Technical Report #88*. Computer Science Department, University of Wisconsin, Madison, WI.

# Appendix

## Chess Glossary

*Advanced Pawn chain*: White/Black's head of a series of pawns in a pawn chain is in the 5-th/4-th rank, respectively.

*Backward pawn*: A pawn that has been left behind by neighboring pawns of its own color and can no longer be supported by them.

*Blocked pawn*: A pawn that is blocked by an opponent's piece which is not a pawn.

*Castled king*: A king that has made a castle.

*Center*: Squares e4, d4, e5 and d5.

*Closed file*: A file with pawns of both colors.

*Doubled pawns*: At least two pawns of the same color on the same file.

*Endgame*: The last and deciding stage of the chess game. In this stage the position becomes simplified and usually contains a relatively small number of pieces.

*Exposed king*: A king without good defence, mainly without a good pawn cover.

*Isolated doubled pawns*: At least two pawns of the same color on the same file that are not protected by any neighboring pawns of their own color.

*Isolated pawn*: A pawn that has no neighboring pawns of its own color.

*Mobility*: Number of potential single moves in the current position.

*Open file*: A file without pawns.

*Passed pawn*: A pawn that has no opponent's pawns which can prevent it from queening.

*Pawn chain*: Two consecutive series of pawns abutting on one another in consecutive diagonals.

*Protected doubled pawns*: At least two pawns of the same color on the same file in which at least one of them is protected by a neighboring pawn of its own color.

*Semi-closed file*: A file with pawn/s of only one's own color.

*Semi-open file*: A file with pawn/s of only the opponent's color.

*Super-Advanced Pawn chain*: White/Black's head of a series of pawns in a pawn chain is in the 6-th/3-th rank, respectively.

# Design of a Case-Based Reasoning System Applied to Neuropathy Diagnosis

Maria Malek[1] and Vincent Rialle[2]

[1] TIMC-IMAG, bat. Lifia, 46 ave. Félix Viallet, 38031 Grenoble, France
[2] TIMC-IMAG, Domaine de la Merci, 38706 La Tronche, France

**Abstract.** The goal of our work is to develop a computer assisted medical diagnosis system in the field of neuropathy (peripheral nervous system diseases). We believe that an efficient medical diagnosis system must integrate the divers reasoning capacities of physicians: logical, deductive, uncertain, and analogical reasoning. A neuropathy diagnosis system based on production rules, called Neurop, has already been developed in our laboratory. However, Neurop is poorly adapted to treat uncertain data or unusual cases.

In this paper, we propose integration of a new module of analogical reasoning to compensate the drawbacks presented by Neurop. The idea is to memorise real treated cases and to construct what we call a memory of prototype cases. This memory is then used during retrieval phase. A learning phase is added to optimise the system reaction and to prevent future diagnostic failures. This is achieved by modifying the contents of the prototype memory. Three principal types of modifications are offered. They are: prototype construction, prototype specialisation and prototype fusion. The proposed reasoning system is planned to function in conjunction with another reasoning system (that could be a human expert) which supervises results and activates the learning mechanisms in case of failure.

## 1   Introduction

In this work, we aim to provide a medical diagnosis system that integrates divers reasoning capacities of physician's such as: logical, deductive, uncertain, and analogical reasoning. In fact, two main sources of knowledge are generally used by a physician when examining a new patient case [10]:

- Academic knowledge, where conclusions are deduced by applying certain production rules to an initial set of factors describing the examined case.
- Practical experience, where knowledge may be presented by an accumulation of conclusions about already treated cases. Resolving a new case, using this type of knowledge, is achieved by using analogical reasoning [6] which is based on the deduction of a behaviour in a new situation in function of memorised information. Similarity or distance notions are important in this type of reasoning [4]. An atypical case of analogical reasoning that was studied and applied to some specific diagnosis or planning problems is Case-Based

Reasoning (CBR)[11]. Another type of reasoning that is strongly related to analogical reasoning is reasoning based on generalisation from examples and on inductive approaches [3].

Actually, we are interested in a specific medical field: the electromyography (cf. 2). A system of aid on neuropathy diagnosis based on production rules, has been designed and implemented. This system, called Neurop uses rule-based knowledge representation and deductive reasoning [9]. Being a rule-based system, Neurop presents two major drawbacks:

- Due to the absence of memorisation of real treated cases, Neurop repeats the same steps even if an already treated case is presented once more.
- Neurop is not able to treat atypical or uncertain cases (Sect. 2).

To compensate for Neurop's shortcomings we propose adding a Case Based Reasoning (CBR) module. CBR is based on the recognition of similarity between a given problem, and one that has already been resolved [2]. The solution found must be adapted to the case under study. Case structure depends on the application domain and must include aspects allowing for measurement of similarities. A CBR system is composed of three main phases [11]:

- The retrieval phase, which permits retrieval of relevant cases from the memory. Many methods exist to decrease retrieval time. Indexing methods determine important features of cases according to the knowledge domain. Unfortunately, this type of knowledge is not always available. Inductive approaches are more suitable when there is a large case memory. They allow the construction of classification tools or architectures, like decision trees [8] which allow an automatic analysis of the new case features with logarithmic complexity. Organising cases in some generalisation hierarchy is an important method for building the case memory [11].
- The selection phase which permits classification of retrieved cases according to their similarities with the case treated. Classifying requires construction of a suitable similarity measure. This measure must take into account two types of criteria: *surface* criteria that depend on the distance between case attributes, and *deep* criteria which take into consideration relationships between attributes.
- The adaptation phase which consists of a set of operations for adapting selected solutions to the presented case. This set contains elements to be reused in the selected solution, elements to be modified, and modification methods.

We design a case hierarchy with two levels of memory. The lower level contains analysed patient cases organised into groups of similar cases. The upper level contains *prototypes*, each of which represents a group of cases. Using a small prototype memory instead of a large memory of patient cases decreases retrieval time . The construction of prototypes is made by applying a simple generalisation method. Prototypes are corrected during the learning phase of the system (Sect. 5).

The remainder of this paper is organised into four other sections. In section two, we describe the application field and the rule-based Neurop system with its limitations. In section three, we present the design of our system and we describe the different phases: initialisation of the memory of prototype cases, diagnosis phase, evaluation and learning phase, and memories reorganisation. In section four, we present our case and prototype structures, and in section five, we describe the learning methods: prototype construction, prototype specialisation and prototype fusion.

## 2 Application Field and Related Work

Neuropathy is an important part of electromyography, a medical discipline that concerns the study of neuromuscular diseases [9]. Four pairs of nerves are particularly tested: the median, the ulnar, the peroneal and the tibial. For each nerve, sensory and motor fibres are studied independently. To localise lesions, we proceed by studying the nerve segment by segment. The nerve is electrostimulated and a signal is detected on each segment. The segment diagnosis depends on the interpretation of the electrophysiological parameters obtained.

- On sensory fibres these parameters are:
  - for the first segment: potential action, velocity, and duration;
  - and on other segments: potential ratio, velocity ratio, and duration ratio.
- On motor fibres these parameters are:
  - for the first segment: amplitude, latency, and duration;
  - and on other segments: velocity, amplitude ratio, and duration ratio.

After analysing these parameters, physicians make a diagnosis on each segment, and then diagnose the whole nerve. The global patient diagnosis is a synthesis of all tested nerve diagnoses.

Neurop is an expert system for neuropathy diagnosis aid. It contains rules that treat the following four levels of neuropathy diagnosis [9]: interpretation of parameters, segment diagnoses, nerve diagnoses and patient diagnosis. The electrophysiological parameters are continuous. They are interpreted by semantic values that take their values in one of the following sets: (normal, decreased very decreased) or (normal, increased, very increased). To determine the appropriate semantic values, some thresholds must be defined. For the moment, these thresholds are determined by a human expert.

When some values of electrophysiological parameters are close to interpretation limits, Neurop fails to give precise diagnosis. This means that some regions of incertitude exist around the given limits. Generally, experts are not able to determine the size of such regions with precision. Figure 1 represents a schema of regions of incertitude for both latency and amplitude parameters.

We have chosen to introduce a new type of reasoning based on analogy and generalisation of examples. This resolves the problem of uncertain cases and completes the expert system by integrating another type of reasoning. We mention here that there exists in the literature several prototype-based systems like

Protos [1] and ARC [7] which was applied to medical diagnosis and which used fuzzy logic.

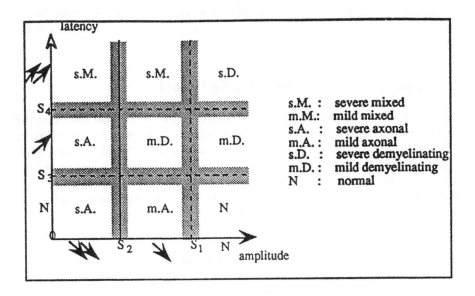

**Fig. 1.** Regions of incertitude for two electrophysiological parameters

## 3   System Design

Our idea is to construct a memory of *prototypes*. This memory is used during retrieval phase instead of the cases memory in order to decrease retrieval time. Thus our system contains two levels of memory which are linked together:

- memory that contains *real patients cases*,
- memory that contains *prototype cases*.

The system is composed of four essential phases:

- initialisation of the memory of prototype cases,
- diagnosis phase,
- evaluation and correction phase,
- memories reorganisation.

Figure 2 illustrates these four related phases. Next we describe each of them in detail.

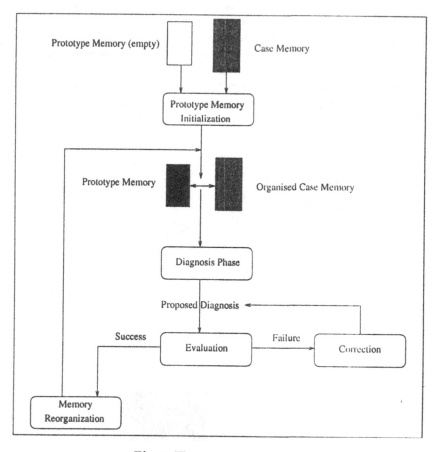

**Fig. 2.** The system cycle life

## 3.1 Initialisation of the Prototype Case Memory

At first, the prototype memory is empty. Our objective is to construct prototypes
that represent sets of *similar* real cases. By similar cases, we mean cases that
have the same diagnosis. The idea is to test the existence of a *sufficient* number
of real cases in the memory having the same diagnosis. *Sufficient* is a system
parameter which is determined by the application user. These cases must be
grouped in the same zone in the case memory. A unique case representing all
these cases is created. This unique case is called a *prototype* and is added to
the prototype memory. This prototype can be modified during evaluation and
memories reorganisation phases. Section 4 illustrates how to construct such a
prototype from a set of cases.

   At the end of this phase, we obtain our case memory divided into many
groups. Each group is represented by an element from the prototype memory. A
memory zone is reserved for cases that are not classified elsewhere. These cases
form a group of *atypical* cases (or unusual cases).

Figure 3 illustrates the architecture of the two memories. We remark that each prototype points to its group.

We would like to mention that during our discussions with physicians on the subject of how they use their experience when diagnosing patients, we concluded that, without quite realising it, they refer to a set of prototype cases when they encounter a new patient case. When the new case can't be associated with an existent prototype, physicians try to refer to individual cases that are *atypical* (unusual cases).

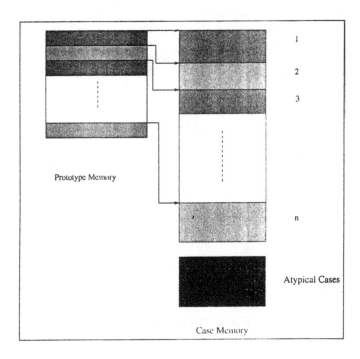

**Fig. 3.** Memories organisation

## 3.2 Diagnosis Phase

In this phase, the system exploits stocked knowledge to propose a diagnosis for the new presented case. This phase is normally composed of the following three sub-phases:

− retrieval phase,
− selection phase,
− adaptation phase.

Prototypes matched to the presented case are extracted from the prototypes memory during the retrieval phase. Both Prototypes and presented cases are expressed by means of Horn predicates. Hence matching two predicates is achieved by using the known *unification* algorithm. If no prototype is matched then the group of non typical cases is retrieved. The selection phase sorts retrieved prototypes or cases according to their similarity to the presented case. The choice of a similarity measurement presents always a real problem. This measurement must depends on the relations that exist among different features of a case. Establishing such relations requires a good analyse of the application field. To simplify, we choose a similarity measurement based only on *surface* criteria. It is based on the measurement of an Euclidean distance among attributes of different cases. The sorted list is used during the correction phase. The first case (the most similar) is selected. Its diagnosis is transferred to the new case.

### 3.3 Evaluation and Correction Phase

An evaluator may be human, or may be another expert system. Our evaluator was either a physician, or the rule-based system Neurop. Neurop can validate a given solution by applying the backward chaining process. The evaluator accepts or rejects the proposed diagnosis.

If accepted, the following learning procedure is executed:

*If* the selected case is a prototype *then*
> the new case is added to the group of the prototype.

*If* the selected case is atypical *then*
> the new case is added to the group of atypical cases.

If rejected, the following learning procedure is executed:

*If* the selected case is a prototype *then*
> this prototype is too general,
> and must be *specialised* to exclude the new case.
> Real cases that do not belong to the new prototype group are deleted
> from the group memory zone and placed into the atypical zone.
> The correction phase selects the next case from the sorted list.
> The diagnosis phase is reexecuted.

*If* the selected case isa typical *then*
> The most similar case is too far of the new case.
> and the system is unable to give a solution.
> The system must learn this new case with its diagnosis.

The *specialisation* algorithm for a prototype is explained below in section 5.

### 3.4 Memories Reorganisation

During the previous phase, many cases can be added to the group of atypical cases. After the evaluation phase affirms a success, this module tests if whether is a *sufficient* number of *similar* cases in the group of atypical cases to form a new group. If so, a new prototype is created.

When a new prototype is created, this module tests the possibility of prototype *fusion*. This prevents constant growth of the prototype memory. We recall that it is preferable to have a prototype memory that is as small as possible. Fusion procedure is given by:

*If* there is a prototype in the memory that is *more general* than the new one,
      the new prototype is deleted.
      the new group is fused with the group of the more general prototype.
*If* there are prototypes that are *more specific* than the new one,
      they are deleted from the prototypes memory
      and their groups are fused with the new one.
*If no* prototype in the memory is *comparable* with the new one,
      this prototype is added to the memory.

The terms *more general* and *more specific* are defined below (cf. 5).

## 4 Case and Prototype Structures

A case should be presented in a way that permits measurement of similarity during retrieval. Additionally, a case structure must contain all the attributes and the relationships between them. To represent all the relationships between the given attributes, we describe a case by a Horn predicate. We then use Horn predicate algorithms for generalisation and specialisation. A predicate presents a nerve case. This predicate contains all nerve electrophysiological parameters, patient age, and nerve diagnosis. A case has the following form:

$$\text{Diagnosis:-Age,}$$
$$\text{Nerve } (\text{fm}(seg_1(Param_{111}, ...Parm_{11n}),$$
$$seg_i(Parm_{1i1}, ...Parm_{1ik})),$$
$$\text{fs}( seg_1(Param_{211}, ...Parm_{21m})$$
$$seg_j(Parm_{2j1}, ...Parm_{2jl})))$$

Where:
Diagnosis represents the nerve diagnosis,
Age is the age of the patient,
Nerve is the name of the nerve (median, ulnar, peroneal, tibial),
fm means motor fibre (fibre number 1),
fs means sensory fibre (fibre number 2),
$seg_k$ is the $k^{th}$ segment of the fibre,
$Param_{ijk}$ is the value the $k^{th}$ electrophysiological parameter of the $j^{th}$ segment of the $i^{th}$ fibre.
As mentioned above, we need to group similar cases which have the same diagnosis and to present them by a simple prototype. The following *prototype* structure is suggested:

Nerve (fm($Seg_1([a_{111}, b_{111}], ...[a_{11n}, b_{11n}])$,
$Seg_i([a_{1i1}, b_{1i1}], ....[a_{1ik}, b_{1ik}]))$,
fs( $Seg_1([a_{211}, b_{211}], ...[a_{21m}, b_{21m}])$,
$Seg_j([a_{2j1}, b_{2j1}], ...[a_{2jl}, b_{2jl}]))$,
$([age_1, age_2])$,
Diagnosis)

**Where:**

$a_{ijk}$, $b_{ijk}$ respectively are the lower and the upper boundaries of the $param_{ijk}$ parameter,

$age_1$, $age_2$ represent also the lower, the upper boundaries of the age parameter.

It is important to mention here that this prototype is presented as a Prolog III predicate. Prolog III allows definition of constraints on predicate variables. This prototype can be modified during learning phase.

## 5 Learning Methods

We have seen that learning methods are used during correction and memory reorganisation phases. Learning is performed by adding new cases to the case memory into the suitable group or by modifying prototype memory. Three types of modification are proposed in our system:

- *construction* of a new prototype,
- *specialisation* of a prototype,
- *fusion* of prototypes.

*Construction* of a new prototype is made when a *sufficient* number of real cases having the same diagnosis are added to the class of atypical cases. These cases compose a group, and are stored in the same zone of memory. A new prototype pointing to this group is created.

On the other hand, when the system gives a wrong diagnosis, the selected prototype must be *specialised* to exclude the current case. This specialisation can be performed by reducing some intervals in the prototype. The choice of intervals reduction is a real problem. Our strategy is to specialise the predicate with the *least possible modification*. This prevents, as far as is possible, obtaining prototypes that are too specific and that will become useless. So we have chosen to reduce one parameter interval. The selected parameter is the one whose intervals need the least modification to exclude the current case. Thus we choose the parameter which has *one* of its interval boundaries closest to the current case parameter:

$$param = min_{ijk}\left(\frac{\min((b_{ijk} - param_{ijk}), (param_{ijk} - a_{ijk}))}{b_{ijk} - a_{ijk}}\right) \quad (1)$$

**Where:**

$a_{ijk}$, $b_{ijk}$ are interval boundaries of $Param_{ijk}$ in the selected prototype,

$param_{ijk}$ is the value of $Param_{ijk}$ in the current case.

One of the following modifications, on one boundary of one selected parameter interval is shown:

$$a_{ijk} = a_{ijk} + param_{ijk} + \epsilon(b_{ijk} - a_{ijk}) \qquad (2)$$

$$b_{ijk} = b_{ijk} - param_{ijk} - \epsilon(b_{ijk} - a_{ijk}) \qquad (3)$$

New prototypes are created continuously. This extends the prototype memory and so, increases retrieval time. Therefore, we have adopted the strategy of prototype *fusion*. Prototypes are compared, and groups of the more specific prototypes are fused into that of the most general prototype (Sect. 3.4). A prototype A is *more specific* than a prototype B if they present the same nerve with the same diagnosis, and if all A´s intervals are included into B´s intervals.

## 6 Conclusion

The quality of an expert depends on both the richness of his experience acquired when analysing a considerable number of real cases, and his academic knowledge domain . The proposed model aims to produce neuropathy diagnosis from an accumulation of carefully analysed cases. We have used a type of reasoning based on analogy and generalisation of examples. This model is based on a large case memory which constitutes the system´s experience. Each case is presented by a Horn predicate. A new level of memory is constructed. This memory contains prototypes, each of them represents a group of real, similar cases. This smaller memory decreases retrieval time.

Learning is done by adding new cases, or by modifying prototypes memory. A new case can be added to a specific group or to the group of atypical cases. This increases the system´s experience. Prototype memory modification can be performed by construction, specialisation, and fusion of prototypes.

An important problem yet to be studied is the integration of this model with the Neurop knowledge base. Such a system will possess both deductive and analogical types of reasoning. Also, it may be closer to human reasoning which integrates both academic knowledge and accumulated experience.

*Acnowledgement: We wish to thank Dr. Annick Vila, Electromyography Laboratory, EFSN, University Hospital Centre, 38043, Grenoble for the medical information she offered us during the design of this system.*

## References

1. Bareiss, R.: Exemplar-Based Knowledge Acquisition: A Unified Approach to Concept Representation, Classification, and Learning. Boston, Academic press, 1989.
2. Barletta, R.: An Introduction to Case-Based Reasoning. AI EXPERT, Volume 6, Number 8, (1991).

3. Buntine, W.: Generalized Subsumption and its Application to Induction and Redundancy. Artificial Intelligence 36- (1988) 149-176.

4. Campbell, J. A., Wolstencroft, J.: Structure and Significance of Analogical Reasoning. Artificial Intelligence in Medicine, 2 (1990), 103-118.

5. Harmon, P.: Case-Based Reasoning III. Intelligence Software Strategies volume VIII, Number 1,1992.

6. Haton, J. p. et al.: Le Raisonnement en Intelligence Artificielle. InterEdition, Paris,1991.

7. Plaza, E., Lopez de Mantaras R.: Learning Typicality from Fuzzy Examples. Methodologies for Intelligent Systems, Vol V, p. 420-427.

8. Quinlan, J. R.: Induction of Decision Trees. Machine Learning 1,(1986), 81-106.

9. Rialle, V. et al.: Heterogeneous Knowledge Representation Using a Finite Automata and First Order Logic: a Case Study in Electromyography. Artificial Intelligence in Medicine, 3 (2),(1991), 65-74.

10. Rialle, V.: Cognition and Decision in Biomedical Artificial Intelligence: From Symbolic Representation to Emergence. Artificial Intellignece and Society, Vol. 9 (1), 1995.

11. Riesbeck, C. K., Schank, R. C.: Inside Case-Based Reasoning. Lawrence Erlbaum Associates, Publishers,Hillsdales, New Jersey,1989.

12. Slase, S.: Case-Based Reasoning: A Research Paradigm. AI magazine Volume 12,Number 1, 1991.

# Controlling a Nonlinear Hierarchical Planner Using Case Replay*

Héctor Muñoz and Jürgen Paulokat and Stefan Wess

University of Kaiserslautern, Dept. of Computer Science
P.O. Box 3049, D-67653 Kaiserslautern, Germany
E-mail: {munioz|paulokat|wess}@informatik.uni-kl.de

**Abstract.** We describe a hybrid case-based reasoning system supporting process planning for machining workpieces. It integrates specialized domain dependent reasoners, a feature-based CAD system and domain independent planning. The overall architecture is built on top of CAPLAN, a partial-order nonlinear planner. To use episodic problem solving knowledge for both optimizing plan execution costs and minimizing search the case-based control component CAPLAN/CBC has been implemented that allows incremental acquisition and reuse of strategical problem solving experience by storing solved problems as cases and reusing them in similar situations. For effective retrieval of cases CAPLAN/CBC combines domain-independent and domain-specific retrieval mechanisms that are based on the hierarchical domain model and problem representation.

## 1 Introduction

Planning for machining workpieces is a crucial step in the process chain of product development in mechanical engineering because it strongly influences the overall product's costs. However, the domain's complexity currently doesn't allow any complete analytical model so that planning must be done based on experience. The task of process planning consists of selecting and ordering machining operations such that all features of a given workpiece can be manufactured by minimal or, at least, by low costs (Cheung & Dowd, 1988). Mostly, the features of a workpiece cannot be treated independently, because steps of a manufacturing plan possibly interact. Positive interactions can be utilized to decrease the cost of manufacturing a feature, e.g. sharing preparatory steps for several processing steps, or compounding manufacturing of several features in one processing step. While positive interactions should be utilized to minimize overall production costs, negative interactions must be resolved because they lead to inconsistencies. For example a processing step for a feature must not be used if it destroys or makes impossible to manufacture another one.

* This research was partially sponsored by the Deutsche Forschungsgemeinschaft (DFG), Sonderforschungsbereich (SFB) 314: "Künstliche Intelligenz - Wissensbasierte Systeme", Project X9 (1991 - 1995).

Theoretically, partial-order nonlinear planning is well suited to support the generation of process plans. Domain-independent conflict resolution techniques that are widely studied can be used for detecting negative interactions between steps. (Conflicts, threats (McAllester & Rosenblitt, 1991; Barrett & Weld, 1993) or clobbering a goal (Chapman, 1987) are used synonymously.) The truth criterion (Chapman, 1987) is an effective way of finding positive interactions. However, in most situations there are many possible treatments of interactions which one has to choosen from. Choosing, however, is a critical step because it influences future planning and finally the execution costs of the overall plan. Past research in planning offers little support on this problem because it was mainly concerned with search for consistent solutions (e.g. (Chapman, 1987; McAllester & Rosenblitt, 1991; Barrett & Weld, 1993)) and the efficiency of the planning process itself (e.g. (Minton, 1988)). Until now some initial work is done on acquiring and representing expertise and controlling a planner to support optimization of plan execution costs (e.g. (Pérez & Carbonell, 1993; Borrajo & Veloso, 1994)).

A main characteristic of human planning for machining is the use of examples that have been found to be successful in similar situations (Humm, Schulz, Radtke, & Warnecke, 1991). In mechanical engineering, there are numerous attempts to build up index structures to support the classification of workpieces and the retrieval of associated manufacturing plans, e.g. (Optiz, 1970). However, these index structures are intended for manual use and only utilize information about the geometry, material of workpieces and the applied technology, e.g. (Zhang, Wright, & Davies, 1988). They completely lack attempts to extract structural information from plans as, e.g., in (Veloso & Carbonell, 1991) to make retrieval more informed.

In this paper, we describe CAPLAN/CBC the case-based control component of the first-principle planner CAPLAN and its application in the process planning domain. Similar to (Kambhampati, Cutkosky, Tenenbaum, & Lee, 1991), CA-PLAN combines specialized reasoners with a general purpose planning approach. In CAPLAN/CBC this hybrid approach is applied to case-based planning by integrating domain-independent and domain-specific methods to organize the case base and to control case retrieval. It extends the ideas of (Paulokat, Praeger, & Wess, 1992), where only domain specific methods are used.

As in PRODIGY/ANALOGY (Veloso, 1992) and contrary to other well-known case-based planning systems like CHEF (Hammond, 1986) case-based planning in CAPLAN/CBC means controlling the planning process of the first-principle planner by reusing control decisions of a case for solving the current problem.

The paper is organized as follows. In the next section, we describe the characteristics of the process planning domain. In section 3 we summarize the concepts of nonlinear, partial-order planning that influenced the architecture of CAPLAN/CBC. Further, we give a survey of the domain model. Section 4 describes our approach to case-based planning and in the last section we discuss our approach.

## 2   Domain Characteristics

The domain we are concerned with is manufacturing planning for rotation-symmetrical workpieces to be machined on a lathe (Paulokat & Wess, 1994). A planning problem is given as a geometrical description of a workpiece and of the raw material that only can be cylindrical in our model (Fig. 1). The description of a workpiece is built up from geometrical primitives as cylinders, cones and toroids that describe monotone areas of the outline, possibly augmented by features as threads, grooves or special surface conditions. In most cases, the outline of a workpiece cannot be machined in one step, but repeated cutting operations are necessary to cut the difference between the raw material and the workpiece in thin layers. These layers are built up from atomic processing areas, that are automatically generated by extending the horizontal and vertical bounding lines of the geometrical primitives. Cutting an atomic area can be seen as an elementary cutting step.

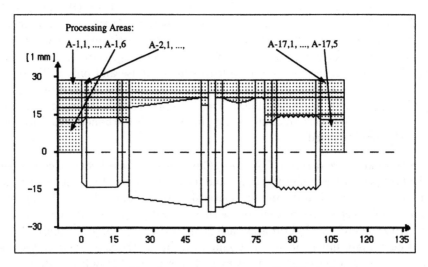

**Fig. 1.** Atomic processing areas of a Workpiece

For machining the workpiece is clamped by a rotating clamping tool, while layers of material are removed by moving a cutting tool along the surface. Standard tools that are normally used for machining large areas have a fixed working direction, i.e., they can be used to cut off material only when being moved either to the left or to the right. Clamping a workpiece hides parts of its surface, therefore, after machining the part which is not hidden, it must be turned and clamped on the other side. Additionally, caused by the geometry of standard cutting tools only horizontal outlines or outlines that are rising along a tool's moving direction can be machined. To machine a descending outline requires tool

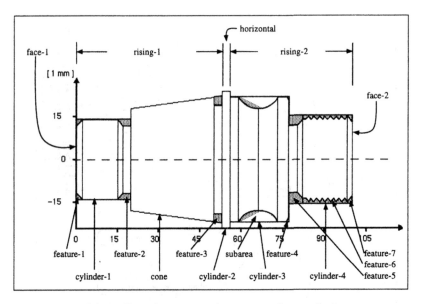

**Fig. 2.** Complex processing areas of a workpiece

changes that increase the overall production costs. But after turning a workpiece and clamping it from the other side, e.g. because this is necessary for machining an area hidden by a clamping tool, a descending outline is now a rising one and can be machined with the same tool. For finding maximally monotonously rising areas, geometrical primitives are grouped to rising areas at both ends of the workpiece and a horizontal area between them (Fig. 2). Each of these compound areas can contain subareas that break the monotonous course of the outline. But from an abstract point of view they do not influence the construction because the monotonous outline necessarily has to be machined first before hidden subareas can be machined. For machining, the horizontal part can be added consistently to one of both rising areas, but choosing an alternative is one of the tasks of the planner because this choice can influence the plan's execution costs. Compound areas can be degenerated to consist of only one geometrical primitive, e.g. the horizontal area in Fig. 2.

The compound areas can be seen as an abstract description of the workpiece resulting in a hierarchical representation whose root node represents the whole workpiece with the compound areas as successors (Fig. 3). The successors of the compound areas are the geometrical primitives and the subareas of the workpiece. A geometrical primitive has successor nodes for its features and the atomic processing areas that are located above it. Subareas, again, can be hierarchically structured, defining their own subtrees. This hierarchical representation of the workpiece is the base for a hierarchically structured planning process.

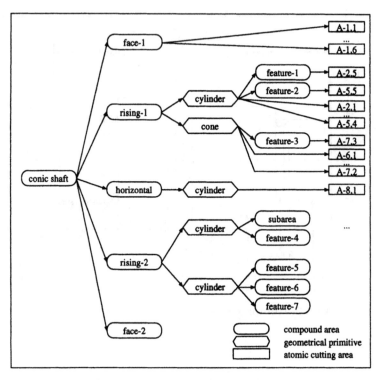

**Fig. 3.** Hierarchical representation of a planning problem.

## 3   Planning in CAPLAN

On an abstract level a planning problem is given by an initial situation, a set
of goals, and a set of possible steps. The task of planning is computing a sequence of steps so that their execution starting from the initial situation results
in a situation satisfying all goals. Planning in CAPLAN is based on the ideas of
systematical non-linear planning (SNLP (McAllester & Rosenblitt, 1991)) and
works on a set of partially ordered plan steps. A new planning problem is represented by two steps $s_0$ and $s_\infty$. The effects of step $s_0$ are the features that
are valid in the initial situation and the preconditions of $s_\infty$ represent the features that are the goals of the planning problem. Step $s_0$ has no preconditions
and is ordered before all other steps of the plan. Step $s_\infty$ has no effects and is
ordered behind all other steps. A goal can be satisfied by every step which is
not ordered behind the precondition's step and which has an effect that can be
matched with the goal's feature. This can be a step already being contained in
the plan or newly added to the plan. Both, the step that adds the effect and
the step the precondition of which is satisfied, are connected by a causal link
that is annotated by the feature. A causal link is threatened by a step if it adds
an effect or the negation of an effect that can be unified with the feature of the

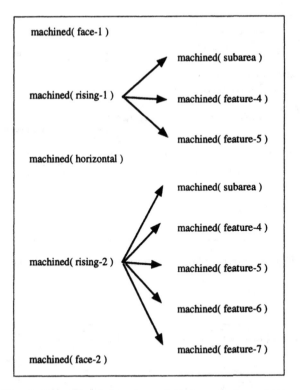

**Fig. 4.** Set of initial goals and their ordering relations.

causal link. Threats must be resolved which can be done by ordering the step that threats the causal link before the step that adds the effect or behind the step whose precondition has been satisfied or by adding constraints that make the unification of the effects impossible.

Planning for machining a workpiece is preceded by transforming the set of compound areas and the set of features of the hierarchical description of the workpiece (Fig. 3) in a problem representation suitable for the planner (Fig. 4). Names, as rising-1 used in the problem description, provide a link to the geometrical representation. They can be used to access further information not explicitly represented in the problem description but which are necessary for control decisions. Fig. 5 shows a part of the plan on the abstract planning level of the hierarchical planning process. First, the planner decided to work on goal machined(rising-1). Therefore, the abstract operator machine(rising-1) is selected, which introduces subgoals to clamp the workpiece and to force the area rising-1 to be free. Then, planning continues with the goal machined(horizontal). Here, the planner can choose between introducing a new step to machine the horizontal component isolated from any other compound component or to utilize the side effects of another plan step. In this example the side effect of step machine(rising-

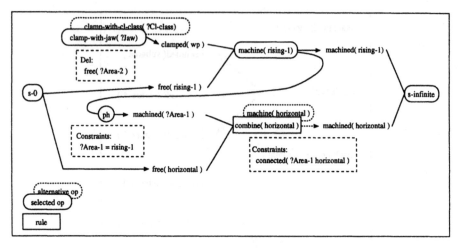

**Fig. 5.** Partial plan on the abstract planning level.

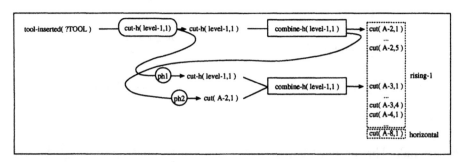

**Fig. 6.** Partial plan on the concrete planning level for the abstract operator machine(rising-1) of Fig. 5.

1) is used. This is supported by the rule combine(horizontal) that introduces a goal that a connected area is machined. (Note: these rules are different from control rules; they are comparable to operators but do not represent actions and are not part of the resulting process plan.) The new goal machined(?Area-1) can be matched to one of the goals of the initial problem description and can be satisfied by a step that is already part of the plan. Using steps already existing is called a phantomization. As different matches are possible, this is a decision point that can strongly influence the execution costs of the plan.

By this phantomization, a decision is made that the compound areas rising-1 and horizontal are processed by one step. This influences the expansion of the abstract plan step machine(rising-1) into a new planning problem on the concrete planning level (Fig. 6). Depending on this decision, the new planning problem is to select and to order cutting operations for the atomic processing areas of the compound areas rising-1 and horizontal. Note that changing the abstraction level means changing the representation language, e.g., the complex processing area rising-1 is replaced by the atomic processing areas A-2,1, ..., A-7,2.

# 4  Case-Based Planning

Three characteristics make manufacturing planning a hard problem. 1) The production cost of a workpiece should be minimized. Optimization of plan execution costs, however, is not supported by AI planning techniques as described in the last section. Nevertheless, they are attractive because they allow an explicit representation of plan steps and reasoning about their interactions and effects. 2) The search space for a manufacturing plan is very large which makes it impossible to generate all alternative solutions and select the best of them. And 3), there is no analytical model of the dependencies between the features of a workpiece, the possible manufacturing steps and the overall execution costs that could be used for choosing between alternatives during the planning process. Instead, human manufacturing planning is based on experience.

If no control knowledge is available, planning in CAPLAN is done by depth-first search or guided by user interactions. For support of planning in complex domains, the planning process can be controlled by a case, e.g., as in (Veloso, 1992). If a case is available the reuse of a decision that has shown to be successful in a similar situation is preferred to search when the planner has to choose at a choice point. If the rationals of a reused decision are satisfied there is a justification that it reduces backtracking and results in a better solution. In CAPLAN there are two kinds of choice points:

- the set of alternative steps to reach a goal, and
- the set of alternative constraints that can be added to a plan to resolve a threatened causal link (McAllester & Rosenblitt, 1991; Barrett & Weld, 1993).

An example for a choice point where the planner has to choose to reach a goal is clamped(wp) in Figure 5. There, the conflict set consists of the steps clamp-with-jaw(?Jaw) and clamp-with-cl-class(?Cl-class).

In CAPLAN the reuse of episodic problem solving experience is done by CAPLAN/CBC. It organizes the case memory and supports case-based planning by retrieving the most similar case and by stepwise reusing the decisions stored in the case. After a problem has been successfully solved and if its solution is substantially different from that of the case it can be added to the case base. An important source for new problem solving experience are user interactions. Storing them as a new case adds control knowledge to the system and increases its planning expertise because knowledge used in these interactions possibly complements the insufficiencies of the model. Adding a case to the case base is preceded by an analyzing step that extracts the relevant features from the problem description which are used for the organization of the case base and for efficient case retrieval.

## 4.1 Case Storage

The organization of the case memory highly influences the efficiency and possibly the result of case retrieval. In (Veloso, 1992) a domain independent architecture for automatic case storage has been described that is based on the assumptions that the set of goals of different problem descriptions are highly varying and that the solution of a problem can be decomposed into independent subplans. These assumptions are not valid in our domain. Machining plans for the considered class of workpieces are highly sequential so that a decomposition is impossible. Further, the goals of planning problems are always similar, i.e., we always have to plan processing steps for one or two rising areas, a horizontal area and for the faces of the workpieces. Optionally, there can be a varying number of workpiece features. On the other hand, there are technological constraints that can be used to classify workpieces and, more important, that are reflected by the manufacturing plan, e.g., the kind of usable clamps depends on the ratio of the diameter of a workpiece to its length.

In our approach, these constraints are compiled into an initial, domain-specific structure of the case memory that spawns a decision tree. In order to add a new case to the case base its relevant category is determined by traversing the decision tree starting from its root to a leaf node. So, every new case is stored as a successor of a leaf node of the domain-specific decision tree which structures the case base. Further, the addition of a new case is preceded by footprinting (Veloso, 1992) the set of features of the initial state as a function of the goal statement and of the particular solution encountered. This process identifies the relevant features of the initial situation with respect to a plan and filters out those features that are not relevant for the plan.

Figure 7 shows the structure of a machining plan for the example of section 2. The footprint is independently computed for the abstract and for every concrete plan. In contrast to the approach in (Veloso, 1992) we don't use the set of goals to index a case, but the hierarchical problem representation described in Fig. 3. It compounds the set of goals and all features of the initial situation. This structure is annotated by the information on the relevance of a feature.

## 4.2 Case Retrieval

The purpose of the retrieval phase is to select a case from the case base that is useful to solve a new planning problem. A good criterion for judging the utility of cases is to consider the modification costs of the corresponding solutions. Unfortunately, it is usually impossible to determine this measure without processing the modification (Paulokat et al., 1992; Smyth & Keane, 1993). Domain-dependent heuristics and domain-independent structural methods (like footprinting (Veloso & Carbonell, 1991)) have been developed to overcome this

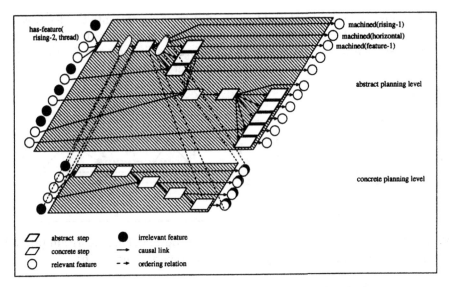

**Fig. 7.** Interactions from a nonlinear hierarchical plan

problem. CAPLAN/CBC combines both approaches by performing its retrieval phase in two steps:

1. A domain-dependent pre-selection using physical constraints and domain knowledge to obtain a small subset of cases, discarting most of the cases in the case base.
2. A domain-independent selection step using a footprint-like similarity measure (Veloso & Carbonell, 1991) which computes structural information about previous generated plans and known problem descriptions (cf. section 4.1).

Given a CAD representation of a new workpiece (Fig. 1) the atomic and the complex processing areas (Fig. 2) are determined. In the next step the hierarchical representation of the planning problem (Fig. 3) and the set of initial goals and their ordering relations (Fig. 4) are computed. The initial goals and ordering relations represent a set of domain dependent technical constraints which must be satisfied by any case, e.g. the groove represented by feature-2 in Fig. 2 can only be processed after the processing areas of cylinder-1 and of the complex processing area rising-1 have been processed.

In the current implementation, case retrieval in CAPLAN/CBC is made by comparing the hierarchical description (Fig. 3) of a new problem with the problem description of stored cases (cf. Déjà Vu (Smyth & Cunningham, 1992)). Using the tree-based problem representation the case match is made by a tree matching algorithm (Tanaka & Tanaka, 1988). The similarity measure is computed as the weighted sum of all adding and deleting operations necessary for transforming the hierarchical problem description of the case into the description of the current problem. Every transformation step is associated with domain-specific costs which are comparable to the effort that is necessary for the modification of the corresponding solutions (Humm et al., 1991).

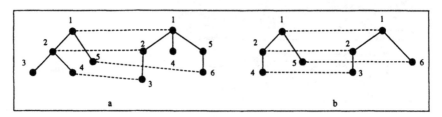

**Fig. 8.** Mapping representations using a structural matching algorithm (a) and generating a reusable solution by deleting the respective nodes (b)

The distance between the case and the problem description is measured as follows: First, a *structure preserving match* (Tanaka & Tanaka, 1988) between the hierarchical structures of the workpieces is computed (Fig. 8a). Second, the difference between the two representations is calculated, i.e. the nodes that were not matched and the nodes that were matched, but are of different type (for example a geometrical primitive of type torroid is matched with one of type cylinder) are counted (Fig. 8b). During this calculation different domain specific weights according to the type of the nodes are processed, since it is easier to replace an atomic processing area than a complex processing area e.g. counting a node which represents a primitive area has a smaller value than counting one which represents a complex processing area. A case qualifies for solving a new problem if the computed transformation costs are smaller than a given threshold.

To determine the relevance of features (Janetzko, Wess, & Melis, 1993) we compare the problem description with the annotated problem description (cf. section 4.1) of the case to determine in detail how many relevant features they have in common. This step corresponds to footprinting in PRODIGY/ANALOGY (Veloso & Carbonell, 1991). Concretely, the groups of features in the annotated problem description of the case that are completely included in the description of the current problem are determined. The relevance of these features is defined as the number of features that are entirely included in the problem description.

## 4.3 Case Replay

Although CAPLAN can autonomously solve problems by depth-first search, it is mainly intended as a planning assistant that provides a control interface for a human planner or external control components, such as CAPLAN/CBC. The input for the case-based control component consists of the problem description of a new planning problem, the case selected (cf. section 4.2) and an association between goals of the new planning problem and initial goals of the plan canned by the case. The associations are computed by tree matching of the retrieval phase. For solving a new problem, the decisions and their rationals of a case are used to choose from the set of alternative planning steps to satisfy a goal or to choose from the set of alternative constraints that can be added to resolve a threat of a causal link. This replaying of a decision of the case is done in four steps. First, the planner computes the set of alternative plan steps or conflict solving constraints that can be applied to the goal or to the conflict currently being worked on. In the second step a match of the alternative chosen by the decision of the case with the possible alternatives of the new problem is made. If there is a successful match, the decision's rationals are verified in the context of the new problem. Third, if the rationals are satisfied the step is chosen and the decision for choosing this alternative is provided with the verified rationals of the case. And fourth, the new subgoals resulting from the step chosen are matched against the subgoals resulting from the replayed decision. By every successful match a new association between a goal of the new planning problem and a goal of the case is generated. As soon as CAPLAN/CBC continues replaying for one of the prematched subgoals the associations to the case are already available, enabling the system to repeat the four steps described above.

Planning for goals that cannot be matched to a goal of the case are delayed until the replay process is completed. The remaining goals are solved by first-principle planning or possibly by user interactions. Because replaying a case and planning by first-principles results in the same representation of a plan, all planning decisions made during case replay can be rejected if they don't allow a completion of a partial plan. The separation of the replay phase from solving unmatched goals is possible because of the partially ordered plan representation and the nonlinear planning paradigm. The first point is in contrast to PRODIGY/ANALOGY where a total-order planner is used which makes necessary interleaving of case replay and first-principle planning for unmatched goals.

## 5 Conclusions

We have described the hybrid planning architecture CAPLAN and its application in a process planning domain. A main characteristic of this domain is that planning is driven by minimizing plan execution costs. Human planning experts in this domain use a large number of heuristics and domain specific reasoning. Since this knowledge is extremely case sensitive its usage is not sufficiently supported by known planning techniques.

In our approach a general purpose planning system, CAPLAN, is combined with a case-driven control unit CAPLAN/CBC which allows to use previous experience in form of recorded cases to guide the problem solving process. If there exists a case which is useful to solve the current problem, its decisions are replayed (Veloso, 1992) in the current context, i.e., a planning decision of the case is only reused if its rationals are compatible with the problem description of the new problem. Thus, our approach is very similar to the work of Veloso (Veloso, 1992), but there are some important differences. First, planning in CAPLAN is based on the ideas of partial-order planning (SNLP (McAllester & Rosenblitt, 1991)), so the underlying planning architecture is different. Second, retrieval of useful cases in CAPLAN is realized as a combination of domain-independent and domain-dependent techniques which constrain the number of cases that have to be inspected during the retrieval phase. The annotated problem description is an extension of the concepts of footprinting (Veloso & Carbonell, 1991) and of interacting goals in PRODIGY. This extension is necessary due to the hierarchical representation of plans in CAPLAN. Third, the overall architecture of the system combines specialized domain dependent reasoners and a feature-based CAD system with general purpose planning (Kambhampati et al., 1991).

Contrary to other well-known case-based planning systems such as CHEF (Hammond, 1986), CAPLAN uses (like PRODIGY) an explicit domain model to describe the plan steps and the constraints that must be satisfied during the retrieval and adaptation phase. The use of domain specific knowledge and techniques for the retrieval of useful cases by calculating a *measure of adaptability* in CAPLAN is similar to the *adaptation guided retrieval* approach in Déjà Vu (Smyth & Keane, 1993).

## Acknowledgements

The authors want to thank Michael M. Richter, Charles Petrie, Manuela Veloso and Frank Weberskirch for their contributions as well as Ralph Bergmann and the reviewers for helpful comments on earlier versions of this paper.

## References

Barrett, A., & Weld, D. S. (1993). Partial-order planning. *Artificial Intelligence*, 67.

Borrajo, D., & Veloso, M. (1994). Incremental learning of control knowledge for nonlinear problem solving. In *Proceedings of the European Conference on Machine Learning*.

Chapman, D. (1987). Planning for Conjunctive Goals. *Artificial Intelligence*, 32, 333–377.

Cheung, Y., & Dowd, A. L. (1988). Artifical intelligence in process planning. *Computer Aided Engineering*, 5(4), 153–156.

Hammond, K. J. (1986). *Case-Based Planning: An Integrated Theory of Planning, Learning and Memory*. Ph.D. thesis, Yale University, New Haven, Connecticut.

Humm, B., Schulz, C., Radtke, M., & Warnecke, G. (1991). A System for Case-Based Process Planning. In *Proceedings of the 1st CIRP Workshop on Learning in Intelligent Manufacturing Systems (IMS)*. CIRP. Budapest, Hungary.

Janetzko, D., Wess, S., & Melis, E. (1993). Goal-Driven Similarity Assessment. In Ohlbach, H.-J. (Ed.), *GWAI-92: Advances in Artificial Intelligence*, pp. 283–298, Springer Verlag.

Kambhampati, S., Cutkosky, M., Tenenbaum, M., & Lee, S. H. (1991). Combining specialized reasoners and general purpose planners: A case study. In *Proceedings of AAAI-91*, Menlo Park, California. MIT Press.

McAllester, D., & Rosenblitt, D. (1991). Systematic nonlinear planning. In *Proceedings of AAAI-91*, Menlo Park, California. MIT Press.

Minton, S. (1988). *Learning Search Control Knowledge — An Explanation-Based Approach*. Kluwer Academic Publishers.

Optiz, H. (1970). *A Classification System to Describe Work Pieces*. Pergamon Press, Elmsford, N.Y.

Paulokat, J., Praeger, R., & Wess, S. (1992). CABPLAN – fallbasierte Arbeitsplanung. In Messer, T., & Winklhofer, A. (Eds.), *Beiträge zum 6. Workshop Planen und Konfigurieren*, in FR-1992-001, pp. 166-169, Forwiss, Germany.

Paulokat, J., & Wess, S. (1994). Planning for machining workpieces with a partial-order, nonlinear planner. In Gil, C., & Veloso, M. (Eds.), *AAAI-Working Notes "Planning and Learning: On To Real Applications"* New Orleans.

Pérez, M. A., & Carbonell, J. (1993). Automated acquisition of control knowledge to improve the quality of plans. Tech. rep. CMU-CS-93-142, School of Computer Science, Carnegie Mellon University, Pittsburgh, PA 15213.

Smyth, B., & Cunningham, P. (1992). Déjà Vu: A hierarchical case-based reasoning system for software design. In Neumann, B. (Ed.), *ECAI-92*, pp. 587-589.

Smyth, B., & Keane, M. T. (1993). Retrieving adaptable cases: The role of adaptation knowledge in case retrieval. In Richter, M., Wess, S., Althoff, K., & Maurer, F. (Eds.), *Proceedings of the First European Workshop on Case-Based Reasoning*, pp. 76-82.

Tanaka, E., & Tanaka, K. (1988). The tree-to-tree editing problem. *International Journal of Pattern Recognition and Artificial Intelligence, 2*.

Veloso, M., & Carbonell, J. (1991). Variable-Precision Case-Retrieval in Analogical Problem Solving. In Bareiss, R. (Ed.), *Proceedings of the Case-Based Reasoning Workshop*, pp. 93-106. Morgan Kaufmann Publishers.

Veloso, M. (1992). *Learning by Analogical Reasoning in General Problem Solving*. Phd thesis CMU-CS-92-174, School of Computer Science, Carnegie Mellon University, Pittsburgh, PA 15213.

Zhang, K. F., Wright, A. J., & Davies, B. J. (1988). A feature-recognition knowledge base for process planning of rotational mechanical components. *International Journal of Adv. Manufacturing Technology, 4*, 13-25.

# A Classification System for Credit Card Transactions

Eliseo B. Reategui and John Campbell

Department of Computer Science
University College London
Gower St., London WC1E 6BT, UK
(e-mail: reategui, jac@cs.ucl.ac.uk)

**Abstract.** This paper describes a system that responds to a significant problem involving credit card theft. After a card has been stolen, some of the transactions processed subsequently have to be granted if it seems that they were carried out by the card owner himself (e.g. by a standing order) while other transactions should be denied authorisation if they were carried out by the misuser of the card. The system developed makes use of a neural network integrated with a Case-Based Reasoning (CBR) component. While the CBR system can use specific cases to determine when a transaction should be granted or denied authorization, the neural network can recognise general patterns of behaviour for the use and the misuse of credit cards and can use this knowledge in the classification task. This paper presents the architecture of the classification system proposed, highlighting the main aspects of each of its components. The system's performance is evaluated and conclusions are drawn.

## 1  Introduction

One of the major problems related to credit card theft is that some transactions which appear after the theft nevertheless have to be accepted and payed for by the credit card companies, as they were carried out by the credit card owner and not by a thief. The credit card companies do not have an efficient way of discriminating between these transactions and fraudulent ones, leading to the loss of large amounts of money every year.

A hybrid architecture integrating a Case-Based Reasoning system (CBR) with a Neural Network (NN) has been devised to solve this problem. The CBR system keeps track of all the transactions carried out with a particular card after the reported theft. When a new transaction appears, the CBR system looks for best matches in the set of previous transactions. The neural network learns general patterns of use and misuse of credit cards through the analysis of old cases, and uses this knowledge to decide when to grant or deny authorization to transactions.

When CBR has been used along with other kinds of knowledge intensive processing, it has been combined mostly with symbolic reasoning mechanisms, as in Lenz (1993), Zeleznikow, Hunter & Vossos (1993) and Skalak (1989). In the latter, four different ways of integrating CBR with rule-based systems have been identified . However, these four approaches can be generalized to describe mixed paradigms for integrating CBR with any other reasoning mechanism:

- Central Control: the CBR and one other reasoning mechanism are controlled by a central device which requests services from one or both of the mechanisms and uses their answers to determine a final result.

- Distributed Control: the control between the two reasoning mechanisms is dispersed between them.

- CBR dominant: the CBR component has the control of the reasoning process and uses the other reasoning mechanism as a support.

- CBR non-dominant: the control of the reasoning process is not held by the CBR component but by the other reasoning mechanism.

The *Central Control* model, being the simplest way to tackle a genuinely hybrid computation, was the model chosen for the new application. We have used such a model to integrate a neural network with a CBR system, direct the reasoning process and supervise the compatibility of answers given by the two reasoning mechanisms. Besides generating a system for the new application, this research should also lead us to some conclusions on how specific knowledge (in the form of cases) and more general bodies of knowledge (in the form of neural networks) can be combined in reasoning.

This paper is organized as follows. The next section presents the basic architecture of our system, detailing each of its components. Section 3 presents validation results obtained from the testing of the system against a set of real cases. The last section gives some final conclusions, compares the system with related research efforts and proposes topics for further development.

## 2  The System Architecture

The system designed to solve the credit card problem consists of 5 main components, as depicted in figure 1.

The next subsections present each component and explain the way in which they interact.

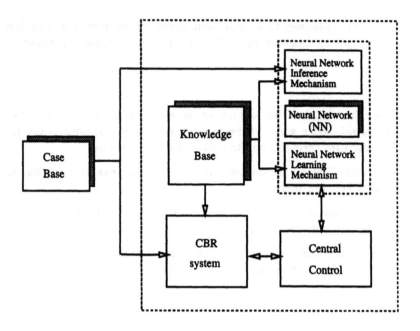

**Fig. 1.** The system architecture

## 2.1 The Case Base

A case is seen here as a collection of transactions for a particular account. The role of the *Case Base* is therefore to provide the cases for the *CBR system* and for the training of the *Neural Network*.

All the transactions that happened after the reported theft in addition to a few transactions that happened before the theft are kept for each case of credit card theft. A typical transaction record is presented in figure 2.

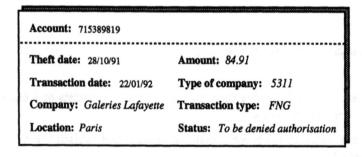

**Fig. 2.** A typical record for a credit card transaction

The field credit card *Account* contains the number of the account of the stolen card, and *Theft Date* refers to the date on which the credit card was stolen. The meaning of the next 3 fields are self-evident. The field *Type of Company* refers to categories in which companies are classified, e.g. supermarkets, restaurants, petrol stations, etc. In the example given in figure 2, the code *5311* refers to department stores. The field *Amount* shows the amount in sterling to be debited in that credit card account. The field *Transaction Type* contains a 3 digit code which breaks down the transactions into categories describing such things as whether the transaction was carried out in Britain or abroad and whether the purchase was for consumables or non-consumables. The field *Status* refers to one of the two categories in which a transaction can be classified, i.e. *to be granted* or *to be denied authorization.*

## 2.2 The Knowledge Base

The *Knowledge Base* stores all the domain knowledge used to process the data coming from the outside world and transform it into appropriate input to the *CBR system* and the *Neural Network*.

The domain knowledge permits representation in an hierarchical frame scheme which makes use of the 4 basic abstraction concepts: generalization, classification, association and aggregation (Hull & King, 1987). Figure 3 presents three excerpts of the frame hierarchy for the credit card system depicting the use of the abstraction concepts.

Besides providing flexible constructs to model the domain knowledge, the abstraction concepts can offer additional pieces of evidence for the inference mechanism. For example:

- the set of transactions called *Company Categories* has been defined in order to inter-relate different *Company types*. For example, the *Company Types*: *Children clothes*, *Men clothes* and *Sports Clothes* can be associated in a group called *Clothing*. Therefore, transactions carried out in companies with different types, which belong to the same category, present a good degree of similarity.
- the aggregation *Country* is composed of counties, which are composed of cities, etc. Transactions carried out in different locations, but in the same city have a good similarity degree, while transactions in different countries, for instance, present a much lower similarity degree.

The *Knowledge Base* is also responsible for storing a symbolic representation of the knowledge present in the neural network (Reategui & Leão, 1993), which is particularly useful when an explanation for the final results has to be provided.

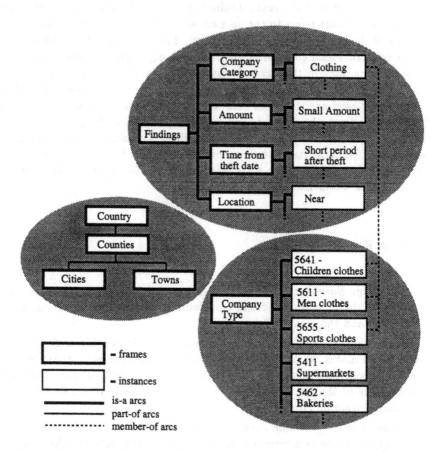

**Fig. 3.** Examples of the use of the abstraction concepts in the frame hierarchy

## 2.3 The Neural Network

We have used the Combinatorial Neural Model (CNM) (Machado, 1989) as our choice of neural network. This neural network was inspired in experts' knowledge graphs described as minimal directed AND/OR acyclic graphs representing the knowledge of an expert for a specific diagnostic hypothesis (Machado, Rocha, & Leão, 1990). This model has been combined successfully with other symbolic approaches to solve problems in the fields of renal syndromes (Machado & Rocha, 1992) and cardiology (Leão & Reategui, 1993). Figure 4 depicts the basic structure of the CNM.

The neural network has a feedforward topology with three layers. The input layer is formed by fuzzy-number cells. These fuzzy numbers (values in the interval [0,1]) represent the degree of confidence the user has in the information that is observed and inserted into the neural network. Cells in different layers are linked by connections with an associated weight which represents the influence

Diagnostic Hypothesis

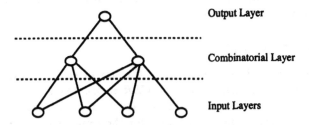

Output Layer

Combinatorial Layer

Input Layers

**Fig. 4.** Basic structure of the Combinatorial Neural Model

of lower layer cells on the output of upper layer cells. The connections of the input layer can be either excitatory or inhibitory. An excitatory connection propagates the arriving signal using its weight as an attenuating factor. An inhibitory connection perform the fuzzy negation on the arriving signal X, transforming it to 1-X. The combinatorial layers are formed by hidden fuzzy AND-cells. They associate different input cells in intermediate chunks of knowledge which are relevant in the classification process. The output layer is formed by fuzzy OR-cells. They implement a competitive mechanism between the different pathways that reach the diagnostic hypothesis. Figure 5 shows the activation functions at the combinatorial and output layers.

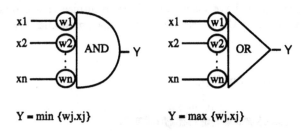

$$Y = \min \{wj.xj\} \qquad Y = \max \{wj.xj\}$$

**Fig. 5.** The activation functions of the CNM

The CNM network uses a punishment and reward learning algorithm, based on the algorithm of backpropagation (Rumelhart, Hinton, & McClelland, 1986), to adjust its connection weights. After the learning period, the *Neural Network* is able to recognize, for instance, that *donations* or *magazine subscriptions* are usually classified with the status *to be granted*, and transactions envoluing large amounts of money are usually classified with the status *to be denied authorization*. The *Neural Network* therefore stores general knowledge about use and misuse of credit cards. The *CBR system* is left with the task of learning how each customer used his or her credit card, and detecting discrepancies in their habitual way of using their cards.

## 2.4   The CBR system

The idea behind CBR is to emphasize the use of concrete case instances in problem-solving (Kolodner, 1993). The *CBR system* takes the transactions carried out with a particular credit card as a source of knowledge to be used in the classification of subsequent transactions for the same card. When classifying a new transaction, the *CBR system* assumes that if there is an old transaction that matches the new one with a good similarity degree, they must both be classified in the same way.

As the number of transactions for each case of credit card theft is not too large, the transactions for each case can be kept in the *Case Base* in a flat structure. Thus, a best match for an incoming transaction can be found by searching serially the set of transactions stored for that same case of card theft. The *CBR system* determines the degree of match between two attributes by measuring the distance between them in a qualitative scale. When the values are within the same qualitative region, they present a good degree of match. For instance, if the interval *Small* for the attribute *Amount of Money* were defined as [0,18], the values *12.00* and *16.00* would be considered small, and therefore would match perfectly. However, having fixed boundaries for the intervals can represent a problem. For example, if the next interval *Average* were defined as [19,50], there would be no similarity between the amounts 18 and 19, while the amounts 19 and 20 would match perfectly. Fuzzy overlapping boundaries for each qualitative region have been defined to minimise this problem. Figure 6 depicts the definition of the overlapping intervals *Small* and *Average*.

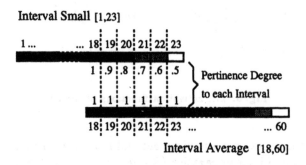

**Fig. 6.** Example of fuzzy overlapping intervals

The *CBR system* also takes into account how important an item of evidence is in the classification process when calculating the degree of match between attributes. For example, the attribute *Location* is more important than the attribute *Company Type*, as *Location* might give the reasoner a better indication of whether the owner or the thief used the credit card for a particular transaction. The importance of each attribute was determined through the analysis of the human specialists' strategy to classify transactions. The similatity between two transactions is thus computed through the formula:

$$Similarity(T_a, T_b) = \sum_{i=1}^{n} (Importance(At_i) \times Match(Val_a(At_i), Val_b(At_i)))$$

where $T_a$ and $T_b$ are the transactions being compared, $n$ is the number of attributes defined for a transaction, $At_i$ is the $ith$ attribute, $Val_a(At_i)$ is the value of the attribute $At_i$ for transaction $T_a$, $Val_b(At_i)$ is the value of attribute $At_i$ for the transaction $T_b$, $Importance(At_i)$ returns the importance of the attribute $At_i$ and $Match(Val_a(At_i), Val_b(At_i))$ returns the degree of match between the values of the two attributes.

## 2.5 The Central Control

The role of the *Central Control* is to request services from the *Neural Network* and the *CBR system* and to mediate their answers. The main steps followed by the *Central Control* algorithm are described below:

1. Verify the *number of previous transactions* existing in the *Case Base* for the same account to which the incoming transaction belongs.
2. If the *number of previous transactions* < *minimum number of cases*[1]
   - Activate the NN for the incoming transaction;
   - Give the answer provided by the NN as a final answer;
   - Store the transaction in the *Case Base* with the appropriate classification result.
3. If the *number of previous transactions* >= *minimum number of cases*
   - Activate both the *CBR system* and the NN for the coming transaction;
   - If the answers coming from the *CBR system* and the NN are the same, give them as a final answer;
   - If the answers are different, the final answer should be the one carrying the higher confidence factor:

   $$Final = Max(\alpha \times CBR_{confidence-factor}, NN_{confidence-factor})$$

   where $CBR_{confidence-factor}$ represents the highest degree of similarity computed in the CBR matching process, $\alpha$ represents a constant used to normalize the value of the result provided by the *CBR system* in relation to that provided by the *Neural Network*, and $NN_{confidence-factor}$ represents the output of the *Neural Network*.

---

[1] The parameter *minimum number of cases* has been set to several different values, the best performance being achieved when the parameter was set to numbers in the interval [5,9] (7 plus or minus two (Miller, 1956))

At this stage, the *CBR system* is given priority by assigning a higher value to the constant $\alpha$, as we believe that the use of specific knowledge can be more accurate than that of general knowledge.

The *Central Control* also keeps track of the incompatibilities between the answers given by the *CBR system* and the *Neural Network*. It is assumed that if some misclassification is carried out at an early stage for a particular case of credit card theft, all the reasoning performed by the *CBR system* up to that point will have been based on wrong premises. Hence, when the number of incompatibilities between the two systems is detected to be too high, all the answers given by the *CBR system* are re-evaluated. In the re-evaluation, however, priority is given to the answers provided by the *Neural Network* by decreasing the value of the constant $\alpha$. This mechanism has proved to be useful in correcting misclassified transactions and adjusting the performance of the *CBR system*.

# 3   Validation

The prototype of the system to control credit card transactions has been implemented in Common Lisp. A total number of 54 findings was described in the *Knowledge Base* for the 2 possible diagnoses (i.e. *to be granted* and *to be denied authorization*). A major British bank provided a database with 172 cases of credit card theft, each case containing an average of 18 transactions, totalising 3237 transactions. Half of the total number of cases was used to train the neural network, and the other half was used to test the system. Table 1 presents the test results for the hybrid CBR x NN system.

Table 1 Test results of the Hybrid CBR x NN system

|  | To be Granted | | To be Denied Authorisation | | Total | |
| --- | --- | --- | --- | --- | --- | --- |
|  | Num. trans. | % | Num. trans. | % | Num. trans. | % |
| Correctly Classified | 64 | 50.4 | 1366 | 92.3 | 1430 | 89.0 |
| Incorrectly Classified | 41 | 32.3 | 44 | 3.0 | 85 | 5.3 |
| Not concluded | 22 | 17.3 | 69 | 4.7 | 91 | 5.7 |
| Total | 127 | 100.0 | 1479 | 100.0 | 1606 | 100.0 |

The general performance of the system was considered to be satisfactory, especially because human specialists (who are not highly trained) are expected to produce a 90% level of performance.

The *Neural Network* and the *CBR system* were also tested separately. The *Neural Network* gave a performance very close to that of the hybrid CBR x NN system (90.0% correct classifications and 7.7% misclassifications). However, the latter still demonstrated more accuracy, presenting a lower number of misclassifications for both *to be granted* and *to be denied authorization* transactions. The *CBR system* presented the lowest number of misclassifications when the answers provided by the system were immediately corrected before storing them in the *Case Base* (2.6% misclassifications). However, when the answers given by the system were not corrected before entering the transactions in the *Case Base* (a more realistic situation), the performance fell off considerably (7.5% misclassifications and 10.5% of not-concluded answers). The number of not-concluded answers was also high because an initial set of correctly classified transactions had to be inserted in the *Case Base* for each case of theft. In the CBR x NN integrated system, this first set of classifications is obtained from the neural network.

# 4 Conclusions

The use of neural networks as an important reasoning mechanism in CBR has been introduced in other papers (Myllymaki & Tirri, 1993; Becker & Jasayeri, 1989; Thrift, 1989), where the neural networks are used mainly for case matching and retrieval tasks. However, the approach presented here is somewhat different in that it proposes a way of using neural networks as a source of general knowledge and a CBR system as a way of using specific instances of cases in problem-solving.

Our tests have shown that the performance of the neural network and that of the CBR system are very close, regarding the number of correct classifications. However, other advantages have been introduced by the combination of the two reasoning mechanisms. For our application, by having the two reasoning components working side by side, we could simulate the behaviour of humans performing the same classification task. When the first transactions for a particular case of credit card theft appear, the human expert can only exploit general knowledge about use and misuse of credit cards to classify this first set of transactions. However, after a certain number of transactions, the observer can start using more specific knowledge related to that particular case; that is to say, the instances of transactions carried out with the same card. The prototype described here behaves similarly, leaving the first set of transactions to be classified by the neural networks and only later activating the CBR system. Furthermore, the use of a CBR component enables the system to retrieve previous transactions that can help the user to understand why a new transaction was granted or denied authorization.

For future developments, other neural network models could be tested in the same domain and evaluated in terms of performance and use of resources, such as processing time and memory. The CBR system could also reduce the amount of main memory used by minimalizing the number of transactions kept for each case. It could maintain only the transactions "worth remembering", i.e. the ones that could lead to correct conclusions more accurately. The transactions leading to misclassifications could also be eliminated from the *Case Base*, or from the CBR matching process.

## Acknowledgements

Eliseo B. Reategui is sponsored by CNPq (Conselho Nacional de Desenvolvimento Científico e Tecnológico), Brazil; grant number 200-414 93-3.

# References

Becker, L., & Jazayeri, K. (1989). A connectionist approach to case-based reasoning. In Hammond, K. J. (Ed.), *Proceedings of the Case-Based Reasoning Workshop*, pp. 213–217 Pensacola Beach, Florida. Morgan Kaufmann.

Hull, R., & King, R. (1987). Semantic database modeling: survey, applications, and research issues. *ACM Computing Surveys, 19*, 201–260.

Kolodner, J. (1993). *Case-Based Reasoning*. Morgan Kaufmann, San Mateo, CA.

Leão, B. F., & Reategui, E. B. (1993). A hybrid connectionist expert system to solve classificational problems. In *Proceedings of Computers in Cardiology* London, UK.

Lenz, M. (1993). Cabata - a hybrid cbr system. In Althoff, K.-D., Richter, K., & Wess, S. (Eds.), *Proceedings of the First European Workshop on Case-Based Reasoning*, pp. 204–209 Kaiserslautern.

Machado, R. J. (1989). *Handling knowledge in high order neural networks: the combinatorial neural model*. IBM Rio Scientific Center (technical Report CCR076).

Machado, R. J., & Rocha, A. F. (1992). A hybrid architecture for fuzzy connectionist expert systems. In Kandel, A., & Langholz, G. (Eds.), *Hybrid architectures for intelligent systems*, pp. 135–152. CRC Press, Boca Raton.

Machado, R. J., Rocha, A. F., & Leão, B. F. (1990). Calculating the mean knowledge representation from multiple experts. In Fedrezzi, M., & Kacprzkyk, J. (Eds.), *Multiperson decision making models using fuzzy sets and possibility theory*, pp. 113–127. Kluwer Academic Publishers, Amsterdam.

Miller, G. A. (1956). The magical number 7, plus or minus 2: Some limits on our capacity for processing information. *Psychology Review, 63*, 81–97.

Myllymaki, P., & Tirri, H. (1993). Massively parallel case-based reasoning with probabilistic similarity metrics. In Althoff, K.-D., Richter, K., & Wess, S. (Eds.), *Proceedings of the First European Workshop on Case-Based Reasoning*, pp. 48–53 Kaiserslautern.

Reategui, E. B., & Leão, B. F. (1993). Integrating neural networks with the formalism of frames. In Grossberg, S. (Ed.), *Proceedings of the World*

*Congress on Neural Networks* Portland, Oregon. Lawrence Erlbaum Associates.

Rumelhart, D. E., Hinton, G. E., & McClelland, J. L. (1986). Learning internal representations by error propagation. In Rumelhart, D. E., McClelland, J. L., & Group, T. P. R. (Eds.), *Parallel Distributed Processing: explorations in the microstructures of cognition*, Vol. 1. MIT Press, Cambridge, MA.

Skalak, D. B. (1989). Options for controlling mixed paradigm systems. In Hammond, K. J. (Ed.), *Proceedings of the Case-Based Reasoning Workshop*, pp. 318–323 Pensacola Beach, Florida. DARPA, Morgan Kaufmann.

Thrift, P. (1989). A neural network model for case-based reasoning. In Hammond, K. J. (Ed.), *Proceedings of the Case-Based Reasoning Workshop*, pp. 334–337 Pensacola Beach, Florida. DARPA, Morgan Kaufmann.

Zeleznikow, J., Hunter, D., & Vossos, G. (1993). Integrating rule-based and case-based reasoning with information retrieval: the ikbals project. In Althoff, K.-D., Richter, K., & Wess, S. (Eds.), *Proceedings of the First European Workshop on Case-Based Reasoning*, pp. 341–346 Kaiserslautern.

# Use of Case-Based Reasoning in the Domain of Building Regulations

Soon-Ae Yang[1], Dave Robertson[1], John Lee[2]

[1] Dept of Artificial Intelligence, University of Edinburgh,
80 South Bridge, Edinburgh EH1 1HN, UK
[2] EdCAAD and Human Communication Research Centre,
Dept of Architecture, University of Edinburgh,
20 Chambers Street, Edinburgh EH1 1JZ, UK

**Abstract.** In traditional legal decision support systems, it has been regarded as natural to represent statutes in terms of decision rules and to link these to a separate case-based reasoning system for handling precedent. Statutory legal rules used in these systems are formal and prescriptive. Building regulations in Scotland are part of statute law and constitute part of a legal system together with case histories. In recent years, the regulations have been becoming less prescriptive and more emphasis has been put onto the interpretive use of the regulations. In developing a system which can assist domain experts in interpreting the regulations, this trend has presented us with difficulties in employing this traditional approach and has led us to a unified case-based model of the regulations and case histories. In this paper, we first describe the characteristics of the regulations and the activities involved in this domain. Second, we explain the reason why we abandoned the traditional approach. Third, we describe the system which has been developed using this case-based model.

## 1 Introduction

Legal and regulatory reasoning is one of the AI application domains where substantial amounts of research have been done over the last twenty years [7]. The law contains "legal rules", which state what should be done in certain circumstances in the context of a legal system. Most of these are expressed in the form of statutes and cases. Building regulations in Scotland are part of statute law and constitute part of a legal system together with case histories.

Since it is normal to view statutory regulations as "legal rules", it is also natural to expect these to be most easily expressed formally in terms of decision rules (perhaps in some propositional language). However, it is becoming increasingly common to make the regulations less prescriptive, with the text of the regulations merely providing a general framework within which the interpretation of the regulations is established through precedent. In these types of system the legal rules do not in themselves allow any decision to be made. Much greater importance is attached to the means by which precedent is accessed and interpreted. A good example of this approach is found in the building regulations of the Scottish Office. These will be used throughout this paper as a concrete example of the more general application.

## 2 The Domain of Building Regulations

The Building Directorate of The Scottish Office is responsible for the drafting and maintenance of building regulations—the Building Standards (Scotland) Regulations 1981 [9]—which set out the statutory requirements affecting building design and construction in Scotland. The Building Directorate is also responsible for the administration of the appeals procedures under the building control system in Scotland.

Building regulations have the generic objectives of safeguarding public health and safety and of conserving energy in the built environment. These objectives express government policy and the principles which bring building regulations into existence. These issues or principles are translated into more detailed issues in the sixteen subject areas: adequate ventilation, drainage and sanitary convenience to ensure the health of people, fitness of materials for durability to ensure the safety of people, structural stability in case of fire to ensure the safety of people, adequate means of escape from fire to ensure the safety of people in case of fire, safe means of passage, etc. These issues or requirements are very general and expressions are highly abstract. The bounds of applicability of this requirement are, intentionally, left unclear at this point. These requirements can be met by compliance with the relevant regulations and provisions set out in the Building Standards (Scotland) Regulations. Requirements stated in these relevant regulations and provisions are a refinement of more general and abstract requirements described above and can be regarded as the description of how those requirements should be interpreted. For example, Regulation D7 (see Fig. 1) requires that building components be constructed of non-combustible materials to maintain structural stability in case of fire.

Requirements are specified only for certain aspects or features of buildings that are related to a particular generic objectives. Other aspects or features unrelated to this particular generic objective are disregarded. In the example in Fig. 1, requirements to achieve structural stability specify only non-combustibility of materials used for particular building components such as compartment floor, floor of any landing or passage within a stairway enclosure and stair within a stairway enclosure. Other factors, for example the thermal transmittance value of materials and the shape and position of stairs are regarded as irrelevant in the subject of structural stability. These requirements do not always apply to every possible building category and different requirements are sometimes specified for different building categories. For example, as shown in Fig. 1, "the floor of any landing or passage within a stairway enclosure" in "a house in occupancy subgroup A2, not being a flat, not more than three storeys in height" does not need to be constructed of non-combustible materials. Cases are also described in the same manner. They do not provide a design of a whole building but provide only the description of aspects or features of a building related to a particular subject area in question.

**D7 Requirements as to non-combustibility**
Every part of a building specified in column (1) of the following table shall be constructed of non-combustible materials, subject to the exceptions if any specified in relation thereto in column (2): ···

| Table to Regulation D7 | |
| --- | --- |
| Requirements as to non-combustibility | |
| Parts of a building required to be constructed of non-combustible materials (1) | Exceptions (2) |
| Compartment floor | |
| Floor of any landing or passage within a stairway enclosure provided so as to comply with Regulation E10 | The floor of any landing or passage within the stairway enclosure of a stair in a house in occupancy subgroup A2, not being a flat, not more than three storeys in height |
| ⋮ | ⋮ |
| stair within a stairway enclosure provided so as to comply with regulation E10 or unenclosed external stairway referred to in regulation E10(1) | 1. Any handrail on such a stair 2. Any stair in a house in ··· |
| ⋮ | ⋮ |

**Fig. 1.** Regulation D7

The relevancy between issues and requirements, which plays a central role in interpretation of the document, is sometimes clearly expressed in the document but in some cases may rely on experts' experience in applying requirements to particular problems.

The interpretation of written requirements also changes through time. At the time of legislation, it is impossible to anticipate all possible circumstances in which a case may arise after legislation. New legal rules are set out in unexpected circumstances or slightly different circumstances and existing legal rules may be relaxed in exceptional circumstances. If it is unreasonable for specific requirements to be applied and these requirements can be met in a less onerous way, existing requirements may be relaxed. In this sense, cases may set out new legal rules but legal rules set out in case histories may or may not apply to new cases. As legal rules from case histories accumulate, they are reviewed when revising statutory regulations. The rulings made in case histories may be generalised and included in the new version of regulations.

An application for relaxation of particular requirements is first submitted to the Local Building Control Authority and if there is disagreement about interpretation between the applicant and the Authority the appeals procedure follows. The argument surrounding each appeal decision is often complex, involving the balancing of a variety of assertions by the parties concerned. Experts make a decision after (if necessary) consulting all information relevant to the given case. In addition to statute and case histories relevant to the given case, experts should refer to all information available to provide justification for their decision within the legal system in which they work. This includes government policies, principles taken for granted in the given field of law, and other related law. It would be ideal to build a knowledge base which includes all this information but that would be too ambitious. The problem is therefore to support the consultation of these loosely expressed legal requirements without being forced to make explicit all the information needed to arrive at a decision.

We do not employ a rule-based approach in our system and employ a purely case-based approach for both statute and precedent. In the next section we explain the reasons why we avoided a rule-based approach.

## 3   Why Not a Traditional Legal Decision Support System in This Domain?

Legal rules are the basic unit of knowledge to be represented in the knowledge base. Legal rules are requirements, which describe a required design *solution* in certain *circumstances*. Given this description of legal rules, conventional if-then rules seem a natural choice for representing legal rules—for example, in the form:

if *circumstances* then *solution*

For example, Regulation D7 can be described in this form as shown below. For ease of understanding, *circumstances* and *requirements* are given not in computer-executable form but in approximate English.

if *the type of building is any and there is a stair in an enclosed stairway used as an exit*
then *the material used for the stair should be non-combustible*

Then some form of rule interpreter might be used to derive information from legal rules represented in the knowledge base. This approach has been taken in Waterman and Paterson's LDS [17], Sergot et al's representation of the British Nationality Act 1981 [10, 11] and Susskind's system [13]. The Scottish Office's Building Directorate has also experimented with this approach in their in-house prototype systems [12]. Legal rules used in these systems are formal and prescriptive. However, the regulations are becoming less prescriptive and more emphasis is put onto the interpretive use of the regulations. This presents us with several difficulties in employing a traditional decision support system approach.

**1.** Legal rules are described at different levels of detail.

In addition to legal rules which are prescriptive and state requirements at a very detailed level, such as Regulation D7, there are legal rules which are less prescriptive and which explain why these detailed requirements should be satisfied in the context of the legal system.

Legal rules are also independently described at various levels of detail. Legal rules at the upper level describe requirements using more abstract terms which have broader meaning. Terms like "safety in case of fire" and "adequate means" are used at this level. Then one or more legal rules are introduced to provide various ways of interpreting these abstract legal rules. Refined legal rules are described using more detailed and concrete terms. For example, what "safety in case of fire" means in the context of achieving "safety" is defined in terms of "structural stability", and then "storeys", "compartment walls", "compartment floors", and so forth. In other words, legal rules at lower levels are a refinement or specialisation or decomposition of legal rules at upper levels.

**2.** There exists a terminological gap between legal rules and cases.

Although appropriate rule structuring might overcome the problem of different levels of detail in statute, the language used in statutory regulations is generally at a more general level of description than that used in describing the objects (buildings) to which the rules apply. The description of the circumstances and required solutions in statutory regulations is the description of requirements generalised from many particular circumstances and solutions in these particular circumstances. Cases arise in one of those particular circumstances and propose one particular solution. For example, in cases, the type of building may be given as "flat" or "house", which are of type "dwelling", or instead of "rooflight" the term "window" may be used. It would be possible to bridge these terminological gaps by introducing domain-specific "bridging" rules, but it is not always possible reliably to bridge this terminological gap in this way, as we demonstrate below.

**3.** The meaning of terms is often in debate.

It is sometimes a matter of debate as to what the regulations mean by basic concepts. For example, does "floor area" include or exclude raised platforms? or is embankment "a place of safety"? This is one of the most common reasons for appealing against the regulations and seeking relaxation, and there are prolonged arguments as to the meaning of terms in the context of the given circumstances in many appeal cases provided by the Scottish Office's Building Directorate. Although it would be possible to encode in rules how these terms are interpreted in particular circumstances, there would remain the serious practical problem of maintaining consistency across the vast collection of these "bridging" rules, given that interpretation of the regulations constantly changes over time and there is always the possibility of conflicts between these bridging rules.

**4.** New legal rules are constantly emerging.

Even if the above theoretical and practical objectives could be addressed, we would still be left with the problem of accommodating new, unexpected or exceptional circumstances within the decision support system, for example if someone invented a new type of building material.

**5.** Legal rules are the generalisation of the rulings made in case histories.

One possible way of solving these problems (1-4) is to use the rule-based model for statutory regulations and to use the case-based model for case histories such as in CABARET [8], GREBE [1] and PROLEXS [16]. These systems assume that legal rules in statutes are open-textured and may (to a limited extent) conflict with each other but they are formal and fairly stable. The problems with open-texturedness and conflicting rules are compensated for by referring to cases.

But we take a different view of statutes and cases. Legal rules in the statutes are the result of accumulation and generalisation of the rulings made in case histories. A case must comply with legal rules in the statutes which are applicable. In this sense, legal rules in the statutes act as "strong" constraints on new cases. Cases provide a way of interpreting a particular set of legal rules in the statutes under particular circumstances, in other words more detailed legal rules than those in the statutes. There may be similar cases and it is possible to derive more generalised legal rules from those similar cases. The interpretation of legal rules in the statutes changes over time, legal rules set out in case histories may or may not apply to new cases. In this sense, legal rules set out in case histories act as "weak" constraints to new cases.

Once we view legal rules in this way (i.e. legal rules are generalised cases) legal rules from both statutes and cases can be represented using only a case-based model. In the system described in the next section, cases are kept in a separate case library, and legal rules, i.e. the generalised cases, are represented as *models*, "strong" models when a model represents legal rules from the statutory regulations and "weak" models when a model represents legal rules set out in a case. Interpretation hierarchies which exist among legal rules can be represented as abstraction hierarchies of models. Each case is relevant to a model or models and links between cases and models can be established using the notion of relevance. There are various matching algorithms which can be used to access models at various levels in the abstraction hierarchies. Models in the abstraction hierarchies are loosely connected to each other so that new legal rules can be added as "weak" models to the existing abstraction hierarchies even when new "weak" models are somehow inconsistent with the existing models.

A prototype system which can assist domain experts in the appeal process has been developed using this approach. The system does not make any decision about relaxation but is intended to provide the experts with relevant information, i.e. relevant legal rules and cases, so that they can arrive at an informed decision. The next section describes each component of the system briefly. [3]

---

[3] A more detailed description of the system can be found in [18].

# 4 The Overview of the System

There are three knowledge bases: the Model Knowledge Base, the Case Library and the Domain Knowledge Base. Legal rules are represented in the Model Knowledge Base. In addition to legal rules, background domain knowledge must be used to bridge terminological gaps between models at different levels of abstraction hierarchies and between models and cases in the retrieval and maintenance of legal rules. Cases and argumentation surrounding each case must be provided to the user. Argumentation surrounding each case is represented in the form of an argumentation network. Background domain knowledge is represented in the Domain Knowledge Base, and cases and argumentation surrounding each case are represented in the Case Library.

A case will be given as $C = (C_{id}, C_g, C_c, C_{cd}, C_{sd})$ where $C_{id}$ is the id number of the case, $C_g$ is the goal given in the case, $C_c$ is the category of the building, $C_{cd}$ is the circumstances description, and $C_{sd}$ is the proposed solution. Given a case $C$, the system first retrieves relevant models by comparing the $C_g$, $C_c$ and $C_{cd}$ of the given case with models in the MKB. Once relevant models are found, the $C_{sd}$ of the case is evaluated against the required solution of the retrieved model. The case is said to be *compliant* if the $C_{sd}$ satisfies the required solution of the retrieved strong models.

If the case is not compliant, there is a possibility of relaxation and the system will explain relevant information stored within the system: principles or issues behind the regulation with which the case is supposed to comply and previous similar cases. The system also checks whether there is conflict between the case and existing models and informs the expert. If the expert decides to grant relaxation, new rulings set out by the case will be integrated into the existing abstraction hierarchy by (if possible) combining new rulings with relevant weak models. The case itself will also be stored in the Case Library. The link between the case and the MKB is established at this point by storing the id numbers of relevant models with other information in the Case Library.

## 4.1 The Model Knowledge Base

Legal rules are represented as *models* and then an abstraction hierarchy is built for each generic objective. In each abstraction hierarchy, a model $M$ is represented as a set of six parts: $(M_{id}, M_{pid}, M_c, M_{cd}, M_{sd}, M_s)$ where $M_{id}$ is the id number of the model, $M_{pid}$ is the id number of the parent model in the abstraction hierarchy, $M_c$ is the category of buildings to which the model applies, $M_{cd}$ is the description of key features of circumstances to which the model applies, $M_{sd}$ is the description of required solutions, and $M_s$ is the strength, i.e. "strong" or "weak". The strength will be given as "strong" if the model is taken from statutory regulations, or as "weak" otherwise. $M_{cd}$ and $M_{sd}$ are described in terms of objects, their attributes and relations between objects. An example of a model is shown in Fig. 2.

Abstraction hierarchies of models are also shown in Fig. 2. The generic objectives are represented in M1–M4: all buildings should be built not to harm the

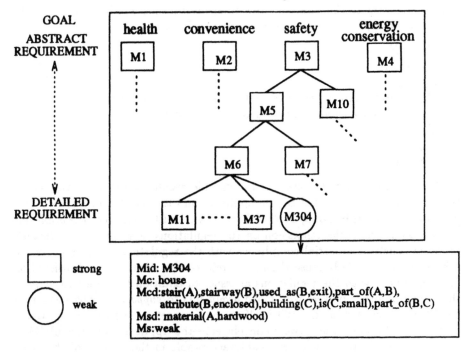

**Fig. 2.** Model Knowledge Base

health(M1) and to ensure convenience (M2) and the safety (M3) of people in and around buildings and the conservation of fuel and power (M4). M3 is interpreted as: all buildings should be built to ensure the safety of people in case of fire (M5) and to provide safe means of passage (M10) to achieve the safety of people. M5 again is interpreted as: structural stability should be maintained in case of fire (M6) and adequate means of escape from fire should be provided (M7). M11–M37 represent the detailed requirements to ensure structural stability in case of fire (M6) in terms of compartments, floors, stairs, walls, etc. M304 represents a ruling from a case, in which the stair of an enclosed stairway used as an exit was allowed to be constructed of hardwood. This ruling can be regarded as another interpretation of M6 and added to the MKB.

## 4.2 The Case Library and Argumentation Structure

The Case Library is a collection of cases processed by the system. In addition to an argumentation network, a case $C$ is represented as a set of eight parts: $C = (C_{id}, C_g, C_c, C_{cd}, C_{sd}, C_d, C_m, C_t)$ where $C_{id}$ is the id number of the case, $C_g$ is the goal given, $C_c$ is the category of the building, $C_{cd}$ is the circumstance description, $C_{sd}$ is the proposed solution, $C_d$ is the decision taken by the Building

Directorate (BD), i.e. "granted" or "refused", $C_m$ is the id number of the model which is relevant to the case, and any other information will be stored in texts in $C_t$. For example, Case 90 is represented as follows.

$C_{id}$: C90
$C_g$: safety
$C_c$: house
$C_{cd}$: stair(a), exit_stairway(b), is(b,enclosed), part_of(a,b)
$C_{sd}$: material(a,timber), fire_resistance(a,1,hour)
$C_d$: granted
$C_m$: M23
$C_t$: nil

Argumentation for the relaxation of specific regulations starts with usually two *positions*, one suggested by the applicant and the another one or two suggested by the Local Building Control Authority (the LBCA). Since the applicant is the player who seeks relaxation on the regulations at issue, the applicant's proposal constitutes partial compliance with the regulations. Appeal cases are submitted to the BD because the LBCA refused the relaxation and insisted on full compliance with the regulations at issue. In addition to these two *players*, there may be other players who make *arguments* to *support* or *oppose* the suggested positions such as the BD itself or the firemaster. The role of the BD is to arbitrate between these two main players—the applicant and the LBCA— and decide which position is reasonably acceptable in the context of the given case. Such argumentation is recorded in the Case Library along with cases in the form of an IBIS-like argumentation structure, which was developed from the IBIS model [6, 2] and Toulmin's model [15] of argumentation. In this argumentation structure, there are two node types, *position* and *argument*, and two link types, *support* and *oppose*. An example of an argumentation structure is shown in Fig. 3. Reasons to *support* or *oppose* a position, e.g. "full compliance", "partial compliance" and "reasonable", are enclosed in brackets ([...]) in this figure.

### 4.3 The Domain Knowledge Base

Knowledge in the Domain Knowledge Base (the DKB) is used in classifying a given case, i.e. to find models whose $M_c$ and $M_{cd}$ are most similar to $C_c$ and $C_{cd}$ of the given case. Specialisation hierarchies are used to represent building categories and concepts used to describe models and cases (e.g. "house" is a subclass of "dwelling", "window" is a subclass of "opening"). Aggregation hierarchies are used to represent structural knowledge about building components (e.g. "stair" is a subpart of "stairway"). Examples of specialisation/aggregation hierarchies are shown in Fig. 4.

### 4.4 Retrieval of Relevant Regulatory Information

Given a case $C = (C_{id}, C_g, C_c, C_{cd}, C_{sd})$, the retrieval is carried out in three steps. First, the system selects an abstraction hierarchy of the given $C_g$ and

argument 1

position 1

support
[practicable]

[applicant]
the building is

models by assessing similarity of circumstances. The system assesses similarity by comparing the features in the $M_{cd}$ of selected models with the $C_{cd}$ of the given case. The system first applies the notion of structural mapping [4, 5, 14]. The system tries to find a model or (models) such that all features in $M_{cd}$ have corresponding features in $C_{cd}$, in other words, for each building component in $M_{cd}$, there is a building component in $C_{cd}$ which is of the same type or of the similar type with the corresponding building component in $M_{cd}$, and all matching building components in $C_{cd}$ have the same or similar attributes, properties and relations with the corresponding building components in $M_{cd}$. Similarity between two concepts (e.g. types of building components, attributes, etc) is measured in terms of semantic distance [3], i.e. the number of links between two types in specialisation hierarchies. In the current implementation, two concepts whose semantic distance is not greater than 2 are regarded as similar. For example, the number of links between "opening" and "window" in the specialisation hierarchy shown in Fig. 4 is only 1 and "opening" and "window" are said to be similar.

If the system fails to find structural correspondence between $C_{cd}$ and any $M_{cd}$ of the selected models, the system tries to bring out similarity hidden under the surface description of $C_{cd}$ using knowledge stored in the DKB (*implied similarity*). The system transforms $C_{cd}$ into an alternative description using knowledge in the DKB and repeats the similarity test using the notion of structural mapping. Heuristic rules used to transform $C_{cd}$ are as follows.

1. Introduce objects which exist in $M_{cd}$ but not in $C_{cd}$ and add "part_of" relations between existing and new objects.
2. Add default properties if properties of objects in $C_{cd}$ are missing. For example, if the occupancy capacity of a storage room is not given in $C_{cd}$ then the default occupancy capacity, 0, is added to $C_{cd}$. Another example is, if there is a storey on the ground/first/second level, then the default height of the floor above the ground/first/second level is added to $C_{cd}$.
3. Infer relations between objects in $C_{cd}$ and add them to $C_{cd}$. For example, if an object A is connected to an object B and B is connected to another object C, a new relation "A is connected to C" is added to $C_{cd}$. Another example is, if an object A is part of an object B and B is part of another object C, a new relation "A is part of C" is added to $C_{cd}$.

Once relevant models are found, the system compares the $C_{sd}$ of the given case with the $M_{sd}$ of retrieved models. If the solution described in $C_{sd}$ is within the range of the solution described in $M_{sd}$ of a model, then the case is said to satisfy the model. For a case to be determined to be *compliant* with the regulations, all "strong" models among retrieved models should be satisfied but "weak" models need not be satisfied.

### 4.5 Acquisition of New Regulatory Information

When the proposed solution $C_{sd}$ does not satisfy any "strong" models retrieved as relevant, there is a possibility of relaxation. The decision on whether the relaxation is to be granted will be made by a human expert. The system only provides relevant information stored within the system:

1. principles or issues behind relevant regulations, i.e. models at the upper levels of retrieved strong models which provide the reason why requirements represented as the retrieved strong models should be satisfied; and
2. previous similar cases, i.e. cases attached to retrieved models.

First, for example, if $(C_{id}, C_g, C_c, C_{cd}, C_{sd})$ of C90 shown in Sect. 4.2 is given to the system, M23 which represents Regulation D7 is retrieved as relevant to C90. The principles or issues behind Regulation D7 are represented as M6, M5 and M3 (see Fig. 2) and these three models are explained as follows.

resolve different issues. Therefore, when a criterion is evaluated for requirements in one issue, all requirements described using the same criterion with respect to other issues are checked and informed to the human expert.

After all relevant information—principles or issues behind the relevant regulations, similar cases and whether or not there is conflict with existing legal rules—is explained, the human expert is asked to make a decision on relaxation. If it is decided to grant relaxation, then the new rulings established in the relaxed case are integrated into the abstraction hierarchies. First, the system will hypothesize the category of buildings to which the new rulings should apply by looking at the $M_c$ of "strong" sibling models which are similar to the case. Second, the system will collect "weak" sibling models which are similar to the case and generate the circumstances descriptions and the solutions by generalising the $C_{cd}/C_{sd}$ of the case and the $M_{cd}/M_{sd}$ of the collected similar "weak" models respectively. A new model will be created from the hypothesised category, the generalised circumstance description and the generalised solution. The strength will be set to "weak". This new model will replace the "weak" models whose circumstances descriptions and solutions are integrated into the new model.

## 5  Concluding Remarks

The Scottish Office records each appeal case in one file which contains documents, letters, drawings and photographs related to the case. 22 appeal cases were randomly selected in different subject areas and were formalised into 25 test cases. The prototype system has been implemented in Prolog using these cases. The regulations related to these 25 cases were also formalised into 102 models and four abstraction hierarchies were built. Background domain knowledge needed for processing 25 test cases was also gathered and formalised in the DKB. 25 test cases were supplied to the prototype system and the results were compared to the results by the human expert recorded in the case files. In 24 cases, the system retrieved models which represent the requirements against which the case appealed. In case 87, the applicant appealed against requirements of mechanical ventilation (represented as M112). Instead of providing some means of mechanical ventilation, the applicant insisted on using windows and doors as a means of ventilation and the system retrieved M108, M109 and M116, which represent the requirements of natural ventilation. Relaxation was granted in 17 test cases and 17 weak models were added to the MKB. There was no case among these 17 relaxed cases in which rulings could be combined with existing weak models (i.e. rulings from previous cases), since issues involved in the selected cases were very diverse and there were no cases which were similar to existing weak models.

A case-based approach as described in this paper has the following advantages over a traditional rule-based approach. First, it allows more flexibility in organising and maintaining legal rules than in a traditional rule-based approach. Although the abstraction hierarchies need to accommodate the representation and handling of exceptions (see Fig. 1 in Sect. 2), the interpretation hierarchies which exist among legal rules have been successfully represented as abstraction hierarchies. Furthermore, since models are loosely connected in the abstraction hierarchies and inconsistency among models is tolerated (to a limited extent), new legal rules can be introduced more easily. Second, the representa-

2. Conklin, J., Begeman, M.L.: gIBIS: A Hypertext Tool for Exploratory Policy Discussion. ACM Transactions on Office Information Systems **6:4** (October 1988) 303–331.
3. Collins, A.M., Quillian, M.R.: How to make a language user. In Organisation of Memory (1972). E. Tulving and W. Donaldson (Eds.). MIT Press.
4. Gentner, D.: Structure Mapping: A Theoretical Framework for Analogy. Cognitive Science **7** (1983) 155–170.
5. Holyoak, K.J., Thagard, P.: Analogical Mapping by Constraint Satisfaction. Cognitive Science **13** (1989) 295–355.
6. Kunz, W., Rittel, H.W.: Issues as Elements of Information Systems (1970). Working Paper. Center for Planning and Development Research, University of California, Berkeley, CA, USA.
7. Rissland, E.L.: Artificial Intelligence and Law. The Yale Law Journal **99** (1990) 1957–1981.
8. Rissland, E.L., Skalak, D.B.: CABARET: Rule Interpretation in a Hybrid Architecture. International journal of man-machine studies **34** (1991) 839–887.
9. The Building Standards (Scotland) Regulations 1981 (1981). Scottish Office.
10. Sergot, M.: Representing Legislation As Logic Programs (1985). Tech. Report. Department of Computing, Imperial College of Science and Technology, UK.
11. Sergot, M,, Sadri, F., Kowalski, R.A., Kriwaczek, F., Hammond, P., Cory, H.T.: The British Nationality Act as a Logic Program. Communications of the ACM **29:5** (May 1986) 370–386.
12. Stone, D.: Intelligent Information Systems for Building Standards. Proceedings of EuropIA 88, Paris (1988).
13. Susskind, R.: Expert Systems in Law (1987). Oxford University Press.
14. Thagard, P., Holyoak, K.J.: Why Indexing is the Wrong Way to Think about Analog Retrieval. Proceedings of DARPA Case-Based Reasoning Workshop (1989) 36–40.
15. Toulmin, S.: The uses of argument (1958). Cambridge University Press.
16. Walker, R.F., Oskamp, A., Schrickx, J.A., Opdorp, G.J.V., Berg, P.H.V.D.: PROLEXS: Creating Law and Order in a Heterogeneous Domain. International journal of man-machine studies **35** (1991) 35–67.
17. Waterman, D.A., Paul, J., Peterson, M.A.: Expert Systems for Legal Decision Making. Expert Systems **3:4** (1986) 212–226.
18. Yang, S.-A., Robertson, D., Lee, J.: KICS: A Knowledge-Intensive Case-Based Reasoning System for Statutory Building Regulations and Case Histories. Proceedings of the Fourth International Conference on AI and Law, Amsterdam, The Netherlands (June 1993) 254–263.

# List of Authors

# Springer-Verlag
# and the Environment

We at Springer-Verlag firmly believe that an international science publisher has a special obligation to the environment, and our corporate policies consistently reflect this conviction.

We also expect our business partners – paper mills, printers, packaging manufacturers, etc. – to commit themselves to using environmentally friendly materials and production processes.

The paper in this book is made from low- or no-chlorine pulp and is acid free, in conformance with international standards for paper permanency.

# Lecture Notes in Artificial Intelligence (LNAI)

# Lecture Notes in Computer Science